Inventing the American Woman

Third Edition

Inventing the American Woman

An Inclusive History

THIRD EDITION
VOLUME 1: TO 1877

GLENDA RILEY
Ball State University

Harlan Davidson, Inc.
Wheeling, Illinois 60090-6000

Library of Congress Cataloging-in-Publication Data

    Riley, Glenda, 1938–
      Inventing the American woman : an inclusive history / Glenda
    Riley. — 3rd ed.
        p. cm.
      Includes bibliographical references and indexes.
    Contents: v. 1. To 1877 — v. 2. Since 1877.
    ISBN 0-88295-957-3 (v. 1: alk. paper) — ISBN 0-88295-958-1 (v. 2: alk. paper)
      1. Women—United States—History. 2. Sex role—United States—History. I. Title.
HQ1410.R55   2001
305.4' 0973—dc21

Cover photos: Northern California woman, portrait by Emma Free-man. *Courtesy, the Newberry Library;* Harriet Tubman. *Library of Con-gress, LC# USZ62-7816;* Sarah Josepha Hale. *From Godey's Lady's Book (author's collection).*
Cover design: DePinto Graphic Design

Manufactured in the United States of America
02 01 00 1 2 3 VP

Contents

Volume 1: To 1877

Reference Contents in Brief for
Volume 2: Since 1877

Introduction

Gender Expectations across Cultures

Since the first edition of *Inventing the American Woman* appeared in 1986, the study of women's history has penetrated the curriculums of most American high schools, colleges, and universities. The widespread response to *Inventing,* as well as subsequent requests for its revision and updating, further demonstrate the tremendous thirst that Americans have developed for knowledge concerning the nation's women and their historical experiences.

Like the first and second editions, this one presents an overview of the history of women in the United States. Intended for use as an introductory textbook supplement in U.S. history or a core text in women's history courses, it combines factual knowledge with a thesis meant to provoke discussion and further thought. More specifically, this volume tracks the evolution of gender expectations and social constructs concerning the essence of womanhood that have played, and continue to play, a critical role in directing and shaping American women's behaviors, responses, and dissatisfactions.

American Indians were the first to establish gender expectations in what is today the United States, yet when European settlers reached America they disregarded or rejected Native peoples' ideas regarding women. Instead, the newcomers established their own beliefs, which soon became dominant and reflected the thinking of a society that argued for the acceptance of certain enduring "truths" regarding women. A real American woman supposedly was, among other things, a devoted mother, a domestic individual who labored most happily and productively within her own home, an unusually virtuous person who remained aloof from the corruption of politics, and a weak-minded, physically inferior being in need of guidance from wiser and stronger people, namely men. Once established as principles, these tenets were embodied in a series of intricate images and prescriptions that defined and limited women's roles. In other words, people invented an ideal American woman.

On one hand, this model of womanhood might be judged harmless. Generally, white middle- and upper-class women best fulfilled its mandates. In turn, it rewarded and honored them. If they remained domestic and unassertive, such women could anticipate the approval of family members, friends, and clergy. Often, such women felt grateful and even revered; they gained satisfaction from meeting their society's expectations of women. For other groups of women, especially Native Americans, African Americans, Spanish-speakers, and Asians, as well as poor whites and those employed outside the home, this model simply appeared irrelevant.

On the other hand, the model should not be underestimated as a form of social control, for it provided a comfortable substitute for careful thought. People generally found it easier to believe that both women and men had a well-defined "place" than to consider the complexities of human society and personality. Such thinking also helped maintain an economic system based on the usually greater physical strength of men, who for centuries had performed the heavy labor involved in hunting, farming, and manufacturing, while women often remained behind to bear and raise children and perform lighter tasks. And these ideas reinforced a political system in which men made more of the public decisions and women more of the private, or domestic, ones.

Gender expectations and social constructs also kept in force power imbalances. Gradually, prevailing beliefs regarding women translated into policies and legislation regulating families, schools, churches, politics, and the workplace. Too often, these codes robbed all women of the opportunity to cultivate their talents and deprived the developing nation of women's nondomestic skills and labor. Such constraints frequently narrowed the range of women's education and socially acceptable literature, often rendering these simplistic and limiting to the mind. They also encouraged the development of impractical, sensuous, and physically restrictive women's clothing and tended to relegate women's pastimes to things trivial.

Consequently, during the 1600s, 1700s, and early 1800s, thousands of women of various social classes and racial backgrounds resisted being molded into the idealized American woman. Typically, women dissidents drew on women's culture, such as female networks, to help them endure the system and to reform it. At the same time, such forces as early industrialization, urbanization, and national expansion not only tested customary prescriptions but demonstrated their unsuitability to a modernizing society.

By the mid-1800s, the idealized American woman sustained open attack. Women's participation in women's rights activism, reformism, religious revivalism, and paid employment all helped erode the model. During the late 1800s and well into the twentieth century, such other developments as Progressivism, world wars, the quest for civil rights, contemporary feminism, and the emergence of double-income families forced many Americans to continue to rethink their beliefs, to recast their ideas in a mold that better fit the reality of all kinds of women living in the United States, including professionals, poor women, lesbians, full-time homemakers, divorced women, and those of color.

And to this day Americans continue to struggle with, and redefine, expectations of women and societal constructs affecting them—and increasingly those affecting men as well. Understanding the historical development of both the nation and its women is essential to these undertakings. Thus, this book considers women and the changes they experienced during various eras of American history.

To assist the reader, each chapter ends with several learning aids. One of these is a checklist of names, terms, phrases, and dates. Also included are several issues to think about and discuss. Finally, a selected bibliography provides the interested reader with additional factual information, varied interpretations, and methodological perspectives regarding women's issues and themes for particular eras.

About terminology: a special attempt has been made in this text to respect sensitivities regarding the labels and language that carry significance in discussing such issues as racism, sexism, ageism, and classism. Some of the relevant style choices and definitions observed include referring to so-called minorities as *peoples of color*. References to *African Americans* and *blacks* are interchangeable. In accordance with present usage, peoples of Spanish-heritage are called *Hispanics*, or *Chicanos/ Chicanas* for Mexican Americans. Upper-case *Native Americans* is used interchangeably with *American Indians* or, where unmistakable, *Indians*.

Except where hyphens are truly necessary to avoid misreading, this text also prefers not to hyphenate groups of people, even when such compounds as African American and Asian American are used as adjectives. Such choices in terminology and style remain an especially important effort in a book that braves generalizations regarding the complex historical experience of so many people—in this case, over half the people of the United States.

This third edition also eliminates a number of examples of women's achievements. Fortunately, women's history has reached such a stage of development and public acceptance that it is no longer necessary to offer long lists of women's names and instances of their accomplishments to "prove" that women indeed participated in such historical events as wars, migrations, politics, or literary and artistic movements. Consequently, the third edition of *Inventing* contains fewer women's names and more examination of women-related issues and transitions. It also has been restructured and reedited to make it more accessible to readers.

In addition, in keeping with American society's growing awareness of the importance of multiculturalism, this edition includes enhanced discussions concerning women of color, that is, Native American, African American, Hispanic, and Asian women. Similarly, women's relationship to nature and participation in the conservation movement is more thoroughly covered, as is women's involvement in sports and the military.

Throughout, the results of new scholarship have been incorporated and suggested reading lists updated accordingly. Because women's history continues to be one of the most energetic and prolific areas of historical investigation, the reader will not only profit from exploring the many books and articles listed here, but by keeping an eye out for recent publications.

Ultimately, this book is about more than American women's past and present. By implication it is also about their collective future, which will witness the emergence of a long overdue development—a reinvented, and far more inclusive, American woman.

1

Women in Colonial America

to 1763

Women's history in colonial America is the saga of different types of people who shared a continent but not a culture. Before 1763, the year in which the American Revolution began to brew in earnest, women of all races and heritages played similar roles as daughters, wives, mothers, and workers; yet different groups—racial, ethnic, and social—saw the world in different ways. Within this wide spectrum of perspectives, values, and beliefs, the meaning of being female varied widely.

The first American women were American Indians (today also called Native Americans) who lived in North America from ten thousand to as many as twenty thousand years before white Europeans arrived. During those centuries, Indian women helped develop the elaborate cultural, social, political, and economic patterns that characterized most of the hundreds of Native groups that spanned the continent.

During the late 1500s and early 1600s, Spanish-speaking women migrated from Mexico to parts of what later became the United States. Especially in such states now called New Mexico, California, and Florida, Spanish-heritage women served in various capacities—as matriarchs of such noted families as the Bandinis and Sepulvadas, as teachers and matrons at Catholic missions, as workers in homes, fields, and businessplaces, and as mothers of children native to the area.

Later, sometime around 1609, European women, primarily English, reached the newly established English settlement of Jamestown in the Virginia colony on the eastern shore of the North American mainland. Although few in number, the first white women who arrived in America usually proved hardy and tenacious. Thus, many other European women soon followed, from such countries as England, Wales, France, Germany, and the Netherlands.

About a decade later, in 1619, the first African women stepped foot on the Virginia shore. Brought against their will and under deplorable conditions, these women proved especially courageous, somehow finding the strength to adapt not only to a wholly new physical and cultural environment, but to their new and most unwelcome status, first as limited-term bond servants and, soon thereafter, as slaves for life.

1

The American Indians and the recently arrived Europeans and Africans all had their own well-established ideas about how women should behave, yet during the 1600s and 1700s European beliefs heavily influenced the thinking of most colonial Americans regarding women. For example, because many white traders and trappers refused to deal with Indian women, Indian men gradually usurped Indian women's long-standing and highly significant role as traders. At the same time, European ideas helped shape the expectations, policies, and laws that white colonial Americans formulated and applied to women of various backgrounds and races.

Native American Women

Eastern Indian Peoples

The many tribes of American Indians who inhabited the continent of North America for thousands of years before Europeans arrived developed rich cultures, including sophisticated economic and religious institutions, intricate social structures, agricultural techniques, and technology. In the northeast region and south along the Atlantic seaboard, at least four different language groups existed: Algonquian, Caddoan, Iroquoian, and Siouan. Each of larger American Indian groups comprised hundreds of different clans, bands, and tribes, united or separated by elaborate kinship structures.

Generally, however, during the 1600s and 1700s East Coast families depended on agriculture for their primary livelihoods, supplemented by hunting, fishing, and gathering. Such families lived in homes made of hide, woven mats, bark, or poles. Furnishings consisted of floor mats, beds of hide and fur, cooking utensils of iron and copper, and pottery of baked clay.

Inside their homes, women cooked over open fires, the smoke exiting through openings in the roofs. Women also served as domestic artisans in supplying their families with a wide range of useful goods. They made thread from bark, grass, or animal sinew; fashioned clothes from textiles and animal skins; wove baskets and mats; and crafted bowls and pots. The intricate designs these Native women created to ornament the clothes and pots they made, as well as the games and rituals they devised, indicate that they enjoyed a modicum of leisure time. Most women living in the eastern American Indian cultures could divorce and remarry without loss of honor.

In about one-third of these Native groups, women operated within a social structure that was matriarchal, matrilineal, matrilocal, or perhaps all three. In matriarchal societies, women ruled families and even tribes. In a matrilineal system, children's lineage descended from mothers. In a matrilocal society, brides brought their grooms to live in their mother's houses.

As a case in point, the northern Iroquois—primarily the Mohawk, Oneida, Onondaga, Cayuga, and Seneca of New York—assigned to men the tasks of hunting, warfare, and diplomacy, and to women the responsibility of running the social and political life of their villages. Iroquois women could select chiefs, participate in politics, initiate warfare, and change spouses without fear of retribution. In addition to this near-matriarchy, the Iroquois were matrilineal, with mothers and daughters forming the primary kin relationships.

In almost all of these groups, women were farmers. Because virtually all native groups venerated women's reproductive and nurturing capacities, they assigned women the role of primary producers of foodstuffs. Rather than an unpleasant chore, raising food was considered an honor. Women worked with hoes they made from shell or wood, following the farming practices handed down from their grandmothers and mothers. Sometimes, women enlisted the help of others. Among the Narragansett (of the Iroquoian language group) during the 1600s, cultivating fields was a community job. Women, men, and children joined in preparing the earth for planting. Although custom did not dictate it, men often helped their mothers and wives with heavy tasks.

As farmers, Native women supplied most of the foodstuffs their peoples consumed. Among the agricultural Algonquians, who lived along the northeastern coast, women farmers produced as much as 90 percent of their people's diet. Observing these women, one white male colonist exclaimed that Native women's output exceeded that of "English farmers," and that at harvest the women gathered large crops, dried them in the sun, and conveyed them "to their barns, which be great holes digged in the ground in the form of a brass pot, sealed with rinds of trees, wherein they put their corn, covering it from the inquisitive search of their gourmandizing husbands, who would eat up both their allowed portion, and reserved seed, if they knew where to find it." In addition, Algonquian women fished, gathered wild plants, processed and stored food, made household goods, and assisted men in hunting.

These women were more than mere laborers, however. In most Native groups, women owned their agricultural tools, controlled the land they planted, and determined the distribution of the foodstuffs they raised. These rights especially belonged to female heads of households, clan matrons, and elders, who, in effect, managed men of their clan through their decisions. For instance, by either releasing or hoarding food supplies, women could enable or prevent men from waging war or going hunting: denied the necessary provisions, men had no choice but to stay home. Such female power was particularly evident among the Iroquois peoples.

Furthermore, Native women wielded influence beyond their homes and fields. They routinely acted as businesspeople and entrepreneurs, offering for sale or barter crops, furs, textiles, and baskets. Women could also rise to the position of leader, commonly called *sachem* or *werowance* among eastern peoples. Although the office of leader was usually inherited, it was retained only by keeping the respect of group members, who supported the leader with contributions of food. One such woman ruler led the Appamatucks against the English settlers in 1611, while a woman named Quaiapan served as sachem of the Narragansetts during the 1660s and 1670s.

In addition, Native women served as *shamans,* or priests. In this role, they acted as both religious leaders and medical practitioners. In some bands, women acted as both shaman and war leader, a position that carried with it much power and respect. Despite a long-standing inattention to Indian women's history, evidence of a number of such cases has survived. During the 1660s and 1670s, for example, a female sachem named Weetamoo led approximately 300 Pocasset Indian men in warfare. Furthermore, Weetamoo was an influential and aggressive leader of Indian resistance to the whites' colonization of their lands. Naturally, a Native woman who spearheaded Indian efforts to dislodge white settlers gained little place in histories traditionally written by white men, and has, until recently, been largely overlooked.

Families among Eastern Indians

Even though roles differed between Native men and women, most Indian societies valued an individual's talent and initiative above his or her gender. In addition, Native American societies esteemed women, according them respect and certain rights. Among some groups, such as the Iroquois, religious beliefs taught that a female figure created the world. Among the Seneca, the Woman's Dance, which celebrated corn, was central to sacred rituals. Thus, Native women who wished to expand their activities and prominence usually had the opportunity to do so.

Typically, however, Native women lived and exercised power primarily within the boundaries of families and kin networks. Young women worked alongside mothers and grandmothers learning to grow such crops as corn, grind it into meal, and bake it into a flat, unleavened bread. Young women also depended on their elders to guide them through such ceremonies as those surrounding the onset of menstruation, which signaled a woman's expanded power and her impending availability for marriage.

Because marriage linked families and kinship groups, courtship involved far more than the couple themselves. Everyone from parents to clan leaders had to agree that the match was a good one. Yet few Native societies forced girls to marry against their will. If a young woman agreed to marriage, a ceremony and feast eventually followed, accompanied by an exchange of presents between the two families concerned. Often, the groom offered a "bride price" to his bride's parents, which showed his esteem for his new wife and compensated her family for the loss of her companionship and labor.

Native communities took other steps to foster harmony between a newly married couple. The Micmac Indians prohibited sexual relations for the first year of marriage, hoping that the couple might use this period of abstinence to develop a strong affectional bond and an effective work partnership. If, however, marital dissension did occur, most Native groups, who cared more about a married couple's happiness and effectiveness than the appearance of stability, offered ease of divorce. In the event of divorce in matrilineal societies, children remained with their mothers. In any case, most Native families graciously absorbed a divorced person as well as his or her children, thereby minimizing the trauma the young ones suffered.

Among most eastern Indian societies, women seemed to control the spacing of their pregnancies. Although Native women left no written records of their birth-control practices, they are believed to have regulated pregnancy through the use of herbal preparations, by prolonging breast-feeding for several years, and by prohibiting sexual intercourse with a breast-feeding woman. Abortion and infanticide also appear to have been accepted practice by a significant number of North American tribes.

Once born, Indian children were raised not only by their parents but by other members of their family, their clans, and their entire villages. Mothers carried infants with them on highly adorned cradleboards, but young children were allowed more freedom. Through praise and criticism, Native children learned, on the one hand, independence and individuality, and on the other, a keen sense of responsibility for group members.

Indian Society Farther West

Yet other American Indian women lived in ways that differed according to tribe and region. Among the Ojibway of present-day Minnesota, for example, mutual respect between spouses and shared child raising characterized the family unit. To make a living, women farmed and men hunted, but it was the women who parceled out both grains and meat, deciding who would get what size portion.

Ojibway women and men cooperated in such other tasks as canoe building and fishing. They also worked together in dressing furs, tapping maple sugar, and harvesting wild rice. But because women had ownership rights over the foodstuffs they produced and the furs they processed, it was they who haggled with the first white traders and set-tlers to reach Minnesota.

Thousands of other Native groups existed in what would become the United States. These included the Hopewell culture in the Ohio River Valley, the hunting-gathering tribes of the Great Plains, and the fishing peoples of the far Northwest. In areas today known as Arizona, Colo-rado, Utah, and New Mexico lived a variety of Native groups, including the Anasazi, who built multistory apartment dwellings of adobe on rock ledges and in crevices of cliffs. As early as 1085, they had completed what is today called Pueblo Bonito. After one hundred years of work, Pueblo Bonito contained over six hundred rooms.

Besides being builders, the Anasazi defined gender roles differently than did most other Native American peoples. Unlike most other Indian groups, Anasazi men cultivated the crops, while women remained in the villages, called *pueblos* by Spanish explorers. In the villages, women processed and prepared food, cared for families, and produced textiles, baskets, and pottery, including water jars, storage vessels, and cooking utensils.

At the beginning of the 1600s, approximately fifty thousand Anasazi Indians lived along the Rio Grande and the present-day New Mexico–Arizona border. Women gathered, prepared, and preserved food, cared for children, crafted pottery, spun and wove cloth, and raised turkeys. They also built houses with mud-plastered walls, which they then owned, for the customs of matrilineal descent and matrilocal residence were widely observed among their people.

Spanish-Heritage Women

Pioneers to El Norte

Among the first people to disrupt the lives of American Indians were Spanish explorers, conquerors, and settlers. After Spain took over Mexico in 1521, this vast territory, hailed as New Spain, constituted the core of Spain's North American holdings. Soon, Spanish officials began to look to the lands north of Mexico as another likely area of expansion. Despite the fact that Pueblo Indians already inhabited the vicinity, Spain viewed it as a frontier to be explored, and eventually settled and colo-nized. Spanish officials, both in Spain and Mexico City, New Spain's capital, realized that success in attracting women to the missions, presidios, and haciendas of what they called *El Norte* would determine Spain's ability to hold that territory as part of the empire.

Especially during the 1600s and 1700s, the Spanish government urged women and children to migrate along with men to El Norte. In re-sponse, a significant number of women helped colonize for Spain the area that became New Spain's far northern provinces and, eventually, the American Southwest. Documents from Mexico's frontier period such as the rolls of pioneering expeditions indicate that women colonists not only existed, but that a significant number of women migrated without men to assist them. During the late 1700s, one such woman, the widow Doña Inez Luz, led a family of two recently widowed daughters and four young grandchildren to Mexico's Far North in hopes of improving their financial status and perhaps finding husbands.

Many such female settlers on the northern frontier engaged in agriculture and raising livestock, while others were attached to the military. Because the highly individualistic Pueblo peoples already living in the territory naturally resented such incursions, Spanish settlers relied on the presence of troops to regulate Indians and to contain frequent rebellions. Thus, women tended to settle their families in or near forts and military encampments. Such was the case of Doña Teresa Varela, who during the 1700s followed her officer husband to his station in El Norte. This formidable woman efficiently ran a household that included two married sons and daughters and their spouses, a grandchild, an unmarried son, and twenty-two servants.

Spanish-speaking women's lives varied further according to their social class and the locale in which they settled. In New Mexico, women pioneers often lived in simple adobe homes. Some of those who resided in Santa Fe, established as the capital of New Mexico as early as 1609, ran small businesses. By the early 1700s, a number of middle- and upper-class New Mexican women owned and controlled land, either with their husbands or individually. By way of contrast, in California some women lived on extensive *ranchos,* which included a *hacienda,* numerous outbuildings, and many acres. At the other end of the social scale were poor women who barely made a living raising crops or animals.

El Norte did not provide a life of ease or security to female settlers. As on any frontier, pioneering women had to adapt customary foods, clothing, and rituals to a different and sometimes harsh environment. They had to learn to grow local plants and herbs to treat their children's illnesses. And they had to endure a rough life that included a high incidence of sexual abuse, such as battery, incest, and rape.

At the same time, Spanish-heritage women generally exercised a variety of rights unknown to white women in either Britain or the American colonies at the time. As Spanish citizens, women in New Spain's northern provinces participated in the judicial system by testifying as witnesses and initiating court proceedings, often without their husbands' assistance or knowledge. During the 1700s, a growing number were literate enough to sign their names on their testimony and other documents.

In addition, owing to a variety of factors including improved female longevity and an increase in male casualties of war, the number of widows increased during the 1700s. According to Spanish law, widows could inherit land, while their daughters received estates on an equal basis with brothers. Thus, numerous widows and some of their daughters owned businesses and land, as well as influencing commercial and public affairs.

Becoming Indigenous

During the 1600s and 1700s Spanish-speaking women resided primarily in the southwestern territory that later became Arizona, California, New Mexico, and Texas. On the southeastern frontier, Spanish-heritage women lived in Florida, from which the Spanish ousted the French between 1565 and 1567. Although many Spanish-heritage women had migrated to these new homes, many others were indigenous, or native-born. In New Mexico, for example, Spanish women arrived sometime during the late 1500s or early 1600s. And Spanish women preceded white women in Florida by nearly fifty years. In both cases, Spanish women settlers produced daughters who were native to their locales.

Another group of native-born people were *mestizos,* or the children of Spanish and Indian parents. As men of Spanish heritage entered Indian lands, they routinely hired local Indian women as guides, interpreters, cooks, domestic servants, field workers, and builders. Gradually, Spanish men and Indian women cohabited or married, thus creating a mixed-heritage population. As early as 1650, mestizos outnumbered Spaniards in New Spain.

Unfortunately, census takers and historians have largely overlooked mestizos, partly because Indian women adopted their husbands' Spanish surnames and thus became invisible in the historical record. In fact, mestizas played an important role in El Norte. These women ranched, farmed, herded, and ran businesses, often alongside men. Some even joined in rodeos, riding horses and twirling ropes with as much dexterity as any *vaquero,* or cowboy. They helped Spain conquer and colonize such parts of the New World as Mexico, New Mexico, and Florida. And they helped establish a complex and flourishing culture that would soon become part of rapidly expanding white America.

Early Accounts of Native Peoples

Reports from White Colonists

In 1607, the English sent a shipload of men to settle at Jamestown in Virginia colony. Hopeful that they would find rich natural resources similar to those discovered by Spanish colonizers in South America, these Englishmen looked to the new land with optimism. Their hopes were soon shattered. After almost destroying themselves in their futile attempts to discover precious metals and other riches, the first English colonists at Jamestown turned to agriculture. Initially growing crops to feed themselves, they turned to the cultivation of a cash crop, tobacco, for export to England.

To establish themselves, early white male settlers at Jamestown and elsewhere along the East Coast encroached on Native peoples' lands. Descriptions of these men's experiences flowed back to Europe in letters, reports, and outright rumors. Often these accounts related positive interactions between white colonists and Native peoples. On other occasions such documents brimmed over with fear and hatred. All these statements, however, reconstructed Indian life and culture only partially, and only from a white perspective.

In judging Native American women, early white male colonists drew on their own personal experiences with Indians. As a result, many settlers developed complimentary attitudes. Some colonists, especially those who were willing to barter with Indian women, giving them needles, machine-woven textiles, kettles, tea, stockings, and shoes in exchange for baskets, hand-produced textiles, and furs, thought highly of Native female traders. Other white settlers married Native women and produced mixed-blood offspring.

Yet other colonists viewed young Native women as beautiful Indian "princesses." To European eyes, Indian women were exotic creatures decked out in beautifully tanned buckskin and fine quill work, both products of their own hands. Some colonists hoped that such Indian princesses might even help them conquer Native peoples. The most famous example was Pocahontas. This Native woman, originally named Matoaka, was the daughter of Powhatan, an Indian ruler in early Virginia. According to unsubstantiated legends, in 1607 Pocahontas intervened with her father to save the life of Captain John Smith of Jamestown.

During following years, the young woman performed many acts of kindness for various Jamestown settlers. In 1613, Pocahontas met John Rolfe, the colonist responsible for introducing the cultivation of tobacco to Jamestown. When she agreed to marry Rolfe, ministers instructed Pocahontas in Christianity and baptized her Rebecca. The couple's marriage in 1614 was the first known interracial marriage in the American colonies. For two years, Pocahontas and John lived in Jamestown and had one child. In 1616, John Rolfe and Pocahontas went to England, where Pocahontas was presented at court and touted as an Indian "princess." In 1617, Pocahontas died and was buried in England. She was later exalted and venerated in art, literature, stage plays and, most recently, an animated feature-length film, so that almost every school child in the United States knows her name.

Unsurprisingly, white colonists viewed in a favorable light other Indian women who proved themselves useful to European settlement and expansion. Examples abound of Native women willing to help white settlers. In colonial America, Mary Musgrove, a part-Creek woman, became an Indian leader friendly to whites. Among the Mohawks, Kateri

Tekakwitha, a convert to Catholicism, stood as a symbol to unconverted Indians. Similarly, Nancy Ward, a Cherokee leader, obtained the title War Woman during the 1750s when she joined a battle against Creek Indians. Other women took an interest in or sometimes participated in war because it was often a family matter, waged in retaliation for the death of a tribesmember.

Some white colonists even advocated marriage between male colonists and Native American women. When Pocahontas and John Rolfe wed, few people considered the racial intermixing that the marriage symbolized. In subsequent years, however, some white colonists argued that interracial alliances would promote harmony between groups of people. During the early 1700s, the Virginia planter William Byrd applauded the apparent willingness of French men to form relationships with Native women in French Canada and Louisiana, where mixed-heritage children were called *métis*. Byrd believed that such racial amalgamation would prove advantageous to both peoples.

Certainly, white colonists often benefited from their relations with Native Americans. Indian men gave whites their services as laborers, guides, and teachers of hunting and other skills, while Indian women served as spouses, companions, traders, craftspeople, and skilled agriculturalists. Indian women paved the way for their white husbands to trade with the people of their villages and tribes. Among many other contributions, the Indian corn called maize facilitated the survival and expansion of the American colonies. Indian culture and arts gave many forms of beauty and originality to the infant white civilization. The Indians' love of liberty and fierce independence helped shape the colonists' conceptions of freedom.

Yet, at the same time, numerous European settlers developed a very different view of Native American women. Unlike John Rolfe and William Byrd, this group was not favorably impressed with the Indians they observed. These Europeans, who viewed Indian women as little more than degraded beasts of burden, described them in highly derogatory terms. Throughout the 1600s and 1700s, disparaging accounts came from missionaries, trappers, traders, travelers, and settlers. Because the majority of such observers regarded Native people as primitive savages to be Christianized, exploited, removed, or exterminated, their accounts frequently tended to magnify, and even create, negative aspects of Indian life.

Because these observers were usually European males from a nonnomadic, agricultural background, they were unaccustomed to a division of labor in which women did the village and agricultural work, while men engaged in hunting, fishing, and fighting. Consequently, Europeans regularly dismissed Indian women by calling them slaves or "squaws," a highly offensive term. One typical description of Native women written by a missionary in the early 1600s characterized Indian women as "poor creatures who endure all the misfortunes and hardships of life." According to this missionary, Indian women were little more than the servants of Indian men. Such damaging characterizations passed along a very unattractive and inaccurate picture of Indian women to subsequent generations of Americans.

In all likelihood, Indian customs confused European observers. For instance, the system of sexual segregation among most coastal Algonquian groups may have misled colonial observers regarding the supposedly "degraded" position of Native women. Women often ate separately from men, performed their own dances, and spent their menstrual periods in special huts. Although the Europeans failed to understand it, such divisions did not signal women's unimportance or subordination. In fact, among most tribes, sexual harassment of women and other abusive behavior was virtually unknown. Rape, when it did occur, constituted a capital offense.

As contact between Native Americans and colonial Americans increased during the 1700s, some colonists did begin to give more balanced reports of Native women. Roger Williams, the religious leader and champion of Indian rights who founded Rhode Island, noted that Native women and men worked together on such tasks as clearing a field for cultivation or harvesting a crop. In addition, a white female captive of Indians during the 1700s reported that Native women's chores were not as demanding as those performed by white women.

White colonists had far less to say about another native group, Hispanics. Unlike Indians and American colonists, Spanish-speaking peoples and American colonists, at least in this early period, seldom met. Numbers of Spanish-speaking peoples were relatively small in what would become the American Southwest; their settlements were scattered along the California coast and throughout present-day Arizona, New Mexico, and Texas. A few American colonists ventured beyond the Appalachian Mountains and the Mississippi River. Those who did were usually ship captains, sailors, explorers, soldiers, traders, or merchants. Through exploration and trade, a few Spanish-speaking women adopted American goods and clothing styles, and some intermarriage occurred. Little of what transpired, however, could predict the antagonism that would develop between the two groups.

From the Native Perspective

Because Native Americans depended on oral rather than written communication, it is difficult to assess their views of themselves or of white Europeans. Clearly, however, growing contact between natives and colonists generally proved unfavorable for Indians. As early as the 1630s, plague and smallpox epidemics ravaged coastal Algonquian language groups, including the Wampanoags and Narragansetts in New

England and the Powhatans in Chesapeake Bay. By the mid-1600s, the mere 10 percent of Indians who survived the diseases introduced by Europeans—to which Natives had no acquired immunity—gradually lost many of their skills and came to depend on such European goods as textiles and weapons.

Most colonists believed such changes were God's intention. As one colonist said, in God's plan "some are mounted on horseback, while others are left to travel on foot . . . some have the power to command, while others are required to obey." Native Americans were less certain that the Divinity had anything to do with it. One Indian woman remembered that her grandparents and great-grandparents had initially stood in awe of white settlers and had even tried to adopt some of their ways, such as moving from hide tepees into roughly hewn log cabins. She recalled that little good had come of such attempts at adaptation. White people seemed to demand more and more of Indians, leaving them in poverty, their family members scattered or dead.

Meanwhile, a few Spanish people left accounts that were not only written, but candid and open. Although Spanish-speaking traders and merchants of the 1600s and 1700s appreciated the benefits that resulted from their commerce with Americans, they judged the "Yankee" mentality too aggressive and profit-minded. Similarly, old Spanish families who initially allowed their daughters to wed white men later regretted their decisions. Such parents complained that white men frequently broke their promises. Nor did they honor family beliefs, including Catholicism.

Spanish-heritage peoples resented the superior attitude of many whites who seemed to think that white customs, beliefs, and religions stood far above everyone else's. As members of an old, well-established, and thriving culture, Spanish people disliked the criticism and condescending attitude that characterized their treatment by many of the white people they encountered.

White Colonial Women

The Arrival of European Women

Obviously, women of various backgrounds had a significant history in North America well before white women arrived during the early 1600s. In addition, sources of discontent and conflict already existed. A few white women entered this potentially volatile scene very early. In 1608 Anne Forest and her maid, Anne Buras, arrived in Jamestown in Virginia colony, the first of the southern colonies. Other women probably completed the transatlantic journey shortly thereafter.

Meanwhile, it was becoming apparent to British officials that colonial enterprises in such places as Virginia would succeed only if they were anchored by the long-term settlement of families who could supply raw materials for Britain, as well as provide a market for English manufactured goods. Of course, such family-based colonization required the presence of women. Not only were women's childbearing abilities essential to the survival of the English colonies in North America, but women's contributions as laborers, religious and social forces, and wives were crucial to the colonies' success.

The English government actively encouraged women to immigrate to the North American mainland, and despite the hazardous ocean voyage, which carried women to a land of sprawling forests and climatic extremes not typical of their homes, they responded. The first significant number of women landed in Virginia in 1619. By their own consent, these women were sold as wives. Two years later, three more ships arrived with fifty-seven potential wives. These included the teenager Jane Dier, the twenty-five-year-old widow Marie Daucks, and the twenty-eight-year-old and never-married Allice Goughe, all of whom hoped to find husbands and happiness in England's far-flung colony.

By 1622, Virginia officials had auctioned off more than 150 "pure and spotless" women for eighty pounds of tobacco and other goods. Yet such efforts hardly made a dent in the gender imbalance of Virginia's white population. Although the London Company of Virginia recognized the need to send women to Virginia if colonial markets and social stability were to develop in the near future, by the mid-1600s men in Virginia still outnumbered women by six-to-one. This disparity left male colonists short of potential wives, who in addition to offering companionship served as domestic artisans and economic partners. It also forced many newly "American" women to learn to survive in a male-dominated society.

In the meantime, another group of immigrants, including some women, headed for the East Coast to establish the first of the New England colonies. In November of 1620, a group of Puritan Separatists, religious dissenters from the English Anglican Church, crossed the Atlantic in a small ship, landing hundreds of miles north of the fledgling settlement at Jamestown. According to the passenger list of the *Mayflower,* eighteen women and eleven girls were among those who disembarked at Plymouth in what soon became the Massachusetts Bay colony. Only four of the women lived until the following spring, while all eleven of the girls survived that first harsh winter. Because the leaders of the Plymouth colony had a vested interest in promoting the increase of families in their colony, more women soon followed. It was not until 1700, however, that the sex ratio began to stabilize a bit in the colony.

As other colonies formed along the eastern coastline, including such "middle" colonies as New York and Pennsylvania, their founders also recognized that women were important, both economically and socially, for a successful enterprise. Lord Baltimore of the southern colony of Maryland advocated the immigration of women to his fledgling colony because he believed that, "it is time to plant with women as well as with men; that the plantation may spread into generations." This policy seemed critical for Maryland, which by the 1650s had approximately six hundred white males and less than two hundred females.

Despite the pressure on women to migrate to America, white men continued to outnumber white women in every settlement. Throughout the South during the 1600s, the gender imbalance stood at as much as five or six men to every woman. This continuing shortage of women throughout colonial America spurred a growing demand for their importation that eventually prompted desperate measures. Besides those women who migrated by their own consent, others came to America as kidnap victims of agents who saw potential gain in selling women as wives. Hundreds of others arrived as petty criminals sentenced to deportation by governments eager to decrease their prison populations.

White Female Indentured Servants

A large number of women migrated to America as indentured servants, that is, people who sold their labor for a term of from four to seven years in return for their passage, support during their indentures, and a small amount of cash and clothing at the end of their terms. Such women were usually unmarried and between the ages of eighteen and twenty-five.

Perhaps as many as half of female colonists came as indentured servants, the earliest going to the southern colonies, and later indentures to the middle and New England colonies. During the 1600s, approximately one-third of colonial families employed an indentured servant, who was considered part of the household. Although these servants engaged primarily in domestic tasks, they occasionally performed field work as well.

During the 1700s, numbers of women who wanted to come to the colonies as indentured servants increased. As a result, the terms of an indenture became less attractive, and labor contracts, if they existed at all, were imprecise and poorly enforced. In 1756, one English girl wrote to her father from Maryland that she toiled "almost Day and Night" and had little but "Indian Corn [hominy or grits] and Salt to eat."

Women who were unhappy with their indentures soon discovered that violations of a contract could lead to severe punishments. A servant who reacted to a master's or mistress's "correction" by striking back verbally or physically ran the risk of having extra time added to her term of service, as did returned runaways or those who became pregnant.

In Maryland alone, one-fifth of indentured women were charged with "bastardy," meaning becoming pregnant while unmarried. Although it appeared that female servants, who were prohibited from marrying until the end of their contracts, had low morals or gave in easily to temptation, their situations were often made difficult by the presence of male masters and other men in the household. A male head of house could especially put sexual pressure on a female servant. As early as 1692, a Virginia law attempted to restrain "dissolute masters" who had "gotten their maids with child."

Despite such stains on their reputations and perhaps a child to raise, virtually all female indentures married, and often married well, at the end of their terms of service. Even though they had reached the advanced age of their mid- to late twenties, female servants were in demand. Not only had the need for wives in colonial America continued, but women freshly released from indentures were greatly attractive to potential husbands: these women already possessed a wide variety of domestic skills, as well as the cash and new clothing mandated by their indenture agreements. Thus, at least during the 1600s and early 1700s, indenture contracts offered impoverished women the opportunity to migrate to the American colonies, learn necessary skills, and eventually establish their own households.

White Women's Status

Because white colonists left behind them a large number of written documents, including diaries, letters, wills, legal proceedings, and business contracts, it is possible to reconstruct white women's lives in a fair amount of detail. Everything from Sir William Blackstone's *Commentaries on the Laws of England* to church records concerning members' transgressions of religious law reveals the restrictions on colonial women. But these documents often stood in sharp contrast to women's actual behavior. In addition, white viewpoints differed from era to era during the long American colonial period, which lasted nearly two centuries. Attitudes additionally varied from colony to colony, ranging from Maine on the northeastern coast to South Carolina on the southeastern shoreline.

Usually, white colonists' beliefs regarding women were custombound. From Europe, white immigrants brought with them the social, economic, and political beliefs and systems that they had known back home. These included traditional western European, especially English, conceptions of gender roles, which assigned to men heavy labor, including farming and manufacturing, and to women child rearing and lighter domestic labor. In addition, most colonists were Christians and, as such, esteemed women primarily in their roles as wives and mothers. In addition, unlike American Indians, colonists tended to view women as both separate and inferior from men.

From the perspective of most white colonists, however, female settlers had the best lives of any women in the world. One pointed out that white colonial women lived in a "Paradise on earth for women" because they could marry if they so desired. George Alsop of Maryland even declared that "no sooner are they on shore, but they are courted into matrimony, which some of them had they not come to such a market with their virginity, might have kept it until it had been mouldy." Like most people of the day, Alsop assumed that all women desired marriage and would experience fulfillment and satisfaction once they entered into it. He would not have thought anything, as modern people might, of the hard life marriage entailed for white women: frequent childbirth, domestic labor, sometimes fieldwork, and often early death. One expert stated that while colonial white men lived on average into their mid-forties, women, largely due to the hardships of childbearing, lived on average until only thirty-nine.

Similarly, in his 1692 guidebook for women entitled *Ornaments for the Daughters of Zion,* Puritan minister Cotton Mather wrote that "for a woman to be praised, is for her to be married." During the seventeenth century, the lopsided ratio between men and women put additional pressure on women to marry and to do so while yet in their teens. During the eighteenth century, however, partly because numbers of white women increased, societal insistence on early marriage relaxed somewhat. Eighteenth-century women usually married between the ages of twenty and twenty-three. Still, throughout the colonial period, nine out of ten white women married at least once.

Those women who remained single suffered discriminatory treatment because people considered them unproductive. White colonists expected unmarried women to join their nearest male relative's household and serve as unpaid help. An unmarried woman performed domestic chores, especially spinning, thus the term *spinster.* Single women, however, enjoyed a legal status known as *feme sole,* or woman alone, that gave them legal privileges denied to married women. Single women could control their personal property and, because they had to support themselves, had the right to engage in business.

Those women who married entered a legal state known as Civil Death or marital unity. This status, derived from English common law and religious tradition, denied legal existence to a married woman. Blackstone's *Commentaries on the Laws of England* clearly summarized the tenets of marital unity. By marriage, the husband and wife became one person in law; that is, during the marriage, the very being or legal existence of the woman was suspended, or at least incorporated and consolidated into that of the husband.

In theory, then, a married woman had no legal existence apart from her husband. Men, who married on average between the ages of twenty-five and twenty-eight, were liable for the support of their wives and children, had to leave two-thirds of their estates to their families, and were responsible for their wives' crimes and debts. In one case, when a Boston court fined a wife for physically abusing her husband, he had to pay the fine assessed her.

Moreover, married women could not sign contracts, own property, vote on civil or religious matters, or retain and control their own earnings. When in 1697 Hannah Duston of Massachusetts killed ten Indians in a daring escape from captivity, her husband collected the cash reward given Hannah by the legislature. Women's restricted legal status, known as *feme covert,* or woman covered, reflected the widespread belief that women were best represented by their fathers, brothers, and husbands, who, as men, had superior knowledge of the world and would speak for women's best interests.

In daily practice, however, white women's behavior often sharply contrasted with legal and societal prescriptions. Especially during the 1600s, civil institutions were unstable and rules laxly enforced. Moreover, in a demanding environment few male colonists stood to benefit from impairing the activities or the effectiveness of women. Women often possessed skills critical to family survival, handled weapons as well as men, and effectively ran the family farm or other enterprise during men's frequent absences for business or military engagements. The Virginia planter William Byrd described one especially dynamic woman of his acquaintance with due respect as "a very civil woman who showed nothing of ruggedness or immodesty in her carriage, yet she will carry a gun in the woods and kill deer, turkeys, and shoot down wild cattle, catch and tye hogs, and perform the most manful exercises as well as most men in these parts."

Local courts of equity played a key role in the expansion of women's rights. Because judges recognized that in actual practice men did not always represent women's needs fairly and that women often suffered distress under the law, they frequently modified legal codes and laws through their decisions. As a result, white American women, especially those of the well-to-do classes, gained a number of privileges not enjoyed by their English counterparts.

Through court decisions, some colonial women won the right to enter contracts, control their earnings, and own land and other property. For instance, in 1643, Deborah Moody of Long Island received a colonial land grant. Another resident of New Netherland, Cornelia Schuyler, later obtained a holding of thirteen hundred acres. In the South, Elizabeth Digges possessed a large plantation, 108 slaves, and a lavishly furnished mansion, while Margaret Brent owned over one thousand acres of land. Brent became such a powerful and respected landholder in Maryland that after Governor Leonard Calvert's death in 1647, she executed his will. Moreover, Brent asked for two votes in the Maryland legislature—one for herself as a freeholder and one as the governor's representative—but the legislature denied her request.

Women continued to own land during the 1700s, by which time the English colonies were better established and one might expect the growing enforcement of English laws to have interfered with such freedoms. In 1701, Quaker Elizabeth Haddon migrated to New Jersey to take over the family holding and serve as a missionary to Indians. Even after Haddon married itinerant minister John Estaugh, she continued to develop her estate, Haddonfield, and exercise as much power and influence as any male landholder of the period. At the same time, Catharyna Brett of New York personally managed her inherited property, expanding her holdings and building a lucrative gristmill.

Safeguarding Married Women's Property

Beginning in the mid 1600s, a few colonial courts tried to safeguard property that wives had brought to marriage as part of their dowries. Among wealthier women, such dowries might include jewelry, furniture, money, land, or slaves. Too often, husbands, who legally controlled their wives' holdings, sold such assets to cover their own bad debts or to expand their farms, plantations, or other businesses. Such liquidation of possessions could leave a woman and her children in dire need in the event of a couple's divorce or a husband's desertion or death. Recognizing married women's jeopardy, several colonial courts attempted to give wives some say in decisions to sell property. In 1646, for example, the Massachusetts General Court ruled that a "wyfe" must formally consent to her husband's sale of their estate.

These measures were stopgaps at best. Protective legislation was needed but would not be realized until the mid-nineteenth century. In the meantime, sympathetic colonial courts obviously attempted to do what they could to help women.

Other men who safeguarded women's dowries had more personal motives. Prosperous fathers disliked seeing the property they gave their daughters in the form of dowries squandered by careless or selfish husbands. Many thus negotiated prenuptial agreements before agreeing to their daughters' marriages. Especially among well-to-do southern planters, fathers preserved their daughters' dowries by helping negotiate premarital contracts. Such agreements provided that married women could control their own dowries, whether those consisted of money, slaves, or land, and that the dowries would pass to the children at the mothers' death. This shielded a family from a future husband's mismanagement, malfeasance, or bankruptcy. It also gave wives some income should their husbands become stingy, abusive, or absent.

Among early Dutch settlers in New Netherlands, such marriage agreements were standard. The customary Dutch marriage contracts ensured a wife's legal rights, including her control over her property. The Dutch example demonstrates that women's experiences could vary widely in colonial America—and could change dramatically over time. When, in 1664, the English took over the Dutch colony and renamed it New York, married women there found themselves limited by the English concept of *feme covert,* which negated earlier Dutch marriage contracts. Thus, a woman who had conducted trade and run a business under Dutch governance could no longer own property or sign contracts under English rule. Eventually, even inheritance laws changed. A wife who had expected to inherit at least one-half of her husband's estate could now anticipate receiving only one-third.

White women seldom sat by passively and allowed men to look out for them, however. Often, white colonial women maximized opportunities that came their way. Colonial American women actually exercised a wide variety of rights and engaged in a large number of nondomestic activities and enterprises. Women proved especially creative in plying income-producing activities within their homes. Among other things, they taught school in their homes and were paid in kind (in goods). In the absence of jails, they boarded prisoners in their homes for a fee. Moreover, women often took advantage of political opportunities, such as the ability to vote occasionally in local and school elections.

Numerous widows were competent and effective. After a spouse's death, many widows, despite inheriting at least one-third of their husbands' estates by law, had to earn a living for themselves and their minor children. Because they usually reverted to *feme sole* status, widows were allowed to own property, sign contracts, and conduct businesses. Although death created hardship and crisis, it empowered women by giving them a chance to manage a business or pursue a trade. During the 1600s, when death ended approximately two-thirds of white marriages before they reached the tenth anniversary, widows not only ran farms and plantations but worked as shopkeepers, merchants, blacksmiths, gunsmiths, and tavern keepers. By the 1700s, widows of substance who remarried frequently asked for, and received, a prenuptial agreement to protect their holdings and their children's futures.

White Women's Work inside the Home

Clearly, work was an important part of white women's lives, whether they were single, married, divorced, or widowed. Despite their social class and family's position, virtually all white women colonists worked. Governor William Bradford of Plymouth observed that when the Pilgrims landed "the women went willingly into the fields and took their little ones with them to set corn."

Throughout the 1600s and 1700s, women assisted in the family business, whether it be a farm, plantation, or shop. And, far from being ladies of leisure, women served as unpaid household labor. They toiled as domestic artisans in the home and as laborers in chicken houses, barns, and sometimes the fields, especially during periods of labor shortages. White men sometimes reciprocated by helping women with domestic chores, especially child care. Gradually, however, as a particular area of the colonies became more settled, white women's work focused on houses and gardens, while men's tasks centered around barns and fields.

Women performed extensive domestic tasks, often under difficult conditions. It was women's responsibility to put to good use the raw materials generated by the men through planting or hunting. Women served as domestic manufacturers as they transformed these raw materials into finished products. In this capacity, women artisans were to their families what factories were to later industrialized societies.

Of all the goods that women produced, food required the most continuous attention. Women raised chickens, milked cows, and tended vegetable gardens. They also prepared and processed food. This involved butchering, cooking, smoking, salting, drying, pickling, and preserving—all processes demanding a great deal of time and expertise. In addition, women manufactured soap from grease and lye, as well as candles from tallow.

Women usually performed such tasks in open fireplaces. In warm weather, they moved outdoors to cook, wash clothes, and make enough soap and candles to last the winter. During the rest of the year, women worked indoors, hauling water from rivers, wells, or rain barrels for cooking, as well as for washing clothes and bathing. When hot water was desired, women had to heat it one bucket at a time over the fire, which they continually needed to stoke. Once dirtied, the bath or laundry water could be used to wash the plank floors; otherwise it had to be hauled away.

Women undertook numerous other tasks. They combed wool and hackled flax that they then spun into thread. Next, they wove the thread into cloth, colored it with their own homemade dyes, and sewed it by hand into clothing. Although women spent untold hours at their spinning wheels and with their knitting needles, they also acted as nurses, doctors, and morticians for their families, friends, and neighbors. In addition, they were accomplished herbalists and apothecaries who produced a large variety of effective medicines. During the eighteenth century, they also bore an average of eight children, taught their children early school lessons, and trained them as laborers.

"On the side," these women brought in cash by selling butter, eggs, beeswax, thread, and other items that they produced. By the mid-1700s, white women conducted such a brisk trade that they began to make the transition to a market economy. A farm wife in New England might have achieved a "competency," that is, she successfully traded on the growing commercial market to ensure financial stability for her family and perhaps provide herself with a few luxuries. In colonial New York, women participated in a consumer society by regularly selling "domestic" goods on regular and frequent market days, and by buying such items as cutlery, fabrics, needles, and buttons. These women kept their own accounts and often sold or bought for cash rather than goods.

Although such emergent capitalism is usually associated with the mid-1800s, colonial women had made the initial breakthrough almost a century earlier.

This brief description of colonial women's domestic work does not begin to do justice to the breadth and complexity of women's duties. Even during the late 1600s and early 1700s, when New England shops sold various kinds of goods, women's work remained extremely taxing. And in the South, the romanticized *grand dame* of the plantation was in reality a hard-working manager, supervisor, hostess, accountant, teacher, and medical practitioner, responsible for a large plantation community.

White Women's Work outside the Home

Moreover, thousands of white female colonists worked outside their homes for wages. In the labor-scarce colonial economy, women could seek, without incurring public censure, other jobs besides their domestic duties. Such employment enhanced women's economic importance in the family and gave them skills to fall back on if they chose to leave their husbands or if disaster struck their families. Thus, colonial women labored as butchers, gunsmiths, journalists, midwives, millers, nurses, printers, proprietors and managers of taverns and boardinghouses, shipbuilders, silversmiths, tanners, teachers, and upholsterers. Because not all husbands exercised their legal right to control their wives' earnings, many women decided for themselves how to spend their wages.

Many wage-earning women learned their crafts from their fathers, brothers, or husbands who practiced a trade in or near the family home. These men frequently needed help from the women of the family, thus creating an opportunity for women to learn and become proficient in the trade. Women frequently ran the family enterprise during men's absence, or marketed their skills to other employers.

Other wage-earning women learned their trades through apprenticeships. Like young men, young women served apprenticeships with local craftspersons, tradepersons, or in family households. A young colonial woman would be apprenticed between the age of eleven to thirteen for a term of service as long as ten years. Female apprentices received training in such skills as silversmithing or upholstery, or such domestic crafts as spinning and sewing. Female apprentices were also taught to read and sometimes to write.

A significant number of colonial women practiced professions, notably that of midwife. During the colonial period midwives delivered most white babies. Some local governments formally licensed midwives, while others informally recognized their competence. These women, who were usually mature and experienced, held respected positions within their communities. They were revered as friends as well as medical practitioners. They would guide an expectant mother through pregnancy, attend her during the birth, and sometimes even remain with her until she could resume management of her household. Midwives also trained other women, passing along their own knowledge and skills through apprenticeships.

Women served as physicians as well. In an era lacking medical schools and licensing of physicians, women as well as men could practice medicine. Occasionally, historical documents reveal the existence of a woman doctor. For instance, during King Philip's War (1675–1676), a Mrs. Allen appeared on the list of army physicians. Because men were needed for the front lines, women filled the void in camp hospitals. In all likelihood, male troops were pleased to have the competent and mother-like hands of women tending to their wounds. Some years later, another woman doctor advertised in a New England newspaper that she treated civilians of all ages and both genders. This woman proclaimed that she followed "the midwife and doctress business; cures burns, salt rheum, canker, scald-head, fever sores, rheumatism, and the piles."

The medical professions were not the only ones open to women. Lines of endeavor that appeared "domestic" in nature were also acceptable. The arts, for example, were something women practiced to enhance their homes and sometimes turned into paid employment. In spite of women's exclusion from formal training, a few women were able to capitalize on their artistic skills. One example was Henrietta Deering Johnston, who migrated to Charles Town (later Charleston, South Carolina) with her husband around 1706. Johnston helped support her family by drawing pastel portraits. After her husband died at sea in 1716, she supported herself in her widowhood by continuing to do portraiture.

White women even entered the male-dominated area of commerce. In fact, during the early years of colonization, labor shortages gave women the chance to pursue business activities that were not even remotely domestic. During the 1660s, Margaret Philipse of New York engaged in general supply and shipping, especially buying and selling furs. Beginning in 1662, Alice Thomas profitably ran a brewhouse in Boston, although she frequently landed in court for committing such crimes as selling alcoholic beverages to Native Americans.

During the 1700s, however, white women's business undertakings appear more closely related to their domestic duties. As colonial society became more "settled," customary ideas about women reasserted themselves. Increasingly, white society expected its women to act more like ladies than pioneers.

Still, the opportunities for women remained numerous. Between 1720 and 1770, women ran 10 percent of the businesses in New England. About the same time, a Philadelphia woman turned her talent with fabric into a successful upholstery business. Although she started out with a traditional domestic skill, Betsy Ross entered the male-domi-

5 BACK
TO
BACK

nated world of commerce. Eventually, Ross employed several young men in her establishment on Philadelphia's Elfreth's Alley. Although Ross is usually characterized as a grandmother who created the American flag from scraps kept in her sewing basket, she was a well-known and respected entrepreneur who brought her considerable skills to bear on the question of a suitable American flag.

White Women's Personal Lives

The varied nature of these women's lives indicates that the history of white female colonists before 1763 does not easily lend itself to generalization. Still, similarities existed in the lives of white colonial women, whether they lived in the South of the 1660s or in New England of the 1700s. Whether she was married or single, the central focus of a white colonial woman's life was her household and family. A typical colonial household might include a married couple, their children, and possibly an unmarried aunt, uncle, or grandparent. Perhaps as many as one-third of these households included an indentured servant, hired field workers, or a number of black slaves.

Although the family was patriarchal (families and groups ruled by men), patrilineal (family lines descended from the father), and patrilocal (married couples live in the groom's father's house), women were to be valued and protected within it. This was not always the case, however. Even in the supposedly peaceful Quaker colony of Pennsylvania, cases of spousal murder and rape were reported. During the 1760s, crime rates were higher in Philadelphia than in London. Much of Philadelphia's criminal incidents stemmed from domestic violence.

Colonial laws compelled husbands to support their wives and remain faithful to them (although men were penalized less severely for adultery than were women). Failure to provide and adultery were punishable offenses. The law also regulated husbands' physical punishment of wives. In 1641, Massachusetts prohibited a husband from abusing his wife "unless it be in his own defense upon her assault." By the 1700s, such laws had less weight in most of the colonies.

In this family structure, spouses generally divided labor according to gender, with women dominating the home and men the fields or other place of business. Such family organization was not necessarily a dictatorship. Rather, colonists usually described marriage as egalitarian. A wedding sermon in Boston in 1750 stated women "are not made of the head to claim superiority, but out of the side to be content with equality." Courts and community opinion, especially in New England, cautioned husbands to extend honor and respect to their wives.

Sexual intimacy was an important part of colonists' married lives. Men, especially among the Puritans, were expected to satisfy the sexual needs of their wives. In Massachusetts and Connecticut, failing to do so, whether through impotence or neglect, was cause for divorce. While believing in sensuality within marriage, most colonists strongly opposed adultery. Courts punished such "inconstancy" with fines, whipping, the pillory, or even death. Legislation in Massachusetts Bay prescribed for the crime of adultery the punishment of whipping and the wearing of the "capital letters A.D. cut out in cloth and sewed on their uppermost garments."

Still, some colonists strayed from their spouses or committed such sexual crimes as seduction. This constituted a lesser offense than adultery and one not always unpleasant or violent. A more-than-willing Virginia woman of the 1600s was so pleased with the outcome of her seduction of a man that she swore to give him "as much cloth as would make him a sheet." Rape, however, was usually a violent, demeaning violation. One disinclined Massachusetts woman of the same era reported that a man flung her down in the street; another, that her master caught her by the wrist and forcibly "pulled her against the side of the bed." Unfortunately for women, by the 1700s, colonial courts received so many complaints of rape that judges became disinclined to treat female victims with respect and trust. Rather, rape complainants had to prove their own good character and modest demeanor.

Because sexuality and childbearing played a prominent role in the lives of colonists, women by necessity devoted a large amount of time to pregnancy and childbirth. The typical married woman could expect to be pregnant every other year. Sarah Stein Place, an average New England woman, wed in 1685. Sarah bore her first child in 1686 and her eighth in 1706. Such frequent pregnancies were likely to take a colonial mother's life in one out of every thirty cases. Those colonial women who survived childbirth could expect to bear their last child at age thirty-nine and to live until age forty-nine. They would spend almost twenty years with an infant at their sides and almost forty rearing their children to adulthood.

Not all women looked forward to such frequent pregnancies, nor were all men anxious to have an additional child to support. Consequently, some couples experimented with forms of birth control, most of which dated back to ancient Egypt and China. Perhaps most popular were herbal concoctions thought to prevent pregnancy, including catnip, pennyroyal, savory, and tansy. Another method believed to prevent pregnancy was *coitus interruptus,* or male withdrawal at the time of ejaculation. And new mothers continued to breast-feed their infants for months in hopes of avoiding an additional pregnancy.

Women who conceived against their wishes could try to induce abortion through the use of botanical remedies or the insertion of an instrument into the cervix. Some of the botanical treatments, such as aloes, oil of cedar, and nightshade, could be poisonous. Desperate women, both single and married, who overdosed themselves on botanicals could seriously impair their health. Abortion through the use of an instrument was even more dangerous. Because abortion was against the law, as well as most religious teachings, women kept their efforts secret. In some cases, however, attempted abortions became public knowledge. Between 1633 and 1699, the courts in Middlesex County, Massachusetts, heard a number of abortion cases and convicted four defendants. Even occasional cases of infanticide, committed by despondent mothers, appear in colonial legal records.

The majority of pregnant white women carried their infants to term, however. Single pregnant women often married, while married women either awaited their babies joyously or simply accepted the inevitable. Until the mid-1700s, these expectant women depended upon midwives rather than doctors to deliver their babies. The word *midwife* comes from an English term meaning "with women." Birthing remained exclusively a female affair during these years. The midwife's primary function consisted of assisting the mother to deliver naturally. She might use herbal teas, wine, or liquor to lessen the pain, but she avoided mechanical devices and drugs.

Throughout the colonial period, white women prepared for childbirth by abandoning corset stays, wearing flat shoes, and refraining from carriage rides. Common advice cautioned women to avoid "sudden frights, strong passions, [and] ungratified longings" to protect her unborn child. Guidebooks advised expectant mothers to pray and to contemplate the possibility of death.

As the day of the birth approached, the mother-to-be's own mother, aunts, sisters, friends, and midwife joined her. They laid out linen, readied basins and towels, told bawdy jokes to lighten the tension, walked the expectant mother about to relieve the pain, and held her by the arms as she delivered her baby through a low stool with an open seat. They then helped care for the mother and newborn while celebrating its birth with a feast. They admitted the father only briefly, and barred other men from the chamber for several weeks. After friends and family dispersed, the new mother returned to her regular round of duties and chores.

White Women's Interests

Not all of the colonial woman's waking hours focused on family and work. One leisure-time activity was the production of handiwork and practice of a craft, especially during the 1700s when some women had slightly more time for such activities. Women's needlework skills resulted in finely stitched samplers, bed rugs, coverlets, pillow shams, and other textiles. Women hooked, embroidered, and appliqued rugs. They painted watercolors and embroidered pictures, portraits, and mourning pictures, which recorded family deaths. They painted stoneware crocks, worktables, sewing boxes, and dishes. And they stitched a large variety of quilts, many of which chronicled births, deaths, marriages, and other significant family events. Surviving examples of women's work include a finely crafted bed rug created by a Massachusetts woman during the early decades of the 1700s, a colorful crewel-worked bed ensemble designed by a Maine woman during the 1740s, and a detailed painting by a Connecticut woman during the 1750s.

Colonial women engaged in other activities as well. By giving handouts from their doors or in their kitchens, or by working through church groups, women provided charity. They cared for widows, orphans, criminals, the disabled, and the poor in a day when social institutions such as hospitals and prisons were virtually nonexistent. In addition, women took an active part in church functions. Although denied full participation and the right to hold church offices, most women attended religious services and ceremonies. Only The Society of Friends, or Quakers, extended to colonial women a reprieve from the doctrine of St. Paul that demanded the silence of women in church. Because Quakers believed in spiritual equality of women and men, and in a lay ministry that included both sexes, they proffered to women a degree of equality.

Some women pursued education. Basic education for women included mainly the "three r's"—reading, 'riting, and 'rithmetic. By the mid-1700s, at least in New England, the illiteracy rate for women began to decline. In fact, New England women were more likely to be literate than were their British sisters or white women in the middle or southern colonies. In the South, some daughters acquired education through the common practice of allowing young women to sit in on sessions given by tutors hired to instruct young men. Those women who sought advanced education, however, were usually taught only such female "accomplishments" as needlework, singing, and playing the pianoforte.

A number of white colonial women even pursued the sciences, at the time (and for quite some time thereafter) believed to be the preserve of men. Some women liked to study plants, animals, and other aspects of the physical world. Although women were supposedly afraid of the larger environment beyond their homes and gardens, such people as Jane Colden of New York City set forth to collect botanical specimens, which she then studied and classified. By 1757, Colden had compiled a catalog of more than three hundred local plants and was respected as a botanist.

At first, colonial women enjoyed a modicum of political involvement. They occasionally voted in early town meetings or spoke out in local gatherings, but increased settlement brought with it consolidation of political power in male hands. By the mid-1600s, in most areas of the colonies the vote, office-holding, judgeships, jury service, and public debate were restricted to men.

On the personal level, however, women wielded political power in their families and among other females. Commonly, white women made decisions for children, enforcing their authority by granting or withholding small privileges that they controlled. Also, white women created local female communities based on complex rules. A woman might extend or refuse neighborliness as a way of condoning or censuring another woman's conduct. An adultress, for example, might find herself shunned by other women for an extended period. A woman might also gossip about another woman, using rumor as another tool to encourage certain "accepted" behavior and punish transgressors thereof. Women recognized that media, in this case verbal gossip, could create or destroy another woman's reputation. Although women may have been excluded from formal politics, they clearly understood and widely practiced the principles of authority and control.

Different Types of White Women

At the same time, similar developments occurred on the edges of society. Along the colonial frontier that slowly pushed southward and, by the mid-1700s, westward toward the Appalachian Mountains, women found that their labor, childbearing abilities, and other important contributions were valued yet not rewarded by inclusion in such aspects of public life as education and politics. On the North Carolina frontier, for example, women worked alongside their men doing the heavy labor involved in clearing forested land for farms, planting crops, constructing homes and barns, and raising stock. Such frontierswomen received little appreciation for their domestic skills or for their abilities outside of the home. As settlement progressed, traditional ideas of women's work and roles took hold once again.

It is important to remember, however, that specific aspects of women's lives differed from group to group and place to place. The Society of Friends, or Quakers, provide an excellent example. Settling primarily in New Jersey and Pennsylvania beginning in the mid-1650s, Quakers believed in the equality of women's and men's souls. According to founder George Fox, Quaker women were free from the Pauline restrictions placed on other Christian women to remain silent and passive. These convictions had many ramifications. Quaker women were encouraged to speak in meeting (church services); organize their own associations in the church and community; and travel around the colonies proselytizing for their religious beliefs.

Quaker women exercised unusual authority over family life. For instance, to enforce their belief that sons and daughters should wed only other Quakers, women supervised their children's courtships and marriages. Because Quaker women believed that God surrounded them with an "armor of Light," they pushed into areas usually closed to women and thus challenged the prevailing interpretation of women's sphere.

A noteworthy case is that of the Quaker women on Nantucket Island, who developed into shrewd traders and maritime suppliers. Although Quakers did not especially encourage the economic independence of women, Nantucket women expanded their roles without criticism from their menfolk. With their husbands away a good deal of the time on whaling or other commercial voyages, women ran the families and farms, sold dry goods produced from their own flax and wool to passing trade ships, and supplied the ships with necessary provisions. A French visitor to Nantucket during the 1770s wrote that Nantucket men saw the benefit of having enterprising wives and thus gave the women full support. Nantucket men, he wrote, who were "full of confidence and love," on their returns home "cheerfully give their consent to every transaction that has happened during their absence and all is joy and peace."

Divorce

Despite the variety of lifestyles available to white women settlers, they did not always adjust easily to their place in colonial society. Some found restrictions on wives and mothers bothersome, while others were discontent with their particular mates and the way in which they wielded the power given to them by a patriarchal system. Court records indicate that spousal and child abuse occurred with regularity. In general, white colonists believed that husbands and fathers had the right—even the duty—to correct their wives and children through such physical acts as slaps and spankings. Abuse that endangered a person's safety, however, was not condoned.

For disgruntled or abused women, divorce was sometimes available. Wives with grievances could sue for divorce in most New England colonies and some Middle colonies. For instance, although Puritan colonists preferred to keep couples together and often fined troublesome spouses or ordered them to "live happily together," they believed that some marriages could not be saved. Because Puritans viewed marriage as a legal contract rather than a religious sacrament, if one party violated the terms of a marital contract the marriage could be dissolved. Thus, a Massachusetts court granted the colony's first divorce to a Mrs. James Luxford in 1639. Five years later, another couple divorced. During the early 1700s, a growing number of women obtained divorces and did so at a greater rate than did men. Still, authorities continued to remind women that they should remain passive and accepting toward their mates. In 1712, a Puritan minister stated that a wife "aught to be under the husband's government."

By the end of the colonial period, Massachusetts alone had granted over one hundred divorces. Courts accepted the grounds of bigamy, nonsupport, desertion, adultery, and, because Puritans stressed the importance of childbearing, impotence. Although judges often ordered at-fault husbands to pay alimony for wives or restore a former wife's dowry, such awards were erratic and difficult to enforce. If a woman was at fault in the marital breakdown, she received nothing; by her behavior she had forfeited all rights to conjugal support. After a divorce, women usually returned to their families, but frequently assumed *feme sole* status in order to manage their own affairs.

Although its population was smaller, Connecticut granted even more divorces than did Massachusetts. The first Connecticut divorce occurred in 1655 when Goodwife Beckwith claimed that her husband had disappeared. Connecticut courts established the first formal list of grounds for divorce in the American colonies: adultery, desertion, and male impotence, or in the words of the legislation, a husband's failure to perform his "conjugall [sic] duty."

In southern colonies, courts refrained from granting divorces. They adhered to English law, which stated that only Parliament could grant divorces, and instead gave limited divorces called separate maintenance agreements. Chancery courts granted these to wives who demonstrated that their husbands treated them in cruel or irresponsible ways. A separated couple lived apart, but, because the husband had caused the marriage to disintegrate, he continued to provide the financial support he had pledged at the time of marriage. Other couples, especially in newly settled areas, simply announced in the newspapers that they had decided to part and were no longer responsible for each other's debts, crimes, or offspring.

Because women divorced and separated in growing numbers, and a majority of widows chose not to remarry, women headed a significant number of households. According to a guidebook published in 1750, *A Wedding Ring Fit for the Finger,* this was perfectly acceptable, for "when the great light goes down, the lesser light gets up." In other words, although a wife was subject to her husband when he was present, she could "be sovereign in his absence." Because death and divorce caused husbands to be absent, former wives could now take on rights and responsibilities previously denied them.

Defying Gender Expectations

Despite the significant variation in white women's lives, the widely accepted image presents colonial women in prim white caps and serviceable dresses, quietly caring for their homes and families. At least in part, this notion originated with the many guidebooks written to shape women's behavior. In the 1660s, for example, the well-known minister Cotton Mather lectured the colonial woman regarding the domestic skills she needed to "enable her to do the man whom she may hereafter have, good and not Evil, all the days of her life." Mather added that because women were more godly and religious than men, and, in his view, had "more time to employ in the more immediate service of their souls than the other sex is the owner of," they should serve as spiritual caretakers of their husbands. He explained that "the curse in difficulties both of subjection and child-bearing," was in fact a blessing for "God sanctifies the chains, the pains, the deaths."

Perhaps it was women's very assertiveness and nondomestic activities that prompted so many colonial writers and speakers to promote restrictive rules and prescriptions for colonial women. Apparently, even though Mather and others supported a model for women that emphasized such characteristics as passivity, virtue, and domesticity, not all colonial women took his advice to heart. For instance, women asserted themselves by running away from fathers or husbands whom they found overly restrictive or abusive. Colonial newspapers during both the 1600s and 1700s carried many advertisements for runaway wives, and church records included many orders for their return. Because of the labor shortage, women could easily find employment in other towns, the rudimentary communications systems of the day assuring them anonymity. Few seem to have responded to either the newspaper advertisements or church directives by returning to their fathers or husbands.

Furthermore, women participated in military engagements, both against American Indians and during periods of civil unrest. When civil war erupted in Virginia in 1676, women joined the fray. More lower-class than middle- and upper-class women acted as spies, couriers, and suppliers of food, medicine, clothing, and gunpowder during Bacon's Rebellion. The lower-class women ignored colonial ideas regarding female behavior to carry intelligence, deliver gunpowder, and even offer to fight. Presumably, lower-class rebellious women felt less bound by gender expectations than did upper-class women, for the latter typically played the more customary female roles of helpmeet, letter writer, and nurse.

Moreover, when the religious revival movement known as the Great Awakening erupted in the colonies during the 1730s and 1740s, women flocked to revival meetings in numbers equal to, or greater than, those of men. Revivalism offered women more opportunity for social interaction and self-expression than more traditional and formal religious services. A proliferation of camp-style meetings, ministers, and sects diffused authority and created an opportunity for women to assert themselves. Women helped to judge members for admission to congregations, to select ministers, and to organize religious services. During the 1760s, a Newport, Rhode Island, woman spoke to hundreds of people in her home each week on religious matters.

In addition to rejecting passivity, women sometimes left virtue behind as well. North Carolina court records reveal that two young women received reprimands for swimming nude with two young men in the Chowan River. The most common crime to appear in North Carolina records was fornication, or engaging in sexual relations before marriage. Moreover, single women often chose their own mates and did not hesitate to elope when their parents opposed their wishes. Once wed, dissatisfied women sought sexual alliances outside of marriage, so illegitimate children were not rare. When widowed, many women chose to remain single rather than to remarry.

Cases of "Deviant" Women

Cases of individual women reveal that domesticity lacked allure in some women's eyes. Apparently, a discrepancy existed between the model established for colonial women and the reality that many achieved. Colonial poet Anne Bradstreet is an early illustration of a woman who grappled with a conflict between the accepted image of womanhood and her own desires. After immigrating to Massachusetts Bay with her husband, Simon, in 1630, Bradstreet not only fulfilled her household duties and bore eight children, but demonstrated her talent as a poet and writer.

Bradstreet was aware of women's accepted roles and duties, for many sermons, statements, and books of the day clearly spelled them out. Two such books, *A Good Wife, God's Gift* and *Marriage Duties,* appeared as early as 1620. If women deviated from the accepted rules, they soon felt the sting of public censure. The venerable and respected governor of the Massachusetts Bay Colony, John Winthrop, declared in 1645 that Anne Hopkins, wife of the governor of Connecticut, had "fallen into . . . the loss of her understanding and reason, by occasion of her giving herself wholly to reading and writing many books." Winthrop added that "If she had attended her household affairs, and such things as belong to women, and not gone out of her way and calling to meddle in such things as are proper for men, whose minds are stronger," Hopkins might have kept her sanity.

Yet Bradstreet felt compelled to go on with her writing, often after a long day's work as the ideal wife and mother. In 1642, she expressed her bitterness regarding the criticism that her work drew. "I am obnoxious to each carping tongue," go the lines of one poem, "who says my hand a needle better fits." She concluded: "If what I do prove well, it won't advance/They'll say it's stolen, or else it was by chance." In 1650, when a book of her poems, *The Tenth Muse Lately Sprung Up In America,* appeared anonymously in London as a result of her brother-in-law's efforts, Bradstreet was soon identified as its author. Her brother, however, took offense and minced no words when offering his opinion of her activities. "Your printing of a book, beyond the custom of your sex, doth rankly smell," he stated in a public letter to her publisher in London. Despite her discouragement over this episode and her increasing acceptance of the idea that "men can do best, and women know it well," Bradstreet continued to write. Six years after her death in 1672, Bradstreet's works appeared in a compilation titled *Several Poems Compiled by a Gentlewoman in New England*.

The well-known religious dissident Anne Hutchinson also stepped beyond the bounds of her domestic world, thus contributing jarring notes to the ongoing debate regarding the nature of women. Like Bradstreet, she was aware of the prescribed behavior for women. Hutchinson, a Biblical scholar, was fully conversant with St. Paul's admonition that women should "keep silent in the churches." Yet after her arrival in Boston with her husband William in 1634, Hutchinson's activities gradually fueled a religious controversy.

Hutchinson believed and taught that individuals could communicate with the spirit of Christ and interpret Biblical teachings and sermons for themselves. Such ideas created a social problem because they stressed the individual's ability to feel God's grace within, a doctrine that minimized ministerial guidance and encouraged women to think and question. Because such beliefs threatened the power of the authoritarian Puritan ministers in Massachusetts, church officials condemned Hutchinson's ideas as heresy, meaning she was anti-authority, both political and religious. Governor Winthrop, fearing the disruption Hutchinson was causing, denounced her, calling her a woman of "a nimble wit and active spirit, and a very voluble tongue, more bold than a man."

In the face of such attacks, Hutchinson continued to defend herself and to teach her religious beliefs. Hutchinson attracted numerous followers, both women and men. Prominent and affluent merchants and craftspeople who felt constrained in their businesses by church rules supported her. Her views appealed to a number of women who seemed restive and in search of a way to express themselves. Yet Hutchinson was not just a rebel and an agitator. She was exemplary in fulfilling her prescribed obligations as a woman. She was a devoted wife, the loving mother of fifteen children, and a beloved midwife and nurse.

Hutchinson attained stature and wide respect, yet church authorities feared her teachings and the growing factionalism in the community that her ideas encouraged. Charging Hutchinson with both religious heresy and behavior unfitting a female, the authorities called her to trial in 1637 and 1638, telling her that "you have rather been a husband than a wife, and a preacher than a hearer." Because Hutchinson had stepped out of her "place" and challenged home, church, and state, Massachusetts courts excommunicated her from the church and banished her from the colony. Along with many of her followers, Hutchinson left Massachusetts Bay and settled in Rhode Island, where she continued her resistance. She later moved to New York where, in 1643, American Indians killed her, two of her sons, and three of her daughters because of a tragic misunderstanding regarding payment for the land Hutchinson occupied.

Neither Hutchinson's punishment nor her death marked the end of the theological debate or women's resistance to the restrictions the Puritan church and society placed on their lives. In 1638, Massachusetts courts ordered a number of other women dissenters whipped or cast out of the church. In 1641, authorities excommunicated Ann Hibbens for slander and denounced her for resisting the supremacy of her husband, "unto whom God put her in subjection." In 1644, officials also excommunicated Ann Eaton, an opponent of infant baptism, for lying and for stubbornness. Twenty-two years after the Hutchinson affair, one of Hutchinson's major supporters, Quaker Mary Dyer, was judged "troublesome" and hanged in Boston.

A similar problem erupted with the women of Salem, Massachusetts. Here, women who questioned religious and other authorities or acted in ways that transcended accepted bounds were branded witches. Apparently, many Puritans, who were going through a bad time economically and politically, sincerely believed the Devil might be at the root of their troubles. People's enormous fear of an evil power that was said to work primarily through the community's women led to legal charges against a large number of women and a few men. During the witchcraft trials of the 1650s and 1660s, Salem courts ordered women whipped, chained to posts, jailed, excommunicated, and executed. In 1648, for instance, one woman was executed for having a "malignant" touch and using suspicious medicines.

In a later outbreak of the witchcraft scare during the 1690s, tribunals condemned as witches many women and a few men in some forty other towns, mainly in New England. Because women were often thought to be evil, partly due to beliefs connected with Eve, they sustained more convictions than did men. Also, like Rebecca Nurse, a seventy-one-year-old woman jailed and then hanged in 1692, the alleged witches were usually middle-aged or older, reputed to be contentious, and involved in community affairs.

Women who achieved even a small bit of economic success, as well as those who enjoyed real wealth, were more likely to be accused of practicing witchcraft than those who did not. Wives or widows active in commerce and business endeavors sustained an unusually high number of charges and convictions. One possible interpretation of these facts is that witchcraft convictions punished women whose economic activities diverged sharply from Calvinist teachings that women should remain quiet, passive, and confined within the home.

During the 1700s, as areas of the American colonies grew more "civilized," rigid gender expectations relaxed somewhat, at least for white women of the middle and upper classes. Still, some women continued to venture beyond the bounds of their usual domains. In the South, for example, young Eliza Lucas practiced her own brand of noncompliance. Because her father served as governor of Antigua in the West Indies and her invalid mother was incapable of running the family plantations in South Carolina, in 1739 seventeen-year-old Eliza began to manage the family's three plantations in the Charleston area. She taught herself bookkeeping, accounting, and other skills needed to run such an extensive business. Eliza also learned all she could about the cultivation of rice, South Carolina's major crop.

The following year, young Eliza wrote a woman friend, "I have the business of 3 plantations to transact, which requires much writing and more business and fatigue of other sorts than you can imagine." She spent her few leisure hours with her "Musick and the Garden," of which she was "very fond." Eliza explained that she avoided becoming "quite moaped" with her way of life because of the encouragement she received from several female friends and through regular correspondence with her father.

Soon, at her father's urging, Lucas began to experiment with other crops. One of these was the indigo plant, which produced a blue dye very much in demand by the British textile industry. Although neighboring planters thought her an eccentric young woman, she believed that indigo might pull the economy of South Carolina out of the doldrums. Lucas worked in the fields alongside her overseer, studying the involved process of "retting" the indigo plant into dye. Finally, Eliza accepted the aid of a knowledgeable indigo maker sent by her father from the West Indies. Because this man thought Lucas unwomanly and feared that her success would undermine his own island's sale of indigo, he quarreled with her and sabotaged her retting equipment.

Despite these difficulties, Lucas finally produced the plantation's first cakes of dye in 1744. Upon observing her success, neighboring planters sought her aid. She graciously gave them both indigo seeds and advice. Eventually, indigo became the second largest export in South Carolina. Also in 1744, after rejecting her father's choices of potential husbands, Lucas chose her own husband, Charles Pinckney, widower of her best friend and twenty years her senior.

Even though she was atypical in many ways, Lucas embodied the well-bred southern woman. She studied Plutarch, Virgil, French, and shorthand. She participated in prescribed female activities, including teaching plantation children, doing needlework, and playing the pianoforte. And she kept a letter-book filled with charming phrases and interesting observations that is one of the most significant collections in existence kept by a colonial lady.

During the 1700s, women of the North also tested the limits. For instance, by 1760, Margaret Cheer had achieved fame as the leading actress on the American stage. Even after her marriage, Cheer traveled with "The American Company of Comedians" until the Continental Congress closed American theaters in 1769. The following year, Ann Catherine Green, the mother of fourteen children, began to publish the *Maryland Gazette,* the only newspaper in Maryland for many years. Noted for her fairness and skill as a commentator and editor, Green became the official publisher for the colony of Maryland. Thus, legal restrictions and gender constructions notwithstanding, numerous colonial women developed their own talents, skills, and interests.

White Women of the Lower Classes

Obviously, such women as Hutchinson and Lucas came from educated, fairly well-to-do families. They had the resources with which to seize opportunities and to buck societal norms. Not all white colonial women were so fortunate, however. At the lower end of the white social structure were uneducated, unskilled, and poverty-stricken women unable to care for themselves adequately.

In desperation, these women often took poorly paying jobs as household servants, washwomen, cooks, or farm laborers. They performed a wide range of tasks, from spinning to harvesting crops. Despite their industry, they could not make a tolerable living for themselves. For women with children to support, their living situations became all but impossible.

As a result, such women often turned to public aid programs. In cities like Philadelphia, a poor woman could go to an almshouse, or poor house, or she might apply for meager assistance in the form of food, clothes, and money. In return, women could be forced to work at highly objectionable jobs or to wear badges marked with a "P" for pauper. They also might see their children scattered, bound out as servants, or lost to them entirely.

The alternative to the acceptance of such humiliating forms of public aid was worse still. Some poor women begged from door-to-door for handouts and lived in back-streets or took shelter in abandoned outbuildings. Others stole food or turned to prostitution, often landing in prison as a consequence.

By the mid-1700s, growing numbers of poor women constituted as much as two-thirds of the desperately poor in some colonies. Their ranks included orphans, single women, abandoned or runaway wives, and widows. Some were indentured servants who had fled intolerable situations. Some had gotten pregnant without benefit of marriage or been caught in an adulterous act. Others had left their homes to escape their husbands' physical and verbal abuse. Still others were too old to work and had no family to help them.

Despite the long-standing image of colonial America as a classless society that offered the promise of a better life to anyone willing to work, the reality was far different for poor white women. Because public assistance programs proved ineffective and demeaning, gradually church organizations and such other groups as Guardians of the Poor extended help. For poverty stricken white women, colonial America remained far from the "paradise on earth for women" that George Alsop of Maryland had described.

African Women

African Women in Colonial America

The situation of another group of women to settle in colonial America was quite different. African women were wrested away from their homelands against their will to provide labor for colonial Americans. Although early generations of slaves left no written documents, colonial records reveal their lives to some degree.

Annals of the London Company show that the first boatload of twenty Africans arrived at Jamestown in August 1619. A Dutch man-of-war, whose crew had seized one hundred African slaves from a Spanish frigate on its way to the Spanish West Indies, brought these twenty survivors to Virginia for sale. The *Treasurer,* an English ship that had sailed with the Dutch ship, had only one slave who had outlasted starvation and ill treatment, a woman her captors called Angela. Other ships followed so that by 1624, Africans accounted for 2 percent of Virginia's population.

In their African homes, these women had served as wives, mothers, traders, farmers, political leaders, and even warriors. In addition, African women represented a wide spectrum of backgrounds and regions, and brought with them a rich history and culture. African female slaves were far more than the "girls" or "mammies" that their white mistresses perceived. Rather, African women reflected the social and regional diversity of Africa and its ethnic variance. Representing every class from royalty to commoners, the African women brought to America came primarily from the West African coast, ranging from Senegambia to Angola, and from the region around the "horn" of the continent to the island of Madagascar. Slave women were taken captive from such tribes as the Dahomey, Ashanti, and Mandinka, and such countries as Sierra Leone, Gambia, and Cape Verde.

Once captured and aboard sailing ships bound to the American colonies, however, African women, regardless of their former status, became "trade goods." Along with gold, ivory, and grain, merchants exchanged African women for iron, guns, gunpowder, whiskey, and foodstuffs. During the so-called middle passage these women endured lack of food and medicine, exposure to foul weather, branding on the breast or face, and sexual assault at the hands of the crew. Because initially slave captains wished to cram as many slaves as possible aboard their "slavers," women usually were made to lie together on their sides spoon-fashion, often shackled together by the ankles. Because such conditions often forced slaves to lie in their own and others' feces, urine, and vomit, disease aboard slavers was rife. In the early years of the American slave trade, the slave mortality rate during the Atlantic crossing ranged from 10 to 50 percent.

Understandably, mutiny commonly occurred on slave ships. Women, as prepared to resist their captors as were men, joined in these mutinies, while many brave souls attempted suicide, fasting to the point of starvation. If they reached the West Indies or the American colonies alive, women submitted to numerous examinations, including rough gynecologic ones. They also saw their supposedly temporary status as indentured servants turn into life-long slavery.

Initially, these and other early African women arrived in Virginia as indentured servants, a temporary status that was supposed to end after a period of years. Unlike colonists in the British and French West Indies, settlers in America hesitated to embrace slavery. Yet, between 1641 and 1750, all colonies legalized slavery. As early as the 1640s, a number of southern colonies, notably Virginia, began to turn indentures into formalized slavery. Virginia court records reveal that Africans and African Americans were sold "for life" and that the status of many black children was that of "perpetual servant." By 1648, Virginia's slave population numbered about three hundred.

Slaveholders also preferred to have ownership of their slaves' *future* children. Because no laws ensured this as yet, purchasers often stipulated it at the time of sale. In 1652, one Virginia planter signed an agreement stating that he had purchased a young black woman as well as "her issue and produce during her . . . Life tyme and their successors forever."

By 1661, Virginia legalized slavery, sealing at least twenty years of practice into law. Although English common law stated that children followed the status of their fathers, in 1662 Virginia law decreed that all black children would automatically inherit their mother's condition. In other words, "all children born in this country shall be held bond or free according to the condition of the mother."

By the 1700s, slave labor played a crucial role in the colonial economy, especially in the southern colonies. In 1711, a North Carolina woman maintained "that there is no living here" without slave help. Although this woman hired a slave girl as a domestic servant and eventually purchased a man, she knew little about slaves. She simply relied on the conventional wisdom that a person might succeed by getting "a few slaves" and beating "them well to make them work hard."

The colony of Georgia, originally founded as a haven for the downtrodden, held out the longest. In 1735, Georgia banned slavery. This provision was difficult to enforce and lasted only fourteen years. In

1750, Georgia officials reversed the earlier stand by making slavery legal in the colony.

Slavery flourished because white colonists faced a dire labor shortage, which they attempted to solve by importing a growing number of African workers, who arrived as indentures but were soon designated slaves. Especially in the southern and middle colonies, a lack of laborers for plantations and large farms galvanized the growth of the slave system. In addition, Africans knew a great deal about the cultivation of crops, especially rice. Also, blacks proved less vulnerable to malaria than did whites. To white planters desperate for workers, the idea of permanently bonded African servants seemed a workable solution

African Women's Work

African women fell outside the colonists' notion that women should be first and foremost wives and mothers. Partly due to acute labor shortages, colonists viewed African women as workers, both in homes and fields. In fact, many African women had been agriculturalists in Africa and were skilled in planting, weeding, worming, and harvesting a variety of crops. Yet, because of the continuing need for field labor, buyers preferred to purchase strong young men for use in tobacco, rice, sugar cane, and corn fields. In South Carolina in the mid-1700s, for example, men sold for upwards of £250, while women brought approximately £200. Although buyers gradually recognized African women's potential as domestic servants, field workers, breeders of future slaves, and even midwives, African women continued to be brought to the colonies in lesser numbers than men. This imbalance frequently left African women bereft of female networks and all the more subject to sexual abuse by white and black men.

In addition, African women had to submit to the system that whites imposed on them. Accordingly, slave women developed roles that would suit their owners and ensure women's own survival. Because slave women were viewed primarily as workers, they had to tailor their domestic duties and cares to fit their new occupations in the field or big house. In so doing, African women tempered their traditional female independence. Some had to forego the leadership positions they had held in African matrilineal societies. Others who may have helped found cities or led warriors against rival kingdoms now had to submit to hard work and a lowly status. And all slave women had to accept the supposed inferiority of women, especially of black women.

At least in part due to Christian teachings equating darkness with evil, Christian colonists thought of black people as more corrupt and as lesser beings than themselves. Because black men and women were inferior, the argument went, Providence clearly meant them to perform brute labor and work for other supposedly superior people. Moreover, the owners of African women counted on them to produce children who would serve as additional slave laborers. At little or no cost, slaveowners could increase the numbers of slaves they held. During the 1600s, however, black women's poor health and the alienation they experienced under slavery suppressed their fertility. The combination of a short life expectancy, created largely by inadequate nutrition and a lack of immunity to unfamiliar diseases, further limited slave women's childbearing abilities. On average, slave women bore three children, many of whom died at birth or shortly thereafter.

Still, slave owners expected women to produce as many children as possible. In 1639, a person visiting Samuel Maverick, the son of an Anglican minister and reportedly New England's first slaveholder, claimed that Maverick forced his slaves to cohabit. The visitor noted that Maverick "commanded" an African slave in his household to "go to bed" with his female slave against her will, although Maverick's slave woman had once been "a Queen in her own Country."

By the early 1700s, many slave women were native-born in the colonies. They no longer had to struggle to learn their owners' languages or stave off diseases for which they lacked immunity. Consequently, many slaveholders encouraged—or forced—matches between slave men and women. Some gave slave women rewards for each child they bore, including days off from work or new clothing.

By the 1720s and 1730s, natural increase among the slave population began to occur. Some women resisted the pressure to produce children by using contraceptives and herbal abortants, while others committed infanticide rather than letting their infants grow up as slaves. Still, plantation records indicate that on average a slave woman bore nine children, thus delivering a child approximately every two years. By 1740, according to one investigator, a total of 23,958 slaves lived in northern colonies, while 126,066 resided in southern colonies.

Besides producing future workers, black women provided cheap labor, even to some degree in the New England and middle colonies, which were made up of farms rather than larger plantations. Here, slave women worked on farms, usually tending stock and cultivating crops, or in farmhouses as domestic servants, washwomen, and nursemaids. By 1690, women constituted a minority of the four hundred black people residing in Massachusetts. One of these was Tituba, from Barbados, bought by Reverend Samuel Parris to work as a domestic servant. Along with her husband, John, Tituba managed the Parris household. Parris also hired Tituba out to a local weaver and John to a tavernkeeper, thus ensuring himself two sources of income.

Tituba often passed dark winter evenings by telling the children and several bound girls (indentured servants) tales of her native land, including stories about talking animals and magic. Unfortunately for Tituba, witchcraft had become a frightening concern in Massachusetts during the early 1690s. When some of her listeners performed strange acts, including barking like dogs, people suspected Tituba of practicing witchcraft. Several of the girls duly accused Tituba and, after Parris beat her, Tituba confessed. In 1692, Tituba became one of the first three women accused of witchcraft in Salem, Massachusetts. A local court convicted Tituba and jailed her for thirteen months. Subsequently, Parris sold Tituba and she disappeared from the historical record.

The New England and Middle colonies did not always treat slave women in such unenlightened ways. Not all colonists believed in the limitations the slave system imposed on black people. As early as 1704 a white male reformer in New York City organized at Trinity Church the first school for slaves in the American colonies. Puritans established a number of similar schools in New England, while Quakers did so in Pennsylvania and New Jersey. Some educated women of color subsequently gained public notice. In 1746, Lucy Terry Prince, educated by her owner, became the first black poet in America. Prince's poem, "A Slave Report in Rhyme," described a battle between American Indians and colonists at Old Deerfield in Massachusetts and was later published in 1855.

In the southern colonies, slave women served as midwives, nurses, apothecaries, cooks, seamstresses, weavers, and dairy maids. Still, 89 percent of slave women labored in the fields. They transferred their agricultural skills from African fields to those of the American colonies, where they tended tobacco, rice, wheat, corn, and indigo. Women worked alongside men, clearing the fields for planting, sowing, weeding, and harvesting. On some plantations, women did separate jobs from men. For example, women hoed and men plowed. On other plantations, or in times of emergency, women performed the same tasks as men, including plowing. In between, women undertook a variety of gender-specific tasks, including caring for and butchering livestock, filling ice houses, spinning cotton, weaving cloth, and cooking. If slack times occurred, the owners of slave women might hire them out to other people to realize extra income.

Other slave women worked in plantation and farmhouses, helping to care for the families who raised crops. Such work could bring benefits in the form of additional scraps of food or items of clothing, but it required long hours waiting in dark hallways and pantries, days spent standing on the rough brick floors of kitchens and washhouses, or nights sleeping on straw mats near children's beds. Nor were mistresses of large houses necessarily easier to work for than were male overseers in the fields. Instances of brutal and abusive mistresses were rife.

Neither did slave women have much hope for their children's futures. During the 1600s and early 1700s, southern slave children sometimes received basic education because planters' wives and daughters often believed it their duty to teach their slaves elementary reading and writing. On some plantations, rudimentary schools even provided classes for slave children. Education for slaves soon disappeared, however, for planters argued that slaves were ineducable and any schooling a waste of time. Other slave owners, who feared that teaching slaves to read and write would help them plot rebellions, actively opposed the educating of slaves.

Slave Families and Communities

During the 1600s, slave women frequently saw their families splintered by sale and death. Once separated from their mates, slave women typically continued to live with their children or form new families with another man. Often, women established their primary bonds with daughters and other women, forming female networks that served as both support and work groups. From women came an effort to conserve what remnants of African culture they could, including birthing practices and the growing of such crops as groundnuts and yams. Too, women devised new folkways to replace those lost in passage, including marriage rituals and work songs used in the fields. A woman, then, often tried to offset the shattering effects of slavery.

During the 1700s, slave women's isolation began to lessen somewhat. Especially on large southern plantations, the number of slaves grew and the ratio of men to women began to equalize. Most native-born slaves spoke English and had converted to Christianity. They lived in slave quarters, a village of sorts usually located out of sight of the plantation house and the overseers' dwelling. These factors allowed slaves to establish a sense of community, and slave women to operate within female and kin networks. By the mid-1700s, a woman might live with her husband and children for many years. In other cases, family members were hired out or sold, thus splintering the family unit that was at the core of slave culture.

In such communities, slave women functioned, like white women, as domestic artisans. Although black women received rations of foodstuffs and minimal clothing from their owners, they supplemented their families' diets by growing vegetables on small plots located near their cabins, raising chickens, and gathering edible plants and roots. Sometimes these women produced surplus goods for sale to itinerant peddlers, local shopkeepers, and even to their mistresses. Slave women's trade goods ranged from vegetables and eggs to pies and handmade baskets. During the mid 1700s, it was not uncommon for such slave women to earn enough cash to purchase such items as thread, cloth, buttons, crockery, and kettles.

Besides this domestic-based economy, slave women recreated customs and rituals from their homeland. Despite the onslaught of Christian teaching and the disapproval of whites regarding African ways,

African and African American women combined old ways with new, thus establishing unique birth, marriage, and burial customs that were reminiscent of Africa yet had Christian elements. Moreover, such women acted as apothecaries, midwives, nurses, and doctors in their immediate neighborhoods. Women's knowledge of roots and herbs served them well in medical situations. In addition, women could barter or sell the potions, liniments, and poultices that they made.

Much like women of other cultures, then, slave women held together families, or remnants of families, providing members with such goods as food, clothing, and medicine. Women conserved traditional practices or created new rituals. Despite frequent pregnancies, these women were productive workers in homes and fields. In addition, burdensome duties failed to keep slave women from developing a life of their own and wielding some power within their families and communities.

Urban Slaves

Slave women also inhabited towns and cities. There they performed domestic labor for wealthy white families. They might labor in the home of a Baltimore shipper, a Richmond merchant, or a Charleston rice trader. Certainly, Georgia planters who escaped malaria by living in Charleston during the summer could not have gotten along without slave women in their households. Even in New England, where small farms and artisan shops had less need for slaves than the middle and southern colonies, female slaves could be found in towns and cities, working primarily as domestic servants.

On the one hand, urban slave women faced a number of disadvantages. Their lodging may have been a cramped attic or musty basement. In addition, they usually lacked a sense of family and community. Few urban households could accommodate a slave's children, and seldom did they have jobs available for a spouse. Even a woman's friends and confidantes necessarily came from the household or immediate neighborhood, thus eliminating the possibility of a wide network to rely on in time of need or crisis.

On other hand, urban life often provided women with a measure of independence and autonomy unknown to their rural counterparts. Rather than living in their mistress's or master's house, they sometimes inhabited small cabins closeby. Some earned extra money by selling such items as catfish, dry goods, and baskets. Especially in Charleston, South Carolina, black women traders combined a keen business sense with a reputation for selling quality wares, notably hand-woven baskets that incorporated traditional African designs.

In addition, during the 1700s, urban markets offered black women an opportunity to function as traders. Naturally, some white Charleston residents feared that women traders would give other African Americans ideas regarding independence. Because whites in Charleston had long feared black rebellion, officials had instituted curfews, prohibited public gatherings of black people, and formed slave patrols to enforce these provisions. Despite these restrictions, in 1739 an uprising occurred at Stono River Bridge, only twenty miles south of the city.

Yet, in South Carolina, the Negro Act of 1740 permitted slaves to act as representatives of their owners in buying or selling produce and other goods. Some clever slave women negotiated deals with their mistresses and masters whereby they could use a portion of the money they earned to buy and sell items for their own profit. Women who worked as market dealers duplicated the roles black women had played in African societies. By the 1750s, the Charleston market was largely run by slave women, who influenced the distribution of the city's daily food supply.

During the next two decades, a growing number of white visitors to Charleston's market described women merchants as "unruly" and "insolent." By the 1760s, some Charleston residents objected to what they called "black profiteering," which drove the price of goods up to an unreasonable level. Yet by this time the number of market women was small, and they remained stifled by their lowly status as women and slaves. Although some whites felt threatened by these traders, Charleston's market women possessed limited power.

White Fears and Black Resistance

Individual slave women and men reacted in different ways to their unhappy situations. Even if a slave woman received some benefits or created opportunities for herself, as did the Charleston market women, she was still a slave, legally "owned" by another person. The arrogance of the concept that one human could possess another is staggering. Certainly slaves recognized the inhumanity of the beliefs that underlay slavery. In addition, many white colonists rejected the idea of slavery or felt extremely uneasy with it. Even the staunchest slaveholders realized that slaves were people who yearned for freedom and were likely to resist their status whenever they could. Such resistance might be passive, such as work slow-downs or purposely misunderstanding instructions, while other slaves might resort to running away or to committing outright violence against their oppressors.

Unsurprisingly, as the number of black people in America grew so did whites' fears escalate. Colonists increasingly viewed slaves who ran away as "troublemakers." Indeed, according to public notices and newspaper advertisements, both slave men and women often ran away. Slaves also frequently revolted. In 1708, for example, a number of Newton, Long Island, slaves revolted and killed seven white people. In punishment, authorities hung three slave men and burned to death one slave woman. The colony passed a law allowing the courts to sentence rebels to death in any manner to maintain "public tranquility."

Other slaves used fire as their weapon of choice against slave owners. In 1740, a Charleston, South Carolina, court condemned a slave woman to death for the crime of arson. The following year, a Charleston, Massachusetts, court ordered that a slave named Kate be executed for setting fire to a house and intending to burn down the entire town. Later, in 1766, when another Massachusetts court sentenced to execution a woman who burned to the ground her owner's house, tobacco house, and outhouse, the prosecutor noted that slaves had already burned two other outbuildings full of tobacco that winter.

Such uprisings led to increased restrictions on the slave population. Worries about runaways and rebellions eventually led to the formal prohibition of education for slaves, as well as written communication between them. Though formally denied a written form of expression, slaves clung to the custom of oral history they brought with them from their African or Caribbean homes. And black Americans relied on this oral tradition to chronicle their history. When excluded from churches, once owners came to fear that slaves might use church meetings to plan rebellions, slaves held their own religious observances, often disregarding Christianity or blending Christian tenets with African traditions. And once owners theorized that they could sell unmarried slaves with less upheaval, slaves were denied formal marriages. Undeterred, slaves responded by holding their own wedding ceremonies, relying on their own communities for recognition.

By the mid-eighteenth century, one appraisal estimates that 48,460 slaves lived in the New England and the middle colonies, while 411,362 lived in the South. Although the women among them played a vital role in the colonial economy, their contributions were frequently overlooked and undervalued. Nor did their lives fit the white colonists' model of womanhood. Black women, especially those in the New England and middle colonies, observed and understood prevailing gender expectations, but few were able to fulfill them. Rather, black women often had to be assertive and strong. Although they did cook, sew, and care for their families, they performed heavy labor, resisted their oppressors, and filled leadership roles. In numerous ways, then, the reality of slave women's lives diverged from the social ideals of the culture at large.

Free Black Women

A slightly different situation existed for free women of color than for slave women. In both rural and urban areas some black women obtained their freedom by working their way out of slavery, receiving it from their owners as a gift, or as a bequest in an owner's will. In the

New England and middle colonies, legal appeals for a slave's emancipation sometimes succeeded as well. In 1766, a forty-six-year-old mulatto named Jenny Slew successfully sued for her emancipation. Because Massachusetts was one of the few states that allowed slaves to bring suit (slaves were usually regarded under the law as property rather than persons), Slew was permitted to argue her case. She claimed that she had been born free because her mother was white. When the judges divided on the case, Slew won her freedom. In addition, the court awarded her £4 and court costs. After attorney John Adams listened to the hearings, he wrote "this is called suing for liberty; the first action that ever I knew of the sort, though I have heard there have been many."

Free blacks sometimes chose to stay with former owners as paid domestic servants, or they hired themselves out as domestics, farm laborers, or workers in other service areas. Some, especially in cities, started their own small businesses, including selling fruits and vegetables from pushcarts. Mary and Anthony Johnson of Northampton County, Virginia, were two successful free people of color. They arrived in separate ships in 1621 and 1622, then met on a plantation where Mary was the only woman. At some point, they obtained their liberty, married, and raised four children. They owned a 250-acre plantation and their grown son John a 450-acre plantation, both of which they sold when they moved to Maryland during the 1660s.

Many other examples of free women of color existed in Philadelphia, where a number of wealthy Quaker professionals and merchants emancipated their slaves during the 1700s, especially after 1740. Although the majority of free women of color worked as domestic servants, washwomen, and nursemaids, many of them could read, write, and figure sums. Other free black women ran small businesses or owned property. One of these, Jane Row, held real estate in Philadelphia and in Southwark and owned two slaves. Another, a widow, owned a lot and several buildings in the Spring Garden section of Philadelphia. Unlike many slave women in Pennsylvania, these free women of color lived with their families and could establish homes, raise their children, and, if they chose to do so, borrow from the ideal American womanhood that white colonists advocated.

Mulattos

From the beginning, interracial unions occurred between Africans and white colonists, creating a new group of Americans called mulattos or black creoles. Some white colonists believed that such intermixing of the races would bring harmony between groups. Others opposed the idea. As early as 1662, the Virginia legislature took a stand against interracial alliances, either between white men and black women or white women and black men. Virginia's 1662 law stated that any "Christian" (meaning a white person) who engaged in "fornication with a Negra man or woman, he or she offending shall pay double the fines imposed."

Other colonies soon followed suit with laws forbidding white-black coupling, whether within or outside marriage. By the mid-1700s, every colony prohibited cohabitation between whites and blacks, although most jurisdictions allowed Africans and Indians to marry. Those who refused to comply were subject to fines, whippings, imprisonment, and banishment. A number of women and men of different races found ways to circumvent laws against miscegenation, which were often laxly implemented, if at all. Some of these black-white unions came about through force, including rape, but a significant number of other interracial relationships were based on strong affectional bonds.

White and black people met in many ways, including in church. In the colony of New Netherland, later New York, Lutheran churches welcomed black members as early as 1660. Ministers conducted wedding ceremonies between free blacks and slaves, as well as between blacks and whites. In 1741, for example, Mary Jorga, a free black woman, wed James Elsworth, an Englishman, in the New York Lutheran synod. The marriage was successful, even though most white Americans of the era increasingly perceived such unions as illicit and perhaps even sinful.

In most colonies, the children of such interracial couples legally assumed the status of their mothers. Thus, many mulatto children were slaves. In some cases, a white father bought a child out of slavery and freed him or her. In others, a father provided extra rations and clothing for mother and child, perhaps freeing them in his will. Yet others ignored the existence of a mulatto child among his slaves and denied any responsibility for the child's existence. If a mother was free, however, her mulatto child was free.

Clearly, the process of inventing the archetypal American woman had only begun during the colonial era. Still, gender expectations regarding women exerted increasing force on white women through public opinion, government policies, and laws. The principles of womanhood had already defined white women's lives in subtle and not-so-subtle ways. Although Sarah Harrison of Surry County, Virginia, might mutter "no obey" at her 1687 wedding to James Blair, many other women assumed and accepted male prerogatives accorded to them in a patriarchal system.

Where did women of color stand in relation to white gender conventions? Although women of color experienced a life cycle similar to that of white women, performed comparable work, and had analogous dreams for their children, they remained separate. The idea of colonial America as a classless society is more fantasy than reality. For over two hundred years such factors as ethnicity, religion, and especially race determined a colonial woman's place among other women. Because white ideology regarding women had become dominant, it also tried to dictate how women of color would live.

The year 1763 marked a turning point in all these women's lives. Although some historians of women have aptly argued that the traditional dates that mark such male-oriented events as wars and depressions are irrelevant to women's history, this contention is only partly true. Cataclysmic national events intruded themselves into women's lives as well as men's. In addition, an ever-expanding knowledge of women's history demonstrates that where men went, women went as well. The year 1763, when the French and Indian War ended and the resistance phase of the American Revolution began, was as significant for women, both white and of color, as it was for men.

Study Guide

Checklist of important names, terms, phrases, and dates in Chapter 1.
Think about what or who each was and why she, he, or it was significant.

matriarchal society
matrilineal society
matrilocal society
Iroquois
Native American farmers
Algonquians
sachem
shaman
"bride price"
Native American divorce
Ojibway
Anasazi
Pueblos
El Norte
indigenous peoples
mestizos
Indian "princess"
Pocahontas
métis
maize
"squaws"
indentured servants
Blackstone's *Commentaries on the
    Laws of England*
gender roles
feme sole
Civil Death
feme covert
courts of equity
Margaret Brent
dowries
Davey v. *Turner*
prenuptial agreements, or marriage
    contracts
widows
herbalists

market economy
apprenticeships
midwives
Betsy Ross
patriarchal society
patrilineal society
patrilocal society
seduction
rape
forms of birth control
women's handiwork
doctrine of St. Paul
Jane Colden
Society of Friends, or Quakers
Nantucket women
1639
separate maintenance agreements
runaway wives
Great Awakening
Anne Bradstreet
Anne Hutchinson
Salem witchcraft trials
Eliza Lucas (Pinckney)
Ann Catherine Green
female paupers
1619
African women agriculturalists
slave women's fertility
Tituba
Lucy Terry Prince
female slave kin networks
Charleston's market women
African oral tradition
free black women
mulattos or black creoles
interracial relationships

Chapter 1 issues to think about and discuss

- How did women's roles and rights differ among American Indians, Hispanics, whites, and blacks? Explain why these cultures came up with different answers to the same question: what is the appropriate work and place of women?
- What factors are responsible for history being recorded largely from the white perspective?
- What problems stand in the way of reconstructing the history of peoples of color?
- If you had to go back in time, in which early North American society would you chose to live? Would it be as a female or male?
- What factors allowed white Europeans to dominate other groups of people living in the American colonies?
- To which colonial female woman does Pocahontas compare: Anne Bradstreet, Anne Hutchinson, or Eliza Pinckney?
- In what ways were the lives of colonial women, both white and of color, better and worse in the 1700s as compared to the 1600s?
- What differences and similarities do you see between the lives of colonial and contemporary women, both white and of color?
- Some people blame men for imposing limits on colonial women. Is this a fair judgment, or did such factors as religion and economics play a role in restricting women?
- For what reasons did some groups, notably the Puritans and most Native Americans, allow divorce? What arguments did contemporary opponents of divorce raise?
- Were the Salem witchcraft trials the result of religious issues or were other, deeper fears responsible?
- If you had been brought to the American colonies as a slave, what coping mechanisms would you use to survive?
- What does it mean to "colonize"? From outside America, that is, the British colonizing the American colonies? From inside America, that is, white people colonizing those of color?
- For what reasons have mixed-heritage peoples been largely left out of historical accounts?
- In what ways do national events affect women? Should the dates traditionally noted in history books be included in a chronology of women's history, or should women's history have a separate chronology?

Suggestions for Further Reading

Native American Women

Anderson, Karen. *Chain Her by One Foot: The Subjugation of Women in Seventeenth-Century New France.* London: Routledge, 1991.

——. "Commodity Exchange and Subordination: Montagnais-Naskapi and Huron Women, 1600–1650," *Signs* 11 (Fall 1985): 48–62.

Anderson, Marilyn J. "The Best of Two Worlds: The Pocahontas Legend as Treated in Early American Drama," *The Indian Historian* 12 (Summer 1979): 54–59, 64.

Buffalohead, Priscilla K. "Farmers, Warriors, Traders: A Fresh Look at Ojibway Women," *Minnesota History* 48 (Summer 1983): 236–44.

Dearborn, Mary V. *Pocahontas's Daughters: Gender and Ethnicity in American Culture.* Section 1. "A Case Study of American Indian Female Authorship," 12–30. New York: Oxford University Press, 1986.

Foote, Cheryl J., and Sandra K. Schackel, "Indian Women of New Mexico, 1535–1680," 17–40, in *New Mexico Women: Intercultural Perspectives,* edited by Joan M. Jensen and Darlis A. Miller. Albuquerque: University of New Mexico Press, 1986.

Green, Rayna. "The Pocahontas Perplex: The Image of Indian Women in American Culture," *The Massachusetts Review* 16 (1975): 698–714.

Higham, John. "Indian Princess and Roman Goddess: The First Female Symbols of America," *Proceedings of the American Antiquarian Society* 100.1 (1990): 45–79.

Hubbell, Jay B. "The Smith-Pocahontas Story in Literature," *The Virginia Magazine of History and Biography* 65 (July 1957): 275–300.

Medicine, Beatrice. "North American Indigenous Women and Cultural Domination," *American Indian Culture and Research Journal* 17 (1993): 121–30.

Perdue, Theda. *Cherokee Women: Gender and Culture Change, 1700–1835.* Lincoln: University of Nebraska Press, 1998.

Shoemaker, Nancy. "An Alliance Between Men: Gender Metaphors in Eighteenth-Century American Indian Diplomacy East of the Mississippi," *Ethnohistory* 46 (1999): 239-263.

Spanish-Heritage Women

Benson, Nancy C. "Pioneering Women of New Mexico," *El Palacio* 85 (Summer 1979): 8–13, 34–38.

Castañeda, Antonia I. "Spanish and English-speaking Women on Worldwide Frontiers: A Discussion of the Migration of Women to Alta California and New Zealand," 283–300, in *Western Women: Their Land, Their Lives,* edited by Lillian Schlissel, Vicki L. Ruiz, and Janice Monk. Albuquerque: University of New Mexico Press, 1988.

Córdova, Teresa, et al. *Chicana Voices: Intersections of Class, Race, and Gender.* Albuquerque: University of New Mexico Press, 1990. Section III.

Gutiérrez, Ramón A. *When Jesus Came, the Corn Mothers Went Away: Marriage, Sexuality, and Power in New Mexico, 1500–1846.* Stanford: Stanford University Press, 1991.

Hernández, Salomé. "Nueva Mexicanas as Refugees and Reconquest Settlers," 41–69, in *New Mexico Women: Intercultural Perspectives,* edited by Joan M. Jensen and Darlis A. Miller. Albuquerque: University of New Mexico Press, 1986.

Monroy, Douglas. *Thrown Among Strangers: The Making of Mexican Culture in Frontier California.* Berkeley: University of California Press, 1990.

Ortíz, Roxanne Dunbar. "Colonialism and the Role of Women: The Pueblos of New Mexico," *Southwest Economy and Society* 4 (Winter 1978/79): 28–46.

Rock, Rosalind Z. "'Pido y Supllico': Women and the Law in Spanish New Mexico," New Mexico Historical Review 65 (April 1990): 145–59.

White Women

Barker-Benfield, G. J. "Anne Hutchinson and the Puritan Attitude Toward Women," *Feminist Studies* 1 (1972): 65–96.

Berkin, Carol. *First Generation: Women in Colonial America.* New York: Hill and Wang, 1996.

Berkin, Carol Ruth. "Within the Conjurer's Circle: Women in Colonial America," 79–105, in *The Underside of American History,* edited by Thomas R. Frazier. 3d ed. New York: Harcourt Brace Jovanovich, 1978.

Daniels, Christine, and Michael V. Kennedy, eds. *Over the Threshold: Intimate Violence in Early America.* New York: Routledge, 1999.

Dayton, Cornelia Hughes. *Women before the Bar: Gender, Law, and Society in Connecticut, 1639–1789.* Chapel Hill: University of North Carolina Press, 1995.

D'Emilio, John, and Estelle B. Friedman. *Intimate Matters: A History of Sexuality in America.* New York: Harper & Row, 1988.

Demos, John. *A Little Commonwealth: Family Life in Plymouth Colony.* New York: Oxford University Press, 1970.

——. *Entertaining Satan.* New York: Oxford University Press, 1982.

Dewhurst, C. Kurt, Betty MacDowell, and Marshal MacDowell. *Artists in Aprons: Folk Art by American Women.* New York: E. P. Dutton, 1979.

Dye, Nancy Schrom. "History of Childbirth in America," *Signs* 6 (Autumn 1980): 97–108.

Farnham, Christie Anne, ed. *Women of the American South: A Multicultural Reader.* New York: New York University Press, 1997.

Gragg, Larry. *The Salem Witch Crisis.* New York: Praeger, 1992

Hull, N. E. H. *Female Felons: Women and Serious Crime in Colonial Massachusetts.* Chicago: University of Chicago Press, 1987.

Kamensky, Jane. "Words, Witches, and Women Trouble: Witchcraft, Disorderly Speech, and Gender Boundaries in Puritan New England," *Essex Institute Historical Collections* 128 (October 1992): 286–309.

Karlsen, Carol F. *The Devil in the Shape of a Woman: Witchcraft in Colonial New England.* New York: W. W. Norton, 1987.

Kessler-Harris, Alice. *Women Have Always Worked: A Historical Overview.* New York: McGraw-Hill, 1982.

Koehler, Lyle. *The Search for Order: The "Weaker Sex" in Seventeenth-Century New England.* Urbana: University of Illinois Press, 1980.

Lang, Amy S. *Prophetic Woman: Anne Hutchinson and the Problem of Dissent in the Literature of New England.* Berkeley: University of California Press, 1987.

Leavitt, Judith Walzer. *Brought to Bed: Childbearing in America, 1750 to 1950.* New York: Oxford University Press, 1986.

Lindemann, Barbara S. "'To Ravish and Carnally Know'—Rape in Eighteenth-Century Massachusetts," *Signs* 10 (Autumn 1984): 63–82.

Main, Gloria L. "An Inquiry Into When and Why Women Learned to Write in Colonial New England," *Journal of Social History* 24 (Spring 1991): 579–89.

McDaid, Jennifer Davis. "'Living on a Frontier Part': Virginia Women Among the Indians, 1622–1794," *Virginia Cavalcade* 42 (Winter 1993): 100–111.

Norton, Mary Beth. "The Evolution of White Women's Experience in Early America," *American Historical Review* 89 (June 1984): 593–619.

Pinckney, Elise, ed. *The Letterbook of Eliza Lucas Pinckney, 1739–1762.* Chapel Hill: University of North Carolina Press, 1972.

Pleck, Elizabeth. *Domestic Tyranny: The Making of American Social Policy against Family Violence from Colonial Times to the Present.* New York: Oxford University Press, 1987.

Porterfield, Amanda. *Female Piety in Puritan New England: The Emergence of Religious Humanism.* New York: Oxford University Press, 1991.

——. "Women's Attraction to Puritanism," *Church History* 60 (June 1991): 196–209.

Ransome, David R. "Wives for Virginia, 1621," *William and Mary Quarterly* 48 (January 1991): 3–18.

Reis, Elizabeth. *Damned Women: Sinners and Witches in Puritan New England.* Ithaca, NY: Cornell University Press, 1997.

Rosen, Deborah A. *Courts and Commerce: Gender, Law, and the Market Economy in Colonial New York.* Columbus: Ohio State University Press, 1997.

Riley, Glenda. *Divorce: An American Tradition.* New York: Oxford University Press, 1991.

Rubinstein, Charlotte Streifer. *American Women Artists from Early Indian Times to the Present.* Boston: G. K. Hall and Co., 1982.

Salmon, Marylynn. *Women and the Law of Property in Early America.* Chapel Hill: University of North Carolina Press, 1986.

Scholten, Catherine M. "On the Importance of the Obstetrick Art: Changing Customs of Childbirth in America, 1760–1825," *William and Mary Quarterly* 34 (July 1977): 426–45.

Sklar, Kathryn Kish, and Thomas Dublin. *Women and Power in American History: A Reader.* Vol. 1. Englewood Cliffs, NJ: Prentice Hall, 1991. Selections 1–6.

Smith, Daniel Scott, and Michael S. Hindus. "Premarital Pregnancy in America, 1640–1671: An Overview and Interpretation," *Journal of Interdisciplinary History* 5 (1975): 537–70.

Spruill, Julia Cherry. *Women's Life and Work in the Southern Colonies.* New York: W. W. Norton and Company, 1972.

Thickstun, Margaret O. *Fictions of the Feminine: Puritan Doctrine and the Representation of Women.* Ithaca, NY: Cornell University Press, 1988.

Treckel, Paula A. *To Comfort the Heart: Women in Seventeenth-Century America.* New York: Twayne Publishers, 1996.

Ulrich, Laurel Thatcher. *Good Wives: Images and Realities in the Lives of Women in Northern New England, 1650–1780.* New York: Oxford University Press, 1983.

Watson, Alan D. "Women in Colonial North Carolina: Overlooked and Underestimated," *North Carolina Historical Review* 58 (January 1981): 1–22.

Wertz, Richard W., and Dorothy C. Wertz. *Lying-In: A History of Childbirth in America.* New York: Free Press, 1977.

African and African American Women

Gaspar, David Barry and Darlene Clark Hine, eds. *More Than Chattel: Black Women and Slavery in the Americas.* Bloomington: Indiana University Press, 1996.

Gregory, Chester W. "Black Women in Pre-Federal America," 53–70, in *Clio Was a Woman: Studies in the History of American Women,* edited by Mabel E. Deutrich and Virginia C. Purdy. Washington, DC: Howard University Press, 1980.

Stevenson, Brenda K. "Slavery," 1045–54, in B*lack Women in America: An Historical Encyclopedia,* edited by Darlene Clark Hine. Vol. II. Brooklyn, NY: Carlson Publishing, Inc., 1993.

Mixed-Heritage Women

Brown, Jennifer S. H. "Métis, Halfbreeds, and Other Real People: Challenging Cultures and Categories," *History Teacher* 17 (November 1993): 19–25.

Hall, Gwendolyn Mildo. *African in Colonial Louisiana: The Development of Afro-Creole Culture in the Eighteenth Century.* Baton Rouge: Louisiana State University Press, 1994.

2

Resistance, Revolution, and Early Nationhood

1763 to 1812

During the mid-eighteenth century, a desire for self-government developed among many white colonists. Despite the efforts of both sides, however, neither could resolve the economic, social, and political differences between England and its colonies in North America. Actual resistance broke out in 1763, leading to more than a decade of protests and violent acts on the part of the colonists. Women of all sorts were actively involved in every aspect of the resistance phase of the coming revolution.

Neither was the war itself a male-only undertaking. The beginning of the American Revolution usually dates from 2 July 1776. On that day, the newly formed Continental Congress voted to fight for the independence of the American colonies from England. When Congress released the news on 4 July, Patriots, who supported the idea of independence, were joyful. Loyalists, however, who backed the English, felt apprehensive and disheartened. Like those men, women's sympathies were split; many women supported the American Patriots, but a significant number of women sided with the British. To defend their beliefs, women maintained the homefront and some even went to the fighting front.

The American Revolution formally ended on 20 January 1783. The new United States was now on its own. It was soon clear that the years of revolution would have far-reaching effects, including modifications in American ideas, law, and policies regarding women. The early years of new nationhood were critical ones for American women, whether white or of color. The emerging concept of Republican Womanhood received a great deal of attention, yet its tenets did not appeal or apply to all women.

At the same time, the American frontier line had been advancing westward, over the Appalachian Mountains and toward the Ohio Valley. As some Americans fought the British, others headed west, disrupting Native cultures and civilizations as they went. What had once been a trickle of Americans toward the West turned into a rushing river. For women, the early westward movement was an eye-opener, in ways both good and bad. For those who stuck to the western venture, rather than turning back, life would never seem quite the same again.

Because of resistance, war, early nationhood, and westward migration, women learned to live with chaos and upheaval. They discovered the truth of the saying that the only constant in life is change. By the time of the War of 1812, or the "Second American Revolution," not only had the young nation changed significantly, so had its women.

Resistance to England, 1763–1776

White Women

The resistance phase of the emerging revolution began in 1763, the year in which the French and Indian War ended. Although most white colonists celebrated the British victory over the French, they soon learned, to their dismay, that the end of the French and Indian War forced the British government to tighten control of its colonies. Huge war debts led British officials to insist on the collection of taxes that the colonists had grown used to disregarding. Britain's shaky economy also persuaded parliamentary leaders to shore up existing trade restrictions and devise new ways to extract revenue from the American colonies. Therefore, in rapid succession after 1763, Parliament approved such legislation as the Currency Act, Stamp Act, Quartering Act, and the Townshend Acts.

Because for many years Britain had been too busy waging war with its European rivals to pay its North American colonies much heed, white colonists had developed a sense of autonomy, regarding the will of the British Parliament and Crown with "salutary neglect." Now that Britain began to demand their compliance, Americans grew harried and annoyed. Within months of the war's end, dissatisfied colonists began to complain about the acts that followed the French and Indian War, especially the restriction on westward migration and the enforcement of old and new taxes. White colonists also opposed the many pieces of legislation that Parliament passed to constrain Britain's unruly American subjects.

The usual historical accounts of this colonial resistance to Britain features such names as Samuel Adams, Thomas Hutchinson, Thomas Jefferson, and Thomas Paine, as well as such organizations as the Stamp Act Congress, the Sons of Liberty, and the Continental Congress.

These descriptions typically omit the many contributions of female Patriots and Loyalists, usually white women who threw their energies into opposing or supporting the British. Although women were supposedly apolitical beings, the furor soon forced women to make political decisions. They had to stand with or against their menfolk, boycott British goods or continue to buy them, generously send goods to the front to supply Patriot soldiers or refuse to participate in the war effort, and decide whether to stay in America and see the conflict to its end or to flee to Canada, the Caribbean, or Europe.

Women who lived in such a highly charged political environment had to become aware of the issues and form some opinions about them. Virtually every shop, street corner, and dinner table hummed with conversation regarding whether the British government was immoral or moral in its actions toward the American colonies. No wonder white women became increasingly interested in the politics of the American Revolution. One such woman was Sarah Jay, who wrote early in the revolutionary era, "What have I to do with politicks?" In a subsequent letter, she admitted that she harbored growing political passions: "I've trangrss'd the line . . . by slipping into politicks, but my country and my friends possess so entirely my thoughts that you must not wonder if my pen runs beyond the dictates of prudence."

Jay, like a huge number of other women, chose to become a Patriot. Typically women Patriots utilized traditional "female" actions to express their sentiments. Employing their feminine charms, young Patriot women refused to court, or even dance with, men who had not declared their anti-English sentiments. Patriot women who were already married pressured men in other ways. Some wives denied their husbands "conjugal rights" until they swore opposition to Great Britain. And a large number of women encouraged their husbands and sons to volunteer as members of the Continental Army.

Other Patriot women wrote letters concerning the chaos in the American colonies. Two of these were Mercy Otis Warren and Abigail Adams, who at first corresponded privately but eventually made their letters public so that other women might understand the current issues. In their voluminous correspondence, these two educated women, the wives of Patriots, discussed political events not only with each other but with a number of men involved in the protest movement. After Warren's and Adams's questions elicited serious and often lengthy replies, the women read the exchanges to a group of interested friends and neighbors. This practice is believed to have provided the basis for the Committees of Correspondence, agencies for communicating insurrectionist ideas and actions from colony to colony.

Other Patriot women contributed to the resistance through economic action. In the North, women supported the resistance effort through their participation in boycotts, refusing to purchase any goods imported from Britain, especially tea. To keep this resistance firm, women formed anti-tea leagues, in which they experimented with brewing herb teas from raspberry, sage, and birch leaves. The most popular home-grown tea, called Liberty Tea, utilized the leaves of loosestrife plants, members of the primrose family that commonly grew in the fields and roadsides of New England.

In the South, in 1774, a Patriot woman convinced a number of other women to sign a boycott agreement against tea and other British imports. In Edenton, North Carolina, Penelope Barker persuaded fifty-one women to sign an agreement boycotting British goods until the British government repealed the tax on tea. To the delight of some and the horror of others, the statement and the names of its signers appeared in the local newspaper. Although these women justified their actions based on their inability to remain "indifferent on any occasion that appears nearly to affect the peace and happiness of our country," they met with unsparing ridicule, especially from British observers.

Besides supporting boycotts and nonimportation, Patriot women eventually rejected customary female restraint in order to express their disapproval of, and resistance to, British rule. For instance, women did everything they could to support local militias, the membership of which armed and marched regularly in preparation for a war that seemed more likely to erupt every day. In 1774, Boston women not only turned out in force on training days, but made cartridges and ran bullets for the men. One observer remarked that the women's enthusiasm for the coming combat surpassed that of the men.

Similarly, at public demonstrations, women increasingly swelled the ranks of men. Sometimes, the very presence of groups of women lent validity to working-class men's assertions that British taxes hurt widows and orphans. Besides protesting rising prices and high taxes, working-class women especially objected to enterprising British soldiers who made money on the side by offering to work cheap, thereby costing American men jobs.

Soon, female Patriots participated in public, sometimes violent actions against the British. Many joined the Daughters of Liberty, who, along with the Sons of Liberty, took to the streets, where they held bonfire rallies and distributed anti-English propaganda. These protestors threatened tax collectors with tarring-and-feathering—sometimes making good on their threats. On several occasions, women helped hang tax collectors in effigy, hanging a stuffed dummy representing the British official.

Other Patriot women organized active demonstrations on their own. Rather than staying quietly at home as "befitted" white women, some women preferred to be in the midst of the action. In fact, a woman named Sarah Bradless Fulton stood behind the largest public challenge to the British, the Boston Tea Party of 1773. Fulton not only initiated the idea of dumping unloaded British tea into harbors, but helped in the plan's execution in Boston. In addition, among the shadowy forms standing along Boston's dock that night were a number of women and their children.

For all these activities, Patriot women received both praise and scorn. On the one hand, some Patriot leaders and ministers encouraged women's aggressiveness in the resistance movement, one minister calling on women "to strike the Stroke" against the British, assuring them they would be "blessed." On the other hand, a number of female and male colonists felt that women's actions in support of rebellion might erode female dignity, as well as undermine men's influence and power. These people snubbed Patriot women or heckled and mocked them publicly. But such derision seldom stopped Patriot women. If anything, is made some women fiercer than ever.

On the other side of the issue stood Loyalist women, who supported the cause of Great Britain. Like Patriot women, female Loyalists demonstrated that white women were not apolitical or passive. Contrary to widely held beliefs of the time, white women were far more than spectators of the brewing conflict. White women demonstrated that "females" could be, and often were, highly political human beings.

Much like Patriot women, middle- to upper-class Loyalist women usually chose a customary female approach to their political expression. These women acted with proper decorum, patience, and willingness to compromise. Through their conversations, letters, and purchases, they tried to convince malcontents who criticized the British government to remember that all American colonists were British subjects who owed loyalty and obedience to the British Parliament and the Crown. At the other end of the social scale were the lower- to middle-class Loyalist women, who readily spoke out in public and marched on behalf of the British.

Because Patriot women increasingly formed a numerical majority, Loyalist women found themselves in a minority, cut off from the support of former friends and sometimes even that of family members who had sided with the Patriots. It was not uncommon for a local Committee of Safety, which had no legal authority, to call a woman to account. One so detained might be asked to explain her lack of support for a boycott or her public words against the Patriots. When in 1775, a Virginia woman refused to back down under such harassment, the committee declared her "an enemy of her Country," and warned her friends and neighbors to stay away from her.

Another woman whose outspokenness cost her dearly was Margaret Draper. After her husband's death in 1774, Margaret took over the publishing of her husband's newspaper, the *Massachusetts Gazette and Boston News-Letter*. For the next two years, Draper edited this newspaper, the oldest in the colonies. In its pages, Draper staunchly defended British actions and policies. Obviously, Draper was neither disinterested in politics nor lacking in opinions of her own. For her willingness to voice her convictions, Draper lost her country. When the British evacuated Boston in 1776, Draper, along with other Loyalists, had to flee the nation. She located first in Halifax, Nova Scotia, and later in England. After American Patriots took over Boston, they seized Draper's property. Only later did the British government reward Draper's continuing allegiance to Britain with a small, life-time pension.

Women of Color

Native American women made up their own minds whether to give their allegiance to the Americans or the British. Sometimes a Native woman's decision depended on her personal relationships. Being married to an American trader, for example, might convince an Indian woman to support the Patriots. In other cases, Native women simply chose the faction they thought had the better chance of winning, thereby hoping to improve their own status after war's end. The promises that British and American officers and other leaders made to Indians weighed heavily with these women. An assurance of returned lands and treaties favorable to Native Americans naturally drew Indian women toward one side or the other.

As a result, some American Indians backed the Americans, and others backed the English. The Senecas of New York, for example, supported the British, largely because American Patriots refused to guarantee the Seneca possession of their territory in case of war. The Cherokee and two Iroquois tribes, however, joined the British to protest white settlement of their lands.

Similarly, African and African American slave women gave their support to whichever side appeared most likely to abolish slavery should it prevail. Much like white Americans, slaves desired independence and liberty. During the prewar years, black persons continually protested the slave system. In 1774, a group of Massachusetts slaves even petitioned the state legislature for their liberation, stressing the destructive nature of slavery on family life: "How can a slave perform the duties of husband to wife or a parent to a child? How can a husband leave his master to work and cleave to his wife? How can the wife submit to her husband in all things?"

Other literate slaves wrote public pleas. In 1761, a wealthy Boston merchant, John Wheatley, had purchased an eight-year-old personal servant named Phillis as a companion for his wife. Susannah Wheatley soon recognized the young girl's nimble mind and gave her opportunities unusual for a slave. Phillis Wheatley became a Latin scholar, poet, and witty conversationalist. In 1774, Phillis penned "A Plea for Equal Rights for Negroes," in which she argued that "in every human Breast, God has a Principle, which we call Love of Freedom." To Wheatley, "the same Principle" lived in black persons, who could not understand the "absurdity" of Christian men and women who believed in liberty for themselves yet held Africans and African Americans in bondage.

Because most colonial officials paid little attention to such entreaties, let alone offering any form of redress, slaves had little loyalty to the American side. Thus, in 1775, when Lord John Murray, Earl of Dunmore and Royal Governor of Virginia, promised to emancipate those slaves who fought for the British, he had a fair number of takers. Other British officials who courted the support of enslaved Americans had similar success. Black wives and daughters watched their menfolk march off to battle under banners optimistically declaring "Liberty to Slaves."

The American Revolution, 1776–1783

White Women

Women realized that the Revolution would touch their lives in some way. Because the conflict was to take place on American soil, battles would be fought nearby. Food and other supplies would have to go to the American army. Thus shortages and inflated prices were sure to result. Wounded soldiers would need nursing; the dead would have to be buried; and the threat of violence to children and to themselves made the impending war all the more frightening to women. The presence of foreign troops in the land and decreasing supplies of food only intensified the chances of contracting potentially deadly diseases such as smallpox and dysentery for women and their children.

As in all wars, rape constituted an omnipresent threat. During the war, a New Jersey man noted that, "many virtuous women have suffered in this Manner." He added that rape victims usually "kept it Secret for fear of making their lives miserable." Not only did public admission of rape hurt a woman's reputation, but local authorities took such cases lightly and seldom investigated them.

Women soon learned that they had to protect themselves and their families. Beginning as early in the war as 1776, British soldiers, frustrated by their inability to halt the rebellion, brutally assaulted women in New Jersey and New York. When German mercenaries known as Hessians arrived in the colonies, women's fears escalated. Hessians drank and gambled to a degree some women considered dangerous. Forced to house Hessian soldiers, a Long Island woman wrote, "we have trying and grievous scenes to go through; fighting, brawls, drumming and fifing, and dancing the night long; card and dice playing, and every abomination going on under our roofs." The faster women could bring the war to conclusion, the safer they and their children would be.

In many ways, then, the Revolution was not just a man's war. Even in the rhetoric and imagery that appeared in the essays, pamphlets, articles, and sermons that flowed from American pens, women were very much present. At the same time that John Adams characterized a true republic as "great, manly, and warlike" and claimed that a republican government demanded "manly" public sacrifice and participation, numerous other commentators described the republican qualities of virtue and sacrifice as feminine characteristics.

Similar themes appeared in colonists' depictions of Great Britain. On the one hand, Britain represented an uncaring mother, who had turned her face away from her child, the American colonies. On the other, some accused Britain of exhibiting the worst attributes stereotypically associated with men: greed, lust, and violence.

Clearly, both the new American republic and Great Britain had some supposedly female aspects and some male. This would prove true of American women themselves. Women demonstrated they had a "feminine" side: they deplored war, feared the death of their men, and wished to behave as apolitically as conventional wisdom portrayed them. But women acted in so-called "masculine" ways as well. Like men, women wanted freedom from outside control, fought when they had to, and operated in the political arena when necessary. Consequently, although some women viewed themselves as weak and passive nonparticipants in the revolutionary struggle, many more threw their energies into helping one faction or the other.

Of all white female activists of the Revolutionary era, Abigail Adams is perhaps the best known. Adams recognized the social implications of the war. She realized that independence would change the direction of the country. Thus, she tried to gain something for women. Contemporary feminists often quote her letters to her husband, John, while he served in the Continental Congress. In 1776, recognizing that Congress would have to devise a new government for the United States, Adams wrote to her husband: "In the new Code of Laws which I suppose it will be necessary for you to make I desire you would Remember the Ladies, and be more generous and favourable to them than your ancestors." Abigail then asked that John and his colleagues not "put such unlimited power in the hands of the Husbands" because "all Men would be tyrants if they could." She concluded with the defiant statement that, "If particular care is not paid to the Ladies we are determined to foment a Rebellion, and will not hold ourselves bound by any Laws in which we have no voice, or Representation."

Abigail Adams was not asking for a complete overhaul of gender roles. She was not arguing that women should vote or hold public office. She was not espousing equality for women or an abandonment of their domestic duties. Rather, Adams envisioned a legal system that would protect women from unlimited power in the hands of men.

John Adams responded to his wife's request in a joking manner. Although John usually showed respect for Abigail's opinions, he found her ideas about women difficult to take seriously. As a result, John wrote that he had heard that the Revolution had "loosened the bands of Government everywhere," even to the point of stirring up American Indians and slaves. He added that her letter was "the first Intimation that another Tribe more numerous and powerfull than all the rest were grown discontent."

In ire at John's reply, Abigail Adams suggested to her friend Mercy Otis Warren that they petition the new Congress regarding the situation of women. Abigail, however, soon dropped the matter with the statement to John that, "I can not say that I think you very generous to the Ladies, for whilst you are proclaiming peace and good will to Men, Emancipating all Nations, you insist upon retaining an absolute power over Wives." Her last words warned "we have it in our power not only to free ourselves but to subdue our Masters, and without violence throw both your natural and legal authority at our feet."

Adams's words were brave, yet in a sense empty. In her day, women's rights and feminism were not major issues. Adams had few allies to support her ideas and to help her mount the revolution of which she spoke. Yet she had identified a theme that would run through the revolutionary era: women were active and involved beings who resented limits on their rights and activities.

Even though Abigail Adams was the most visible, and probably the most vocal, woman of the Revolutionary era, she did not stand alone. Numerous other white women violated the dictates of the female role in order to follow their own interests and convictions. Mercy Otis Warren not only composed patriotic poetry, but was a historian, playwright, and arch propagandist of the Revolution. She wrote three anti-British satirical plays during the war years. And by the late 1770s Warren had begun her major literary work, the three-volume *History of the Rise, Progress and Termination of the American Revolution,* which finally appeared in 1805. Warren's work indicated that she was not only a supporter of the principle of American liberty but an early advocate of female independence. Warren once commented to a friend that women might accept their "appointed subordination" for the sake of "Order in Families," but never due to any inferiority on women's part.

Across the colonies, many other women spoke out or took a variety of actions. Whether they wrote letters and tracts, engaged in political activities, fought alongside men, or pursued other "unfeminine" endeavors, their activities challenged the model of American womanhood. Like the many assertive and irrepressible colonial women who had preceded them, women of the war years displayed a high degree of independence of thought and spirit. Not content with the passivity and submissiveness that many Americans believed were inherent female traits, these women defied convention to follow their own desires, talents, and activities.

White Patriot Women

In many cases, white women were able to undertake "male" activities without much public or private censure. It was, after all, a time of national crisis that demanded the relaxation of the rules. Women who wrote, worked, or fought for American independence were usually thought patriotic and loyal to their country, if not to the dictates of their gender roles. Women who neglected the female sphere in order to participate in the larger public realm were indeed Patriots of the first order in many people's eyes.

Even as men continued to discuss and debate the abstract issue of whether women could be political beings, women were showing that they could indeed act in highly political ways. Women who supported the Patriot cause simply assumed they were part of what one revolutionary called "the people." They believed that, like men, they were struggling for liberty, "everyone's birthright." Women were, in other words, as politically minded and aware as men.

By the time the Revolution began, women had become expert at "making do." Few British products or goods brought to the colonies in British ships appeared on their tables if they could possibly avoid it. In 1777, one Patriot woman assured a British officer: "I have retrenched every superfluous expense in my table and family." She added, "Tea I have not drunk since last Christmas, nor bought a new cap or gown since your defeat at Lexington: and, what I never did before, have learned to knit, and am now making stockings of wool for my servants: and this way do I throw in my mite for the public good." She revealed that she was a very politically oriented woman indeed when she concluded that, "I know this, that as free I can die but once: but as a slave I shall not be worthy of life."

Patriot women also kept their boycotts in place. In 1777, for example, several Massachusetts women forcibly opened the warehouse of a merchant who was hoarding goods in order to sell them later at inflated wartime prices. One observer reported that "a number of females, some say a hundred or more, assembled with a cart and trunks, marched down to the warehouse and demanded the keys, which he refused to deliver." A large woman grabbed the merchant by his neck, pushed him into a cart, and seized the keys. After opening the warehouse, the women hoisted out hogsheads of coffee and drove off with them while a large group of men stood by in amazed silence, apparently incapable of comment or criticism.

Other women became involved in the Patriot cause because of their technical know-how. By managing colonial businesses and serving apprenticeships, many women possessed skills critical to the wartime effort. For instance, in 1775 Mary Katherine Goddard had been appointed postmaster of Baltimore and was probably the first woman to fill such a post. By the time of the Revolution, she was a successful and respected businessperson in Baltimore. As a leading Baltimore printer and publisher of *The Baltimore Journal,* Goddard received the government contract to print the official version of the Declaration of Independence. In 1777, the members of Congress demonstrated their faith in Goddard by asking her to reproduce the document that explained the American Revolution. And why not? Goddard ran one of the largest, most respected printing businesses in America.

Goddard fully understood the importance of this occurrence. As an avowed feminist, she recognized its historical importance. As a result, she deviated from a printer's usual practice: rather than placing her (the printer's) initials at the bottom of the document, she spelled out her name, letting others know that a woman had printed one of the most important statements in history.

As the war accelerated, Patriot women pushed their men toward the front lines, even though men's absence would mean great sacrifice for women. In many cases, women had to run family farms and businesses by themselves, as well as sell produce to supplement their husbands' irregular soldier's pay. Despite the hardships, most women responded without hesitation. When John Adams urged Abigail to "rouse your whole attention to the family, the stock, the farm, the dairy" in his absence, she became an expert farm manager. It was Abigail's hope that, in time, she would have the "reputation of being as good a farmeress as my partner has of being a good statesman."

In addition, female Patriots organized women's associations that devoted untold hours to sewing clothes, rolling bandages, and preparing foodstuffs. As in all nineteenth-century wars, during the War for Independence troops counted on women to meet many of their basic needs. Before widespread industrialization, supplies had to come from the mothers, wives, and daughters of fighting men. In response, women shifted aspects of domestic manufacture to the war effort, replacing, for example, fancy embroidery with plain sewing on soldier's shirts and trousers.

Women also spent huge amounts of time and energy organizing charity fairs and other events to raise money for food, clothing, and sanitary goods, such as bandages and medicine for the wounded. In these endeavors American women showed themselves extremely capable of managing business affairs, allocating money, and delivering supplies. In a fund-raising broadside printed in 1780, a Philadelphia woman explained that the members of the newly organized Ladies Association were motivated by the "purest patriotism" in aspiring "to render themselves really useful." Among other feats, these women raised $7,500 and contributed 2,005 shirts.

Colonial leaders were extremely grateful to Patriot women and expressed their appreciation on many occasions. In 1781 George Washington publicly praised the Ladies Association of Philadelphia, which included Benjamin Franklin's daughter, Sarah Franklin Bache, for their fund-raising efforts. They had "embellished" the American character, Washington stated, "by proving that the law of country is blended with those softer domestic virtues" of women. He added that these women deserved "an equal place with any who have preceded them in the walk of female patriotism."

Women not only assembled food and other goods. They also destroyed critical resources rather than letting them to fall into the hands of the British or their mercenaries. Implementing a scorched-earth policy, women gladly demolished their own stocks of food for the American cause. Given the destruction already caused by the war, such sacrifices were especially admirable. Whether British or American, troops had moved across the land like locusts, eating all the food they could find, appropriating everything from carts to horses, and taking over homes for their headquarters and officers' quarters.

Yet women took the expedient course of action. A Patriot woman in Albany, New York, set fire to her fields of wheat to prevent the enemy from seizing their output. In South Carolina another woman, determined to rout English soldiers from her home, personally handed flaming arrows to colonial soldiers who aimed and fired them at her house. She quietly proclaimed, "I am gratified with the opportunity of contributing to the good of the country."

During the war women also engaged in heavier tasks usually thought of as men's work. Women collected lead, melted it down, and produced the shot used by the Patriot army. Women manufactured and assembled arms. And women converted their businesses to wartime production. One woman in Salem, Massachusetts, transformed her tool factory into a Patriot arsenal, while another, a smith known only as "Betsy," lent her expertise regarding cannon and other arms to the Patriots. At the same time, the women traders on Nantucket Island ran the British blockade of the American coast to supply the Patriots.

Yet other women aided the Revolution by acting as saboteurs and spies. Although sabotage and spying were usually male tasks, women discovered that they could perform such duties with great effectiveness. As women, they could gain access to places where men were not permitted. For instance, a Quaker woman in Philadelphia eavesdropped at the door of a room in her home, which British officers had taken over for meetings. When she overheard her unwanted lodgers reading attack orders, she penetrated the British lines on the pretense of needing to get some flour milled. Once across, she located an American officer to whom she entrusted her secret. A few days later, she placidly observed a British officer's dismay at finding American cannon mounted and prepared to receive his assault. "We have marched back here like a parcel of fools," he fumed.

Perhaps the most creative female spy was Emily Geiger, who volunteered to carry a message after the male soldiers in camp declined to do so. When a British scout detained her, Geiger ripped up the document and swallowed it. The next day she promptly delivered the message that she had quickly committed to memory.

Daring women disguised as men thwarted yet other onslaughts. Because women found their efforts successful, they became increasingly audacious. In Massachusetts, for example, a group of women dressed themselves in their husbands' clothes and carried pitchforks to guard a nearby bridge. Here they forcibly unhorsed and searched a British courier. When they discovered dispatches concealed in his boot, they conducted him to the local jail for detention. Even supposedly decorous southern women engaged in such subterfuge In South Carolina, Elizabeth Marshall and her daughters-in-law dressed as men. They, too, accosted a courier and seized his dispatches, thus blocking the passage of essential military intelligence.

White Patriot Women at the Front

Women served at the front in one of two capacities: 1) as wives and camp-followers who accompanied and assisted soldiers and officers, 2) as soldiers fighting alongside male troops or in independent women's units.

Over the course of the war, the first category—wives and camp followers—numbered perhaps as many as twenty thousand women and included some of the legendary women of the Revolution. One of these was Mary Ludwig Hays McCauley, who worked as a nurse, camp cook, and washwoman. Reportedly, she was known as Molly Pitcher because she carried so many pails and pitchers of water to the men. It is likely that no real Molly Pitcher existed at all—that she was a folktale symbolizing the many heroic women at the front.

Mary McCauley, however, was authentic. Like so many other women on the front line, McCauley watched her husband fall, mortally wounded. Rather than wailing and moaning, she took over her husband's cannon, which she kept firing for the duration of the Battle of Monmouth in July 1778. Later, soldiers who survived the battle described McCauley as a warmhearted, energetic woman who swore volubly and chewed tobacco. Not until 1822 did the Pennsylvania legislature reward McCauley's military service with a small pension.

Throughout the Revolution, military officers usually considered camp women a necessary nuisance that helped men survive the rigors and dangers of battle. Especially in a homefront war, camp followers formed an important part of the military community. In 1776, the American Articles of War even stated that "all sutlers [traders] and retainers to a camp, and all persons whatsoever serving with the armies of the United States," constituted military personnel. Outside this definition fell perhaps a few prostitutes and consorts, but it included most female camp-followers—traders, nurses, cooks, and wives who followed their husbands in order to assist them and their fellow soldiers. Many of these women hoped to contribute to the revolutionary cause. "If opinions and manners," one said, "did not forbid us to march to glory by the same paths as the men, we would at least equal, and sometimes surpass them in our love for the public good."

Accordingly, scores of women flocked to the camps of the Continental Army, pledging to help in any way possible. Martha Washington was one such camp follower. Martha wintered with her husband at Valley Forge. There, she went from hut to hut carrying food to the sick and consoling the dying. Yet another task that camp women often performed was combing the battlefields for the dead, whom they identified and gave proper burial.

Less is known of those women who actually bore arms in the Revolution. Yet, apparently, a number of women served as soldiers. Although Continental Army regulations prohibited the recruitment of women, women could enlist. Their names appeared on company rolls, they drew their pay along with men, and they wore men's clothing. Women served not only with the Continental Army but with militia units that joined General George Washington's forces or fought Native Americans along the lines of advancing white, frontier settlement.

One of these was Margaret Corbin, who became a soldier through necessity. Corbin followed her husband to the front, where she served as a nurse, cook, washwoman, and soldier. In the Battle of Fort Washington in November 1776, Corbin's husband fell at her feet. Despite her shock and grief, Corbin took his place. She filled her husband's battle post until she was disabled by three grapeshot that permanently cost her the use of one arm. In 1779, she received a small pension, thus becoming the first female military pensioner in the United States.

A number of other women dressed as men, took male names to conceal their gender, and enlisted in the Continental Army. Known only by her pseudonym, Samuel Gay served until she was wounded and her true gender discovered. She was duly discharged from the army.

White Loyalist Women

All white colonial women were not Patriots, however. On the opposite side stood Loyalist women who supported the British throughout the American Revolution. As a consequence of their allegiance to Britain, many women lost their livelihoods, homes, and property, while their social class standings plummeted.

In one case, Grace Growdon Galloway, wife of attorney Joseph Galloway who had served as speaker of the Pennsylvania Assembly between 1766 and 1774, saw her Loyalist husband branded a traitor and her own estates seized by the Patriots. After Joseph fled Philadelphia in 1774, taking the couple's only child with them, Grace lived near the poverty level. She watched as Patriots confiscated Galloway lands. Grace's final humiliation came when she learned that only her husband's name appeared on the deeds to her father's property, which she had brought to her marriage as part of her dowry. By the time of her death in 1781, Grace Galloway had lost everything, including friends who wanted nothing to do with the wife of a Loyalist to the British Crown.

In another case, Catherine Van Cortlandt, a Loyalist wife whose husband had run away from home to escape arrest, found her home surrounded by nearly twenty men who hoped to intercept her husband. When additional Patriot troops arrived, they commandeered the Van Cortlandt's home as a headquarters. Catherine lamented that "the frequent frolics of the Officers in the House," as well as their habit of feeding their horses from the Van Cortlandt's granary had reduced her and her nine children to living on a "mere pittance." Because of her husband's Loyalist leanings, even neighbors whom Catherine had once helped through a crisis refused to assist her.

Such bitterness against Loyalists continued throughout the Revolution. The state government of New York alone obtained nearly $4 million from the sale of Loyalist lands. As late in the Revolution as 1782, South Carolina passed a Confiscation Act that not only impounded Loyalists' property but banished some Loyalists from the state. As the revolution neared its end, which formally occurred in January of 1783, some 7,000 loyalists set sail for Canada or Europe.

American Indian Women

During the Revolution, thousands of Native Americans lost their lives, villages, and fields to the ravages of war. Not uncommon were reprisals by American militiamen against one band of Indians or another who had chosen to support the British. In addition, Native women were raped and both they and their children were shot by both British and American troops.

Soon after white Americans had declared their independence, American Indians discovered, to their dismay, that the new American government regarded Native groups as foreign nations. Congress intended to deal with Indians not as inhabitants of the United States but as adversaries. In line with this thinking, the U.S. government planned to dispatch troops to negotiate treaties with or simply conquer Indian peoples, obtaining Native lands on the premise of war gains. Thus, the revolutionary war and the American government's new policies often proved catastrophic for America's Indian peoples.

The case of the women of New York's Seneca Indians constituted one of the most poignant. At the time of the Revolution, Seneca female agriculturalists had already lost a degree of stature within their traditional culture. These women often fell prey first to warfare, then to epidemics, and finally to the consequences of trade. During the Revolution,

American troops, in reprisal for the Seneca support of the British, destroyed forty Seneca towns composed of communal longhouses. In these search-and-destroy raids American soldiers laid waste to Seneca orchards, fields, and crops. Next, smallpox, undoubtedly contracted from the unwanted visitors, ravaged the tribe, keeping women out of the fields and causing a decline in their numbers. Finally, increasing trade between Indians and whites undercut Seneca women's craft production. Iron scissors and needles made obsolete implements of bone, while textiles replaced fur garments and glass beads supplanted porcupine quills as ornaments. Although Seneca women retained some of their political power, that too began to decline as treaties with the American government reduced the amount of land women controlled.

Native women typically responded to such changes by adapting to them. Among the Seneca, women replanted their crops, while women of other tribes learned to grow or produce different kinds of goods in higher demand. Many took advantage of the new white trade goods for their own purposes. For instance, many Native women used glass beads to construct highly saleable Indian craftwork. Rather than purchasing beads from white traders, some women figured out how to manufacture glass beads themselves.

In addition, Native women developed new areas of influence in their communities. They established female associations, networks, and other bonds to assist each other and enhance women's importance. There is no evidence that native women became subordinate to native men or imitated white society in any other way.

Yet the dream of Native American women that the end of the Revolution would bring relief to their people came to nothing. The Seneca had made the wrong choice, the British. However, even those Indians who had backed the Americans were soon disappointed. Because the new U.S. government promptly classified Indians as foreign nations, the lofty ideals of the Declaration of Independence apparently did not apply to Native American groups.

Slave and Free Black Women

For black women, whether free or slave, the war proved especially debilitating. Besides the omnipresent threat of rape and physical abuse, families were torn asunder. Free black Lucy Terry Prince of Northfield, Massachusetts, encouraged her two eldest sons to enlist and serve with the militia even though this meant leaving Prince and her husband, Abijah, alone on their small farm.

Separation of family members occurred for other reasons as well. Troops who appropriated horses and cattle for their own use also carried away slaves. A husband might be taken by one detachment of troops, a wife by another. Children were frequently left behind. Or slaveholders, especially Loyalists, might flee the state or the nation, taking their slaves with them. Often, a family who owned a husband went one direction, while a family who held the wife went another.

The presence of British armies contributed to the upheaval. Officers not only encouraged slaves to escape their owners, but often harbored runaway slaves and granted them liberty as a means of weakening the efforts of Patriots, especially those in the South. In British encampments, runaway female slaves worked as cooks, laundresses, and nurses.

Yet other slaves escaped in family groups that included women and children. Over half of the twenty-three slaves who fled Thomas Jefferson's Virginia plantation during the war were women and girls. Although not separated from each other, such escapees faced a life of chaos and uncertainty.

Slaves who stayed put during the war made what contributions they could, especially by keeping households and plantations running. Like white women, slave women who backed the Patriots produced cotton and other goods for the war effort. Among these were a number of unidentified women. One was a free black domestic servant who gave most of her meager wages to the war effort. At the same time, black women harboring Loyalist sentiments did what they could to disrupt revolutionary efforts.

Some free black women also joined the American propaganda effort. A notable case was that of Phillis Wheatley, who wielded her pen to keep people fighting and shore up American spirits. One of her most celebrated poems, "Ode to General Washington," appeared in the *Pennsylvania Magazine* in 1776. The poem marked Wheatley as a Patriot and gained her a personal invitation to visit General Washington's headquarters in Cambridge, Massachusetts.

Other free black women fought at the front. In 1782, Deborah Sampson, generally believed to be a mulatto, enlisted in the Continental forces under the name of Robert Shurtleff. Her unusual height, strong features, and great stamina protected her from discovery until she was hospitalized with a fever and was discharged in 1783. She later wrote that she had "burst the tyrant bonds which held my sex in awe and clandestinely, or by stealth, grasped an opportunity, which custom and the world seemed to deny, as a natural privilege." In 1792, the U.S. Congress granted Sampson's heirs her pension as a war veteran.

Scores of other overlooked or unnamed women contributed to the American victory. In 1778, for example, Phoebe Fraunces, General George Washington's black servant, stopped a British plot to murder Washington. An unidentified free woman of color took soup and bread to imprisoned Patriots.

For a short time, it appeared that slaves might gain their freedom after all. In a burst of wartime enthusiasm, many Americans advocated the abolition of slavery. A number of slave owners in the upper South chose to free their slaves. Other Americans began to form antislavery societies. As longtime opponents of slavery, the Quakers stood in the forefront of this activity, founding their first antislavery society in 1775.

Such abolitionist societies, organized especially in Philadelphia and elsewhere in the middle states, sought to convince Americans that the freedom they cherished should extend to Africans and African Americans. Using the Declaration of Independence as a basis, the abolitionists claimed that liberty for one and all should transcend distinctions of color.

During the war years, the Pennsylvania legislature took another valiant step to erase the contradictions between the nation's quest for independence and the servitude of some of its citizens by adopting the Gradual Abolition Act. Although earlier Pennsylvania legislation had discouraged manumission, prohibited social gatherings, and stipulated that a free black person who married a white person could be sold into slavery, the Gradual Abolition Act expressed a desire to lessen tyranny against the state's black population. Among other provisions, no child born after the passage of the act would be a slave and black people would have the right to court trials. This legislation inadvertently fostered an increase in the state's African American population. The Census of 1790 recorded 10,301 blacks in Pennsylvania—6,540 freed men and women and 3,761 slaves. The state's abolition provisions attracted such an influx of enslaved people, many via the early Underground Railroad, that the total jumped 176 percent by 1800. Pennsylvania's black population numbered 16,270 by 1800—14,564 free and 1,706 enslaved.

Several other states experimented with emancipation provisions. In 1780, the Massachusetts Constitution included a Declaration of Rights stating that "all men are born free and equal." Under this provision some slaves sued for their liberty. In 1781, with the assistance of an attorney, Elizabeth Freeman (also known as Mum Bett) petitioned a Massachusetts court for her emancipation, arguing that the new state constitution guaranteed her liberty. Freeman stated that she had heard a "paper" read that said "all men are born equal, and that every man has a right to freedom." She now intended to secure her own freedom and thereby establish a principle for other slaves. The court agreed with Freeman and issued the first decision that construed a state constitution as inconsistent with slavery. The Freeman ruling was significant, yet remained an exception. Although Freeman gained her liberty, and her case established the principle of inconsistency, it did not result in statewide emancipation.

Clearly, the ideals of freedom and liberty stated in the Declaration of Independence proved troublesome when applied to black women and men. In a society that had long harbored racist attitudes and needed cheap labor, many Americans thought slavery necessary and acceptable.

Women after the Revolution

Slave Women

Whether of color or white, many women expected to receive certain liberties of their own once the United States secured its independence. Black slave women wanted emancipation; free black women wanted better economic conditions; and white women wanted some of the privileges given only to men. While every type of woman experienced some changes after the Revolution, for most the reality fell far short of the desired effect.

When the Revolution ended, black women and men longed to see the eventual abolition of slavery. After the war, the British transported over 3,000 Loyalist slaves, of which some 900 were women, to Nova Scotia in Canada. Although this evacuation of Loyalist slaves further splintered families, most of these women regarded their migration as a wondrous opportunity for new lives in a free land.

At the same time, some Americans argued that slaves who had participated in the Revolution on behalf of the Patriots should be rewarded with their liberty. In practice, however, this idea was seldom implemented, especially regarding women. In 1782, a female slave who had attended an American colonel for forty years made an impassioned, yet futile plea for liberation. Another African American woman who had served as a bullet runner for American troops remained a slave until she was nearly eighty years old, at which time she escaped to Canada.

Slave women were justifiably disgruntled by the situation. The freedom of which they had long dreamed proved illusory once again. A few reacted to their disappointment by seizing their liberty. Although Silvia Dubois, born a slave in New Jersey in 1768, saw her father gain his freedom by joining the Patriots in the Revolution, she remained a slave at war's end. Eventually, Silvia struck her mistress and ran away.

The new U.S. Constitution, ratified in 1789, did not ease the situation for Africans and African Americans. Although the Constitution advocated equality and rights for all, it included three clauses protecting the institution of slavery. Indeed, if one defined a slave as property rather than a human being, no contradiction existed in this brave new document. In addition, the Constitution expressly allowed the importation of slaves into the country for twenty years, or until January of 1808. The founding fathers hoped that slavery would have disappeared in the United States by that time.

Still, slavery's demise seemed entirely possible. In 1790, the nation's first census listed 3,172,444 white people, 59,557 free black people, and 697,624 slaves. With the growth of industrialization in the North during the 1790s and early 1800s, slavery gradually declined in that region.

In the South, however, a far different scenario unfolded. Because of the huge appetite of English textile mills for cotton and Eli Whitney's invention, under planter Catherine Green's sponsorship, of a workable cotton gin in 1793, the cotton culture and an accompanying demand for slaves increasingly characterized the South. Thus, by 1800, the black population in southern states had jumped to 1,002,037, of whom 893,602 were slaves. The acquisition of the Louisiana Territory in 1803 brought into the Union additional slave territory.

As profits from cotton began to rise, white slave owners intensified their efforts to extract the most labor possible from slave women. Owners usually regarded these women as chattels. They listed slave women in property inventories of plantations by first name, age, and monetary value. On the sale block, auctioneers held women up to public scrutiny much like livestock. One observer at a slave sale reported that a potential buyer "took one of the prettiest women by the chin and opened her mouth to see the state of her gums and teeth, with no more ceremony than if she had been a horse." Women were further dehumanized by having their childbearing and sexual features pointed out.

Once purchased, slave women labored as nursemaids, midwives, domestic servants, and field hands. On the larger plantations, they served as seamstresses, nurses, poultrymaids, and dairymaids. Since the number of trades and crafts opened to women were limited as compared to those open to male slaves who worked as, among other things, smiths, coopers, and overseers, more women worked in the fields than did men. The female field hand was routinely expected to perform domestic tasks as well. One Virginia planter of the late 1700s described a favored slave as "a stout able field wench and an exceedingly good washer and ironer."

After the Constitution abolished the Atlantic slave trade in 1808, owners urged their slave women to bear as many children as possible. Slaveholders frequently offered time off work, eventual emancipation, and other rewards to slave women who bore ten or more children. Such women sometimes received better housing or a larger ration of food.

In spite of the indignities and degradation of the slave system, women held slave families together. Although familial ties were extremely important to slaves, they lived with the constant threat of separation from their kin. To offset the deleterious effects of separation, women formed close bonds with their remaining children and tried to establish a new relationship with an unmarried slave or one who had lost his wife through sale or death.

Female slaves also resisted the system whenever they could. Naturally they resented their own situations, but they also detested the very concept of slavery. Running away was just one form of rebellion, one that could result in a slave's beating or death. Because their husbands, children, and other family members tied slave women to plantations, they became geniuses at small acts of revenge against whites. Every chicken that disappeared from the henhouse, every piece of fabric that was ruined by inaccurate cutting, every insolent look and toss of a head behind a mistress's back counted heavily in the slave woman's struggle to maintain her self-respect and pay back her oppressors for her ill treatment.

Free Black Women

Nor did the circumstances of free black women markedly improve after the Revolution. During the postwar depression that hit the new United States, free black women were the last hired and the first fired. Even when the economic situation improved during the early 1800s, free black women had a difficult time finding find employment; when they did, the wages were impossibly low. In addition, free black women faced the ever-present threat of being kidnapped and sold back into slavery.

During the postrevolutionary years, a number of women took matters into their own hands. As early as 1787, free women of color began to work on behalf of such goals as economic autonomy and religious separatism. This early black nationalist movement developed in response to racism and the degraded position of most African Americans. During the postrevolutionary period, the movement especially led to the establishment of benevolent societies. These included the Free African Society of Philadelphia founded in 1787, the Benevolent Daughters in 1796, and the Daughters of Africa in 1812. Such organizations assisted black women, men, and children in need and helped free women of color find employment. They also sustained black churches and their social-service groups, and helped establish churches as dynamic forces in black communities.

Other free blacks worked for abolitionism through both black and white churches. Although Quakers required free women of color to sit on back benches during meetings, free blacks still applied for church membership. Although Quakers publicly advocated the abolition of slavery, apparently they had a difficult time putting racial equality into practice.

After the Revolution, the number of black women in the Catholic Church increased because of the immigration of Catholics from Haiti. Concentrated mostly in Maryland, Catholic women began to campaign against slavery using as precedents a number of emancipation cases in the state's history, especially those in which mulatto women had been freed. By the 1790s and early 1800s, these women opened schools for children. They also offered education to adult women and initiated plans for an order of Catholic sisters, or women Religious as they are now called.

Despite the difficulties facing free women of color after the Revolution, a number of them proved that economic success could occasionally be achieved. Catherine (Katy) Ferguson, born c. 1774 on a slave ship headed for New York, excelled in business. Ferguson used the proceeds from her catering business to establish in 1793 an integrated school that would endure for forty years. Similarly, Elleanor Eldrige, born in 1784 in Warwick, Rhode Island, and freed with her family because her father and brother had fought on the American side during the Revolution, had by age fourteen learned to spin and weave. Among other items, Eldrige made exceptional carpets and bedspreads. She worked for Captain Benjamin Green's family until 1812, then went into business for herself, weaving, nursing, and producing soap.

Still, despite their financial status, these free women of color had far fewer rights and freedoms than did their white counterparts. Typically, free black women lived in near poverty and fear of being returned to slavery. For them, the Revolution had brought about little relief.

White Women

Among white women, Loyalist women fared the worst after the revolution. Special commissions established by the British judged how much Loyalists should receive in compensation for the homes, lands, and businesses that the Patriots had seized. The commissions tried to resolve the significant question of whether married Loyalist women could, as females, make political decisions on their own. Had women themselves been Loyalists? Or were they simply following their husbands' leads?

Certainly, throughout the resistance phase and the armed conflict a large number of women had held their own convictions and resisted their husbands' influence. During the war, Lucy Flucker Knox had let her husband know that she had a mind of her own. In 1777, Knox wrote her husband that she enjoyed making her own choices and had no intention of resuming a subordinate status when he returned from the war. "I hope you will not consider yourself as commander in chief of your own house," she declared, for "there is such a thing as equal command."

Despite such brave declarations concerning independent action, most white Americans believed that Loyalist women had simply obeyed their husbands and, thus, should be excused for their actions. Loyalist women must have been torn. Should they cling to their Loyalist sentiments and live a life of privation and scorn after the Revolution's end? Or should they blame their husbands for forcing a Loyalist stance on them?

For many desperate women, who often had children to support, the latter strategy seemed the most practical. After all, the revolution was over; the American Patriots had succeeded in their quest for independence. By the mid-1780s, there was little reason to remain Loyalist. And surely some of these women *had* simply adopted their husbands' Loyalist philosophy.

Consequently, women who had supported the British, often through their own choice, now backpedaled. Rather than sticking to a defunct political philosophy, many Loyalist women let necessity guide them. In South Carolina alone, more than sixty-five women sought from the courts redress for the effects of the Confiscation Act. They asked either for the return of their property or monetary "damage" awards. Most of these female plaintiffs claimed, and the court believed, that they had been passive, innocent victims. For example, Jane Linwood's attorney told the court that "as a Lady," Jane could not "be deemed Guilty of any Act inimical to the American Cause." The widespread assumption that women were apolitical and simply receptacles of their husbands' ideas saved Jane Linwood's property. In 1784 the court removed Linwood's name from the confiscation list.

Meanwhile, many white women who had supported the cause of the American Patriots expected their energy and courage to be rewarded with some of the fruits of the Revolution. Some even hoped that traditional beliefs regarding the weakness and inferiority of females would fall by the wayside as a consequence of women's courageous deeds. Surely, the postrevolutionary years would allow women to partake of the democracy that was so widely discussed throughout the new nation, especially as many women had a hand in securing independence.

In recent years, historians of women have devoted a good deal of time to exploring whether the American Revolution did in fact produce any marked improvements in the lives of white women. On the one hand, some argue that the American Revolution had negative results for women. The war pushed America toward industrialism, a system that would move many women into poorly paying and low-status factory jobs. Women would thus lose whatever respect and autonomy they had as commanders of their households. Furthermore, the ideology of the new nation demanded that women become Republican wives and mothers, nurturers who would train their sons for future citizenship and their daughters for future domesticity. Neither one of women's new roles—factory worker or Republican wife and mother—offered women improvement in their situations.

On the other hand, a number of historians believe that the Revolution may have had a positive effect on white women's lives. The economic and social disruption that it created gave women the opportunity to take over farms, plantations, businesses, trades, and professions while men carried out war-related duties. Thus, reform for women did not consist of rewriting legal codes, granting the vote to women, or developing a strong feminist movement. Rather, it appeared in women's heightened aspirations and in the views that Americans held regarding white women.

For one thing, the war soured many people against taking violent action. Although violence continued to characterize American life in such port cities as Baltimore, Maryland, a number of people hoped to introduce peace into their homes. Especially white, middle- and upper-class men and women wanted to introduce a new civility into marriage and family life. To this end, in 1787, Vermont listed "intolerable severity" as grounds for divorce. In 1791, New Hampshire adopted a law against "extreme cruelty."

Courts punished abusive spouses by granting their mates divorces, property, alimony, and child custody. In addition, wronged wives often aired their grievances in newspaper announcements that could lead to profound embarrassment for their husbands or former husbands. One such woman "posted" her husband for "jamming her until she was black and blue," as well as treating their five children in a similar manner. Occasionally an irate husband would charge his wife with sloppiness in her household duties, neglecting their children, or throwing things at him. No longer was physical violence in marriage widely accepted practice.

For another, the war's philosophy supported divorce for those who wanted to flee unfulfilling marriages. If, such women asked, the nation could seek independence and happiness, why must individuals remain in unhappy situations? The incidence of divorce not only increased after the war, but now such terms as "tyranny," "misrule," "injustice," and "happiness of the individual" crept into petitions. In 1789, for example, Abigail Abbot Bailey finally left the husband who mistreated her and sexually abused their daughter. Even though her husband tricked Abigail into going with him from their home in New Hampshire to New York, where the laws gave husbands greater control over wives, she persevered in bringing about what he termed "a revolution" in their marital status. Although Abigail recognized that her husband had "lawful government and authority" over her, she felt he had violated his marriage vow to care for and protect her. Thus, she was determined to flee from her oppressive marriage and set her "feet on the ground of liberty."

The concept of "liberty" continued to have an effect on women through the 1790s and early 1800s. In 1800, one teenager considering her future was thankful that she had the "liberty" of refusing a man she did not like and the "liberty" of choosing for a husband someone she did like. "Principles" also received a great deal of discussion by women. At the end of the 1810s, even middle- and upper-class women occasionally questioned the "principle" underlying husbands' legal authority over their families, as well as the "principle" that men should work outside the home and women only inside it. Apparently, the rhetoric of the

American war for independence inspired some women to apply revolutionary ideas to their own situations.

In addition, some important changes had occurred in the way people perceived women. Before 1776, American colonists viewed white women primarily as wives, helpmates, and ornaments. But colonial Americans did not idealize women. Nor was wifehood and motherhood glorified. Even child raising was seldom seen as exclusively a female duty. Mothers were so busy with their many chores that they often relied on their husbands or other adult members of the household to care for their children. Because men worked in or near the home during the years of settlement, they were able to help rear their children.

After the American Revolution, these casual attitudes changed dramatically. Drawing on the contemporary work of Scottish philosophers and other theorists who had considered women's roles in the polity, American thinkers argued that white women constituted indispensable halves of Republican marriages, who, in their capacity as mothers, were instrumental in the raising of effective and moral citizens for the new Republic. The new Republic depended upon public virtue: who better to instill it than domestically oriented wives and mothers?

One factor that brought about this change in thinking was the strong women of the revolutionary era who provided examples for others. For instance, Abigail Adams proved herself an accomplished business manager and self-proclaimed "farmeress" when John was away, which was a good deal of the time. In addition, she demonstrated that women could develop business acumen. Abigail's wise investments and sound management provided funds to send her sons to Harvard University, underwrite John's political career and finance the furnishing of several foreign legations and the newly constructed White House. Abigail's financial strategies supported herself and John after his retirement from the presidency. As Abigail's son John Quincy Adams wrote after her death, "her life gave the lie to every libel on her sex that was ever written."

Moreover, Abigail Adams established a model for other women when she wrote and spoke about the sensitive topic of slavery. She firmly believed that the slave system destroyed the character of individual citizens and that of society as a whole. In 1797, Adams sent a free black servant boy to evening school. When her neighbors visited to make known their objections, she strongly advocated the principle of "equality of Rights." Arguing that the young man was a free man, Adams maintained that he therefore had a right to an education. "Merely because his Face is black, is he to be denied instruction? How is he to be qualified to procure a livelihood?" she asked. As a result of her impassioned defense of the young man's right to an education, Adams's neighbors withdrew their objections.

Meanwhile, a number of social changes helped produce a modified perception of white women's roles. Many men now worked away from the home, regularly leaving the care of children in the hands of women. The increasing availability of certain factory-produced goods began to lessen the burden of incessant domestic labor, thus giving women more time for childcare. Women read more than ever before, including the rapidly growing literature on motherhood. And, because of the growing availability of manufactured goods, white women, at least of the middle- and upper-classes, had more leisure time.

Also, it is likely that many women recognized that the concept of Republican Womanhood in a way upgraded their inferior status. Thus, by the end of the 1700s such topics as discipline and the instilling of morality in young children elicited the attention of American ministers, guidebook writers, and physicians, among others. The moral mother, who bore and reared future citizens of the new United States, was now increasingly responsible for championing virtue and morality among children and in families.

Not only women but men gradually accepted the idea that females were innately more loving and nurturing than males. During these years, white society began to tout mother's love as an inborn instinct and to highly acclaim maternal fondness and tenderness toward children. Americans idealized, romanticized, and sentimentalized motherhood, believing that the future of their new nation somehow depended on it.

Republican Women in the Early Nation

The Rhetoric

The concept of Republican Womanhood applied primarily to white women, the mothers of future citizens, and even more directly to white women of the middle and upper classes, who could devote their full-time energies to childcare. Working, farm, and poor white women seldom had the opportunity to adopt such ideals. Because even white men had to own property to qualify as voters and office holders, few considered women of the lower classes capable of rearing future voters and office holders.

Despite the limitation of Republican Womanhood's applicability, thinkers and writers of the time implied that such ideals suited all white women. One such commentator was Hector St. John de Crevecoeur, a New York farmer of French background, who in 1782 published his impressions of America, *Letters from an American Farmer*. He described an ideal wife and mother much like his own wife, always spinning, knitting, or nursing a child. He claimed that American men did not expect a dowry with a wife, for they realized that a "wife's fortune consists principally in her future economy, modesty, and skillful management." According to Crevecoeur, if a farmer were "blessed with a good wife," he had the opportunity to live better than "any people of the same rank on the globe."

Similarly, Thomas Jefferson in his *Notes on the State of Virginia,* which appeared in published form in Paris in 1782 and in London in 1787, described white women in terms of their industry, ability as helpmates to men, and motherhood. He lauded the beauty of their "flowing hair," "symmetry of form," and fair skin, which revealed "the expressions of every passion by greater or less suffusions of color."

When he turned to Native American women, Jefferson made it clear that they were very different. Because they were not regarded as citizens, Indian women would not raise their sons as citizens of the new Republic, nor mold their daughters as eventual Republican women. In addition, Jefferson noted that Indian women were forced to submit to "unjust drudgery," as was the "case with every barbarous people." They bore fewer children than did white women, for, as "with all animals, if the female be badly fed, or not fed at all, her young perish." To Jefferson, such "obstacles of want" were simply nature's way of limiting "the multiplication of wild animals." He concluded that, when married to a white man and fed properly, exempted from "excessive drudgery," and protected from danger, an Indian woman could bear as many children as did white women.

Jefferson displayed a similar bias when he focused his attention on slave women, who were usually regarded as property and never as citizens. After maintaining that black people slept frequently, he explained that an "animal whose body is at rest, and who does not reflect, must be disposed to sleep of course." Jefferson lamented that the "veil of black" gave women's faces an "eternal monotony." Jefferson dismissed the work of black poet Phillis Wheatley as an example of religious zeal, rather than of talent: "The compositions published under her name are below the dignity of criticism." If the charges against Jefferson of taking as his mistress his own slave, Sally Hemmings, are true, his statements become all the more ironic, for he apparently found a black woman worthy of his intimate companionship.

Jefferson's writings demonstrate that even educated, liberal observers adhered to prevailing gender expectations and models. While he discussed white women largely in terms of their domestic roles, he viewed Native and black women primarily in terms of their race. And although the statesman extolled white women's contributions to the nation, he denigrated those of Indian and black women. It is unlikely that ordinary citizens of the time would have been any more informed or open-minded.

Ideals of Marriage and Motherhood

Republican ideals not only provided enhanced status for white women, but such beliefs encouraged white women to hold greater expectations of marriage and motherhood. Surely, many concluded, wives and mothers would gradually gain more respect and wield more influence than ever before.

Demographic shifts accompanied, and perhaps helped create, these ideas. White women's personal status was indeed modifying. White women now controlled more personal and real property. For those women who wed, the age of marriage gradually rose, while family size slowly declined. During the late 1700s and early 1800s, women of the Virginia gentry began to complain about bearing an average of eight children. Accordingly, they decreased the number of children they bore by marrying later, lengthening the period of sexual abstinence after a birth, and experimenting with birth control devices.

At the same time, birth itself rapidly became a more complicated and notable matter. No longer did the average white woman expect to bear a child in her own home with the help of a female midwife. During the colonial period, pregnant women had delivered their babies with the assistance of other women. During the war era, Dr. William Shippen of Philadelphia had led the revolution in birthing techniques. After studying medicine, including midwifery, in London, Shippen returned to Philadelphia in 1762. He brought with him British standards concerning hospitals, medical training, and professionalism. At his urging, the only hospital in America, the Pennsylvania Hospital, in 1763 initiated formal medical training and lectures in midwifery, including the use of obstetrical forceps. By 1807, five medical schools in the United States offered courses in midwifery to male students. The increasing presence of trained male doctors in the delivery room brought instruments and anesthesia into regular use, and the Cesarean section became a common emergency procedure.

Many women still preferred female midwives, however. One of these midwives, Martha Ballard, attended 814 births between 1787 and 1798. By horseback, wagon, and sometimes canoe, Ballard traveled to homes where she delivered women of what she called a "fine" daughter or son. Ballard was more than a midwife. She was a confidante to women who suffered at the hands of men, inside and outside their families. As a midwife, Ballard gave not only medical assistance, but a form of psychological counseling as well. The latter was something that few medical doctors cared to provide. By the time Martha Ballard died in 1812, some women preferred that doctors attend their deliveries, but others still insisted on receiving the personal attentions of a female midwife.

Another consequence of the growing emphasis on motherhood was an interest in childcare practices. Manuals such as *Mother's Catechism and Maternal Instruction* appeared in large numbers. The prevailing view of children became less one of miniature adults in need of rescue from original sin and more one of pliable and innocent beings whose upbringings demanded specialized equipment, including toys and books. Thus, childhood came to be seen as a discrete period in a person's life that included maternal care, training in ideals and values, and specific paraphernalia.

Women in Politics, or Not

After the Revolution, the political realm proved a source of great frustration for white women. They soon learned that the Declaration of Independence's grand statements regarding "freedom and liberty for all" excluded them. They did not seem to be part of "the people" after all, nor was liberty *their* "birthright."

Leaders of the new Republic did debate the nature of women's place in the new United States of America. John Adams argued that while women were theoretically part of the new U.S. government, they should exercise their influence in the home rather than in any public capacity. Adams maintained that women's power lay in their influence over men and children, whom they could steer toward the adoption of "proper" republican values. Adams wrote to a friend that, like men without property, women lacked decisiveness, while "their delicacy renders them unfit for practice and experience in the great business of life."

Similarly, Thomas Jefferson, the author of the Declaration, believed that "the tender breasts of ladies were not formed for political convulsion." Like John Adams, Jefferson thought that women should remain in the protected privacy of home, while men fought the daily battles in the public and political arenas. Although he carried on extensive correspondence with Abigail Adams, Jefferson remained convinced that neither he nor his fellow citizens were ready for women voters and office holders.

As a result of such attitudes, when voters discarded the Articles of Confederation and ratified the new Constitution in 1789, Republican women found that the document included no rights or protection for them. Nor were women released from coverture (*femes covert*) and the limitations of marital unity. Also, thirteen years after the Declaration of Independence, no female representatives sat on governing bodies and no women served as emissaries to the first political parties. Of course, the new constitution reflected patriarchal principles of the era.

Still, the new Constitution did include such gender-inclusive terms as *citizens, inhabitants,* and *persons,* which suggests that the Founding Fathers envisioned women as part of the body politic of the new United States, or perhaps intended to expand women's political rights in the future. The Constitution also counted women for representation in the new U. S. Congress.

On the state level, only New Jersey experimented with including women in politics. From colonial days, New Jersey had a tradition of adhering to liberty of conscience, civil rights, and taxation only by representation. In New Jersey, which adopted its state constitution as early as 1776, property requirements for office holding were lower than in nearby states. New Jersey was also the first state to ratify the Bill of Rights. In harmony with these leanings toward democratic ideas, in 1790 the New Jersey state constitution included an election law that employed the terms "he or she," thus allowing women to vote. State officials made it clear that women had the right to vote if they so chose. In 1797, a contingent of women voters helped decide a close election in Elizabeth, New Jersey. Ten years later, the defeated candidate of 1797 ran successfully on a platform that would disenfranchise women. Because no other state had followed New Jersey in venture into woman suffrage, New Jersey's women lost the vote in 1807.

Clearly, the many political ramifications of the Revolution and the new nation's government did not extend to women. Some women accepted this situation as inevitable. Like her husband John, Abigail Adams believed that political participation might sully women. Although she had argued for an expansion of women's rights, her list did not include participation in politics. Rather, she thought that women played their most critical role in the home. Adams was a woman who took mothering seriously, once writing to her son John Quincy, then a student in England: "I would rather see you find a grave in the ocean you have crossed than see you an immoral, profligate or graceless child."

Other women, barred from expressing themselves politically, did so personally, especially regarding the question of marriage. Long before the twentieth-century feminist movement coined the slogan during the 1960s, some women recognized that the *personal was political*. For instance, although women could not vote or hold office, they could demand the right to choose their own mates or refuse to marry at all. During the 1780s and 1790s, more women in the Northeast chose not to marry rather than select a less-than-suitable mate. Daughters, especially of eastern, well-to-do families, exercised their "independence" in the marriage market.

During the early 1800s, Laura Wirt of Washington, D.C., wrote, "it will never do for me to be married." She did not want to sacrifice her legal rights, for by common law a husband held legal and economic power over his spouse. Nor did Laura wish to spend the rest of her life bearing children. Although southern women like Laura had fewer alternatives than their counterparts in the North and experienced more social pressure, perhaps as many as one-fifth remained single. Among other things, they feared marrying men who might turn out to be authoritarian or aloof to them. When Laura Wirt finally succumbed to marriage in 1826, she unfortunately found her anxieties verified. She spent the years of her unhappy marriage on a Florida plantation, bearing four children. Laura died in childbirth in 1833.

Unlike Wirt, a number of other women abided by their decisions to remain single. When an increased number of women in the general population relieved some of the pressure on women to marry, the proportion of single women in the United States grew. By 1796, for example, women headed 8 percent of Baltimore's households; one-third of these women were never married.

The growing availability of divorce, except in South Carolina, also helped swell the number of unwed women. Women successfully sued for divorce in larger numbers than did men. This statistic can be interpreted as a consequence of an enhanced spirit of independence among women, along with their rising expectations of marriage and unwillingness to tolerate anything less than they had anticipated. In addition, a new ideal of companionate marriage was developing. An anonymous article of the 1790s declared that an ideal marriage was one based on "mutual esteem, mutual friendship, mutual confidence, begirt about by mutual forbearance." Possibly the heightened worth of motherhood raised expectations regarding the contributions of men to marriage and family relationships. And having become ever more emotionally and professionally invested in their children, women were perhaps no longer, for their children's sake, as willing to endure a husband's adultery and alcoholism.

Women who chose not to marry, who divorced their spouses, or were widowed, supported themselves by working as seamstresses, laundresses, dyers, starchers, lace makers, and mantua (gown) makers. They also ran small businesses supplying groceries, dry goods, millinery, hardware, and other goods. For some women, supporting oneself meant a life of poverty and hard work; other women found the notion empowering and thrived, providing positive models of single, independent women for others who doubted their ability to stand alone.

Improved Female Education

In the course of the young republic, white women gained far more in the realm of education. A corollary of Republican Womanhood, that mothers must have some education to raise Republican children, soon spurred a reconsideration of women's education. Although the rhetoric of the 1780s and 1790s declared that reason and rationality were masculine qualities not common among women, at the same time, many Americans believed that women must be better educated for their roles as Republican mothers.

As "improved female education," as it was then called, became an ongoing debate, it was obvious that many Americans believed that the new Republican woman should be rational, competent, and self-reliant. This view did not favor "intellectual" women or the departure of women from the home as their primary sphere. Rather, it emphasized the idea that women's duties in the home had achieved a new significance. One trustee of a southern women's school hoped for neither "excessive refinement nor extreme erudition." He simply wanted female students to develop a "rational, well-informed piety."

Some reformers, however, wanted more for women students: they hoped for them an education equal to that given men. In her letters to her husband, Abigail Adams explored the meaning of the Revolution for women's education. Adams understood that women's primary duty was to cultivate wisdom and loyalty in their children, thus preserving virtues, especially those supposedly female traits of selflessness and purity, necessary to an independent republic. How would women train "heroes, statesmen and philosophers," she wondered, if they themselves were not "learned"? In 1778, she reminded John of the "narrow contracted Education" of women in the new United States. "You need not be told," she wrote, "how much female Education is neglected, nor how fashionable it has been to ridicule Female learning."

At the same time, Judith Sargent Murray, an author and early feminist, became one of the first Americans to argue publicly for equitable educational opportunities for women. In 1779, writing under the pen name of Constantia, Murray declared that men and women had equal minds that deserved an equivalent education. "Are women deficient in reason?" she asked. "We can only reason from what we know, and if an opportunity of acquiring knowledge hath been denied us, the inferiority of our sex cannot fairly be deduced from thence." If women were "allowed an equality of acquirements" in the area of education, they would "meet on even ground" in their achievements.

Abigail Adams continued to worry about the matter and, by 1787, concluded that women were "rational beings" whose minds "might with propriety receive the highest possible cultivation." Although she recognized that an educated woman would "draw upon herself the jealousy of the Men and the envy of the Women," she believed that the only "way to remedy this evil" was "by increasing the number of accomplished women," thus forcing their acceptance by society.

The celebrated Dr. Benjamin Rush of Philadelphia explained it this way: "Let the ladies of a country be educated properly and they will not only make and administer its laws, but form its manners and character." In 1787, Rush presented at the recently established Young Ladies Academy of Philadelphia an address that urged the inclusion of academic subjects in the curriculum. Rush urged students to act in a "womanly" way so as not to inflame Americans' fear that education would "unsex" women. The course of study at this academy, which claimed to be the first of its kind chartered in the United States, included reading, writing, arithmetic, English grammar, composition, rhetoric, and geography. This curriculum represented a major alteration in ideas regarding white women, for prominent men had, for the first time, devoted their time and energy to advocate the concept of a sound education for women, at least for those of the upper social classes.

Strong evidence indicates that the male founders of the Young Ladies' Academy wanted to lessen women's discontent while improving the education of the mothers of the new country's future citizens. Yet there were other reasons as well to improve women's education in the new nation. Like many upper-class Americans of the day, the academy's founders were sons of the Enlightenment and, as such, valued knowledge for its own sake. They recognized that in times of peace and that of war, women would teach children at home and in schools. In addition, women would act as what Rush called "stewards" of farms, plantations, and businesses, thus making their acquisition of basic skills in reading and arithmetic necessary. Moreover, white women of the middle- and upper-classes would have to educate children, servants, and slaves, and therefore needed their own educational foundation. Finally, it was reasoned that educated women would prove more socially adept and make a better companion for an educated man.

Still, as Rush's remarks suggested, the academy's founders did not intend the establishment of the school to mark "an Era altogether new." Consequently, some women who gave graduation addresses reflected their continuing acceptance of the *status quo*. "I believe I must give up all pretensions to profundity," one stated, "for I am more at home in my female character." Others, however, mentioned such ideas as equal education for women and widening the accepted female sphere. One who viewed education as a "prize" and a "conquest," long denied to women, proclaimed, "shall not our sex be ambitious of gaining the summit?"

A short time later, in 1792, a bold new experiment in women's literature, the *Ladies Magazine and Repository* published in Philadelphia, revealed a similar double-sided approach to women's education. On the one hand, the editors emphasized that women should read such intellectually expanding works as Mary Wollstonecraft's *A Vindication of the Rights of Women* (1792), which argued for a reformed female education that would do more than leave women in a "state of perpetual childhood," prepared only to attract and please men. On the other hand, the editors featured such male writers as Noah Webster and Benjamin Rush who argued that women's education should enlarge only to the point of allowing women to understand Republican ideals.

As a consequence of the growing interest in women's education, a number of schools attracted more female students than ever. The Linden Hall Seminary, which grew out of a Moravian (Methodist), or United Brethren, day school established in Lititz, Pennsylvania, in 1764, expanded its facilities and programs after the Revolution. By 1790, it enrolled a dozen female students. Applications increased so rapidly that in 1799 one teacher wrote, "We cannot increase our numbers for want of teachers, every one must wait for a vacancy." A renovation allowed the enrollment to expand somewhat, and, by 1804, seventeen female day pupils and fifty-two boarders attended the school. During the 1790s, northern young women could attend a wide variety of other schools in Philadelphia or Boston, or enroll in such New England small-town schools as Sarah Pierce's Litchfield Academy.

In the South, planter's daughters could select either northern boarding schools or female academies, especially in North Carolina and Georgia. Southern women's academies moved away from superficial education in "female accomplishments" to training in subjects that would contribute to women becoming more effective mothers and more informed citizens. In 1805, a Virginia planter requested that his daughter send a complete account of her academy education: "I wish to know how each day is employed—what proportion is devoted to study, to writing, to cyphering, to reading, to sewing, to amusement, to idleness." Southern women flocked to academies in order to gain, if not equality, at least an improved quality of life as wives, mothers, and plantation mistresses.

The Growth of "Women's" Literature and Art

The concept of Republican Womanhood encouraged a number of novelists to write explicitly for women, notably white women. The resulting didactic tales usually ended with a highly moral message directed especially to future as well as present wives and mothers.

The most popular example of the genre was Susanna Haswell Rowson's novel, *Charlotte Temple, A Tale of Truth,* first published in 1794. On the third page, Rowson explained that, as author, she would guide the reader through a "perusal of the young and thoughtless of the fair sex." Rowson intended her tale of Charlotte Temple's involvement with an evil man named Montraville to prove instructive to young female readers. In the novel, after Charlotte marries and is deserted by Montraville, it becomes clear that women have responsibility for their own fall from virtue. By the early 1800s, this cautionary saga of seduction reportedly sold more copies than any other book in the history of British or American publishing to that date.

Such stories reinforced the growing belief that women acted as moral forces and purveyors of virtue in the new American republic. Such literature created a unified female reading audience that increasingly believed in women's moral superiority over men, and it opened a wider area of employment to female writers.

After the Revolution, white women also moved into the arts, competing with male artists by creating conventional works of art. They did so without the benefit of formal training or study abroad because these activities were believed unseemly for women. The families of such women did not want them to attend classes with unclothed models, and certainly objected to their daughters traveling to, and living in Europe, alone.

Despite these restrictions, several women gained public recognition for their pastel drawing, which required supplies easily available to them. In addition, they were largely self-taught and had erratic careers due to the interruption of domestic duties. For instance, a Connecticut pastelist named Sarah Perkins produced portraits during the 1790s. Her career was brief, however. She first had to take charge of her seven brothers and sisters at the age of twenty. Later, Perkins married a widower with five children, and then had four children of her own. She now had little time to pursue the talent that had given her and others so much pleasure.

Other women artists worked in the medium of watercolor. They staved off criticism or charges of being unwomanly by combining their art with some aspect of women's roles. One combined her watercolors with exquisite embroidery, which was an acceptable female craft. Others concentrated on religious themes, such as the parable of the prodigal son. As long as such women artists limited their work to moral teachings, they were thought to be following women's "proper" path.

The best-known female artist of the early 1800s was Sarah Miriam Peale. She trod where other women were unable, or afraid, to go. As the youngest daughter of James Peale, a renowned miniaturist and portrait painter, and the niece of acclaimed natural history painter and portraitist Charles Willson Peale, Sarah had artistic advantages not available to other women. Trained by her father and her uncle, Sarah Peale became an accomplished portrait and still-life artist. Her clients included heads of state and generals, and Peale was the first woman to have her work exhibited at the prestigious Pennsylvania Academy of the Fine Arts.

The Feminization of Religion

Changes for women occurred in religion as well. Because far more women belonged to churches than did men, most congregations had a majority of female members. As church audiences became largely female, ministers began to "feminize" their message to meet better the needs of their listeners. The clergy also turned their attention to topics of special concern to women, such as the family, public and private morality, the refinement of society, and missionary endeavors. The clergy stressed the crucial role of godly mothers and the importance of women's morality, thus adding the church's voice to the growing emphasis on motherhood.

With religion in America thus feminizing, women were quick to seize new opportunities. Beginning in 1776, "Mother" Ann Lee promoted a new sect, Shakerism, known for its female participation and leadership. This Protestant, celibate, and communitarian sect envisioned Lee as the female incarnation of Christ, as well as the female aspect of a God who had both male and female components. Lee believed that sexuality constituted the primary barrier to human perfectibility, a message she intended to deliver to humankind. To her, celibacy was the key to salvation: once everyone rejected sex, the end of the world would come and God would have the opportunity to make more perfect beings to inhabit the Earth. Lee and her followers became known as Shakers because of a ritualistic dance they performed in which they "shook" off the devil from their hands and feet. Lee died in 1784 of injuries, perhaps inflicted by a mob, but the sect she founded continued to follow her teachings.

When the religious revival movement known as the Second Great Awakening began during the early 1800s, women spurred it onward as members, lay speakers, and exhorters. Revivalist Jemima Wilkinson especially attracted numerous followers with her charisma and exceptional speaking abilities. As a popular and effective preacher, she helped legitimize the highly emotional nature of the Second Great Awakening, which allowed women to express their religious sensibilities freely.

As religious, impassioned, and highly moral beings, women began to see themselves as the inculcators of virtue not only in children but in men as well. They actively recruited men for conversion, an act that implied the superiority of their female religious nature. In an 1810 sermon, one preacher agreed: "We look to you, ladies, to raise the standard of character in our own sex." Women openly expressed anger against authority, particularly that of ungodly men and controlling ministers, thus venting some of the tensions created by the remaining limitations on their lives.

Similarly, in the Catholic Church women gained a degree of visibility. Elizabeth Ann Seton, a widow who converted to Catholicism in 1804, founded a community of women Religious in 1809. Located in Emmitsburg, Maryland, Seton's order founded the first Catholic parochial school in the new nation. Later, in 1812, Archbishop John Carroll confirmed the rules and constitution of Seton's Sisters of Charity, making it the first American community of women Religious.

Women on the Western Frontier

American Indian Women

Before the French and Indian War, waves of white settlers had already begun to trickle into Indian lands. After the French and Indian War ended in 1763, the frontier formed a jagged line across the Appalachian region and the South. The emerging American frontier was a zone in which white settlers and Native peoples often encountered each other. Both sides were curious about the other, and at first were often friendly and helpful to each other.

As a result of the American Revolution, the new United States, rather than Britain, claimed and controlled the trans-Appalachian West. In 1785, the new American government officially "opened" the lands beyond the Appalachian Mountains for settlement. The Appalachian district became the "West" of its era. Because of such factors as high taxes or worn-out farm land at home, white Americans migrated to the Appalachian West, elbowing out Native Americans as they went. With them, white settlers carried a lot of cultural baggage, including long-held assumptions regarding race and gender.

Indians themselves facilitated western development. Indian men and women acted as traders in furs and other goods, and eventually as porters, laborers, guides, bridge builders, explorers of routes, and suppliers of food and other necessary commodities to migrants. Such Indians acted out of friendship or for payment in trade goods or coins. Most Indians had no idea how many white settlers would follow these first few interlopers, or how devastating the great white migration would be for Indian peoples.

From the white perspective, settlers owed a debt to many Indians. The brisk trade that whites conducted with Indians in furs and other goods significantly aided the economic development of the white American frontier. And more than one party of white settlers avoided getting lost or starving to death due to the efforts of the Indians who helped them.

Yet, white migration usually proved disastrous for Native Americans. The Indian policy of the new American republic soon developed into a "seize-and-settle" process. In acquiring Native land through war or treaty, American agents, officials, lawmakers, and settlers became increasingly impatient with Indian concepts of communal landholding. Puzzled by the Indian belief that land belonged to everyone and thus could not be transferred to an individual through a piece of paper, whites often resorted to threats and trickery to get Indians to agree to land sales. Convinced of the validity of "private property"—and believing they had a God-given right to the land—whites pushed Indians farther and farther to the South and West.

Once Native Americans understood that whites had arrived intending to seize Native lands, they resisted white migration and settlement. Understandably, many Native Americans now became "hostile" to whites. Indians had no desire to see their crops and game disappear or their families broken and scattered. Conflict between the two groups soon ensued.

For Native American women, the arrival of whites further undercut their already weakened position. The American fur trade especially impaired the status and power of Indian women. At first, native women merchants bartered furs for white-style goods. But because whites treated Indian women with scorn and refused to negotiate with them, Indian men took over women's traditional function as traders. Instead, whites hired Indian women only as poorly paid and low-status interpreters, workers, and liaisons.

At the same time, such factory-produced items as cloth and blankets began to undermine Native women's production of goods. As industrialization came to the United States during the 1790s and early 1800s, white mountain men and peddlers carried westward manufactured items, which they swapped for furs. In relatively short order, calico shirts and trade blankets replaced the beautifully tanned and decorated animal-hide clothing that Indian women had been producing for their families for centuries.

Meanwhile, white attitudes regarding the inferiority of women spread along the frontier. In white eyes, an Indian woman had two strikes against her. Although some white people idealized Indian women as romanticized "dark damsels of the forest," many others judged them savage and immoral. As a consequence of the latter reaction, whites shamelessly disrupted Native women's personal lives. For instance, fur trappers and traders carried to Native women venereal disease and introduced them to the practice of prostitution. Moreover, Native American women who married white men often found themselves and their mixed-heritage children abandoned and forced to return in shame to their tribes.

Gradually, the importance of Indian women in fur-trade societies decreased. This, in turn, led to a decline in women's opportunities to become political leaders of their communities, or to act as shamans or warriors. In Iroquois society, for example, female elders had long served as sachems on tribal councils, the most powerful Iroquois ruling body.

Among the Seneca of New York, white teachers and missionaries further disabled women. During the 1790s, teachers and missionaries encouraged Seneca women to spin and weave, while men took over the farming. Farther south, Choctaw and Cherokee women discovered that white Americans wanted to convert them from farmers to housewives. Rather than being mothers of green corn they were to spend their time indoors.

Apparently, whites wanted to reshape Indian societies that would mirror their own, in which women wove and men farmed. No doubt, whites believed their way was the best way and would help the Seneca live happily among encroaching whites. For Seneca women this shift in responsibilities meant they could no longer follow women's traditional duty of supplying food to their people. Seneca women also lost the power and influence they had held by determining the distribution of food. In addition, Seneca women watched their men, once mighty warriors and hunters, reduced to home-bound laborers made to undertake women's customary work, farming.

In the South, Cherokee societies experienced similar disruption. Traditionally, Cherokee women held property, kept their children in case of a divorce, and decided the fates of captives. But as a result of intermarriage with whites and the U.S. government's new "civilization" policy, the Cherokee gradually abandoned the custom of matrilineal descent. Instead, they adopted the white concept of a patrilineal pattern of inheritance. During the late 1790s and early 1800s, Cherokee women lost more ground. Because white migration had depleted the Cherokees' supply of wild game, men who had once been esteemed hunters now took over the agricultural tasks that previously had belonged to women.

As among these eastern tribes, Indian women who lived along advancing lines of white settlement in the West and the South suffered. A typical story was that of a Mohawk medicine woman named Coocoochee. After undertaking five forced moves across hundreds of miles, she ended up in Kentucky. After her husband died in war in 1790, Coocoochee took refuge with the Shawnees. Here, she acted as a spiritual leader and a Mohawk historian, for she feared that she and her children were the last of the Mohawks. This once-proud woman ended her life torn from her own people and culture.

At the time, however, most whites understood little about the damage that white migration inflicted on Native Americans. Whites knew even less about the deteriorating position of American Indian women. Typically, white people were interested only in those Native women who had helped them to achieve their ends. Between 1804 to 1806, Sacagawea, an Idaho Shoshone, gained historical fame among whites. By aiding the Lewis and Clark expedition as an interpreter and guide, Sacagawea became a heroine to whites. Even today most school children know her name.

As clearly as can be determined, the legendary Sacagawea was probably born sometime during the 1880s to a Lemhi Shoshone family. As a girl, Sacagawea was taken captive by the Minnetares and Hidatsa Indians on the Missouri River. In 1804, an old and disreputable fur trapper, Toussaint Charbonneau, chose the young Sacagawea as one of his "wives." Shortly after Sacagawea bore her first child, a son named Baptiste, she found herself included, along with Charbonneau, in the Lewis and Clark expedition, dispatched by the U.S. government to explore the upper portion of the Louisiana Purchase. The indomitable Sacagawea foraged food, explained Indian customs, and convinced the Lemhi Shoshone to help Lewis and Clark. This Indian woman, who Captain William Clark described as being of "great service" to him as a pilot and interpreter, appears to have died in 1812 at age twenty-five. Sacagawea's deification as "the beautiful Indian princess" who guided the Lewis and Clark expedition to the Pacific Ocean began during the early nineteenth century. Women were looking for historical heroines and white people hoped to find something other than hatred and bitterness between their own people and Native Americans. As a result, although many twentieth-century Indians view Sacagawea as a traitor to her own people, her story is still celebrated among whites.

Sacagawea did not stand alone. Other similar cases existed of Native women assisting whites, usually a result of their own personal relations with white men or because they hoped that Indians and whites could learn to coexist in harmony. One of these was Marie Dorion, an Iowa

Indian. Dorion was the only woman on the famed 1811–1812 exploring expedition to Astoria on the Columbia River. Like Sacagawea, she explained Indian ways to the white explorers and warned them of Native attacks.

Spanish-Speaking Women

Growing numbers of Spanish-speaking women lived along parts of the American frontier line during the years of the Early Republic. Unlike American Indian women, most Hispanic women, or *Hispanas,* were not yet inhabitants of the American frontier. The tide of white settlers and government officials had only begun to threaten the lands they called home. Yet their culture was soon to meet, and eventually become part of, white American society.

Hispanas not only lived in different parts of the frontier but were of disparate backgrounds, social classes, marital statuses, and age groups. Some Spanish-heritage women migrated to, or were born in, Spanish-held Florida on the southern frontier. Others lived in the French-dominated Louisiana territory. In the Southwest, Spanish-speaking pioneer women contributed greatly to the settlement of *El Norte,* the northern provinces of New Spain and then Mexico. These women helped found and develop the towns and cities that were as yet only fascinating names to most white Americans: Los Angeles, San Antonio, San Francisco, Santa Fe, and Tucson. Others were scattered across the rich valleys and semi-arid areas of what later became Arizona, California, New Mexico, and Texas.

Generally, such Spanish-speaking women were Roman Catholics. Because the Roman Catholic Church stressed family well-being and the collective good above individual gain, both single and married Hispanic women gave their primary allegiance to their families. Among their duties were the care of children and the aged, as well as holding families together. Especially among the middle- and lower-classes, Hispanic women were well versed in plant medicine, midwifery, and other domestic skills. And Hispanic women of all classes kept alive a sense of fiesta and celebration, thus maintaining traditional culture wherever they went.

Even in this patriarchal, family-oriented system, women exercised a great deal of influence. According to Spanish law, women could inherit and hold family property. Wealthy matriarchs ran large families, distributing land and power as they saw fit. Even among the lower classes, women shared in, or made, family decisions. And women played active parts in community life, either as volunteers or as wage workers. For instance, much like white midwives in the United States, *curanderas,* or healers, often received as pay food, clothing, or small amounts of cash. Women could also be found working as teachers and matrons in the Catholic missions strung from Texas to the California coast.

In a culture that honored and revered women, it is unsurprising that strong women frequently became heroines. Stories of female mettle, in which intrepid women overcame adversity and made contributions to Hispanic culture, abounded. One such woman was the daughter of Don Jose Dario Argüello, *comandante* of San Francisco during the early 1800s. After she lost her betrothed in a sea disaster, she led a life of piety and charity, always helping the ill and poor. In 1851, at age sixty, Doña Concepcíon joined the Dominican order. Renamed María Dominica, she became California's first woman Religious. This intrepid woman spent the remaining six years of her life in benevolent works, thus supplying a model for generations of young Hispanic women.

White Women

Even though Native American and Hispanic women already inhabited what Americans thought of as their frontier, white women migrated to the region. Because whites thought of Indians and Hispanics as few in number and inferior in culture, they had few misgivings over taking these peoples' lands.

For most whites, the journey to the West was a long and difficult one. Usually travelling by covered wagon, these pioneers embarked on a trip that could consume months and might cost them their lives. Because wagon trains only covered three to ten miles day, it took as long as four months to travel from a farm in New England to new land in present-day Ohio or Kentucky. While women brought with them as much clothing and equipment as possible, they nonetheless feared that they might prove unprepared, psychically and psychologically, to meet the demands of the new environment.

Once on the frontier, however, white women soon learned that they were not only willing but able to fight alongside their men in wresting land from its Native owners and in working to clear it with oxen, mules, horses, and primitive machinery. Despite their contributions to frontier society, white women found only limited opportunities in it. Although religion and education held out some leadership roles to women, the political realm barred them. As in their former homes, formal politics was for men only. Although women aided in the formation of the new states entering the union after the Revolution—Kentucky in 1792, Tennessee in 1796, and Ohio in 1803—they continued to lack political privileges. Even in such supposedly egalitarian frontier regions as those along the Cumberland River, women remained outside of the political realm throughout the late 1700s and early 1800s.

The domestic domain demanded much of women, however, and kept them busy. As in the East, women adopted those standards of Republican Womanhood that suited their western lifestyles. All along the frontier line, white women struggled to raise their children as educated "proper," virtuous, and democratic men and women. At the same time, women managed homes, chicken coops, and dairies—all complex and arduous responsibilities requiring training and skill.

Frontierswomen learned to run farms and handle crises on their own while their men were absent on long trips. Married to hunters, traders, trappers, surveyors, and politicians, women stayed home and minded the family enterprise. Daniel Smith, for example, was gone from his family more than a year when he helped to survey the North Carolina–Virginia line in 1779–1780. Thus, women often tilled the fields, built houses and outbuildings, bred animals, and did a multitude of heavy chores.

A small number of women could be found at the western posts that dotted the area. Officers often had the privilege of bringing wives and children to the posts they commanded. Other women followed the army hoping for employment as cooks, laundresses, or nurses. Yet others intended to work as prostitutes in locations that had a very high ratio of white men to very few women.

When she arrived at Fort Wayne in Indiana during 1811, Captain Nathan Heald's wife realized a primitive and isolated lifestyle. Fort Wayne sat in the center of a military reserve, surrounded by Indians lands. Because settlers were not yet allowed in the region, there were few white women for Heald's wife to meet. Yet she preferred fort life to waiting back East for her new husband's return. Other women of her social class that may have been present were wives of Indian agents, traders, interpreters, or other officers. Such women spent their time much like white female settlers, arranging to feed and clothe their families. During the early 1800s, the Fort Wayne "factory," or shop, carried spinning wheels, needles, and all kinds of thread. Lists of possessions owned by officers indicated that such families owned large amounts of kitchen equipment, including tea trays, cork screws, looking glasses, and silver soup ladles.

Army wives had a multitude of other duties. Because churches were rarely available, women held religious services and Bible readings. Women cared for and instructed children. Because no or few schools existed within or nearby early forts, mothers often returned "home" when their children reached school age. Fort Wayne's social life depended on the number of women present. In 1799, a new agent's wife was delighted that Fort Wayne had witnessed three balls, or dances, since her arrival, one each night. In 1807, a new officer at Fort Wayne judged life there "agreeable," but "destitute of society." A holiday that Fort Wayne never missed celebrating was the Fourth of July. In 1805, the ceremony consisted of discharging "Seventeen rounds from a Piece of Ordnance," a concert by the fort musicians, and an extra "Gill of Whiskey" for all officers and for women who were entitled to draw rations.

Across the western frontier, whether settlers or military personnel, men often recognized women's labor and management abilities in their wills, which commonly left property to wives and assigned them as executors of estates. After losing their men, many frontier widows continued to work on their own. It has been estimated that Indian wars widowed almost two-thirds of early women settlers in Tennessee by the 1790s. Yet few of these women chose to leave the frontier in order to live with families in the more settled eastern regions. Widowed in 1781, Leah Lucas stayed on the Cumberland frontier, farming the family land and raising five children.

Other women attained single status by divorcing their spouses. By the early 1800s, when statistics were not yet compiled, it appeared that western divorces outnumbered those in the Northeast and the South. A study of Kane County in northern Illinois indicates that after a newly formed circuit court granted the area's first divorce, the number of divorce requests grew rapidly. In these cases, women petitioned for divorce more often than men did, primarily relying on the grounds of desertion, bigamy, and fraud. Evidently, westward migration placed a definite strain on marriages, especially when one spouse refused to go along with the other. The reluctant party was often the wife but not always; some wives disappeared westward, never to be seen by their husbands again.

With their mobile population, hastily adopted laws and policies, and emphasis on independence and personal satisfaction, western settlements often provided fertile ground for divorce. As in Kane County, anecdotal evidence and surviving records suggest that far more women than men took advantage of the availability of divorce in newly settled western sections of the country than in the older regions.

Slave and Free Black Women

Despite myths and media images that present light-haired and fair-skinned women as archetypal westerners, frontierswomen included slave and free black women. Such slave and free women of color went west as domestic workers, nursemaids, riverboat cooks, and farm laborers, until they trickled into almost every western locale. For instance, of the forty-four settlers who founded Los Angeles in 1781, at least twenty-six were black women, men, and children.

The frontier offered many attractions to African Americans: good farming land, few people to ask questions, and jobs in the towns and on the riverboats. In 1787, the Confederation Congress passed the Northwest Ordinance, which, among other things, prohibited slavery in the areas that would form the states of Illinois, Indiana, Michigan, Ohio, and Wisconsin. But the provisions of the Northwest Ordinance lacked means of enforcement so whites in the territory who already held slaves continued to do so. Still, the ordinance's barring of "involuntary servitude" in this area attracted free blacks, who worked for fur trappers, traders, soldiers, and farmers, or farmed on their own.

As a growing number of blacks went west, however, white settlers began to fear them. White people saw people of color as different and were afraid that black workers would take over local jobs by providing cheap labor. As a result of such anxieties, white legislatures passed measures restricting black men and women. In 1804, the Ohio state legislature enacted the first of a series of "black laws" limiting the rights and mobility of free African Americans in the Northwest. Neither black men nor women could own property, while exclusion laws barred them from residing in certain towns, counties, and states. Such states as Ohio and Indiana even required that free blacks post a bond of as much as $500 to guarantee that they were indeed freedmen and women rather than runaway slaves or to ensure their good behavior. If they turned out to be slaves or caused trouble, they would forfeit their bond.

Despite these drawbacks, free blacks continued to head "Out West" in hopes of finding better jobs and less prejudice there. This was not to be. Although a few whites did not hold racial prejudices or were abolitionists, the majority of pioneers had brought ideas concerning racial inferiority westward with them. Most white settlers gave migrants of color a cool reception and hired them only in times of dire need. Antagonistic whites might even use such violent means as tarring-and-feathering to convince black newcomers to look somewhere else for a new home.

African American women were especially disappointed in the climate of opinion they found in the Old Northwest. Although black women usually received paltry wages, like every other wage earner they had to pay taxes. Yet their children were not allowed to attend public, tax-supported schools. In addition, black women met with racial discrimination everywhere, including the hospitals and orphanages that their tax-dollars helped support. Although some black women had made it to a new home on the American frontier, they soon learned that the West's promise of freedom and opportunity did not apply to them.

Sharing a World

Classifying types of women by race and culture is convenient. In many respects, such categorization is fairly accurate. Obviously, Indian and Hispanic women, though both early inhabitants of North America, experienced different lifestyles during the late 1700s and early 1800s. So did white and black women fare differently during the years of the early American Republic.

Yet race did not always constitute an impenetrable barrier between such women. In the pueblos of El Norte, soon to become the American

Southwest, numerous Indian and Hispanic women worked side by side, perhaps grinding corn or making baskets. On southern plantations, white and black women stuffed featherbeds or cooked maple syrup into sugar. On the Appalachian frontier, Indian and white women traded with each other for foodstuffs and clothing.

Such women shared the same physical space at the same time. They learned bits of each others' customs and folklore. They taught each other languages and skills. And, they occasionally fell in love with each others' menfolk. Although laws forbidding cohabitation and marriage between people of two different races existed in America well into the twentieth century, women and men found ways to circumvent them. Mixed-heritage children resulted, including mestizos, metís, "halfbloods," and mulattos. These were truly the children of the new world, combining two or more racial and cultural heritages with a life-time spent growing up, maturing, and dying in America.

Often scorned by their own people, mixed-heritage women and men spent their lives trying to find a niche, trying to determine where they belonged in a country run largely by white people yet filled with throngs of people of color much like themselves. Were they misfits? Perhaps in some ways they were, yet they often played important roles that have gone largely unrecognized. Many women, for example, acted as cultural intermediaries, going back and forth between their people and those of their spouses, weaving both into an intricate and fragile web.

That the present generation of Americans tends to view its historical past as one torn asunder by race is an illuminating comment on the present rather than a reflection of actual events. Intersections did occur between women and men of diverse racial backgrounds. Too often such meetings resulted in conflict, yet cooperation existed as well.

Beginning in 1763, then, the chaos of resistance, revolution, and early nationhood tested the hardiness of the concept of an invented American woman and her "sphere." By 1812, social, economic, and political upheaval in the new nation resulted in changing ideas about white women, especially those of the middle- and upper-classes. These beliefs included the ideal of companionate, or partnership, marriage and an increased respect for motherhood. The idea of the legitimacy of women's education had gained ground. There was even talk of enhanced self-esteem for women. Yet for white women of the lower classes, gender expectations, whether pre- or postrevolutionary, continued to offer little more than unrealistic goals.

Nor did women of color see many positive developments. Native American women seemed destined for removal from their homelands or for degradation, disease, and death. African and African American women feared that emancipation had become more illusory than ever. Although women of these groups exercised their agency in numerous ways, including passive resistance and clinging to their own cultures, they lived on the margins of a white-dominated nation. While some of their white sisters may have experienced some gains between 1763 and 1812, women of color would have to continue to wait and to hope.

Study Guide

Checklist of important names, terms, phrases, and dates in Chapter 2.
Think about what or who each was and why she, he, or it was significant.

Patriots
Loyalists
1763–1776
resistance phase of the American
    Revolution
French and Indian War
Patriot women
Mercy Otis Warren
Abigail Adams
anti-tea leagues
boycott agreements
Daughters of Liberty
Sarah Bradless Fulton
Loyalist women
Margaret Draper
Seneca Indians
Cherokee Indians
Phillis Wheatley
1776–1783
Mary Katherine Goddard
women's associations
charity fairs
scorched-earth policy
female saboteurs and spies
wives and camp followers
Mary Ludwig Hays McCauley, or
    Molly Pitcher
Martha Washington
female soldiers
Margaret Corbin
Grace Growdon Galloway
Catherine Van Cortlandt
South Carolina Confiscation Act
Seneca female agriculturalists
Deborah Sampson
manumission
Pennsylvania Gradual Abolition Act
Massachusetts Declaration of
    Rights
Elizabeth Freeman, or Mum Bett
Loyalist enslaved women
U.S. Constitution
1789

allowance of importation of slaves
cotton gin
1808
black women's benevolent
    societies
Republican Womanhood
Thomas Jefferson's views of
    women
Dr. William Shippen
obstetrical forceps
Martha Ballard
companionate marriage
improved female education
Judith Sargent Murray
Young Ladies Academy of Phila-
    delphia
Mary Wollstonecraft's *A Vindication
    of the Rights of Women*
Linden Hall Seminary
didactic tales
Susanna Haswell Rowson's
    Charlotte Temple, A Tale of Truth
Sarah Miriam Peale
"feminization" of religion
"Mother" Ann Lee
Shakers
Second Great Awakening
Elizabeth Ann Seton
"seize-and-settle" process
Iroquois women
Seneca women
Cherokee women
Sacajawea
Hispanas
El Norte
curanderas
army wives
Northwest Ordinance of 1787
"black laws"
exclusion laws
posting a bond
mixed-heritage women
cultural intermediaries

Chapter 2 issues to think about and discuss

- In what ways did white culture and laws change the roles and status of American Indian women during the revolutionary era. For what reasons did white people push their ways on Indians?
- What motivations did white women and those of color have for becoming either Patriots or Loyalists?
- What kinds of changes did Abigail Adams hope for as a result of the Revolution? Why did these changes fail to occur?
- In what ways was the American Revolution a women's war?
- What did women, both white and of color, lose or gain as a result of the American Revolution?
- If the differences between the British and Americans could have been resolved peaceably, rather than through war, what would white women and those of color have gained?
- White Americans wanted liberty and self-government yet could not understand that such other groups as Indians and African Americans wanted the same things. Why?
- Why did the American Revolution fail to free slaves in the new United States?
- Why was the U.S. Constitution so conservative regarding women and slaves?
- What use to women, both white and of color, was the concept of Republic Womanhood?
- What rationales underlay white peoples' conquering of the frontier?
- How did life differ for women on the Hispanic frontier of El Norte and women on the American frontier?
- What roles have mixed-heritage people played in American history? What does their very existence tell us about frontier culture and society?

Suggestions for Further Reading

Women during Resistance and Revolution

Akers, Charles W. *Abigail Adams: An American Woman.* Boston: Little, Brown and Company, 1980.

Bloch, Ruth H. "The Gendered Meanings of Virtue in Revolutionary America," *Signs* 13 (Autumn 1987): 37–58.

Buel, Joy Day, and Richard Buel, Jr. *The Way of Duty: A Woman and Her Family in Revolutionary America.* New York: W. W. Norton & Co., Inc., 1984.

Coker, Kathy Roe. "The Calamities of War: Loyalism and Women in South Carolina," 47–70, in *Southern Women: Histories and Identities,* edited by Virginia Bernhard, Betty Brandon, Elizabeth Fox-Genovese, and Theda Perdue. Columbia: University of Missouri Press, 1992.

DePauw, Linda Grant. *Founding Mothers: Women in the Revolutionary Era.* Boston: Houghton Mifflin, 1975.

—. "Women in Combat: The Revolutionary War Experience," *Armed Forces and Society* 7 (Winter 1980): 209–26.

Gundersen, Joan R. "Independence, Citizenship, and the American Revolution," *Signs* 13 (Autumn 1987): 59–77.

Hoffman, Ronald, and Peter J. Albert, eds. *Women in the Age of the American Revolution.* Charlottesville: University Press of Virginia, 1989.

Nash, Gary B. *Race and Revolution.* Madison, WI: Madison House, 1990.

Newman, Debra L. " Women in the Era of the American Revolution in Pennsylvania," *Journal of Negro History* 61 (July 1976): 276–89.

Norton, Mary Beth. *Liberty's Daughters: The Revolutionary Experience of American Women, 1750–1800.* Boston: Little, Brown and Company, 1980.

Mayer, Holly A. *Belonging to the Army: Camp Followers and Community during the American Revolution.* Columbia: University of South Carolina Press, 1996.

Westbury, Susan. "Women in Bacon's Rebellion," 30–44, in *Southern Women: Histories and Identities,* edited by Virginia Bernhard, Betty Brandon, Elizabeth Fox-Genovese, and Theda Perdue. Columbia: University of Missouri Press, 1992.

Zagarri, Rosemarie. *A Woman's Dilemma: Mercy Otis Warren and the American Revolution:* Wheeling, IL: Harlan Davidson, Inc., 1995.

Women after the American Revolution

Alexander, Adele L. *Ambitious Lives: Free Women of Color in Rural Georgia, 1789–1870.* Fayetteville: University of Arkansas Press, 1991.

Baker, Paula. "The Domestication of Politics: Women and American Political Society, 1780–1920," 85–110, in *Unequal Sisters: A Multicultural Reader in U.S. Women's History,* edited by Vicki L. Ruiz and Ellen Carol DuBois. 2d ed. New York: Routledge, Chapman, & Hall, 1994.

Banks, Amada Carson. *Birth Chairs, Midwives, and Medicine.* Jackson: University Press of Mississippi, 1999.

Basch, Norma. *In the Eyes of the Law: Women, Marriage and Property in Nineteenth-Century New York.* Ithaca, NY: Cornell University Press, 1982.

Bloch, Ruth H. "American Feminine Ideals in Transition: The Rise of the Moral Mother, 1785–1815," *Feminist Studies* 4 (June 1978): 101–26.

Brodie, Janet Farrell. *Contraception and Abortion in Nineteenth-Century America.* Ithaca, NY: Cornell University Press, 1994.

Bogdan, Janet. "Care or Cure: Childbirth Practices in Nineteenth-Century America," *Feminist Studies* 3 (June 1978): 92–99.

Boydston, Jeanne. *Home and Work: Housework, Wages, and the Ideology of Labor in the Early Republic.* New York: Oxford University Press, 1993.

Chambers-Schiller, Lee Virginia. *Liberty, A Better Husband: Single Women in America, The Generations of 1780–1840.* New Haven, CT: Yale University Press, 1984.

Clinton, Catherine. "Equally Their Due: The Education of the Planter Daughter in the Early Republic," *Journal of the Early Republic* 2 (Spring 1982): 39–60.

Clinton, Catherine, and Michele Gillespie, eds. *The Devil's Lane: Sex and Race in the Early South.* New York: Oxford University Press, 1997.

Cody, Cheryll Ann. "Naming, Kinship and Estate Disposal: Notes on Slave Family Life on a South Carolina Plantation, 1786–1833," *William and Mary Quarterly* 39 (January 1982): 192–2ll.

Dewhurst, C. Kurt, Betty MacDowell, and Marsha MacDowell. *Artists in Aprons: Folk Art by American Women.* New York: E. P. Dutton, 1979.

Dye, Nancy Schrom. "History of Childbirth in America," *Signs* 6 (Autumn 1980): 97–108.

Dye, Nancy Schrom, and Daniel Blake Smith. "Mother Love and Infant Death, 1750–1920," *Journal of American History* 73 (September 1986): 329–53.

Farnham, Christie Anne, ed. *Women of the American South: A Multicultural Reader.* New York: New York University Press, 1997.

Gelles, Edith B. *Portia: The World of Abigail Adams.* Bloomington: Indiana University Press, 1992.

Jabour, Anya. *Marriage in the Early Republic: Elizabeth and William Wirt and the Companionate Ideal.* Baltimore: Johns Hopkins University Press, 1998.

Jensen, Joan M. "Native American Women and Agriculture: A Seneca Case Study," 70–84, in *Unequal Sisters: A Multicultural Reader in U.S. Women's History,* edited by Vicki L. Ruiz and Ellen Carol DuBois. 2d ed. New York: Routledge, Chapman, & Hall, Inc., 1994.

Kerber, Linda K. "'I Have Don . . . much to Carrey on the Warr': Women and the Shaping of Republican Ideology After the American Revolution," *Journal of Women's History* 1 (Winter 1990): 231–43.

———. *Women of the Republic: Intellect and Ideology in Revolutionary America.* Chapel Hill: University of North Carolina Press, 1980.

Kerber, Linda K., Nancy F. Cott, Robert Gross, Lynn Hunt, Carroll Smith-Rosenberg, and Christine M. Stansell. "Beyond Roles, Beyond Spheres: Thinking about Gender in the Early Republic," *William and Mary Quarterly* 46 (July 1989): 565–85.

Lasser, Carol. "Gender, Ideology, and Class in the Early Republic," *Journal of the Early Republic* 10 (Fall 1990): 331–37.

Leavitt, Judith Walzer. *Brought to Bed: Childbearing in America, 1750 to 1950.* New York: Oxford University Press, 1986.

Lewis, Jan. "The Republican Wife: Virtue and Seduction in the Early Republic," *William and Mary Quarterly* 44 (October 1987) 689–721.

———. "'Of every age sex & condition': The Representation of Women in the Constitution," *Journal of the Early Republic,* 15 (Fall 1995): 359-87.

Lewis, Jan, and Kenneth A. Lockridge. "'Sally Has Been Sick': Pregnancy and Family Limitation Among Virginia Gentry Women, 1780–1830," *Journal of Social History* 22 (Fall 1988): 5–19.

Nash, Margaret A. "Rethinking Republican Motherhood: Benjamin Rush and the Young Ladies' Academy of Philadelphia," *Journal of the Early Republic,* 17 (Summer 1997): 171-91.

Perdue, Theda. *Slavery and the Evolution of Cherokee Society, 1540–1866.* Knoxville: University of Tennessee Press, 1979.

Shells, Richard D. "The Feminization of American Congregationalism, 1730–1835," *American Quarterly* 33 (Spring 1981): 46–62.

Smith, Daniel Blake. "The Study of the Family in Early America: Trends, Problems, and Prospects," *William and Mary Quarterly* 39 (January 1982): 3–28.

Soderlund, Jean R. *Quakers and Slavery: A Divided Spirit.* Princeton, NJ: Princeton University Press, 1985.

Ulrich, Laurel Thatcher. *A Midwife's Tale: The Life of Martha Ballard, Based on Her Diary, 1785–1812.* New York: Alfred A. Knopf, 1990.

Wertz, Richard W., and Dorothy C. Wertz. *Lying-In: A History of Childbirth in America.* New York: Free Press, 1977.

Wilson, Lisa. *Life After Death: Widows in Pennsylvania, 1750–1850.* Philadelphia: Temple University Press, 1992.

Zagarri, Rosemarie. "Morals, Manners, and the Republican Mother," *American Quarterly* 44 (June 1992): 192–215.

Women on the American Frontier

Clark, Ella E., and Margot Edmonds. *Sacagawea of the Lewis and Clark Expedition.* Berkeley and Los Angeles: University of California Press, 1979.

Conley, Frances R. "Martina Didn't Have a Covered Wagon: A Speculative Reconstruction," *Californians* 7 (March/August 1989): 48–54.

Dawson, Jan C. "Sacagawea: Pilot or Pioneer Mother?" *Pacific Northwest Quarterly* 83 (January1992): 22–28.

Devens, Carol. *Countering Colonization: Native American Women and Great Lakes Missions, 1630–1900.* Berkeley: University of California Press, 1992.

Enríquez, Alfredo, and Mirandé Evangelina. *La Chicana: The Mexican-American Woman.* Chicago: University of Chicago Press, 1979.

Faragher, John Mack. "The Custom of the Country: Cross-Cultural Marriage in the Far Western Fur Trade," 199–216, in *Western Women: Their Land, Their Lives,* edited by Lillian Schlissel, Vicki L. Ruiz, and Janice Monk. Albuquerque: University of New Mexico Press, 1988.

Foster, Martha Harroun. "Of Baggage and Bondage: Gender and Status Among Hidatsa and Crow Women," *American Indian Culture and Research Journal* 17 (1993): 121–53.

Gutiérrez, Ramón A. "Honor, Ideology, Marriage Negotiation and Class-Gender Domination in New Mexico, 1690–1846," *Latin American Perspectives* 12 (Winter 1985): 13–26.

Hernández, Salomé. "No Settlement Without Women: Three Spanish California Settlement Schemes, 1790–1800," 309–38, in *Southern California's Spanish Heritage: An Anthology,* edited by Doyce B. Nunis, Jr. Los Angeles: Historical Society of Southern California, 1992.

Hurtado, Albert L. *Sex, Gender, and Culture in Old California.* Albuquerque: University of New Mexico Press, 1999.

Jacobs, Sue-Ellen, Wesley Thomas, and Sabine Lang. *Two-Spirit People: Native American Gender Identity, Sexuality, and Spirituality.* Urbana: University of Illinois Press, 1997.

Looney, Rebecca. "Migration and Separation: Divorce in Kane County, 1837–1869," *Illinois Historical Journal* 89 (Summer 1996): 70-84.

Lothrop, Gloria Ricci. "Rancheras and the Land: Women and Property Rights in Hispanic California," *Southern California Quarterly* 76 (Spring 1994): 59–84.

Niethammer, Carolyn. *Daughters of the Earth: The Lives and Legends of American Indian Women.* New York: Macmillan Publishing Company, 1977.

Perrone, Bobette, H. Henrietta Stockel, and Victoria Krueger. *Medicine Women, Curanderas, and Women Doctors.* Norman: University of Oklahoma Press, 1993.

Shoemaker, Nancy. "The Rise or Fall of Iroquois Women," *Journal of Women's History,* 2 (Winter 1991): 39-57.

Van Kirk, Sylvia. *Many Tender Ties: Women in Fur-Trade Society, 1670–1870.* Norman: University of Oklahoma Press, 1983.

Wright, Mary C. "Economic Development and Native American Women in the Early Nineteenth Century," *American Quarterly* 33 (Winter 1981): 525–36.

3

"True" Women in Industrial and Westward Expansion

1812 to 1837

During the 1810s, 1820s, and 1830s a fever of growth and expansion burned its way across the United States. Even the Panic of 1819 was a short-lived interruption to the "boom psychology" that encouraged investors to sink money into everything from cotton lands to new industries. Such hopefulness caused people to migrate. They moved from rural America to cities, from the East and South across the Appalachian Mountains toward the beckoning frontier, and from other nations largely to the northeastern and western United States. Although historians once gave the women of this era short shrift, it is now clear that women's physical labor, childbearing ability, and creativeness helped energize the sweeping changes that turned the fledgling United States into a player on the international scene.

During the years between the onset of the War of 1812 and the Panic of 1837, the long-standing image of women as primarily wives and mothers endured. At the same time, however, women's changing activities, entry into paid employment, and willingness to travel to western frontiers challenged the idealized concept of separate spheres for women and men. So many etiquette-book writers and other advisors urged women to aspire to Republican Womanhood—increasingly called "domesticity" or "true womanhood"—that the concept of women as submissive and domestic beings seemed firmly entrenched. Clearly, in the ideology of the day, women were supposed to inhabit a separate world from men: while men ran the public world of business and politics, women were to fill domestic roles in which they would remain virtuous, pious, and submissive to men.

A closer look at life in the early-nineteenth-century American South, North, and West reveals that such beliefs hardly fit the situations of most women, including whites, black slaves, and American Indians. Indeed, in their daily lives, more women deviated from the model of American womanhood than practiced it.

The South

Slave Women

In a very real way, the South's enslaved African and African American women helped underwrite the Industrial Revolution in the North. The labor and sacrifices of enslaved women made increased cotton production possible—and greater quantities of cotton fueled the development of the textile industry in the northern states.

In the fields of southern plantations, women cultivated the soil and planted and harvested crops, especially cotton. Some slave owners and overseers grouped women, boys, and elderly men into hoe gangs, and organized robust men into plow gangs. Although picking cotton by hand is an arduous and painful task, women made especially adept pickers, with one slave woman able to bring in as much as 150 pounds of raw cotton a day. Smaller plantations and farms seldom had enough slaves to divide workers into gender-specific gangs. According to one woman on such a smaller concern, women's work was difficult to distinguish from men's: "I have done everything on a farm what a man done 'cept cut wheat. I split rails like a man. I used a iron wedge drove into the wood with a maul. I drive the gin, what was run by two mules."

Therefore, on most southern plantations and farms, in addition to field work slave women performed a wide variety of taxing jobs, ranging from the unskilled to skilled. In the "big house" on southern plantations, women labored long hours at domestic tasks. There, or in adjacent outbuildings, they cooked, butchered, preserved, spun, wove, sewed, and knitted. Although these women worked indoors and might glean the odd scrap of food or clothing, they endured constant surveillance by whites, harsh punishment, and isolation from black friends and family members. And while house slaves may have shared the same gender with their mistresses, race and class differences effectively distanced most black women from their white supervisors. Moreover, mistresses of the house usually expected their house slaves to learn white ways of speaking, acting, keeping house, and rearing children, a process of cultural assimilation that sometimes alienated domestic slave women from their own people.

Other slave women worked in skilled positions, including as artisans and midwives. One slave woman who was trained as a midwife at the age of thirteen earned substantial sums of money for her owner but derived no pay or other benefits from her own work. In her words, "I made a lot o' money for old missus. Lots of times, didn't get sleep regular or git my meals on time for three-four days. Cause when they call, I always went."

Yet other slave women labored away from plantations. In southern industry, they performed heavy work in cotton and woolen mills, turpentine camps, sugar refineries, food and tobacco factories, hemp manufactories, foundries, saltworks, and mines. They also worked as lumberjacks and ditch diggers and helped build roads and levees and lay track for railroads. In cities, slave women toiled as chambermaids, nursemaids, hairdressers, seamstresses, domestic servants, and vendors. Usually these women's wages reverted to their owners. Only occasionally were slave women permitted to keep part of their pay or to apply a portion thereof toward buying themselves out of slavery.

In spite of their large economic contributions to the development of the southern economy, slave women were generally denied not only wages but privileges and other recognition of their labor. Most of them found their daily roles and lifestyles dictated by the slave system. One unspeakable abuse was the effort of white southerners to deprive slaves of a basic right, learning. In short, slave women had little control over their domestic lives, childcare practices, or even the moral climate in which they lived.

In addition, slave women encountered gender-related difficulties, especially sexual coercion and rape by both white and black men. Although white servants had some legal protection from rape, black women had little or none. In some cases, women impregnated through coercive unions with their masters lacked the time and resources to care for their children properly. In other cases, children of black unions were seized at birth or sold away from their mothers as young children. Frequently, African American women rebelled against such sexual and economic exploitation by avoiding sexual relationships altogether, aborting unwanted fetuses, and committing infanticide to save a child from slavery.

Despite such resistance, women were encouraged to reproduce as frequently as possible. Even though Caribbean and other non-African peoples had become an important source of slaves, the southern agricultural system demanded more hands all the time. Owners sometimes threatened women with beatings, solitary confinement, or sale if they refused to bear children, or promised women extra food, additional clothing, or larger cabins if they willingly did so. Some black women degradingly referred to as "breeders" even brought higher prices at auction and elicited special care from their owners. As one woman noted, the more children she had, the more she was worth.

Slave mothers often saw their children turned into miniature workers. At an age long before most white children had to give up childhood, enslaved black children ran errands, gathered firewood, and fed the chickens. It was not unusual to see a small child wielding a large broom in an effort to sweep out the yard or clear the carriage drive. Cotton sacks were even made shorter so that children might use them in the fields. Other children were assigned to the "big house," where they helped in the kitchen and learned how to serve at table. Most would never return home again to eat, sleep, and play near their natural mothers. Rather they would become servants in training who, to be sure, enjoyed better nutrition and clothing than their brothers and sisters but who were on call twenty-four hours a day with no family to call their own.

In the face of such adversities, slave women usually proved independent and strong, managing to perform their daily work and still resist slavery in ways both subtle and blatant. On the one hand, a woman might steal food, lie, plot against her owners, or feign illness or pregnancy to gain a few days' reprieve from the fields. Some even committed suicide, which they believed would return them to their original families and countries in the spirit world. On the other, a woman might rebel by striking an overseer or running away. Newspaper postings offering rewards for runaway slaves indicate that women accounted for only 10 to 15 percent of the total runaways, for most slave women remained bound to plantations by ties to their husbands and children. In 1834, the *South Carolina Gazette* carried the following advertisement: "Run away about five weeks ago from Hugh Campbell, a Negro wench named Flora, she has a scar on her forehead." Campbell offered a reward of thirty shillings for the return of Flora, who, if captured and returned, could expect punishment ranging from whipping and branding to mutilation.

Despite such fortitude, black women could not always stand on their own. Indeed, numerous black women found the will to survive in slavery by drawing strength from their marriages, which they regarded as a critical part of their lives. Such marriages, however, often ended prematurely through the death or sale of one spouse or the other. Death terminated approximately 45 percent of slave marriages, while sale destroyed another 32 percent. As one black minister noted, slaves married "until death or distance do you part." As a result of the instability of marriage under slavery, women often raised their families without the aid of men. In addition, enslaved women devoted much of their energy to maintaining kinship ties and to creating new kin networks when slavery destroyed old ones. They bonded with their children and with other black women through such special events as childbirth or get togethers to spin, weave, or sew useful items. Thus, even in slavery women drew meaning and a sense of identity from the black community, to which they had a strong commitment.

One type of black community emerged when slaves preserved what they could of their African cultures. In slave quarters on plantations and in certain sections of southern cities, slaves held "festivals" or "gatherings" at which they danced, sang, played music, and chanted. On such occasions black women were highly visible in roles as dancers, musicians, singers, and leaders of chants. In New Orleans, for example, enslaved peoples met in Congo Square on Sunday afternoons, where they performed traditional African music with an American flair. Such impromptu concerts not only laid the groundwork for the eventual emergence of jazz, but gave slaves a sense of individuality and strength of spirit that, at least in their own minds, elevated them above their status as bound chattels.

In other words, black women helped create a subculture far away from the world of white overseers, masters, and mistresses. Although enslaved women learned to present a blank face to white eyes, they developed an inner identity and self-respect. Still, hard work, poor nutrition, threats to their families, and resistance to sexual exploitation wore these women down and contributed to a lower birth rate for slave women than for many other groups at the time. Slave women in the upper South carried and bore only an average of five to six children rather than seven to ten, while women in the lower South bore slightly more. Typically, those who became mothers formed extremely close bonds with their children. Some owners allowed slave women time off for birth and childcare, but others continued to work expectant and new mothers at their regular tasks. Pregnant women even labored in the fields, and, in between planting or hoeing, new mothers often nursed babies shuttled out to them by elderly women. In spite of such difficulties, many strong mother-child bonds developed. In other instances, slave women were, as mentioned, denied the right to raise their own offspring at all.

To preserve a sense of themselves as women, slave women often followed a strict division of labor in their own homes, for this was the one realm in which true womanhood had any meaning for them. Even in one-room cabins with dirt floors, they could act as the women they could not be in the fields or the "big house." Thus, slave women performed most housekeeping tasks and childcare chores themselves, maintaining their homes with pride and tending their families with care. In these tiny realms, slave women could put aside the deferential behavior they displayed to owners and overseers, teach their children respect for their race, and cling to African or African-American customs.

Free Black Women

The number of free black women in the South grew during these years through a variety of means. Some slave women gained an owner's permission to work away from the plantation for pay, usually on Sundays. These women saved their wages and might eventually buy themselves and their children out of slavery. In other cases, free black men occasionally bought out of slavery women they wanted to marry. Finally, some white slave owners freed their female slaves in their wills, even leaving property and homes to them, which the newly freed black women sometimes converted into boarding houses or other businesses.

But whether born free or newly liberated, free black women were only slightly better off than slave women. Composed of approximately half African American women and half Caribbean women who hailed from such countries as Haiti and Jamaica, the population of free American women of color typically earned some amount of money for their toil. Free black women also had the right, at least theoretically, to protest injustices against them and to use the courts.

Yet most free black women were underpaid and denied opportunities for education or advancement. They held exhausting jobs and sometimes headed households formed by circumstance rather than their own choice. In the South, women, who constituted 53 percent of all free blacks, usually lived in cities, where they could procure jobs, join churches and other organizations, or even start small businesses. In the streets of Charleston, South Carolina, as mentioned, women vendors hawked everything from vegetables to fish.

Nonetheless, in a number of cases, southern free black women achieved some wealth and influence. Although the South grew more conservative and rigid as each year passed, some free women of color ran such profitable businesses as restaurants and dressmaking establishments. Especially in New Orleans, free black women owned property and often held respected positions in the community. Some of these women were so successful that they even owned slaves who labored on their farms and in their other businesses. Such black female slave owners usually bought and sold slaves as casually as did white slave owners. Some, however, were a bit more helpful to others of their race. One of these, Eufrosina Hinard, purchased slaves, hired them out, and allowed them to buy their freedom with their savings. She was a determined businesswoman who helped herself, and, along the way, helped others.

Indeed, a dedication to community service characterized many free black women. For instance, in 1827 Elizabeth Lange established a Catholic school in Baltimore for French-speaking black students, who, like Lange herself, were born in French colonies in the Caribbean. Because of Lange's commitment to education and to the church, the Pope allowed her to found the first community of black women Religious, later known as the Oblate Sisters of Providence. These dedicated African American nuns kept Lange's school going, even though the sisters had to take in laundry during times of financial hardship.

Another case was Marie Bernard Couvent, also of New Orleans. One legend had it that she was a former slave transported from Guinea, West Africa, at such an early age that she had no memory of her own parents, while another story says she was born in New Orleans in 1757. In any event, this determined woman gained her freedom and married a free black man. Between them, the Couvents accumulated some property. In 1832, as a widow, Couvent decided that her property would one day support a school for orphans. Couvent, who died in 1837, provided

in her will for the "establishment of a free school for orphans of color."
Couvent's school accepted a number of black children who were prohibited from attending New Orleans' schools. Later named Holy Re-
deemer School, the institution is now recognized as the oldest black
Catholic school in the United States. Like white parochial schools, this
and other similar schools offered academic and religious instruction but
also gave vocational training to their students. Such schools sometimes
offered to black Catholic families extension courses in agriculture,
health, and home economics.

White Southern Women

White women in the South ranged the social scale from poor laborers
and the wives of tenant farmers to independent mistresses and the
wives and daughters of plantation owners. Like northern women,
southern women grew up believing they would one day become "domestic" or "true" women. Sometimes southern writers and speakers referred to the ideal of "Southern Womanhood." Whether North or South,
women were supposed to live domestic and pious lives dedicated to
wife- and motherhood. But regardless of the region in which women
lived, such goals were nearer the grasp of elite white women than those
of any other class.

To most southern women, family, work, and religion constituted the
most enduring themes in their lives. Despite the ups and downs of the
southern economy or the growing political fight regarding black slavery,
white women sustained themselves through family ties, necessary labor, and religion. This was true of women of all social classes.

Of all white women, poor women had the hardest lives. Their families lived on the infertile edges of good land, as well as in the sandy
foothills and rock-strewn mountains. These women bore large families,
which lived a hand-to-mouth existence. Poor women did what they
could to bring money into their cash-starved families. In addition to
their myriad daily duties, women produced such craftwork as quilts or
surplus agricultural products for sale or trade. In spite of these women's
efforts, however, poor children received little schooling and, due to inadequate nutrition and improper sanitation, were vulnerable to a host
of diseases, especially hookworm. Because poor whites seldom had
enough money to supply their children with shoes during the summer
months, hookworms easily entered young people's bodies through their
bare feet.

Above poor white women on the social yardstick were women of the
yeoman class. The owners of small farms and plantations, the yeoman
farmers ranked well below the southern gentry dominated by large
planters. On average, women of the yeoman class married between the
age of eighteen and twenty, usually choosing husbands from their own

social level and locale. Increasingly after the War of 1812, such young women looked for romantic love, while their parents continued to show more concern with a potential husband's economic prospects. Parents recognized that a man's ability to support a family would be crucial to the success of their daughter's marriage.

Once married, yeoman women bore as many children as possible. After all, each child was a potential worker on the family farm, as well as a potential companion and helpmate for the overburdened mother. If expectant mothers and their infants survived the frequent threat of malaria or puerperal fever (an infection of the womb usually caused by unsanitary conditions), these women breastfed their own babies. Despite the natural immunities infants acquire through their mother's breastmilk, infant mortality remained high in the South. Yeoman-class children contracted a wide variety of maladies, including tapeworms, commonly found in spoiled or undercooked food, and diarrhea, from drinking well water polluted from the run-off of latrines and graves. Unsurprisingly, southern graveyards had a high proportion of tiny markers among the gravestones.

In addition to the demands of child raising, yeomen women functioned as domestic artisans within their homes, producing the food and clothing their families needed to survive. Processing and preparing sufficient food for four to five meals a day was a never-ending task. In addition, weaving, spinning, making clothes, and keeping garments mended were continual chores. Sometimes, white yeoman women enlisted the help of one or two black slave women, whose husbands worked in the fields alongside the woman's husband.

Besides raising their own vegetables and fruit, yeoman women often helped in the family struggle to produce enough cotton or sugar cane to make a small cash profit. Such women were a crucial part of the southern labor force, working next to husbands, sons, brothers, and fathers in the struggle to eke a living from marginal farmland located in lowlands along the southern coast, along riverbanks, and in delta areas near the mouths of rivers.

Undoubtedly, women wore down under the burden of heavy responsibilities and seemingly endless chores. Yet, yeomen women had the reputation of being more audacious, outspoken, and assertive than other white women in the South. Perhaps their economic contributions gave them more power and voice in family decisions, which translated into public confidence. Certainly, the churches that such women chose, primarily Baptist and Methodist sects, welcomed female participation. When the revival movement known as the Second Great Awakening swept the South during the first third of the nineteenth century, male ministers increasingly tailored their sermons to women, who constituted a growing proportion of their congregations. Ministers expected their female listeners to relay religious messages to the men and chil-

dren in their families, a role that helped create a sense of self-impor-
tance among women.

Above yeoman women, at the top end of the South's social register,
were wives and daughters of wealthy planters, as well as an occasional
woman who owned and managed a plantation outright. Some women
who owned and managed plantations had never married, but others
were divorced or widowed. Although many of these women had chosen to remain single to avoid the highly patriarchal marriages typical
of their class, single and divorced women often had to contend with
scorn from friends and neighbors. Widows were acceptable in southern
society because they, in accordance with social expectations, had been
married. Because they received by law one-third of their deceased husbands' estates, widows, at least those of the upper classes, usually had
some land and slaves with which to support themselves.

Most elite, white southern women married, however. Nonetheless,
for the wealthy and well-bred white woman, finding an appropriate
mate could be difficult, especially if she lived on an isolated plantation.
Such social events as balls (dances), receptions, parties, horse races, and
weddings gave young women the opportunity to meet men of their social standing. A significant number of white women married men from
their neighborhood or county, while others wed male cousins. In some
ways a cousin-marriage was reassuring. The potential spouses not only
had a long acquaintance, but they had family ties to bolster their relationship. In addition, such a union often consolidated familial land holdings, so that the couple might eventually inherit a sizeable estate, along
with slaves to work the land.

Once married, white plantation women held the status of lady. Supposedly freed from household duties by the presence of slaves, plantation mistresses were to enjoy leisure and pursue such activities as
visiting relatives and other ladies and attending balls. Romantically portrayed in novels and the popular press as glamorous and idle southern
belles, most southern women, even those of the planter class, were hard
working and competent.

Besides overseeing household servants, white plantation women
maintained vegetable and flower gardens, managed dairies and chicken
houses, knitted and sewed, and provided medical care for white and
black people, including children, living on their plantations. Supposedly
delicate and passive, those women might also supervise such foul
chores as the annual winter hog butchering. Plantation women had
firsthand knowledge of washing clothes in iron kettles over open fires,
preparing tallow dipped candles and soap from lye and leftover fat,
gathering medicinal herbs from fields and swamps, and fashioning
clothes for a plantation population that might number two hundred or
more persons.

What of the gracious southern belle sitting under a magnificent Mag-
nolia tree with her satin skirts draped gracefully as her guests swirled

around, full of compliments for her beauty and grace? Upper-class southern women certainly could be lovely and charming, and they did entertain. Indeed, entertaining was another of plantation women's many duties and cares. Seldom, however, did these white plantation women reveal the hard-working reality of their lives. Because of the tensions inherent in an economic system based on slavery, as well as women's love and concern for family honor, plantation women affected an exaggerated coyness and gentility that reflected well on their men. In effect, they had to work hard at appearing hardly worked. In practice, however, southern women often disliked the restrictions placed on their lives by genteel society as well as the slave system with which they lived. Whether they approved of their situations or not, they refrained from airing their views in public.

During the era of the early American republic, only a few white women living in the South spoke out for societal reform of any kind. One of these was Scottish-born reformer Frances Wright, who had few ties and little allegiance to the southern economic and political systems. In 1826 Wright founded a community called Nashoba in Tennessee to educate black Americans. Members of Wright's community rejected the idea of marriage in hopes that an absence of the institution would prevent men from exercising "rights of power" over women and would encourage women to maintain an "independent existence." Wright lectured widely on the need for public education for all Americans, including women. "Until women assume the place in society which good sense and good feeling alike assign to them," Wright reasoned, "human improvement must advance but feebly." She concluded that, whereas "men establish their own pretensions upon the sacrificed rights of others, we do in fact impeach our own liberties, and lower ourselves in the scale of being."

White Women/Black Men

Despite the reticence of white women to speak out against state-sanctioned racism, the rigid separation of white and black people in the South was not as widely supported by white women as is usually thought. Women's diaries demonstrate that many plantation women were compassionate toward male and female slaves. Some white women even believed that slavery should be abolished and all slaves emancipated. Because southern white women feared reprisal should they express such shocking views out loud, they often confided them to their diaries or perhaps in whispers to a sister or close friend. To these white women, slavery was a system that fostered abuse of other human beings.

Other white women defied the slave system and its underlying racism by establishing relationships with African American men. Although much has been said about white men taking sexual advantage of women slaves, little has been revealed regarding white women who formed liaisons with black men. Most southern whites believed that affection and consensual sexual relations between a white woman and a black man was impossible, that any white woman would find even the suggestion of such a relationship revolting. In truth, however, cross-race alliances existed, many of them based on strong affectional ties between the couple.

Some small, rural communities handled such affiliations by keeping them matters of local gossip, but in other instances liaisons between white women and black men became a matter of public scandal and jurisprudence. For example, divorce records indicate that courts were often sympathetic toward white husbands who sought divorces because their wives had borne mulatto children. In fact, the first divorce granted in Virginia (in 1803) was to a husband whose wife had borne mulatto babies and publicly admitted that the child's father was a black slave. In other cases, judges proceeded cautiously. They were aware that such charges by a white husband against his white wife might be untrue, meant to slander or retaliate against her for some reason. In a 1814 divorce suit, the wariness of legislators to believe that Peggy Jones's baby "was the offspring of some man of color," as her husband claimed, led to the impaneling of a special jury to investigate the matter.

Another example of relationships between white women and black men entering the courts occurred when a white man, upon learning of a woman's secret romance, filed an accusation of rape against the black man involved on her behalf. Sometimes women, eager to avoid public condemnation, went along with this ruse willingly, but others gave in to the demands of irate husbands and fathers only unwillingly. Although false rape charges could save a white woman's reputation, it also could prove disastrous for the black man involved, who might lose his life as punishment. Such rape complaints inflated the number of rape indictments against black men, thus giving white men another rationale for fearing and restricting black men.

Finally, anecdotal evidence reveals the existence of interracial unions. In one case, a woman's public confession indicates that white husbands and fathers occasionally accepted the illicit activities of their wives and daughters and tried to move on with their lives. In southern Virginia, a white husband who returned from service in the War of 1812 to discover that his wife had borne two mulatto daughters forgave his wife and adopted the children. Other men were less forgiving and tried to control recalcitrant wives through physical punishment, which sometimes resulted in violence and even murder.

Obviously, sexual and affectional ties between white women and black men could create havoc in southern society. Especially when white women professed their love for black men, as happened on more than one occasion, white men had to confront squarely their supposition of black inferiority. Unsurprisingly, local and state lawmakers reacted by attempting to curb cross-racial relationships by law. A variety of antimiscegenation provisions appeared, which specifically made such relationships illegal and punishable. At the same time, rape laws were reinforced and widened. Those in power were determined to reinforce the existing social order and to force white women into the "proper" mold.

Divorce

Of course, some southern marriages turned out badly for numerous reasons. During the colonial period, southern colonies had only granted divorces of bed and board, much like today's legal separations. During the years following the American Revolution, most southern states adopted a new attitude and more freely offered divorces to white couples. Because white courts did not recognize the marriages of African Americans and Native Americans, people of color seldom appeared in divorce courts except as corespondents in adultery cases.

The first divorce in the South occurred as early as 1790 in Maryland. State legislators granted this divorce to a white man who proved to their satisfaction that his white wife had borne a mulatto child, whose father was a black man. By the mid 1830s, the Maryland legislature was approving slightly more than thirty divorces each year, with wives more often seeking divorces than husbands. Although this divorce rate seems quite low when compared to modern figures, it demonstrates that some white women had legal recourse against adulterous, drunken, or absent husbands.

In addition, except for South Carolina, all other southern legislators heard divorce cases. In North Carolina, divorce seekers submitted 266 applications between 1800 and 1835. More than one-third of the petitioners stated that their mates had deserted them. Several women noted that their husbands had migrated to "the western country." Another 8 percent of divorce seekers accused their spouses of committing adultery with African Americans. Yet others used a variety of allegations, including adultery with a white person, cruelty, bigamy, impotence, incompatibility, nonsupport, ill temper, and indecent conduct.

Similarly, in Virginia, members of the General Assembly approved 135 divorces between 1803 and 1850. Although one might expect state legislators to be inaccessible to female petitioners because of women's exclusion from politics, the General Assembly gave more divorces to women than it did to men; women received about 51 percent of early Virginia divorces, while men obtained 49 percent.

Overwhelmed southern legislators gradually moved divorce hearings to the courts, so that for a number of years a petitioner might go to either the legislature or the courts. Because courts often showed more leniency, especially to women, the number of divorce petitions gradually increased during the late 1820s and early 1830s. Acceptable grounds for divorce also expanded. In 1832, an Alabama court ruled that cruelty no longer had to be life threatening to suffice as due reason for divorce. Female divorce seekers soon cited a string of other indignities to which their husbands had subjected them, ranging from rudeness and ridicule to vulgarity and abusive language.

Obviously, the white patriarchal family in the South was not as stable as its supporters claimed. Especially revealing is the fact that so many women applied for divorce, even though most of them were financially dependent on their husbands. With an eye toward the future, female petitioners often asked legislators and judges to grant them part of their husbands' estates, alimony, or a return to *feme sole* status so that they could conduct their own business affairs. White male legislators and judges often showed southern women sympathy and leniency by honoring such requests.

Some desperate wives simply ran away from their husbands. Notices in southern newspapers indicate that "runaway" spouses were common. Although one might expect primarily husbands to desert their mates, these same announcements indicate that a significant number of wives walked away from situations they found intolerable.

The North

Enslaved and Free Black Women

In northern cities, a very different situation existed. Because slavery constituted an expensive and ineffective labor system for small farms and factories during the 1810s, the number of female slaves in the North steadily declined. By 1821, northern states had abolished slavery. Because of racial prejudice, however, factory owners usually avoided hiring free women of color. Employers turned instead to white women and girls as laborers.

Thus, approximately two-thirds of the North's free black women sought employment as domestic servants, usually working for white women who expected them to remain docile and passive. White employers usually required black domestics to live in and treated them much like surrogate slaves.

Other northern free black women maintained their own residence but took in sewing or laundry, often for the fee of one cent per shirt. Still others engaged in hairdressing, flower selling, hat cleaning, or personal services, including prostitution. Some were not able to find jobs at all. In 1827, a black newspaper, *Freedom's Journal,* listed forty-three black women paupers in New York City alone.

Like their slave counterparts, free black women worked diligently to cultivate meaningful values and activities in their own lives and those of family members. Unlike slave women, free women of color enjoyed far more opportunity to establish homes, enjoy families, and try to better their lives. They could also incorporate aspects of domestic ideals, true womanhood, and piety into their lives.

Thus, a small, but vocal black middle class emerged, centered in such cities as Boston and especially in Philadelphia. Women of this class often tried to "uplift" the situation of other black people as well. These women formed clubs and organizations and worked together through their churches. They wrote and published widely, contributing heavily to magazines and the more than one hundred works of fiction, protest, and autobiography written by free blacks between 1810 and 1860.

More specifically, free women of color in the North emphasized the importance of education for freed black people. Because they realized that education paved the road to better jobs, entry to the professions, and a larger measure of acceptance of black people by the larger society, free black women made education of other blacks a very high priority. A number of them opened schools for children and experimented with adult education. They not only hoped to see their children advance, they hoped to improve themselves at the same time.

Because adult schools were difficult and expensive to establish, a number of free black women organized self-education groups. In 1831, free women of color created the Minerva Literary Association of Philadelphia, a study and reading group intended to "cultivate the talents entrusted" to its members and thus "break down the strong barrier" of racial prejudice in the United States. The following year, a group of Boston women formed a similar self-education group, the Afric-American Female Intelligence Society.

At the same time, free black women exercised their womanly moral influence through the formation of reform societies. As early as 1818, women established the Colored Female Religious and Moral Reform Society in Salem, Massachusetts. Among those in Philadelphia were the Daughters of Africa (1812) and the Daughters of Erin (1819). By the late 1830s, Philadelphia alone had 119 aid societies, more than half of them founded and run by women.

During the 1820s and 1830s, a number of free black women supported the temperance campaign against the use of alcoholic beverages. Although white women's temperance groups occasionally accepted black women as members, women of color usually backed the temperance cause within black associations. Members of such groups spoke and prayed for people, usually men, addicted to alcohol.

Churches offered free black women yet other opportunities to initiate change. Because the Great Awakening embraced both white and black people, black women participated in everything from prayer meetings to religious revivals. In 1816, Philadelphia women participated in the establishment of the African Methodist Episcopal Church, which adopted a policy of welcoming women members and even female preachers. Such black leaders as traveling preacher Jarena Lee championed the importance of addressing black issues, including civil rights, employment, and education. Lee later explained that during her sermons she felt as if her "tongue was cut loose," that "the love of God, and of his service, burned with a vehement flame" within her. Lee had an enormous influence on women, black and white.

Most important, however, the North's free black women crusaded for the abolition of slavery. By the late 1820s and early 1830s, the voices of free black women reached growing numbers of black and white people. As early as 1831, for example, Mary Prince's *The History of Mary Prince, A West Indian Slave* exposed the horrors of Caribbean slavery. Meanwhile, Maria Stewart, a black domestic in Connecticut, began to write and lecture. Stewart spoke to racially mixed audiences of men and women regarding the abolition of slavery, increased opportunities for black Americans, and the need in a supposedly democratic United States for equality between the races.

The following year, 1832, when the Pennsylvania legislature considered a bill requiring all blacks, free and enslaved, to carry passes, Sarah Mapps Douglass, a free black born in Philadelphia who ran a school for free black children there, became a political activist. "One short year ago, how different were my feelings on the subject of slavery!" she exclaimed. Now that she felt the sting of racism firsthand, Douglass experienced an important turning point and determined "to use every exertion" in her power "to elevate the character of my wronged and neglected race."

The next year, too, saw progress. In 1833 Sarah Louisa Forten, a regular contributor of poems and essays to the abolitionist newspaper *The Liberator,* recruited her mother and two sisters to help her found the Philadelphia Female Anti-slavery Society. It was Sarah Forten and Sarah Mapps Douglass who helped shape the group's policy and tirelessly organized antislavery sewing circles and charity fairs. From this point until the outbreak of the Civil War, the "two Sarahs" were among the most articulate and persistent voices in the antislavery movement.

White Women as Factory Laborers

Opposed to hiring free blacks, northern factory owners relied on white women and girls as their labor force. The story of white women as factory workers began in 1789, when the first factory for carding and spinning yarn in America was established in Rhode Island. Because most men engaged in agriculture, proponents of the American factory system suggested hiring women, preferably white farm women. These advocates of industry recognized the need to keep men in the fields, producing foodstuffs for nonfarming people, especially those living in northeastern cities. Besides, it seemed natural for women, who had spun and woven in their homes, to continue their customary work in a new venue.

In his Report on Manufactures of 1791, U.S. Secretary of the Treasury Alexander Hamilton advocated factory employment for women because it made development of the new industrial system possible "without taking men from the fields." He added that factory employment would render women "more useful than they otherwise would be," while farms would prosper as a result of the income brought in by the "increased industry" of farm wives and daughters.

These arguments multiplied many times over during the following years. One avid supporter of manufacturing argued that "the portion of time of housewives and young women which were not occupied with family affairs could be profitably filled up" by factory work. This view soon expanded to include the claim that a factory was actually a blessing to a community because it furnished employment for women.

Of course, women had always worked; they had labored in cabins, farmhouses, and outbuildings without wages as a reward. Now they shifted their place of employment to the new factories and expected paychecks in return. They did so in large numbers because of the growing need of farm families for cash income during the early 1800s and the increasing availability of factory jobs. The War of 1812 resulted in an upsurge in industrialization that created an expanding demand for workers and offered women not only wages for their toil but an escape from farmlife.

After the War of 1812 ended, the U.S. Congress appointed the first congressional committee charged with investigating the situation of women workers. In 1816, the committee identified 100,000 industrial workers in the United States, two-thirds of whom were female and usually white. The committee's findings revealed that, among other things, industrialization transformed household production, drew huge numbers of women from their homes into paid employment, and shaped new social classes of women.

Lady Operatives

During the years following the War of 1812, thousands of young farm women in New England left their families to relocate in the new mill towns. The best known of these factory villages was Lowell, Massachusetts. Here, women workers lived together in company-owned boardinghouses. Often, these "mill girls," usually in their teens and early twenties, sent part of their meager wages home to their families, while their brothers remained on the farm to provide agricultural labor or attended college, paid for by their sister's earnings.

Lowell women often aspired to the tenets of true womanhood. They hoped that one day they would be wives and mothers with enough leisure time to raise and help educate their children. In the meantime, however, they toiled in Lowell's factories. The Lowell women commonly worked twelve to fourteen hours a day, tending two or more spinning jennies or looms for about $2 a week. Although matrons supervised the boardinghouses, factory women possessed a certain amount of independence. They also enjoyed cultural benefits the mill-company provided, such as lending libraries and the opportunity to write for the company-sponsored literary journal, *The Lowell Offering.*

As early as the mid-1820s, however, conditions began to change for Lowell and other factory operatives. Wages failed to increase, but the pace of work increased. Although operatives worked at a faster rate, hours remained long. At the same time, working conditions worsened in the factories and boardinghouses became overcrowded, while goods in the company stores grew increasingly expensive.

In 1824, a group of women protested against low wages and bad conditions by walking out of a mill in Pawtucket, Rhode Island. Although many similar strikes, or "turnouts," followed in other areas, women workers did not make much progress with these protests. After all, women workers were expendable because there were always more young women or, by the late 1830s, Irish immigrants of varying ages willing to fill the places of the protestors. Women had difficulty organizing or supporting labor organizations on their low wages. Also, since women were denied knowledge of, and access to, such other important avenues of power as public office-holding, they remained powerless to initiate workplace reform.

Despite the growing problems associated with factory employment, women who found it necessary to help support their families continued to enter industrial occupations in large numbers. By 1828, nine out of ten textile workers in New England were female. As immigration increased during the late 1820s and 1830s, a growing number of such women were foreign born. Because parents of young, unmarried immigrant women routinely expected them to help support their families, almost 60 percent of young, single Irish women worked. German and other immigrant groups followed similar employment patterns, though to a lesser extent. Even in conservative Italian families, daughters often held jobs to provide temporary relief for an overburdened family budget. In many Jewish families both single and married women worked, sometimes so men could continue the much-revered study of the Torah, especially if the men aspired to the respected position of Rabbi. Despite having to work both inside and outside the home in their new land, such women usually felt that they had more opportunities in the United States than they did at home.

This diverse female workforce labored primarily in textile factories, cotton mills, the needle trades, and shoe factories. Employers thought of them as "lady operatives" who worked cheaply and could be hired and fired as needed. In other cases, women held atypical industrial jobs. Census data reveal that, among other occupations, women toiled as coopers, glass engravers, ironworkers, and tinsmiths. By the 1820s and 1830s, however, the number of women engaged in such heavy occupations began to decline.

Yet other women called pieceworkers labored for wages within their homes. They produced parts that factory workers would later assemble; for this, they earned "piecework" wages, a minimal fee per part. The country's largest shoe factory, located in Lynn, Massachusetts, depended on the needle skills of women pieceworkers to bind, meaning to stitch, shoe uppers in their homes. Still other women worked at home as seamstresses. After observing Philadelphia seamstresses in 1829, one commentator noted: "It takes great expertness and increasing industry from sunrise to 10 and 11 at night, constant employment which few of them have, to earn a dollar and a half per week."

These types of women constituted a new female working class, one whose lives were driven by the market economy. Yet, because of the fluidity of the women's labor market and the scattered nature of their workplaces, these women remained largely isolated from each other as well as from other types of women. They tended to focus on improving their own immediate situations, including obtaining better pay and improved working conditions. Because such issues as education, property ownership, and the right to vote had little relevance to their lives, such women did not form the basis of a women's rights campaign. Instead, they provided a nucleus of the emerging American labor movement.

Northern White Women in Nonindustrial Occupations

Yet another group of northern women earned wages by using their domestic skills in employers' homes. In early America, many families had "hired help," who assisted with domestic tasks and were accepted as part of the family. By the late 1700s and early 1800s, "domestics" did the same tasks that had always been expected of household help, but now they were seen as paid servants and assigned specific menial chores performed apart from the household's family members. An increasing influx of immigrant women, especially Irish, provided a source of needy, untrained women for the domestic service market.

Domestics toiled at such chores as cooking, food processing, and child-care. They usually assisted middle- and upper-class white women, who now exchanged money for the goods they needed rather than producing them at home. Although pleased to have help, female employers generally treated domestics coolly due to ethnic and class prejudices and paid them poorly. In fact, domestic servants, who lacked an opportunity to organize on their own behalf, were probably the most underpaid of all working women. In 1837, one observer commented that "a woman who goes out to wash works as hard in proportion as a wood sawyer or a coal heaver, but she is not generally able to make more than half as much for a day's work."

A very different type of employed women was the growing number who provided sexual services for pay. In New York and other cities, many destitute seamstresses and servants turned to prostitution as a relatively lucrative pursuit. In New York, one report claims that between twelve hundred and seven thousand prostitutes existed by the 1820s. In Philadelphia of the 1820s and 1830s, thousands of other "disorderly" women walked the streets, parks, and amusement places openly. In Nanny Goat Alley, Ram Cat Alley, and on Baker Street, women solicited business. Especially in New York City and Philadelphia, prostitutes were overwhelmingly between the ages of fifteen and twenty-five, and largely urban born. Rather than being arrested for prostitution, these women were brought before the law for vagrancy, theft, or drunk and disorderly behavior. Apparently most urban dwellers regarded prostitutes as a necessary nuisance.

Yet other women, especially heads of households and widows, kept their hand in at operating small businesses, especially those catering to other women by supplying millinery, yard goods, or notions. These shops often became gathering centers for women who wanted to visit with other women and express their opinions on public affairs. Women also established businesses that appealed to both women and men. These included street peddlers, market vendors, and tavern and boardinghouse keepers.

One especially successful business woman was Sarah Todd Astor, who helped her husband, John Jacob Aster, parlay her dowry of $300 into a lucrative fur business, the American Fur Company. While John traveled to locate and trade furs, Sarah managed the business, processed and graded furs, and eventually gave birth to eight children in rooms above their shop. Due to the Astor's investment of profits earned by the American Fur Company in New York real estate, the Astor fortune was reputed to be the largest in the country at the time of Sarah's death in 1832. Still, Sarah remains largely unknown, while her husband is celebrated as one of the great entrepreneurs of early industrialism.

Rebecca Pennock Lukens was another woman who contributed greatly to a family business. On his deathbed, Lukens's husband asked her to take over the family iron mill in Pennsylvania. As a Quaker, Rebecca was well educated and had always been encouraged to take an interest in the family metal-working enterprise. Lukens not only saved the mill from bankruptcy but expanded it to include iron plate rolling, supplying boilers for steamboats and locomotives. Lukens was so successful that she was worth $100,000 at the time of her death in 1854.

White Women's Unpaid Labor

Another large component of women labored within their homes or on family farms without wage compensation. After all, domestic work demanded full-time attention and energy, while the concept of true womanhood had long assured such women that childcare should be their first and foremost duty. Because the newly industrializing society measured people's worth by the wage they earned, many Americans overlooked or even denigrated the work such women performed.

Despite the lack of pay or recognition, however, thousands of women labored in kitchens, nurseries, dairies, barns, chicken coops, and gardens. Others worked on the land, either on their own or as "farm wives." Although census takers failed to categorize such women as "farmers," these women agriculturalists added considerably to the nation's economic growth.

The New Leisure Class

Industrialization and accompanying urbanization redistributed millions of Americans and changed their work and social patterns. White women had once labored in their homes while their husbands worked outdoors in the nearby fields, or couples had worked together in a family enterprise. Now, especially in the Northeast, large numbers of men reported to jobs and professions in factories and offices some distance from the house while their wives remained homebound.

Throughout the course of these developments, "woman's place is in the home" became a popular maxim. In addition, it was no longer enough to be a Republican wife and mother. Now, elite women had to exhibit qualities associated with domesticity and true womanhood. Such qualities as knowledge of "proper" domestic skills and holding such values as piety, virtue, and submissiveness supposedly defined a true woman.

In all likelihood, in an era when millions of women left their homes for paid employment, some Americans felt a pressing need to protect and expand the traditional idea of women as wives and mothers. From an economic standpoint, the argument that women's "real" jobs were in their homes was used to justify low wages and kept female workers segregated in the needle trades and other areas dependent on cheap labor. Moreover, the ideology of domesticity encouraged increased consumption of factory goods by full-time homemakers, as well as holding home-bound women in reserve as an emergency labor supply.

In reality, the tenets of domesticity never applied to the majority of American women. Among white, working-class people, few married women remained at home during the day. More often than not, economic necessity drove them to join their husbands in taking employment in urban factories. According to one 1816 estimate, some sixty-six thousand white women worked in the northern cotton textile industry. When such women returned home at night, they completed domestic chores and childcare as best they could. They were thus among the first women to experience what has since been termed the "double day."

Among the white middle- and upper-classes, however, women often stayed at home full time. Because men pursued banking, trade, insurance, shipping, and other businesses in cities some distance from home, no longer could women learn trades and professions from fathers, brothers, and husbands. Nor, given their husbands' incomes, did these women need to do so. For the first time, a group of American women experienced leisure. Known by the evolving term "ladies," they had the time to pursue creative homemaking, and to achieve superb domesticity and true womanhood. They could serve as status symbols for their husbands, who were anxious to prove their own abilities as "bread-winners" by giving their wives leisure time and paid household servants. In addition, these women served as undisputed guardians of virtue and morality, thus allowing men to engage in such morally compromising business practices as selling slaves, safe in the belief that all at home was pure and decent.

Throughout the nation, middle- and upper-class ladies were the only women with the resources necessary to pursue such idealized notions as true womanhood seriously. Yet the concept of domesticity—or true womanhood—soon reached the status of a widely held ideology that preached such virtues for all women. Even farm women, mill girls, and poor women began to aspire to true womanhood, only to find in reality that few in their situation ever achieved such glorified domesticity.

Therefore, in the Northeast, even as middle- and upper-class white women practiced true womanhood in pleasant homes on the periphery of industrializing cities, working- and lower-class white families lived in shantytowns, tenements, and slum districts. In such blighted urban areas, disease and epidemics were rife, fire remained a constant threat, and the crime rate was reputed to be the highest in the world. In addition, domestic violence, including wife and child abuse, was common. Given these dangerous conditions, working women naturally wondered how they could achieve any aspect of ideal womanhood and establish an aura of "morality" in their overcrowded and shabby homes. In the first place, it was impossible for them to properly train and rear children who were already engaged in full-time factory labor by the age of seven or eight.

Ladies

In order to help ladies—and other women who aspired to true woman-hood—understand their prescribed roles and lifestyles, a plethora of prescriptive literature, ranging from guidebooks and etiquette manuals to didactic novels, began to flow from the presses, especially in the North. Authors continually stressed the need for a woman to marry, to ensure her happiness and economic survival. "Her family is the source of all her joy," one proclaimed. One popular guide cautioned a lady to keep secret any "learning" she might possess, "especially from the men, who generally look with a jealous and malignant eye on a woman of . . . cultivated understanding." Another book advised women to draw on their own natural morality to instill virtue in children, men, and servants.

Extensive discussion ensued regarding what many Americans referred to as the "proper spheres of the sexes." It was generally agreed that men were to provide income and take care of public affairs. Women were to establish homes that would "dispel the gloom and restore the ease and comfort" of men after long days spent coping with weighty matters. Men would rule the public world, while women would preside over the home.

In this system, such fashionable "accomplishments" as playing the piano and speaking French became more important than ever for women who wished to attract a "suitable" husband. One young lady duly learned all the appropriate graces, including how to curtsy and dance. When she was about to wed, her mother told her that she must "please and make [her] husband happy."

In daily living, ladies were expected to enjoy the finer aspects of life. Because household chores and overseeing servants consumed only a portion of their days, ladies sought out a variety of other activities, including dressing lavishly in order to display their husbands' earning abilities and status. Ladies spent hours selecting clothing, which was usually ornate and overdone. Ribbons, flowers, flounces, and ruffles bedecked almost every outfit. Intricate hats and bonnets were absolute necessities, as were gloves, a parasol, reticule (purse), and high-buttoned shoes. These outfits contained as much as 100 yards of material and, in combination with whalebone stays and hoops, weighed fifteen to twenty pounds. When chemise, pantaloons, corset, corset cover, petticoats, and hoops were added, getting dressed was a one- to two-hour project. Once dressed, poring over samples of yard goods, ribbons, or bonnet makings in a favorite shop could consume many more hours.

In addition, white ladies paid considerable attention to their complexions, which they believed should be delicate and pale. They protected their hands and face from the sun and avoided the use of "paints" on their face. A lady's pallor demonstrated her leisure, for paleness indicated little activity. She avoided exercise other than maneuvering her hoopskirts into carriages and through doorways. Inactivity combined with tight corseting made the fainting couch a necessary piece of furniture for women who often felt overheated, weak, and dizzy.

Ladies took similar care with their decorum. They avoided discussing politics and current events, speaking only of approved ladylike topics. They used proper language that indicated their modesty: "limb" for "leg" and "female" or "lady" for "woman." European visitors reported that some American ladies were so modest that they even covered piano "limbs" with frilled trousers and placed drapes around nude statues.

Ladies spent their spare time on a variety of activities. Most of them busied themselves with such fancy needlework as embroidery and such craftwork as the making of hyacinth stands and glove boxes. They read, but limited themselves to "morally improving" works of literature and poetry. They also spent a good deal of time visiting other women during morning calls or afternoon teas. In fact, many ladies formed close ties with other women. In 1834, the popular writer Catharine Sedgwick wrote that strong, affectionate relationships between women were "nearest to the love of angels."

Raising children also required a lady's attention. Once again, the expanding American publishing industry celebrated the importance of American mothers. Authors of advice books and other writers, who believed that mothers shaped children's character, advised mothers to mold and train their children into virtuous and responsible people. Women were further cautioned to "let thy children be the darlings of thy tenderness." It was widely assumed that women's maternal love, now believed to be innate, would guide women in the proper disposal of their motherly duties.

In reality, most ladies spent few hours with their children, who were often with nannies and tutors. When in their mother's company, boys were allowed to run and play certain games, but girls were expected to sit quietly sewing or reading. Briefly at dinnertime, children saw their fathers, often in the male role as primary disciplinarians of the family. The closeness of the colonial American family was clearly unknown to these middle- and upper-class children of the new republic.

Ramifications of Domesticity or True Womanhood

The belief that women should be wives and mothers, cloistered in their homes, led to limitations for women in certain areas. For instance, newly established medical and law schools barred the admission of supposedly "delicate" women, while practicing physicians and attorneys refused women internships.

By the 1820s, all but three states required licenses for medical practitioners. Because licensing examinations included questions regarding such techniques as the use of forceps, taught only in medical schools, women were incapable of passing such tests even if they had been permitted to take them. Nonetheless, women continued to train in the medical arts through apprenticeships and to practice as doctors and midwives without the benefit of formal licenses, especially in rural areas.

At the same time, numerous licensed doctors and self-styled experts increasingly counseled women that female reproductive organs determined women's physical health as well as their social roles. For example, male medical practitioners of the day believed that a malfunction of the uterus, then thought to be linked to the entire nervous system, could cause backaches, headaches, insomnia, irritability, and a whole gamut of "nervous" disorders. "Female ailments," as they were termed, supposedly determined a woman's emotions and achievements. Common treatments of women's illnesses included painful and traumatic procedures such as cauterizing the uterus, injecting saline into the uterus, and inserting leeches into the vagina.

Discontent among Ladies

Domesticity or true womanhood was not as pervasive and powerful as it appeared, even among the North's middle- and upper-class women. Although women generally found the endeavor of being ladies amusing for a few years, a growing number gradually turned to an examination of more serious topics, especially the many reform issues that characterized the 1820s, the so-called "Age of the Common Man." Democratization had spawned demands for widening the vote, expanding property ownership, and instituting workingmen's reforms. Soon, ladies, who came together regularly in small groups for social activities, began to discuss what democratization and reform might mean to them.

Other factors motivated middle- and upper-class women to think and talk about possible improvement in American society and law. The concept of separate spheres for women and men aggravated women's discontent. First, many women railed against limitations imposed on them by the idea of women's proper roles. Rather than spending their time in frivolous pursuits, they preferred to develop their own talents and skills.

Second, woman's separate sphere caused a group consciousness to develop among middle- and upper-class women, which in turn led them to identify common problems. Because such women spent so much time together, they came to see themselves as a type of woman, living under restrictions that kept them from controlling family size, obtaining more than a superficial education, using their unique moral powers in the world outside their homes, or engaging in the arts or business.

Third, the growth of the idea of companionate marriage, in which women and men would give each other romantic love and companionship, made many women less willing to release their husbands to the demands of "men's sphere," including business and the professions.

And despite the stereotypes that Victorians were prudish, women spoke of sexual relations as the highest expression of romantic love and companionship. They described Victorian men as highly affectionate and sexual. How, such women wondered, could they achieve the new ideal of establishing warm and loving marriages if their husbands spent six days a week away from their homes?

Little wonder, then, that the leaders of the first women's rights' movement came from middle- and upper-classes, largely in the North. Such catalysts as leisure, wealth, and the idea of separate spheres had helped create in women discontent, along with a willingness to test the bounds of their "female sphere."

Gynecology and Obstetrics

Among white women, rebellion often began quietly and privately with concerns that dominated and shaped women's lives for most of their adult years—obstetrical and gynecological care. For thousands of women who relied on patent medicines heavy with opium, morphine, or alcohol rather than seek treatment from a male physician, modification of the medical establishment seemed absolutely necessary. Women resisted unenlightened medical practices in obstetrics and gynecology by exploring such supposed cures as diet reform, animal magnetism, and phrenology. They also followed the advice of health reformers who stressed exercise, fresh air, and the consumption of grains.

Moreover, women sought out unlicensed practitioners such as Dr. Harriot K. Hunt, who, after having completed a medical apprenticeship, began practicing as a "female physician" in Boston in 1835. During the late 1830s, Hunt pursued homeopathic, preventive medicine and studied the psychological basis of women's medical problems. Licensed physicians derided Hunt's efforts; in her words, she was "entirely shut out from the medical world." Despite such opposition, she practiced successfully for over four decades.

In addition, women sought ways to control the numbers of children they bore. Although many forms of birth control such as abortion, douching, withdrawal, and the use of condoms date back to ancient times, they were not widely used in the United States. By the 1820s, however, women were not only asking about birth control but were apparently utilizing various forms of it, including pessaries (devices to cover the cervix), condoms, withdrawal, and abortion, for the birthrate began to drop, at least among white women in urban areas. This alarmed many Americans who feared population loss. Thus, beginning in 1829, many states began to pass laws against abortion. In 1832, when a male doctor in Massachusetts advocated "checks to conception," officials arrested and fined him.

In the matter of birthing, women acted on their fears regarding mother and infant mortality by marshaling anywhere from two to ten other women to help them through their pregnancies and deliveries. Such helpers often assisted a woman during a difficult delivery, spoke for her when necessary, nursed her through recovery, and performed her household and other duties until she was on her feet. Although doctors tried to limit the number of helpers in a delivery room, they recognized their importance to the women under their care.

Divorce

Increasingly, women realized that divorce could provide an answer to their difficulties. Although some reformers argued that easy divorce was a birthright in a democratic country, others viewed the increasing availability of divorce as a protective device—sort of an escape clause—for women who faced mistreatment or desertion.

Unlike the South, most northern states had mechanisms in place for granting divorces. Pennsylvania legislators were especially progressive in their thinking. By expanding grounds for divorce and making the process easier, legislators and other reformers hoped to decrease fraud during courtship, prevent cruelty in marriage, and lower the suicide rate. Thus, in 1815 Pennsylvania lawmakers added to an already generous list of grounds two more provisions: cruel treatment by a husband and "indignities" that made a wife's situation intolerable. In 1838, a new constitution did away with legislative divorce, so that all divorce cases would be heard in courts.

Except for New York, which accepted only adultery as a reason for divorce, most other northern states recognized such causes as consanguinity (relationship by blood), bigamy, adultery, impotency, extreme cruelty, alcoholism, imprisonment for a felony, and willful desertion. Some states even adopted omnibus clauses, meaning that a petitioner had only to convince the court of a breakdown in his or her marriage to get a divorce.

Certainly, divorce in the northern states gave women more legal recourse than had been available to their mothers or grandmothers. Divorce also offered northern women legal relief unknown to women in most other countries at the time. Despite the uncertainty regarding whether a female petitioner would receive alimony and custody of her children, a growing number of northern women took advantage of divorce. Fortunately for them, the decades since the American Revolution had witnessed a change in the old idea that fathers "owned" their children and would automatically get custody of them should a marriage dissolve. The postrevolutionary idealization of motherhood had led to a new belief—that children, especially young ones, were better off with their mothers.

As early as 1813, the Chief Justice of Pennsylvania had handed down a startling decision regarding child custody. Although the defendant's husband divorced her on the ground of adultery, the judge ruled that the children should stay with their mother. He explained that because the children were of "tender years" they need the kind of care and affection "which can be afforded by none so well as a mother."

By the mid-1830s, it was apparent that a dissatisfied wife in the North had alternatives available to her. Still, because of their financial dependence on husbands, wives had to consider carefully before seeking a divorce. Also by the 1830s, it was increasingly clear that more Americans, especially women, were looking for companionate marriages, a partnership of friends and equals. Rising expectations that marriage would include the three "Rs"—respect, reciprocity, and romance—challenged the customary idea of marriage as a patriarchy. Such new beliefs often primed women for disappointment in marriage, especially when the union turned out to be more patriarchal than companionate after all.

Women's Literature and Publishing

Another important step in the evolution of women's rights, especially among white women, was the new generation of women's literature and publishing. Partly because industrialization had encouraged the development of improved machinery that produced an accessible and inexpensive print media, women's books and magazines began to proliferate. Increasingly, middle- and upper-class women had the education, money, and leisure time to procure and read such journals as the *American Monthly Magazine,* which in 1829 argued that laws prohibiting women from owning property made husbands greedy and wives mean and concealing. Even in the conservative South, ladies could buy and read such reform literature as Mary Wollstonecraft's *A Vindication of the Rights of Women,* which maintained that women needed and deserved liberation.

In addition, these women also turned to a new wave of periodicals aimed at improving women's lives and minds with domestic recipes and hints, romanticized stories, and didactic tales. A leading producer of such women's literature was writer and editor Sarah Josepha Hale of Boston. After her husband's death in 1823, Hale began a millinery business and, on the side, built a sound reputation as a poet and novelist. After Hale's 1827 novel *Northwood* achieved renown, she founded in 1828 a woman's journal called the *American Ladies' Magazine.* In her first issue, Hale assured men that she intended to help women become more competent in their domestic duties and more agreeable as companions. She would achieve these ends by working for the improvement of "female education," which, in turn, would increase women's effectiveness as the moral and purifying force of America.

Hale's approach proved appealing to both female and male readers. As a result, her competitor, Louis Godey, bought Hale's *Ladies' Magazine* and persuaded her to join him in Philadelphia. In 1836, Hale left Boston to become the editor of *Godey's Lady's Book*. As editor of *Godey's,* Hale became one of the primary proponents of the concepts of women's sphere and the moral powers of women. In the first issue of *Godey's* in January 1837, she explained that the magazine's mission was to "carry onward and upward the spirit of moral and intellectual excellence in our own sex, till their influence shall bless as well as beautify civil society." Hale soon demonstrated, however, that she planned to create a subtle subversion by using the concept of women's sphere to expand women's activities. During her tenure as editor, Hale argued that highly moral women would make perfect social workers, teachers, Sunday school leaders, ministers, nurses, doctors, and writers of family and children's literature. Hale instituted a practice of hiring women writers and illustrators, and encouraging the work of other talented women.

Improved Female Education

Women's rights reformers recognized that education was a crucial issue for white women. As early as the 1810s, advocates of "improved female education" began to dispute the widely accepted idea that women's minds were smaller and weaker than men's, thus making women ineducable. In 1818, Hannah Mather Crocker, granddaughter of Cotton Mather, stated in *Observations on the Real Rights of Women:* "There can be no doubt but there is as much difference in the powers of each individual of the male sex as there is of the female: and if they receive the same mode of education, their improvement would be fully equal." Other proponents of women's education similarly argued that if women were given "equal advantages" with men, they would soon prove that they were indeed educable.

Critics responded that there was no reason for women to obtain education since they were confined to domestic vocations. What difference would it make if women's minds were equal to men's since women did not need to use them in the same ways? Reformers turned the principles of domesticity to their own ends when they answered that motherhood demanded education if motherhood was to produce responsible adults. While reformers did not wish to see a woman "emulate the schoolmen's fame," they did believe that a woman's "mental and moral improvement" was necessary for her success as a mother.

Several women tried to resolve this debate by educating women in "serious" subjects. Emma Hart Willard upgraded her Middlebury Seminary to show what women could do with such topics as algebra, trigonometry, history, and geography. In 1819, she appealed to the New York legislature for state aid for women's education. She had come to believe that female education could be equal only if it were publicly supported, as was men's. Not only was Willard's request refused, but a newspaper commented that "they will be educating the cows next." Willard resisted defeat and in 1821 founded the Troy Female Seminary in New York, the first school in the United States to offer a high school education to women.

Northern reformer Catharine Beecher attempted to implement this philosophy. Throughout the 1820s, Beecher ran the Hartford Female Seminary with her sister, Mary. During these years, Catharine proposed that schools for women be endowed, argued that teachers' assignments be limited to a few fields, and advocated the training of young women in domestic science and teaching. In the 1830s, Beecher established the Western Female Institute in Cincinnati, where she collaborated with William H. McGuffey on his famous readers. Beecher joined the temperance movement and wrote extensively about women's domestic sphere, although she herself had decided not to marry.

In the meantime, other reformers concentrated on higher education for women. Mary Lyon of Massachusetts argued for separate women's colleges. Dissatisfied with her own meager training, Lyon decided in 1834 to found the first women's college in the United States. She wrote: "My heart has so yearned over the adult female youth in the common walks of life, that it has sometimes seemed as if there was a fire shut up in my bones."

Indeed, Lyon pursued with a fiery zeal her plan for "a residential seminary to be founded and sustained by the Christian public." She personally appealed to women for "five or ten dollars of hard-earned money, collected by the slow gains of patient industry." Although critics condemned her for traveling alone, Lyon persevered, and in 1837, her college, Mount Holyoke, enrolled its first student. The three-year course of study included Latin, science, and anatomy; tuition, room, and board cost $60 a term. When Mary Lyon died in 1849, Mount Holyoke had attained a reputation as an outstanding teacher-training institution.

White Women as Teachers

Other educational reformers added another dimension to the discussion when they raised the issue of women as teachers. As men left teaching for jobs that paid more and offered continuous, year-round employment, American society in general accepted women's entry into teaching in men's stead. Teaching, it seemed, was a logical extension of women's domestic duties. Supporters of women as teachers emphasized women's innately high character, capacity for affection that would make students respond to them, and maternal instincts that would allow women to build a greater rapport with their pupils than would be proper for the "other sex," but pointed out that women still needed adequate training. These supporters issued an early call for improved education not just for women but for women who would serve as teachers of the nation's youth.

Despite low pay, little status, and no security, women rushed to fill the teaching posts left by men. Most women could live with the drawbacks of the job because they planned eventually to marry and attain their domestic destinies rather than hold these positions for life. Consequently, teaching became classified as "women's work," with all the attendant disadvantages.

The Arts and Entertainment

Some women tested societal boundaries through the fine arts. Of course, many women continued to produce quilts, rugs, bed coverings, wall hangings, and other craftwork in their homes. The teachings of domesticity and true womanhood reassured women that if they created homes of "order and purity," women could exercise "a power that will be felt round the globe." Consequently, many talented women satisfied themselves with needle and thread instead of brush and paint and worked with pieces of cloth instead of stretches of canvas.

A number of women, however, refused to accept such teachings and challenged the words of commentators who warned that "art is the most difficult—perhaps, in its highest form—almost impossible to women." Barred from enrolling in art schools and displaying their work in galleries, women artists did indeed have a difficult time learning the necessary skills. Women were believed to have a "natural repugnance" to drawing from "life," or in other words, from nude models. According to one minister, "no virtuous and delicate female . . . would desire to abate one jot or tittle from the seeming restrictions imposed upon her conduct."

Several women soon proved him wrong; they taught themselves and became practicing artists. One of the most notable of these women was Eunice Pinney, who reared five children while in the process of becoming a prolific watercolorist. Her vigorous and forthright work included landscapes, mourning pictures, and religious, historical, and literary scenes. A few women artists flaunted convention in other ways as well. For instance, painter Mary Ann Willson lived openly with another woman, whom Willson described as her "romantic attachment." Highly original and lively, Willson's works were done with paints made from berries, brick dust, and vegetable dyes.

Nor did women hesitate to get involved with popular entertainments, especially live theater. Women wrote plays, acted, and managed theaters. Some women alternated careers as actresses and theater managers. Although New York City was the center of the entertainment world, women also found theatrical opportunities in such other cities as Philadelphia in the North, New Orleans in the South, and San Francisco in the West.

Women theater managers seldom challenged public tastes. Instead, they tended to present the most popular of British and American plays, as well as showcasing the era's leading actors and actresses. They did demonstrate that women were perfectly capable of ruling over an assorted lot of stagehands and acting personnel. Thus, they opened the way for subsequent generations of theater-minded women.

Religious Participation

Female evangelism, which continued to characterize the Second Great Awakening throughout the 1810s, 1820s, and 1830s, helped women's reforms. Because the Awakening welcomed female participants, women took part in prayer meetings, special services, and revivals. In an effort to convert men, women directed a militant piety against ungodly and unchurched men. Despite women's efforts, female converts outnumbered male by three to two.

As women became the majority of congregates, clergy continued to feminize their teachings. For example, in response to mothers' protests against the harsh doctrine of infant damnation due to innate human sin, ministers began to agree with women that good Christian nurturing might offset original sin. This growing feminization of religion resulted in an emphasis on introspection and morality. Women learned to assess their own characters and believe in their strengths—two abilities that propelled them toward independence rather than toward domesticity. The stress that religion placed on brotherhood and equality of men before God became, for many women, a sense of sisterhood and equality of women before God.

Women dominated the Sunday schools that were appearing in many churches. By claiming that their inherent virtue qualified them, rather than men, to instruct children in religious values, women essentially seized positions of power within their congregations. Their roles as Sunday-school teachers effectively allowed women to ignore the Pauline doctrine that advocated women's silence in church.

In some sects, women even became preachers. The Freewill Baptists especially welcomed women as ministers. It is likely that several hundred women preached during the 1810s, 1820s, and 1830s, while a number achieved a measure of eminence. Harriet Livermore of New Hampshire was one of the best-known white women evangelists. Through their devoted and selfless commitment to religion, such women created for themselves and others a perception of women as capable religious leaders.

Moral Reform and Other Causes

Female moral reform societies similarly enlarged women's roles. These groups emphasized the moral influence of women and urged their members to exert active control over the ethics and actions of their friends and neighbors. In 1834, another group of women reformers founded the New York Female Reform Society dedicated to the credo that "it is the imperious duty of ladies everywhere and of every religious denomination, to cooperate in the great work of moral reform." This society published a journal called *The Advocate* intended to denounce "sin" in all forms; hired several ministers to aid the needy in hospitals, jails, almshouses, and brothels; and stood vigil and prayed outside brothels.

During the 1830s, such female societies proliferated rapidly, comprising large numbers of women. In 1835, seventy white women founded the Boston Female Moral Reform Society to assist needy women and combat prostitution; they soon attracted hundreds more members through rural auxiliaries. By 1837, the neighboring New York Female Reform Society counted 250 auxiliaries and 15,000 members.

Besides moral reform, other causes attracted women. Thousands of women joined the American Temperance Society's crusade during the 1820s and 1830s, either as members of men's temperance groups, in which they soon found their level of participation strictly restricted, or as founders of their own organizations in which they could vote, hold office, and set policy. During these early years of the prohibition movement, women engaged primarily in exhortation and moral suasion to bring about temperance among drinkers.

White women also championed abolitionism. One of the first to do so was author and editor Lydia Maria Child. Widely known for her editorship of *The Juvenile Miscellany,* a children's magazine, and her authorship of *The Frugal Housewife,* a household hint book, Child published the first American antislavery book in 1833. Entitled *An Appeal for that Class of Americans Called Africans,* Child's tract asked for justice and equality for black Americans. She pointed out that the "Negro woman is unprotected by either law or public opinion" and is thus "entirely subservient to the will of her owner." After Child's readers turned against her for her "unfeminine" involvement in political matters, she became the editor of the *National Anti-Slavery Standard* and devoted the rest of her career to abolitionism.

About the same time that Child's book appeared, a Quaker teacher, Prudence Crandall, accepted a black student into her Canterbury Female Boarding School in Connecticut. Local authorities warned Crandall that if the young woman stayed, they would "ruin her school." Crandall bravely replied "let it sink, then. I shall not turn her out." When all of Crandall's white students withdrew, she converted her school, with the help of abolitionist editor William Lloyd Garrison, into the High School for Young Colored Ladies and Misses, which opened in April 1833. A storm of protest erupted in the town of Canterbury, and a group of irate citizens declared that "the Government of the United States, the nation with all its institutions, of right belong to the white men, who now possess them."

Crandall attempted to carry on with her school, but was jailed during the summer of 1833 under a newly passed law that forbade the teaching of African Americans in the state of Connecticut. After the abolitionist press aired Crandall's case around the world, she was finally freed on a technicality. At this point Crandall bravely returned to her school and to the continued harassment of townspeople who threw manure into her well, smashed the school's windows, threatened the students, and set fire to the building. After mob violence in September 1834, Crandall finally gave up. Recently married to an abolitionist minister, she moved with her husband to Illinois, where she maintained an interest in reform until her death in 1890.

These initial attempts to help black slaves proved largely ineffectual, but they alerted many white women to the need to organize antislavery societies. Beginning in 1832, the formation of the New England Anti-Slavery Society, the Connecticut Female Anti-Slavery Society, and others in numerous states and regions marked the entry of women into the largely male abolitionist movement.

White women's increasing involvement in the abolitionist cause received national attention in the mid-1830s because of the activities of two southern-born women, Sarah and Angelina Grimké. Raised in Charleston, South Carolina, as proper young ladies, the Grimké sisters grew up detesting slavery and resenting the restrictions inherent in true womanhood. In 1821, at age twenty-eight, Sarah moved to Philadelphia and joined the Society of Friends. Angelina followed Sarah to Philadelphia and into the Quaker fold in 1829. Angelina soon joined the Philadelphia Female Anti-Slavery Society, noting in her diary, "I am confident not many years will roll by before the horrible traffic in human beings will be destroyed."

The year 1836 proved a turning point for the sisters. When the American Anti-Slavery Society published Angelina's *Appeal to the Christian Women of the South,* indignant citizens in the South publicly burned copies of the pamphlet, while officials warned Angelina never to return to her home there. Soon, both women began to lecture against slavery. Their willingness to speak to gatherings that included both women and men, so-called promiscuous audiences, caused a great deal of public indignation. Undaunted, Angelina wrote a second pamphlet in 1837, *An Appeal to the Women of the Nominally Free States,* which argued that as long as slavery existed in the South it hurt the North as well.

The West

True Womanhood and Western Women of Color

In western areas, the idea of domesticity or true womanhood had little meaning for most women of color. Their lives were configured more by race, religion, and the hard denials of survival than by white ideas re-garding domesticity. Of course, some women of color, especially free African American and Spanish-speaking women of the middle and up-per classes, already practiced their own version of true womanhood. Many women of color had not even heard about the idealized American woman, while others had little interest in such abstract notions. And even those who did realized that their lives of toil and instability offered little opportunity to develop domestic "virtues," act "feminine," or raise children in "proper" ways.

Even though beliefs regarding true womanhood had little meaning for women of color, its implicit racism often exerted widespread and negative influence on them. For one thing, ideals of white womanhood underwrote policies and laws that affected women of color, frequently in a destructive manner. As a case in point, government officials in Washington, D.C., helped destroy the influence of Native American women through mandates that Indian women give up their customary pursuit of agriculture and learn instead to sew, weave, and keep house like white housewives.

White society also used standards established for white women to judge women of color. Generally, white Americans regarded women of color as coarser in appearance and far less attractive than white women. Because dark skin carried a negative connotation in white culture, only the occasional Indian "princess" or Mexican "señorita" was thought at-tractive—in an exotic and alien way.

Women of color usually faced a dismaying situation in regard to their actions as well. If a free black woman worked at heavy labor to support her family, critics deemed her unfeminine rather than energetic. And if a Spanish-speaking woman preferred the ease of low furniture and floor mats to upholstered sofas and carpets, white observers thought her undomestic, incompetent, and even lazy.

A third way that the concept of true womanhood impinged on women of color in the West was by disrupting their traditional cultures. As American traders, merchants, and settlers fanned southward and west-ward over the continent, they not only carried white standards with them but inculcated the same wherever they went. Because the travelers simply assumed that white culture and goods were superior to those they encountered, they did not hesitate to force them on local populations. For instance, in 1821 when American merchants reached Santa Fe in New Mexico they offered local women such American products as whale-oil lamps, what-not stands, and commodes, objects that, once women em-ployed them, forced women to spend more time cleaning and doing housework, acting "domestic" in the approved white sense of the term. The newcomers also expected these Mexican women to learn English, learn to cook American-style dishes, and to desert their families and reli-gious affiliations once married to or living with white men.

American Indian Women

The early 1800s proved to be especially upsetting for Native American peoples. With the white population doubling every twenty-five years, it was clear that Thomas Jefferson's prediction that Native peoples could live in peace west of the Mississippi River for many decades to come fell short. Instead, as early as the 1810s and 1820s settlers swept across the Ohio and lower Mississippi valleys, and by the late 1820s they began to cross the Mississippi River, pushing American Indians along ahead of them or simply destroying Native peoples and their societies.

In the process, white settlers continued to borrow what they could from American Indians. Indian women served as guides, sexual partners, domestic servants, and teachers of agricultural methods yet seldom received recognition for their ingenuity and expertise. In Minnesota, trader Jean Baptiste Faribault bartered with Dakota women who brought him tanned furs, maple sugar, and sometimes corn. In exchange, Faribault gave them awls, axes, beads, hatchets, hoes, iron knives, silver ornaments, and tin kettles. These women used such tools as awls to punch holes in leather before stitching it together with deer sinew and decorating the leather with quills or beads and metal tinkling cones.

Settlers offered little thanks to Indian women. Instead, they recognized only those native women who helped them achieve their objectives. One of these, Milly Francis, a Creek Indian woman, received a congressional medal and a small pension for saving a white captive from death at the hands of Creek people in 1817.

Like the trappers and traders before them, white settlers tended to impose their own ideas on Native Americans. For instance, during the 1830s, the United States Commissioner of Indian Affairs classified the Cherokee as a hunting society simply because Cherokee men hunted. This view overlooked the fact that Cherokee women for centuries had been and still were adept and productive agriculturalists. The Commissioner's office declared that Cherokee women must come in from the fields and be taught to spin and weave while the men must be taught to farm. Not only did this prescription slight women's work, but it further disrupted Cherokee culture by forcing men to grow crops, long considered uniquely women's prerogative.

Nor were settlers very accepting of Natives who took on gender roles associated with the opposite sex. For Native women who became warriors and spent their lives hunting, fighting, and taking wives, white people had little but scorn. For Native men who adopted the ways of women the situation was even worse. Although Native American tribes ranging from the Creek to the Hopi and the Navaho to the Zuni accepted homosexuality, white settlers and government agents often opposed or denied its existence.

Regardless of how white settlers viewed Native Americans, one constant remained: they wanted Indians moved out of their way. During the 1820s and 1830s, President Andrew Jackson's removal policy forced thousands of Native Americans onto the westward trail. The route these Indians traveled—forcibly marched at gunpoint by the U.S. Army—between their homes in the southeastern United States and the new Indian Territory in (present-day) Oklahoma, earned the designation the "Trail of Tears" because of the illnesses, deaths, and other tragedies that the Indians suffered on it. The "Five Civilized Tribes," especially the eastern Cherokee, lost not only land but saw many of their people and much of their culture destroyed in the process of removal to the West.

Indian women frequently responded to destructive policies and treatment by shielding Indian history and customs from the view of whites, by fighting alongside native men to stave the white advance, and by refusing to cooperate with the U.S. government's removal policy. White settlers often commented on the ferocity and passion of enraged Native women, but they seldom, if ever, speculated that their own policies and attitudes had elicited such reactions. When whites found Native American women aggressive rather than accepting, they branded them as "hostile" rather than "protective" of their families and cultures.

Spanish-Speaking Women

During the early 1800s, an influx of white settlers and American government policies disrupted and disheartened a large number of Spanish-heritage people. For instance, as early as 1819, Spanish-speaking women living in the Old Southwest frontier discovered that they had become American citizens. After the Adams-Onís Treaty, in which Spain renounced all claims to West Florida and ceded East Florida to the United States, women in these areas learned that they no longer lived under Spanish law and custom but those of the United States. As a result, those women who enjoyed property and other rights under Spanish law soon lost them, an event that established a precedent for other Spanish-background areas that eventually entered the United States.

In a few decades, during the 1810s, 1820s, and 1830s, a similar fate would befall the thousands of other Spanish-speaking women who lived just outside America's southwestern boundaries, in El Norte, Mexico's northern frontier—today's Texas, New Mexico, Arizona, and California. These women were usually Catholic, community- and family-oriented, and accustomed to male authority. Most lived in patriarchal families linked through an intricate system of kinship and godparents. Although daily work roles usually divided by gender, women assisted men in family enterprises. In Texas women helped men establish great cattle ranches based on a Spanish-derived system of land titles. In New Mexico and Arizona, families farmed, traded, or mined, especially copper in Arizona. In California, women helped to trade by sea or worked farms, cattle and sheep ranches, and mines.

In 1821, when Mexico declared its independence from Spain, it appeared that Mexico would rise to wealth and fame. It proved difficult, however, for people scattered over more than 850,000 miles to develop their holdings and restrain land-hungry Americans. By such routes as the Santa Fe Trail to New Mexico and the Old Spanish Trail to Los Angeles, Mexican lands were well within reach of American explorers, traders, merchants, and settlers.

Shortly after Mexico became an independent nation, Mexican officials opened the province of Texas to American settlers who promised to convert to Roman Catholicism and assume Mexican citizenship. Four years later, some 2,000 Americans lived in Texas, including nearly 450 black slaves who worked on American-owned cotton plantations. When American settlers in Texas neglected to fulfill their promises and remained blatantly American in their loyalties, the Mexican government adopted the Colonization Law of 1830, which forbade further settlement in Texas by Americans and prohibited the entrance of any more slaves. In 1836, the Texans declared their independence from Mexico, establishing the Republic of Texas after a series of clashes with the Mexican army.

A similar process occurred in New Mexico. Again in 1821, Missourian William Becknell pushed American trade into the Mexican province of New Mexico. Local people welcomed American traders; women appreciated American cooking utensils, household goods, and rich American fabrics and styles. Middle- and lower-class women began to replace their skirts, blouses, and shawls with outfits featuring full skirts, petticoats, and hoops. Soon trade routes linked St. Louis, Santa Fe, and San Francisco, bringing west in addition to goods American migrants, some of whom married Spanish-speaking women.

In the Rio Arriba Valley, the center of Spanish culture in the Southwest, as many as 75 percent of foreign-born men married local women, usually of the lower and middle classes. Because church marriages were expensive and Spanish frontier society accepted cohabitation, another group married by common law. By the 1830s, the majority of men who married New Mexican women listed the United States as their place of origin and such occupations as trapper, trader, or merchant as their trade. In addition to acquiring wives and families, these men gained certain trade and land ownership privileges and naturalization as Mexican citizens. The native women obtained successful husbands and might bear lighter-skinned children, considered at the time as higher caste than those of dark complexion.

More than two-thirds of white husbands stayed with their wives and children, establishing long-term relationships, adopting *tortillas* and *frijoles* as standards of their diet, and learning at least enough Spanish to function on a daily basis. The rest, however, disappeared, leaving their wives and children to support themselves. Thus, although intermarriage aided cultural adaptation of the two groups, it disrupted kin networks and caused some Spanish-speaking women to mistrust American men.

Other problems developed between Spanish-speaking residents and white migrants across the region that became the American Southwest. Legal systems clashed, as they had in California, where American expatriates favored legal codes that fostered more individualism than did existing Mexican laws. In time, white antimiscegenation laws prohibited interracial marriage, a long-standing tradition in the region. In addition, as more white women entered the area, they tended to judge Spanish-speaking women by their own standards of domesticity and true womanhood. As a result, white women usually misinterpreted and misunderstood local women's behavior. They sharply criticized local women for their religious practices, or for dancing, drinking, and gambling—all socially acceptable pastimes for women in Spanish frontier society of the time.

As more Americans poured into Texas, New Mexico, and California during the mid-1830s, and in far smaller numbers into Arizona, friction increased. In East Texas, for example, *Tejanos* (Texas Mexicans) withdrew from the white population, forming their own communities. Throughout the Southwest, women, especially of the upper classes, often thought Americans rough, boorish, and dishonest. They increasingly relied on their own churches, families, and organizations as sources of support. At the same time, Americans frequently judged Spanish-speaking women, especially those of the lower classes, loud, unkempt, and immoral. These vastly overdrawn stereotypes revealed not only the clash of two different cultures but the racial prejudices of the era that would soon drive these groups even further apart.

White Women Moving Westward

White women also lived in the American West. During the 1810s, 1820s, and 1830s, white settlers poured into the Old Southwest, filling areas that became such states as Arkansas, Florida, and Texas. In the Old Northwest, settlers eventually formed Indiana, Illinois, Missouri, and Michigan. By the early 1830s, some settlers crossed the Mississippi River into Iowa and Wisconsin, while by the middle of that decade some migrants were already on the Oregon Trail, heading west toward Oregon or California. In 1836, Eliza Hart Spalding and Narcissa Whitman became the first white women to cross the Rocky Mountains; both entered the Oregon Territory as missionaries.

Men often made the decision to migrate, dictating that wives and daughters pack their things, or ordering slave women to load their goods and themselves into wagons. In other cases, women favored the move; they could appreciate the chance of restored health for a family member in a more favorable climate, the opportunity to recoup a financial disaster sustained by the family, a fortune to be gained from the utilization of natural resources, or the potential of a prosperous future on cheap, available land.

Women found migration attractive for other reasons as well. Army wives followed their husbands to frontier forts. Religious orders of women relocated to nurse and educate native peoples. Single women chose to migrate in order to find husbands, procure employment, take up land, or serve as missionaries and teachers. And European women wanted homes where their families could enjoy land ownership, practice religious toleration, or escape tyrannical governments.

For many reasons, then, women began the trek west with husbands, families, and friends in conveyances that ranged from stagecoaches and railroad cars to the legendary Conestoga wagon. Wagons, either the smaller emigrant wagon or the larger prairie schooner, were popular because they contained abundant space for people and possessions. Men equipped wagons with running gear, trained horses or oxen, and prepared tools, firearms, and stock. Women stitched wagon covers and readied food, clothing, bedding, and medicines.

While these arrangements progressed, people began to prepare themselves for the coming traumatic separation from the friends and family with whom they had spent their lives. After tearful and often prolonged partings, the migrants were on their way. Once on the trail, they were far from alone. Their diaries tell of meeting old friends and neighbors and of making new friends. Women visited with other women and exchanged recipes and bits of useful trail lore. One woman's diary contained frequent references to storytelling, song, music, and merrymaking.

Although loneliness was not part of the trail routine for women, hard work surely was. A family's daily living had to continue despite the harsh trail environment. Women cooked meals over campfires, laid beds out under the stars, and washed clothing in streams, while men frequently set up tables, started fires, and even cooked. Because of trail conditions, women's work became more complex and more wearying than it had been before departure. In addition, many trail women were pregnant or nursing infants, which further complicated their numerous trail duties.

Yet women's complaints were not overwhelming. Westering women seemed to draw strength from the tenets of domesticity and true womanhood. Kitturah Belknap, on her way to Iowa in the 1830s, prided herself on her "housekeeping." She took "good earthen dishes" backed up with tinware and "four nice little table cloths" that she made. Belknap supplemented her family's food by buying fresh produce from farms, baking bread that she set to rise on the warm ground under the wagon during the night, and producing rolls of butter by letting the motion of the lurching wagon operate the churn inside it.

Women utilized the teachings of domesticity to get them through hard times. They rallied as wives and mothers, providing strength and support even when the weather was frightful, wagons broke down, oxen died, and people fell ill and died. Women helped with men's work such as driving the wagon or herding stock, while at the same time doing their best to protect their children from the many hazards of the trail.

Most women recognized that their efforts were crucial to the success of the migration. Any domestic routines that they could establish en route, any help that they could offer, any support that they could give were all hedges against the disintegration of the undertaking. In addition, most female migrants were farm women familiar with the tasks demanded of them. They approached the trail experience as a time of transition, during which they could hone their skills and prepare mentally for what lay ahead. One migrant stated simply, "I never thought about its being hard. I was used to things being hard."

White Women Settlers

Once they reached their destination, women often had mixed reactions to their new homes. Many reported feelings of dismay regarding Native peoples, cold winters, wet springs, hot summers, mosquitoes, and "wild beasts." Some women grew discouraged and gave up. As one explained, "some liked the new country, but others returned to their native states."

Most women stayed on, whether they liked the area or not. As one woman recalled, "when we got to the new purchase, the land of milk and honey, we were disappointed and homesick, but we were there and had to make the best of it." Another pragmatically wrote to her mother: "I can't say I like the West as well as I do New England yet I think it is better for me to be here."

At the same time, other women felt ecstatic at the sight of rolling valleys, flowing rivers, and miles of untilled land. One young woman claimed not to be disillusioned even when she saw the primitive log cabin that was her new home. In "girl fashion," she explained, "I considered it very romantic."

Most women, however, were less pleased with their first western houses, which ranged from the wagons that had carried them westward to a corn-crib, abandoned outbuilding, lean-to, tar-paper shack, sod hut, or log cabin. Regardless of the nature of those first shelters, women turned their energies to converting them into homes for their families and workplaces for themselves. In the Old Southwest, these housekeepers suffered from scorching sun, oppressive humidity, torrential rains, insects, and snakes. In the Old Northwest, women often complained of frost on the walls, snowflakes on the blankets and table, and ice on the floors. In some regions, wind was the major problem because it continually carried dust onto clothing, cooking utensils, and food.

Women endured all because they realized that their early homes represented the youth of the frontier and marked a rough stage through which every raw community must pass. So women hung quilts as room dividers, papered walls with newspapers or painted them with lime, and created household furnishings out of packing crates and rope.

With her workplace established, the frontierswoman turned her energies to producing candles, soap, clothing, foodstuffs, and a wide variety of other domestic goods, all of which demanded ingenuity, expertise, and incredible amounts of time to produce. In addition, women bore many children, educated them, and trained them as domestic or field laborers. Women were expert herbalists who served as apothecaries and morticians to their families and friends. And they brought in all the cash that many families would ever see through the sales of excess butter, eggs, knitted goods, and other products.

Most frontierswomen found that the worst was over in about two years. By that time many moved into better homes, could purchase many useful items from stores in newly sprung towns, and had friends and neighbors to relieve the initial loneliness. Eventually churches and schools appeared, which gave women other social outlets.

Typically, women left the fields as soon as they could. They then limited themselves primarily to the house, garden, and barn. Thus, the frontier, contrary to popular belief, did not break down the usual division of labor along gender lines. Rather, after a transitional period following arrival, frontierswomen reestablished the same labor system within the family that they had always known.

Nor did the frontier eradicate laws and policies restricting women. When Indiana applied for statehood in 1815, women there could not make wills, convey property, or control their own incomes. Indiana became the nineteenth state on 11 December 1816, but nearly thirty years would pass before Indiana adopted legislation protecting married women's property and Hoosiers began to discuss the possibility of women voting.

Ideas regarding domesticity and true womanhood also accompanied the migrants. Many of the frontierswomen who had managed to leave the fields attempted to reestablish domesticity and other feminine values in their huts and cabins. For example, although hoops often swept skirts into open fireplaces where they singed, women continued to wear them. They also wore sunbonnets to protect their faces from the sun and retain their pale complexions. And they decorated their homes with craftwork and folk art, particularly exquisite quilts that often told a story or recorded family history. One Kentucky woman devised a "coffin" quilt on which she recorded family deaths. When a family member died, she took his or her "coffin" from the quilt's border and sewed it in the graveyard at the quilt's center.

At the same time, however, frontierswomen resisted some tenets of domesticity and true womanhood. Although women wanted to look good and act "properly," they did not want their rights restricted. Especially in the Northwest, they sought education in the country schoolhouses and early women's seminaries, for coeducation constituted an accepted practice in the West from the beginning. Only six years after the Black Hawk Purchase Treaty opened Iowa for settlement in 1833, a Dubuque woman announced the founding of an academy that would provide a "good English education" to both men and women. In 1833, the Utopian community of Oberlin, Ohio, which encouraged women to enhance their powers through advanced education, founded Oberlin College, the first coeducational college in the nation. Women rapidly moved into teaching and also took paid employment as railway station agents, team drivers, shepherds, store clerks, prostitutes, lawyers, musicians, artists, authors, journalists, and a wide variety of other jobs. And they sometimes voted in local elections and discussed such issues as equality, land ownership, and the right of suffrage.

In many ways, the West appeared to offer more opportunities to women than had their former homes. At least for some white women, the West was a place to grow and to pursue a few women's rights.

Divorce

In the West, white women had the legal right to apply for a divorce. During this era, virtually no African Americans or American Indians used white, western courts to dissolve marriages. As in the South and the North, in the West courts received more divorce petitions from women than from men. The ratio of women seeking divorce to men was higher in the West than in any other region of the country.

Frequently, western legislators borrowed from the legal codes they had known back home, then added their own innovations. The most startling of these new ideas dealt with a glut of divorce petitions by divorcing more than one couple in the same bill of divorcement, thus saving legislators time and expense. In 1825, for example, an Illinois court parted two couples with one legislative action. Other western states soon adopted this practice, divorcing as many as a dozen or more couples at a time.

Because in newly established western towns and counties discontented spouses could easily disappear, desertion was rife. Women as well as men took advantage of this situation. And when deserters reappeared in another part of the West, they simply identified themselves as single or widowed. Without modern forms of communication and record keeping, who could have known the difference?

The West soon gained a reputation for its liberal notions regarding divorce and desertion. After all, many westerners believed in the American dream of happiness and freedom. If they did not find happiness in a marriage, they sought freedom from it. At the same time, westward migration was very hard on family unity. Some men went west leaving wives and children behind them. Although many such emigrants hoped they would eventually reunite with their wives, others knew that they had left home for good. Migration also put huge strains on those family members who went west together. Stories abound of marital outbursts: a woman who set fire to the wagon in which her husband slept; a wife who stole out of a cabin one night never to return; or a wife and mother who packed her children into a wagon and vowed to return home, with or without her husband and her children's father. Under such stressful circumstances it is little wonder that western legislators and judges faced a large number of divorce applications.

Black Women in the West

Black women saw promise in the West. Some slave women, who hoped for eventual emancipation once away from the South, begged their departing owners and others to take them along, especially those headed to California. Notably, many migrants bound for the Old Southwest and adjacent areas intending to raise tobacco or cotton did indeed take slaves with them. For instance, in 1822 some settlers from Virginia brought four slave valets and a slave woman called only "Mammy" to Missouri. During the first years after the party's arrival, the four black men helped break and farm the land outside the cabin, while Mammy helped inside.

At the same time, some free black women chose migration because they anticipated less prejudice "out west." African Americans assumed that because parts of the West outlawed slavery, black people would gain acceptance there. They soon discovered, however, that racial prejudice and discrimination was the cultural baggage of most white settlers.

Indeed, in the Southwest, white settlers often tried to establish laws and policies similar to the ones they had used in their former homes to keep black people enslaved. In Texas, for example, white settlers confronted an awkward situation. During the years of Spanish and Mexican rule, free black persons were recognized by law. As a result, during the early 1800s, Texas became a haven for runaway and freed slaves from the nearby American South. Yet, in 1823, when the impresario Stephen F. Austin led white settlers into Texas, he received permission from the Mexican government to bring slaves as field laborers and domestic servants.

Meanwhile, additional free black women entered Texas. Some came with white or black husbands; others settled in Texas on their own. One of these, Emily Morgan, known as Emily D. West, gained fame as "The Yellow Rose of Texas." According to legend, in 1836 Emily not only informed American leaders of Mexican general Santa Anna's location, but distracted him while the Texan forces approached. Thus, she ensured the Texan army's victory at the deciding battle of San Jacinto. Despite Morgan's help and the assistance of free black men who fought alongside the Americans against Mexico, the newly independent government in Texas first banished free blacks from the area, then allowed about 150 free blacks to stay without full rights of citizenship. Clearly, racist sentiment was stronger than gratitude for the help of free black men and women in establishing the Republic of Texas.

Even in the Old Northwest, where the Northwest Ordinance of 1787 prohibited slavery, black and white people faced confusing circumstances. Although settlers initially helped each other regardless of race, as areas became more settled racial lines reappeared. During the 1810s and 1820s, white settlers flowed into Ohio, Illinois, and Indiana. Others poured into Michigan and Wisconsin by the 1830s. During this period the status of black people became unclear. Antislavery statutes seemed to apply to some people but not to others. As a case in point, in 1820 officers at Fort Snelling, Minnesota, reported for duty along with their slaves (both male and female) with no apparent opposition from the slaves or the other inhabitants of the fort. A mere decade later, abolitionist sentiment had grown tremendously. In 1835, a slave woman named Rachel who resided at army posts in Minnesota between 1831 and 1834 successfully sued for her freedom.

Rachel's case did not prove a landmark decision for other blacks in the Northwest. Rather, a good deal of white resistance appeared to the idea of freed black men and women living there. Fearful whites talked about the possibility of "black incursions," that is, a substantial number of African Americans moving to northwestern areas. As a result, some northwestern jurisdictions passed "exclusion laws" to keep out free black Americans, or simply denied property and other rights to free blacks. Some jurisdictions required free blacks to register, give evidence of their freedom, and post cash bonds guaranteeing their proper behavior. Illinois and Indiana frequently barred black people from entering their boundaries, while the Indiana legislature appropriated funds to expel black people from the state, a program that was never implemented. Meanwhile, the threat of re-enslavement hovered over the heads of free blacks living in the Old Northwest.

As a result, free black women who migrated to the Old Southwest and Old Northwest hoping for fair treatment were in for an unpleasant surprise. Prejudice and poverty characterized their lives during the 1810s, 1820s, and 1830s. Although they worked hard, they were not allowed to send their children to public schools. Clearly, the opportunities the West offered to white women were largely unavailable to black women. Furthermore, the meaning of domesticity and true womanhood remained elusive for the West's women of color.

What, then, was the real essence of the American woman between 1812 and 1837? Visitors from other countries offered contradictory answers to the question. In 1835, French observer Alexis de Tocqueville described the American woman as protected and elevated, while he interpreted the American family as a miniature democracy, with the man as its head and the woman and children as its citizens. Only two years later, however, English writer and traveler Harriet Martineau reported that the American woman's intellect was confined, her morals crushed, health ruined, weakness encouraged, and strength punished. Unlike de Tocqueville, Martineau thought the American family "a poor institution" in which "one sex overbears the other."

The reason for this apparent discrepancy is that no single type of "American woman" existed. Despite the teachings of domesticity and true womanhood, American women remained disparate in talent, interests, and abilities. Their lives varied according to their race, ethnicity, and social class. Nor did they all adhere to the dictates of true womanhood. At the same time that women helped foster the twin forces of industrialization and national expansion, they often challenged, or ignored, the idealized image of the American woman.

Study Guide

Checklist of important names, terms, phrases, and dates for Chapter 3.
Think about what or who each was and why she, he, or it was significant.

domesticity
true womanhood
Industrial Revolution
hoe gangs
"big house"
"festivals" or "gatherings"
Elizabeth Lange
Marie Bernard Couvent
Southern Womanhood
hookworm
poor white women
women of the yeoman class
puerperal fever
tapeworms
southern widows
"cousin-marriage"
southern belles
Frances Wright
antimiscegenation provisions
runaway spouses
self-education groups
free black women's reform
    societies
African Methodist Episcopal
    Church
Jarena Lee
Mary Prince's *A History of Mary
    Prince, A West Indian Slave*
Maria Stewart
Sarah Mapps Douglass
Sarah Louis Forten
The Liberator
lady operative, or "mill girls"

Lowell, Massachusetts
The Lowell Offering
pieceworkers
Lynn, Massachusetts
domestics
"disorderly" women
Sarah Todd Astor
ladies
"proper spheres of the sexes"
companionate marriage
patent medicines
Dr. Harriot K. Hunt
pessaries
Sarah Josepha Hale
Godey's Lady's Book
Hannah Mather Crocker
Emma Hart Willard
Troy Female Seminary
Catharine Beecher
Mary Lyon
Mount Holyoke
female evangelism
female moral reform societies
American Temperance Society
Sarah and Angelina Grimké
Cherokee women
Rio Arriba Valley
Kitturah Belknap
Oberlin College   1833
Emily Morgan, or "The Yellow
    Rose of Texas"
Northwest Ordinance of 1787
"exclusion laws"

Chapter 3 issues to think about and discuss

- Would white women in the North and South and African American women in the North and South have been better off without the Industrial Revolution?
- What aspects of life did black enslaved and elite white women in the South share? Were there similarities between free black and yeomen white women?
- How do historians know that relationships existed between some white women and black men in the South?
- How would you feel if you knew a member of your family was enslaved? What actions would you take?
- Despite their numbers, "mill girls" seemed to lack the power to better their situations. What more could they have done to improve their condition?
- In what ways did women's unpaid labor contribute millions of dollars to the American economy every year?
- What "jobs" were ladies expected to perform? How did such tasks effect the economy?
- Women of color in the American West had little use for domesticity, or true womanhood. Yet these doctrines affected their lives. What factors made it possible for eastern, white philosophies to exert so much influence in the West?
- Women are often seen as reactors rather than actors, as respondent to change rather than initiators of it. In what ways was this true, and what ways false, for American women living between 1812 and 1837?
- Was it true that more women deviated from the concepts of domesticity, or true womanhood, during this era than adopted them as life goals?

Suggestions for Further Reading

Women in the South

Alexander, Adele Logan. *Ambiguous Lives: Free Women of Color in Rural Georgia, 1789–1879*. Fayetteville: University of Arkansas Press, 1991.

Clinton, Catherine. *The Plantation Mistress: Woman's World in the Old South*. New York: Pantheon Books, 1980.

—, ed. *Half Sisters of History: Southern Women and the American Past*. Durham, NC: Duke University Press, 1994.

Davis, Marianna W. *Contributions of Black Women to America*. Vol. II. Columbia, SC: Kenday Press, 1981. Pages 21–69 (on slavery).

Ellison, Mary. "Resistance to Oppression: Black Women's Response to Slavery in the United States," *Slavery and Abolition* 4 (May 1983): 56–63.

Fox-Genovese, Elizabeth. *Within the Plantation Household: Black and White Women of the Old South*. Chapel Hill: University of North Carolina Press, 1988.

Gutman, Herbert G. *The Black Family in Slavery and Freedom, 1750–1925*. New York: Pantheon Books, 1976.

Hagler, D. Harland. "The Ideal Woman in the Antebellum South: Lady or Farmwife?" *Journal of Southern History* 65 (August 1980): 405–18.

Hine, Darlene. "Female Slave Resistance: The Economics of Sex," *Western Journal of Black Studies* 3 (Summer 1979): 123–27.

———, and Kathleen Thompson, *A Shining Thread of Hope: The History of Black Women in America.* New York: Broadway Books, 1998.

Hodes, Martha. *White Women, Black Men: Illicit Sex in the Nineteenth-Century South.* New Haven, CT: Yale University Press, 1997.

Hutson, C. Kirk. "'Whackety Whack, Don't Talk Back: The Glorification of Violence against Females and the Subjugation of Women in Nineteenth-Century Southern Folk Music," *Journal of Women's History* 3 (Fall 1996): 114–42.

Jones, Jacqueline. "'My Mother Was Much of a Woman': Black Women, Work, and the Family Under Slavery," *Feminist Studies* 8 (Summer 1982): 235–69.

Lebsock, Suzanne. "Free Black Women and the Question of Matriarchy: Petersburg, Virginia, 1784–1820." *Feminist Studies* 8 (Summer 1982): 270–92.

———. *The Free Women of Petersburg: Status and Culture in a Southern Town, 1784–1860.* New York: W. W. Norton Co., Inc., 1983.

McMillen, Sally G. *Southern Women: Black and White in the Old South.* Wheeling, IL: Harlan Davidson, Inc., 1992.

Schweninger, Loren. "Property-Owning Free African-American Women in the South, 1800–70," *Journal of Women's History* 1 (Winter 1990): 13–44.

Sterling, Dorothy. *We Are Your Sisters: Black Women in the Nineteenth-Century.* New York: W. W. Norton & Co., Inc., 1984.

Stevenson, Brenda K. "Slavery," 1055–70, in *Black Women in America: An Historical Encyclopedia,* edited by Darlene Clark Hine. Vol. II. Brooklyn, NY: Carlson Publishing, Inc., 1993.

White, Deborah Gray. "Female Slaves: Sex Roles and Status in the Antebellum Plantation South," 20–31, in *Unequal Sisters: A Multicultural Reader in U.S. Women's History,* edited by Vicki L. Ruiz and Ellen Carol DuBois. 2d ed. New York: Routledge, Chapman, & Hall, Inc., 1994.

Women in the North

Billington, Louis. "'Female Laborers in the Church': Women Preachers in the Northeastern United States, 1790–1840," *Journal of American Studies* 19 (December 1985): 369–94.

Blewett, Mary H. Men, *Women, and Work: Class, Gender, and Protest in the New England Shoe Industry, 1780–1910.* Champaign-Urbana: University of Illinois Press, 1988.

Boydston, Jeanne. *Home and Work: Housework, Wages, and the Ideology of Labor in the Early Republic.* New York: Oxford University Press, 1990.

Boylan, Anne M. "Evangelical Womanhood in the Nineteenth Century: The Role of Women in Sunday Schools," *Feminist Studies* 4 (October 1978): 62–80.

Braude, Ann. *Radical Spirits: Spiritualism and Women's Rights in Nineteenth-Century America.* Boston: Beacon Press, 1989.

Brown, Irene Quenzler. "Death, Friendship, and Female Identity During New England's Second Great Awakening," *Journal of Family History* 12 (October 1987): 367–87.

Brownlee, W. Elliot. "Household Values, Women's Work, and Economic Growth, 1800–1923," *Journal of Economic History* 39 (March 1979): 199–209.

Carlisle, Marcia. "Disorderly City, Disorderly Women: Prostitution in Ante-Bellum Philadelphia," *Pennsylvania Magazine of History and Biography* 110 (October 1986): 549–68.

Clifford, Deborah Pickman. *Crusader for Freedom: A Life of Lydia Maria Child.* Boston: Beacon Press, 1992.

Cott, Nancy F. *The Bonds of Womanhood: "Woman's Sphere" in New England, 1780–1835.* New Haven, CT: Yale University Press, 1977.

Coultrap-McQuin, Susan. *Doing Literary Business: American Women Writers in the Nineteenth Century.* Chapel Hill: University of North Carolina Press, 1990.

Curry, J. K. "Petticoat Governments: Early Women Theatre Managers in the United States," *Journal of American Drama and Theatre* 6 (Winter 1994): 13-39.

—. *Nineteenth-Century American Women Theatre Managers.* Westport, CT: Greenwood, 1994.

Dewhurst, C. Kurt, Betty MacDowell, and Marsha MacDowell. *Artists in Aprons: Folk Art by American Women.* New York: E. P. Dutton, 1979.

Dublin, Thomas. *Women at Work: The Transformation of Work and Community in Lowell, Massachusetts, 1826–1860.* New York: Columbia University Press, 1979.

—. *Farm to Factory: The Mill Experience and Women's Lives in New England, 1830–1860.* New York: Columbia University Press, 1981.

—. *Transforming Women's Work: New England Lives in the Industrial Revolution.* Ithaca, NY: Cornell University Press, 1994.

Dudden, Faye E. *Serving Women: Household Service in Nineteenth-Century America.* Middletown, CT: Wesleyan University Press, 1983.

Epstein, Barbara Leslie. *The Politics of Domesticity: Women, Evangelism, and Temperance in Nineteenth-Century America.* Middletown, CT: Wesleyan University Press, 1981.

Foner, Philip S., and Josephine F. Pacheco. *Three Who Dared: Prudence Crandall, Margaret Douglass, Myrtilla Miner-Champions of Antebellum Black Education.* Westport, CT: Greenwood Press, 1984.

Friedman, Jean E., William G. Shade, and Mary Jane Capozzoli. *Our American Sisters: Women in American Life and Thought.* 4th ed. Lexington, MA: D.C. Heath & Co., 1987. Chapters 6–7.

Golden, Claudia. "The Economic Status of Women in the Early Republic: Quantitative Evidence," *Journal of Interdisciplinary History* 16 (Winter 1986): 375–404.

Gordon, Jean. "Early American Women Artists and the Social Context in Which They Worked," *American Quarterly* 30 (Spring 1978): 54–69.

Gordon, Linda. "The Long Struggle for Reproductive Rights," *Radical America* 15 (Spring 1981): 74–88.

Handler, Bonnie. "Prudence Crandall and Her School for Young Ladies and Little Misses of Color," *Vitae Scholasticae* 5 (Spring/Fall 1986): 199–210.

Hardesty, Nancy A. *Women Called to Witness: Evangelical Feminism in the 19th Century.* Nashville: Abingdon Press, 1984.

Harley, Sharon. "Northern Black Female Workers: Jacksonian Era," 5–16, in *The Afro-American Woman: Struggles and Images,* edited by Sharon Harley and Rosalyn Terborg-Penn. Port Washington, NY: Kennikat Press, 1978.

Hoffert, Sylvia D. *Private Matters: American Attitudes Toward Child-bearing and Infant Nurture in the Urban North, 1800–1860.* Champaign-Urbana: University of Illinois Press, 1988.

Jensen, Joan M., and Sue Davidson, eds. *A Needle, a Bobbin, a Strike: Women Needleworkers in America.* Philadelphia: Temple University Press, 1984.

Karcher, Carolyn L. *The First Woman in the Republic: A Cultural Biography of Lydia Maria Child.* Durham, NC: Duke University Press, 1994.

Kessler-Harris, Alice. *Out to Work: A History of Wage-Earning Women in the United States.* New York: Oxford University Press, 1982.

—. *A Woman's Wage: Historical Meanings and Social Consequences.* Lexington: University of Kentucky Press, 1994.

Lazerow, Jama. "Religion and the New England Mill Girl: A New Perspective on an Old Theme," *New England Quarterly* 60 (September 1987): 429–53.

Leavitt, Judith Walzer. "Under the Shadow of Maternity: American Women's Responses to Death and Debility Fears in Nineteenth-Century Childbirth," *Feminist Studies* 12 (Spring 1986): 129–54.

Lerner, Gerda. "The Lady and the Mill Girl: Changes in the Status of Women in the Age of Jackson," *American Studies* 10 (Spring 1969): 5–15.

McCall, Laura. "With All the Wild, Trembling, Rapturous Feelings of a Lover: Men, Women, and Sexuality in American Literautre, 1820–1860," *Journal of the Early Republic* 14 (Spring 1994): 71-90.

Okker, Patricia. *Our Sister Editors: Sarah J. Hale and the Tradition of Nineteenth-Century American Women Editors.* Athens: University of Georgia Press, 1995.

Osterud, Nancy Grey. *Bonds of Community: The Lives of Farm Women in Nineteenth-Century New York.* Ithaca, NY: Cornell University Press, 1991.

Premo, Terri L. *Winter Friends: Women Growing Old in the New Republic, 1785–1835.* Champaign-Urbana: University of Illinois Press, 1990.

Scott, Ernest L., Jr. "Sarah Josepha Hale's New Hampshire Years, 1788–1828," *Historical New Hampshire* 49 (Summer 1994): 59-96.

Sklar, Kathryn Kish, and Thomas Dublin. *Women and Power in American History: A Reader.* Vol. I. Englewood Cliffs, NJ: Prentice-Hall, Inc., 1991. Parts 7–15.

Stansell, Christine. *City of Women: Sex and Class in New York, 1789–1860.* New York: Alfred A. Knopf, 1986.

Suitor, J. Jill. "Husbands' Participation in Childbirth: A Nineteenth-Century Phenomenon," *Journal of Family History* 6 (Fall 1981): 278–93.

Van de Watering, Maxine. "The Popular Concept of 'Home' in Nineteenth-Century America," *Journal of American Studies* 18 (April 1984): 5–28.

Welter, Barbara. *Dimity Convictions: The American Woman in the Nineteenth Century.* Athens: Ohio University Press, 1976.

Wilson, Carol. *Freedom at Risk: The Kidnapping of Free Blacks in America, 1780–1865.* New York: W. W. Norton & Co., 1994.

Woloch, Nancy. *Women and the American Experience.* New York: Alfred A. Knopf, 1986. Chapters 5–6.

Women in the West

Blackwood, Evelyn, "Sexuality and Gender in Certain Native American Tribes: The Case of Cross-Gender Females," *Signs* 10 (Autumn 1984): 27–42.

Bradley, Martha Sonntag. "'Seizing Sacred Space': Women's Engagement in Early Mormonism," *Dialogue: A Journal of Mormon Thought* 27 (Summer 1994): 57–70.

Cashin, Joan. *A Family Venture: Men and Women on the Southern Frontier.* New York: Oxford University Press, 1991.

——. "Black Families in the Old Northwest," *Journal of the Early Republic* 15 (Fall 1995): 449–75.

del Castillo, Richard G. "Neither Activists Nor Victims: Mexican Women's Historical Discourse: The Case of San Diego, 1820–1850," *California History* 74 (Fall 1995): 230–243, 355–57.

Craver, Rebecca McDowell. *The Impact of Intimacy: Mexican-White Intermarriage in New Mexico, 1821–1846.* El Paso: Texas Western Press, 1982.

Gutiérrez, Ramón. "Honor, Ideology, Marriage Negotiation, and Class-Gender Domination in New Mexico, 1690–1846," *Latin American Perspectives* 12 (Winter 1985): 81–104.

——. *When Jesus Came, the Corn Mothers Went Away: Marriage, Sexuality, and Power in New Mexico, 1500–1846.* Stanford, CA: Stanford University Press, 1991.

Holland-Braund, Kathryn E. "Guardians of Tradition and Handmaidens to Change: Women's Roles in Creek Economic and Social Life During the Eighteenth Century," *American Indian Quarterly* 14 (1990): 311–44.

Jeffrey, Julie Roy. *Converting the West: A Biography of Narcissa Whitman.* Norman: University of Oklahoma Press, 1991.

Jensen, Joan M., and Darlis A. Miller. "The Gentle Tamers Revisited: New Approaches to the History of Women in the American West," *Pacific Historical Review* 49 (May 1980): 173–214.

Katz, William Loren. *Black Women of the Old West.* New York: Atheneum Books, 1995.

Kaufman, Polly Welts. *Women Teachers on the Frontier.* New Haven, CT: Yale University Press, 1984.

Kolodny, Annette. *The Land Before Her: Fantasy and Experience of the American Frontiers, 1630–1860.* Chapel Hill: University of North Carolina Press, 1984.

Langum, David J. *Law and Community on the Mexican California Frontier: White-American Expatriates and the Clash of Legal Traditions, 1821–1846.* Norman: University of Oklahoma Press, 1987.

Lecompte, Janet. "The Independent Women of Hispanic New Mexico, 1821–1846," *Western Historical Quarterly* 12 (January 1981): 17–35.

Lothrop, Gloria Ricci. "Westering Women and the Ladies of Los Angeles: Sisters Under the Skin?" *Californians,* 12 (1995): 12-23.

Maestas, José Griego, and Rodolfo Anaya. *Cuentos: Tales from the Hispanic Southwest.* Santa Fe: Museum of New Mexico Press, 1980.

Malone, Ann Patton. *Women on the Texas Frontier: A Cross-Cultural Perspective.* El Paso: Texas Western Press, 1983.

Marín, Christine N. *The Chicano Experience in Arizona.* Tempe: University Libraries, Arizona State University, 1991.

Miranda, Gloria E. "Hispano-Mexican Childbearing Practices in Pre-American Santa Barbara," *Southern California Historical Quarterly* 65 (Winter 1983): 307–20.

Myres, Sandra L. *Westering Women and the Frontier Experience, 1800–1915.* Albuquerque: University of New Mexico Press, 1982.

——. "Mexican Americans and Westering Whites: A Feminine Perspective," *New Mexico Historical Review* 57 (October 1982): 317–33.

Perdue, Theda. "Cherokee Women and the Trail of Tears," *Journal of Women's History* 1 (Spring 1989): 14–30.

Spector, Janet D. *What This Awl Means: Feminist Archaeology at a Wahpeton Dakota Village.* St. Paul: Minnesota Historical Society Press, 1993.

Trulio, Beverly. "White-American Attitudes Toward New Mexican Women," *Journal of the West* 12 (April 1973): 229–39.

Winegarten, Ruthe. *Black Texas Women: 150 Years of Trial and Triumph.* Austin: University of Texas Press, 1995.

Images
and Images
and Images
and Realities
Realities
Realities

Ætatis suæ 21. Aº. 1616.

Top: Pocahontas,
after the 1616
engraving by Simon
van de Passe.

Bottom: A Spanish
illustration of the
"heathens" who
came to the Jesuit
missions near the
modern Arizona-
Mexico border in
the early eighteenth
century.

155

Top: Mary Gibson
Tilghman and sons,
1789.

Bottom: Batting
cotton.

Top: Phillis
Wheatley (ca. 1753–
1784), poet and first
African American
published author.

Bottom: *The Market
Plaza*, by Thomas
Allen.

The Wife, 1831.

The working women of Lynne, Massachusetts, protest, early 1840s.

Left: *"Madonna of the Prairie,"* painting by W. H. D. Koerner, 1921.

Right: Ma-ke and Kun-zan-ya, St. Louis, 1848.

Bottom: Harriet Tubman.

160

Right: Engraving from *Godey's Lady's Book*, 1845, features a number of achievement-oriented women, including several popular authors.

Below: Sarah Josepha Hale, editor of *Godey's Lady's Book*.

Above: A nineteenth-
century New England
schoolroom, painting
by C. Bosworth.

Below: Sojourner Truth
(ca. 1797–1883),
abolitionist.

162

Left: The water carri-
ers, ca. 1880.

Below: Southern
women, photographed
around 1860.

Right: Indian woman
with baby.

Below: Pawnee Indian
Wind Lodge, ca.
1868–1870.

Above: Apache camp, ca. 1885.

Bottom: "Chicago Joe," Mary Josephine Welch Hensley, who established the Red Light Saloon in Montana before the state outlawed dance halls.

Above: Lithograph of a
nineteenth-century revival
meeting after a painting by
A. Rider.

Below: Dancing girl, Virginia
City, Nevada.

Above: Hunting along
the Red River, 1870s.

Below: Annie Oakley,
early publicity photo.

Above left: Wedding picture,
William and Anna Belle
Steintemp, 1881.

Above right: Wedding
portrait, Mr. and Mrs. James
Sullivan, ca., 1870.

Bottom: Portrait of Old
Crow and his wife, 1880.

168

Former slave, Tillie Brackenridge, in San Antonio, ca. 1900.

Left: Na-tu-ende,
Apache, ca. 1883.

Below: Mormon
settlers, Arizona,
ca.1885.

170

Right: Dr. Mary
Walker, ca. 1865.

Below: American
tennis club, ca.1887.

4

"Moral" Women Reshaping
American Life and Values

1837 to 1861

The United States fell on hard times during the late 1830s. The Panic of 1837 brought an abrupt halt to the nation's economic boom. During the lean years that followed the depression, many Americans questioned the popular and widespread belief that the United States was the promised land. Critics pointed out that, from the economic structure to the political system, American institutions demanded reshaping. Others argued that many aspects of American peoples' lives also clearly required revision.

Consequently, during the 1840s and 1850s the term "reform" became common currency among men and women. Especially in the North, white and free black women of the middle and upper classes declared themselves ready to help their country, as well as to improve women's status. Female writers, speakers, and reformers explored America's problems from every angle and suggested scores of changes. Gradually, women dedicated to the idea of improving the American nation argued that destroying slavery was of primary importance.

Such women had hundreds of other ideas as well, ranging from prison reform to a betterment of their own rights. In 1848, the first woman's rights meeting convened in New York. Although it garnered more criticism than compliments, by the end of the 1850s, gender expectations would be well shaken and the landscape set for future quakes. In the meantime, problems in need of resolution seemed innumerable.

Women in the South

Black Slave Women

Even though African slavery had started as an economically feasible way of obtaining sufficient workers for the American colonies, by the 1840s and 1850s the institution had turned into one characterized by meanness, rigidity, and racist assumptions. Fear was rampant, especially in the antebellum (pre–Civil War) South. Not only did slaves fear their masters and mistresses, but white slave owners lived in a high state of

172

anxiety regarding slave rebellions. In addition, white husbands and fathers drove themselves into a frenzy worrying about black men raping
their wives and daughters. Consequently, even though female slaves
had no legal recourse against rape, southern states regularly added new
laws protecting white women.

Obviously, antebellum slavery, a volatile system that could ignite into
a blaze at any time, cried out for reform. Everything about slavery con-
tradicted the ideals of freedom and democracy worshiped in the United
States. For most black women, slavery meant hard work on the South's
larger farms and plantations. Such women seldom had the right to
choose their mates or limit the number of children they bore. They had
no control over their bodies for sexual or breeding purposes. Even
though they could not desert abusive husbands, they could be torn from
loving husbands through sale. And, threat of physical punishment could
force them to accept a new spouse after the sale or death of a mate in
order to keep producing children.

One of the few considerations slave women received on some plantations was an occasional lightened workload while pregnant. One Virginia planter warned his overseers that "breeding wenches you must be
Kind and Indulgent to, and not force them when with child upon any
service or hardship that will be injurious to them." When not pregnant,
however, slave women were expected to maintain an exhausting work
schedule.

Despite the prevalent division of labor along gender lines, many
owners expected slave women to take part in all necessary tasks from
plowing to building fences. In 1853, an observer in South Carolina saw
male and female slaves carrying manure containers on their heads to
fields where they applied it by hand to the earth around cotton plants.
In North Carolina, he observed women hoeing, shoveling, and cutting
down trees to create roadbeds. Slave women were sometimes hired out
to cotton and woolen mills, sugar refineries, and tobacco factories. In
1860, about five thousand slave women were so employed.

Only about 5 percent of slave women attained the relatively privi-
leged status of house servant, serving as cooks, personal attendants,
nursemaids, and wet nurses. Aged slave women worked hard at such
tasks as sewing, weaving, spinning, canning, and caring for babies and
young children whose mothers were in the fields. In addition, these
aged "grannies" often served as nurses and midwives.

Slave women frequently rebelled against their heavy workloads.
"She'd git stubborn like a mule and quit," one overseer complained. Another slave woman might strike an overseer across his head with her
hoe or run away into the woods to hide as a "truant." One Florida
woman even chopped her overseer to death after a reprimand. Rather
than commit such violence, some women became concubines and mistresses to escape heavy labor. Others would "sham," for example, claim-

ing aches and disabilities due to their menstrual cycle or pregnancy. Another more subtle form of rebellion involved slave women's adherence to traditional divisions of labor within their own quarters. By adhering to a small bit of true womanhood through the customary performance of the roles of wife and mother, slave women mocked their owners, who treated them as pseudo-men and beasts of burden. In addition, by acting as the force that held the black family together in the face of daily adversity or that formed new kinship ties in times of crisis, slave women defied owners' casual attitudes toward the institutions of marriage and family among slaves. In preserving their families from the dehumanizing aspects of slavery, black women engaged in the ultimate revolt against the system.

Yet others fought the system by seeking education. Although "black codes" forbid the educating of slaves, secret schools existed in many areas. Milla Granson of Natchez, Mississippi, for example, learned to read and write from her owners' children and then taught hundreds of other slaves late at night in what they called Milla's Midnight School. Another woman opened a secret school in Savannah, Georgia, which she operated undiscovered for twenty-five years.

By 1860, the population of the South included 7,033,973 whites, 3,838,765 slaves, and 258,000 free blacks, with slaves at the bottom of the scale in every way. Slave women living on certain plantations might find their lot softened by an owner who allowed their bondspeople "frolics," which included dancing and playing courting games, or provided material goods that raised their slaves' standard of living slightly above the average. Most slave women, however, had to take matters into their own hands. A prime example was Harriet Brent Jacobs, who told her story, *Incidents in the Life of a Slave Girl,* under the pen name Linda Brent. She told a tale of cruelty and licentiousness. Edited and published by abolitionist Lydia Maria Child in 1861, the book included Jacobs's statement regarding her owner: "I was his property; that I must be subject to his will in all things."

Rather than being weakened by slavery and its many restrictions, slave women often exhibited a huge amount of personal will and agency in achieving their goals. The very rigidity of slavery inspired some women to resist barriers by developing a measure of autonomy and power. Still, despite slave women's exercise of personal agency within slavery, the system demanded reform from the outside.

Free Black Women

Among the South's free women of color, the same type of strength prevailed. Often, these women were of mixed racial backgrounds. They either had some skills or had received some education. A few held property, including slaves. Most free black women lived in towns and cities where they worked at a variety of jobs or ran businesses, especially boardinghouses. Consequently, virtually all southern cities included a number of free blacks in their populations. In Mississippi, for example, such cities as Vicksburg and Natchez had black communities. New Orleans, however, had the largest number of free black women in the South.

Often, free women of color tried to help those who had less. As a result, benevolent organizations appeared in many southern cities and towns during the 1850s. These groups dedicated their efforts to providing relief—or charity—for people in need. For instance, in New Orleans, the Colored Female Benevolent Society helped the needy and gave its members insurance benefits. Such groups also provided an important source of support and female networks for the South's free black women.

Because by this time white southerners had established rules regulating all black people in the South, free African American women found their opportunities more restricted than in earlier eras. Too often, they saw their legal rights shrinking. Apparently, southerners' fear of enslaved blacks spilled over to mistrust of free blacks as well. With the South's free women of color caught in such a bind, help came from a newly energized source.

White Southern Women

Logically, one might think that white women would want to come to the aid of their black counterparts. In a slave society, however, racism frequently proved stronger than sisterhood. Some white women acted as harshly toward their bondspeople as any overseer personally beating certain slaves and ordering harsh punishments for others. Fortunately, this response did not characterize all white women in the antebellum South.

In the decades before the Civil War a significant number of white women felt outrage at the inhumanity of slavery that they saw all around them. And white southern women had good reasons to oppose slavery. They lived with the constant dread of a slave revolt, which might end with their own deaths as well as those of their children. White women also disliked their own heavy workloads in supervising and training enslaved dependents. They experienced guilt about oppressing African Americans, and most of them deeply resented their husbands' sexual liaisons with slave women.

Yet many southern women's social status and financial security rested on the continuation of the slave system. Economic dependence on planter fathers and husbands hedged in southern ladies, who seldom dared to voice antislavery sentiments for fear of reprisal or abandonment. In 1854, a male social theorist explained that "Women, like children, have but one right, and that is the right to protection . . . if she be obedient, she stands little danger of maltreatment."

Plantation mistresses usually confided their thoughts to their diaries rather than to spouses and friends. Frances Kemble, a distinguished English actress who married Georgia planter Pierce Butler in 1834, recorded her emotions in her diary during the winter of 1838–1839, when she lived in the big house of Butler's Sea Island plantation. When she later divorced Butler and released her diary under the title *Journal of Residence on a Georgian Plantation* (1863), Kemble's jottings divulged feelings that other women shared before the war but were more hesitant to express. Of her time on a plantation, Kemble wrote: "It appears to me that the principal hardships fall to the lot of the [slave] women." Kemble's journal reveals that during her time as mistress of the plantation slave women continually appealed to her to lighten their work, soften their punishments, and extend their time of rest after childbirth to the customary four weeks. Kemble felt overwhelmed by the women's stories, especially one involving a woman who had borne sixteen children, fourteen of whom were dead. According to the woman's own words, she had been lashed by "a man with a cowhide [who] stands and stripes" slaves. Kemble added, "and when I said: Did they do that to you when you were with child? she simply replied: Yes, missis." Incensed, Kemble wrote, "to all this I listen—I an Englishwoman, the wife of the man who owns these wretches, and I cannot say: That thing shall not be done again."

When other white women's diaries finally came to light they contained similar passion. In 1858, another Georgia woman had recorded her conviction that "Southern Women are all at heart abolitionists" in her journal. She added that "the institution of slavery degrades the white man more than the Negro. . . . The happiness of homes is destroyed but what is to be done?" Plantation mistress Mary Boykin Chestnut, whose husband later ranked high in the Confederate government, concurred; versions of her extensive diaries published in 1905 and 1981 indicate that numerous southern women condemned the slave system.

Besides slavery, another problem for elite southern white women was the growing complexity of their lives. Compared to northern middle- and upper-class women, southern women had less education, married earlier, and bore more children. Southern women lived in more rural areas, managed complicated households of whites and blacks, and died younger than northern women of the elite classes. Despite these drawbacks, most plantation women were strong and hard working.

In addition to their domestic responsibilities, women had to learn the business side of family plantations. When husbands left for business or political reasons, or died, wives took over the running of plantations. One Alabama widow managed her deceased husband's plantation for eighteen years, including hiring out her slaves and directing the day-to-day operations of a cotton farm. To her credit, she kept the plantation financially stable and raised her children to adulthood.

While such women appeared to support the pre–Civil War patriarchal system, most only tolerated it, straining against its dictates whenever possible. Just as they were abolitionists at heart, many antebellum southern women were what would today be called feminists. Rather than forming abolitionist and woman's rights groups, which would have brought severe criticism down on their heads, such women supported charitable associations. In Charleston alone, women organized numerous societies, including the Ladies Benevolent Society and the Juvenile Industry Society.

Younger women seemed more assertive. Girls of the planter class used the widespread belief in female virtue to gain for themselves improved educational opportunities. Daughters assured fathers that educating young women would help to maintain the "tone" of the planter class. Those fathers who bought the argument agreed to establish female academies or to send their daughters to existing southern schools.

Neither daughters nor fathers, however, had a clear idea of how women should be educated. While planter-class women certainly had to be raised as ladies, the only existing model for establishing women's academies and seminaries was that of boys' schools. Borrowing from existing curriculums, girls' schools gradually moved away from the "female accomplishments," including playing the piano and doing fancy embroidery work, toward more "masculine" subjects as English and mathematics. In addition, the study of logic and science were also considered suitable for young women, who needed to learn mental discipline. Botany was an especially common offering in women's schools. After all, a wife and mother could easily continue to pursue this subject in her morning-room or parlor.

By the 1850s, most southern educators agreed that women had the ability to learn. Those Protestant clergymen and young northern teachers who had gone south to teach hoped that expanded course offerings would not only develop a woman's mind, but help define her moral values. Still, the well-bred southern woman had to possess a working knowledge of the female accomplishments, including speaking French and the writing of a proper letter. It was also important that she develop the ability to organize gracious social functions. Music education was especially attractive because a woman musician could provide in-home entertainment for years to come. Accordingly, music lessons required an additional fee. Regardless of the scope of the curriculum offered, female students seemed to cherish their opportunity to gain a better education. Nonetheless, most recognized that intellectual development would take a back seat to marriage, casting them into roles much like those that their mothers filled.

The growing number of southern white women who remained single, however, believed they that enjoyed more liberty than their married sisters did. Although their families despaired and people called single women "old maids" and "spinsters," many wrote in their journals about the wonderful independence they enjoyed. They maintained that being single was not as lonely as stereotypes portrayed it. Rather, the absence of a mate allowed women to develop their minds and to administer their estates as they wished.

Among the middle and lower classes in the South, a different situation existed. Most white women of these groups actively engaged in agricultural work. On small tobacco, cotton, and subsistence farms, women regularly joined men in planting, weeding, and harvesting crops. In addition, women transformed the raw materials of the fields into finished goods and continued to provide cash income through the sale of their surplus products.

Women of the yeomanry (small landowners) played an important economic role in their families and frequently participated in the making of financial decisions. A significant number of yeoman-class women worked outside the home, especially as teachers. These women usually chose their own mates and sometimes determined the number of children they would bear. Some abandoned abusive, negligent, or lazy husbands, while others bore children out of wedlock and headed their own households.

Such women were important forces who, along with women of the planter class, challenged restrictive norms when and where they could during the 1840s and 1850s. Southern women gained property rights in several states during the 1850s, and common practice often protected women's ownership of land, looms, cattle, and furniture. Meanwhile, a rise in southern women's activism laid the basis for an eventual women's rights movement in the South. Even though southern white women found ways to develop a sense of self and recognized their own contributions to society, most hoped for far more in the way of meaningful reform and civil rights.

Divorce

While antebellum southern divorce courts offered hope to white women trapped in bad marriages, no courts would hear the pleas of African American petitioners. Rather, black southerners sought divorces through family courts, public hearings in the slave quarters, or a slave owner's verbal decree. Although black families tended to be stable, some unions broke down. As with white couples, black couples experienced such marital ills as domestic violence. Technically, black spouses in such troubled marriages could divorce at will, since slaves were not married according to white law. But since most slave couples felt very much married according to custom, spouses who had decided to separate often wanted some event to mark the change in their marital states.

Divorce courts were for white divorce seekers, who appeared before judges in growing numbers. Because southern women functioned in a conservative agrarian society, however, they were not as effective in breaking down male suspicions regarding female divorce petitioners as were their northern counterparts, who had the advantage of operating in an industrial, relatively progressive world. Southern women soon learned that if they acted docile and submissive while presenting their claims that adulterous, drunken, abusive, neglectful, or felonious husbands had wronged them, they were likely to gain a judge's sympathy. Thus, they stood a chance of receiving awards of marital property and alimony, as well as control of their children.

Throughout the South, women's divorce petitions revealed a significant amount of domestic abuse. After all, everything from advice books to ballads told men to act in forceful ways in personal relationships. To be masculine was to be decisive and persistent. Although southern men were advised to keep their strong passions in check, some attempted to control their wives and families through physical action. Ideas regarding southern chivalry, as well as social class, dictated what forms of brutality husbands might use on their wives, but the patriarchal system approved of a certain amount of "correction" by husbands. Consequently, even middle- and upper-class women told divorce courts about beatings that had turned them black-and-blue. One woman claimed that her bone corset stays saved her life by stopping the knife blade with which her husband attacked her.

Such dramatic tales often influenced southern judges to grant divorces to more women than men. For example, between 1800 and 1860 twenty-one women in Alabama sued for divorce as opposed to seven men. Eleven of the disgruntled wives obtained final decrees, while only two of the husbands did so. In Louisiana, sixteen wives sought divorces as compared to six husbands. Seven of these women secured divorces, while only one man was able to do so.

Although these divorce figures are low compared to modern statistics, they indicated that, for a number of women, southern patriarchy was not a fulfilling, or safe, way of life.

Women in the North

The Argument for Women as Moral Guardians

At the same time—the late 1830s, 1840s, and 1850s—thousands of women enlarged their domestic roles to include acting as moral guardians, first for their families and next for their larger communities. The belief in women as moral guardians was an outgrowth of years of discussing and preaching the tenets of Republican Womanhood, domesticity, and true womanhood. If women were indeed more virtuous than men were, the thinking went, then women should act as the moral stewards not only of men and children but of all things that affected family welfare.

Even though the concept of women as society's moral keepers gained support in the South and the West, it especially caught hold among the North's white and free black women of the middle and upper classes. These northern women were not restricted in the same ways as southern women, and, unlike western women, they did not have to devote their energies to settling frontiers. Relatively speaking, they enjoyed a greater measure of freedom and leisure time. And because most of them lived in urban areas, they were exposed daily to such societal ills as inadequate and overcrowded housing, a rising crime rate, overflowing prisons, prostitution, and public drunkenness.

Consequently, these women's burgeoning sense of moral stewardship—and confidence in their own abilities—gradually turned the majority of them into reformers. In fact, by the late 1850s, the willingness to improve American society became a deep-seated value of elite women in the North, especially in New England and New York state.

Women learned about their innate morality from many sources, ranging from sermons to books. In addition, a variety of women's literature continued to preach that women must do everything they could to preserve the moral tone of spouses and children in particular, as well as of American citizens in general. In *Godey's Lady's Book,* editor Sarah Josepha Hale repeatedly emphasized that because men had to engage in necessary, and often unethical, business practices and public affairs, women acted as the moral keepers of home and family. In 1847, Hale expressed this principle in verse: "He must work—the world subduing/ Till it blooms like Eden bright/She must watch—his faith renewing/ From her urn of Eden light."

At the same time that Hale maintained that women wielded great influence in the home, she subtly enlarged the domestic sphere to take in the school room, the Sunday school, and public parks. Some of Hale's favorite causes were improved female education and simplified clothing styles that would afford women increased physical mobility. She argued for "moral" women as teachers of the young, as authors of "moral" literature and poetry, as missionaries, and as medical practitioners. Her approach to widening women's sphere was so nonthreatening that generations of American readers of all ages revered both Hale and *Godey's Lady's Book.*

Many other editors and writers offered their interpretations and perspectives regarding the concept of the moral American woman. Legions of women writers wrote books that became immediate bestsellers during the late 1830s, 1840s, and 1850s but have since languished on library shelves. Domestic novels, as they were called because of their homey themes, frequently went through multiple and worldwide editions.

In part, such books achieved popularity among women because they presented women as virtuous, strong beings capable of resolving any situation they confronted. Caroline Lee Hentz was one the era's most prominent women writers. During the late 1830s, Hentz, with Hale's encouragement, published her first stories in *Godey's*. Because of her husband's lack of business success, Hentz soon turned to writing full time to support her family. By the 1850s, Hentz gained renown for such novels as *Ernest Linwood* (1856). While she seemed to uphold all the usual ideals associated with women's domestic sphere, Hentz's story lines revolved around decisive, all-suffering female heroines who—much like Hentz herself—rescued ill, mindless, or morally crippled men. Understandably, female readers felt comfortable with Hentz's prose, for it did not remove women from their supposed realm—the home. Also, Hentz's strong, highly moral female characters always triumphed in the end.

Novelist Lydia B. Sigourney also followed a literary career due to the decline of her husband's business. Known as "the Sweet Singer of Hartford," Sigourney wrote for over half a century and produced more than fifty books. Like other domestic writers, Sigourney lauded the traditional virtues of home and family in such works as *Whispers to a Bride* (1850) and *The Daily Counsellor* (1859). Yet, in her own career and personal life, Sigourney rejected such themes. The lesson seemed to be that in times of need, women could, and should, do whatever was needed to save themselves, their men, their communities, or even their nations.

A contemporary of Hentz, E. D. E. N. Southworth, removed men from the scene entirely. In such novels as *The Deserted Wife* (1851) and *The Discarded Daughter* (1852), Southworth sent men off to war, the West, or in pursuit of pretty young women. The women the men left behind proved self-dependent, energetic, and capable of supporting themselves and their siblings or children, often achieving fame and fortune in the process. When the guilt-ridden father, suitor, or husband returned, his generous daughter, fiancé, or wife always forgave him. That men could not function without the strength and morality of women formed Southworth's overriding message.

Elizabeth Fries Lummis Ellet took a slightly different approach to women's roles. She reconstructed the history of women in a way that demonstrated that women had served as prominent nurturers and guardians of American democracy. Ellet argued that women fulfilled a variety of social functions, did jobs considered to be "men's work," and contributed significantly to the settlement of the frontier. Her best-known work, *The Women of the American Revolution,* which appeared in two volumes in 1848, went into its fourth printing by 1850.

Increasingly, women looking for examples of strong womanhood did not have to search very hard. They could simply turn to "morally improving" domestic literature, which presented subversive ideas in such a palatable form that few Americans questioned them.

Implications of the "Morality" Argument

At least on the surface, these and other wildly popular women writers preached all the fashionable beliefs regarding true womanhood. They idealized the customary view of the family and women's place, especially as moral guardians of home and family. When read closely, however, contradictory themes in the literature become apparent. Deep discontent riddled these authors' portrayals of domesticity. On the one hand, they characterized men as sinful, obsessed with a desire for wealth and social position, and in need of reform. On the other, they presented women characters as superior beings, responsible for families, and clearly capable of guarding society against evil.

This assignment of women as moral keepers had wide implications. For example, the moral guardian theory underwrote the argument that women had to gain an understanding of politics in order to influence male legislators wisely. Women rather than men must teach school to instill children with virtue. Women had a God-given mission to form charity organizations to exercise their goodness on behalf of the poor and destitute. In short, as morally superior beings, women must confront any corrupted social situation.

This line of thought made it easier for women to stay in their own "sphere," for that sphere was growing to include more of the everyday world. Although American cultural values still promoted such "male" qualities as aggressiveness, economic achievement, and shrewdness, American beliefs began to encompass such "female" values as flexibility, moral success, and lack of guile. This partial feminization of American cultural beliefs gave women a measure of potency and prestige, which many women seized and amplified.

By this time the reform of American ills was a crucial part of women's agenda. The logical extension of women's moral guardianship was that women had a mission to improve society. In reality, however, only well-bred women had the time and financial resources to pursue reform causes. Sometimes, white and black reformers worked together. On other occasions, white women shut black women out of their organizations. In addition, women of color often preferred to work in segregated groups because they wished to direct their energies toward such race-specific problems as abolishing slavery, educating free blacks, and providing health care for black urban children. Gradually, reformism drew in employed, poor, rural, immigrant, and other types of women, but, for the time being, female reformism rested largely in the hands of middle- and upper-class white and black women, who happily carried similar social class and religious values to other types of Americans.

Adding to women's zeal were the teachings of the Second Great Awakening, the religious revival movement that had swept westward from New York state beginning during the early nineteenth century. By the late 1830s and 1840s, Protestant ministers assured their listeners that they possessed free will and personal agency. Thus, dedicated individuals not only had the power to improve themselves, but American society as well. In a sense, such sermons held up Protestantism as a means of social change. Much as Protestant revivals altered a person's life, reform efforts based on Protestant beliefs could modify the entire United States for the better.

Between people like Sarah Josepha Hale proclaiming that "woman" was "God's appointed agent of morality" and ministers who reinforced the idea that moral women had a calling to fulfill, women could not ignore the point: they must become reformers. And in so doing, they need not even step too far from women's traditional roles, for they would exert a particularly feminine influence. As educational reformer Catharine Beecher put it, "Woman is to win every thing by peace and love."

Women first formed auxiliaries of men's church, reform, and other groups. From these experiences, women learned two lessons. The first was that men's organizations were unlikely to give women the right to vote or even speak. The second was that women could learn organizing and other skills from men, then move on to found female-only groups in which members could pursue reform in ways that suited their own ideas. Women were initially satisfied to bring about reform through female morality, while men operated in the less attractive world of politics, primarily voting and passing legislation.

Improved Female Education

Female reformers often started close to home. For instance, women's limited educational opportunities had long been of concern to reform-minded women. Because such women believed that better education would heighten their natural moral sense, they experimented with self-education. Those who could afford books and magazines not only read widely, but went far beyond the "domestic" literature that improved their skills as wives and mothers. Such women passed books from hand-to-hand, established circulating libraries, and founded reading clubs. Working outside formal institutions of learning, women often became learned, yet that was not enough to satisfy them.

Women tirelessly crusaded for "improved female education." As long as men dominated schools and colleges, they argued, women would never learn the skills they needed to advance. The questions of how much education women should have and just how they should use it had no easy answers, especially when conservatives continued to cling to customary beliefs regarding women. Widely quoted in the United States in this time were the words of the eighteenth-century French commentator Jean Jacques Rousseau:

> The whole education of women ought to be relative to men. To please them, to be useful to them, to make themselves loved and honored by them, to educate them when young, to care for them when grown, to counsel them, to console them, and to make life sweet and agreeable to them—these are the duties of women at all times, and what should be taught them from their infancy.

Hardly satisfied with this traditional ideal of women's education, beginning in the 1840s, reformer Catharine Beecher presented her own views regarding "proper" education for women. In addition to speaking and writing on behalf of improved education for women, Beecher argued that women teachers should be sent West to educate and morally improve Native peoples, children, and unprincipled men. Beecher also campaigned for the establishment of teacher-training, or normal, schools in western areas. She also personally organized missionary societies, which recruited and sent female teachers westward, and founded a number of women's schools, including the Dubuque Female Seminary (Iowa) and the Milwaukee Female College (Wisconsin), in the West.

Despite her active and vigorous crusades on women's behalf, however, Beecher never strayed from her conviction that women were by nature domestic creatures. Her schools trained women to work as teachers before marriage and to serve as homemakers afterward. Because she believed that such "higher" subjects as mathematics and philosophy would weaken the female constitution and interfere with a woman's ability to bear children, Beecher's curriculum stressed health, home economics, and English. In her many books, including the popular *Treatise on Domestic Economy* (1841), Beecher offered household hints and recipes, always emphasizing that domesticity was an honorable and worthy profession.

Another prominent female educator of the era, Almira Lincoln Phelps, took a more progressive position. She wanted to help women escape the restrictions of women's sphere. In 1841, Phelps and her attorney husband took charge of the Patapsco Female Institute in Baltimore. Phelps included such subjects as science in the institute's curriculum and wrote several botany textbooks. She became the second woman admitted to the American Association for the Advancement of Science. After her husband's death in 1849, Phelps ran the school by herself until her retirement at sixty-three.

Beecher and Phelps diverged in many ways, but both educators agreed that female students should act appropriately at all times. For instance, they and other women instructors offered rules regarding attachments that students formed among themselves. Female students often paired off and showed affection for one another by holding hands and sending notes. At Patapsco and elsewhere these young women were advised not to hold hands, put their arms around each other's shoulders, or sit too closely to each other. Recently, historians have wrestled with the thorny question of whether such alliances were sexual. The consensus is that schoolgirl "romances" were not lesbian in nature, yet they were vexing to such teachers as Beecher and Phelps.

Another goal of female educators was to get students to exercise. They counseled young women to abandon stays, corsets, and other fashionable but unhealthy accessories. Arguing that the performance of women's roles demanded a robust physical condition, including stamina and endurance, Beecher and Phelps designed exercise programs for their students, regularly prescribing activities to improve posture, gracefulness, and general good health.

Still, these and other reformers of the day believed that women's bodies could sustain only a limited amount of moderate exercise. Women, for example, were encouraged to ride horses using a sidesaddle and wearing an appropriate riding habit. *Godey's Lady's Book* stressed this idea, urging women always to preserve their feminine grace and delicacy while horseback riding. Racing and riding to the hounds were definitely frowned upon, but, by the 1850s, women began to compete in "female equestrian" events at county fairs.

Pedestrianism, or foot racing, constituted another acceptable sport for women during the 1840s and 1850s. In 1852, one American woman competed in a British race in which she covered five hundred miles. Most women's magazines, however, only recommended moderate walking and sedate dancing as acceptable exercises. They advised women to proceed with caution, for, as one counseled in 1858, when the body is "too much exercised, it is apt to produce ganglions on the ankle joints of delicate girls, as wind galls are produced on the legs of young horses who are too soon or too much worked."

Clearly, women reformers focused on white, middle- and upper-class women's education. Only a few concerned themselves with the education for other types of American women. A few reformers tried to help indigent and delinquent white women. The Lancaster (Pennsylvania) Industrial School for Girls offered moral instruction and vocational training for girls between the ages of seven and sixteen. The school also provided medical care, a temporary home, and an employment service.

A handful of other women tried to help educate free women of color, who especially understood the crucial importance of education. In 1837, the Society of Friends, or Quakers, established the Institute for Colored Youth in Philadelphia. Soon, the school became a center of African American education. Free black Grace Mapps taught at the school during its formative years and helped shape its curriculum. Later, Grace's daughter, Sarah Mapps Douglass, became a teacher and an administrator at the Institute. As a free woman of color in Philadelphia, Sarah was especially dedicated to training black public school teachers, who could, in turn, educate black children. In addition, Sarah insisted on teaching science to female students, even though science was thought "too difficult" for female minds.

Free black Fanny Jackson Coppin also joined the Institute. Coppin was born a slave in Washington, D. C., but her aunt purchased Coppin's freedom. Coppin began her education while working as a domestic servant in Newport, Rhode Island. Coppin first hired a tutor, then attended the segregated Newport schools. In 1859, she completed the teacher-training course at the Rhode Island State Normal School. In 1860, she enrolled in the only integrated college in the United States—Oberlin College in Ohio. After graduating, Coppin went to Philadelphia as principal of the Institute for Colored Youth. She was the first African American to hold such a position, which she used to introduce a teacher-training program and eventually industrial training as well. Coppin had such an impact on the school that it later was renamed Coppin State College in her honor.

Family Size

Still at issue was women's inability to control the number of children they bore. Clearly, many women desired to exercise control over their bodies and childbearing. In addition to marriage and motherhood, they wanted their lives to include other activities. At the same time, changes in the American economy, especially the rising cost of living, and urban overcrowding increasingly made large families less desirable.

A few outspoken women publicly advocated the practice of limiting family size, while others privately practiced abortion. By the 1840s, a dramatic rise in the abortion rate occurred, especially among married white women. These trends led to a demand for information regarding contraception. During the mid-1840s, women's rights' leaders issued a call for "Voluntary Motherhood," arguing that women who actively chose to bear children would be better mothers than those who were denied a say in the matter.

A decline in the white birth rate from an average of 7 children in 1800 to 5.4 in 1850 demonstrated women's willingness to use birth-control methods. Besides abortion, these included abstinence, coitus interruptus, pills, pessaries, and an improved rubber condom made possible by the 1843 discovery of the vulcanization of rubber. Regularly advertised were such products as "Preventive Powders" at $5 a package and a rubber diaphragm called a "Family Regulator, or Wife's Protector," at $5 each. Alternatively a woman might choose "Female Monthly Regulating Pills," supposedly abortifacients guaranteed to cure "all cases of suppression, irregularity, or stoppage of the mensus." Although religious and other leaders spoke against Voluntary Motherhood, no laws restricted the dispensing of such information or the providing of birth-control assistance to women.

Medicine

A related issue was the improvement of obstetrical and gynecologic care. The pioneer in medical reform was Elizabeth Blackwell. In 1847, as a twenty-six-year-old teacher in Kentucky, she decided to enroll in medical school and eventually treat women patients. Although Blackwell applied to numerous schools, twenty-nine of them rejected her. Only at New York's Geneva College did students and faculty vote to accept Blackwell's application. Unaware that the College intended to use Blackwell as proof that women were incapable of medical practice, Blackwell entered Geneva in November 1847. After some ridicule and an unsuccessful attempt to bar her from classes teaching human anatomy, Blackwell proved herself an exceptional student.

In 1849, Blackwell not only received her medical degree but graduated first in her class. She then served a residency as a student midwife in Paris. In 1850, St. Bartholomew's Hospital in London admitted her to its residency program, yet barred her from practicing gynecology and pediatrics. The following year, Blackwell returned to New York and shortly wrote to her sister Emily that "a blank wall of social and professional antagonism faces a woman physician and forms a situation of singular and painful loneliness, leaving her without support, respect, or professional counsel."

Despite such discrimination, in 1853 Blackwell opened a small clinic in New York City's slum district. In 1857, Blackwell incorporated the clinic as the New York Infirmary and College for Women. Composed largely of women, the institution's staff included Blackwell's sister Emily, whom Elizabeth had encouraged to pursue a medical degree. In 1854, Emily Blackwell received her degree from the medical school of Western Reserve University in Cleveland, Ohio. She joined Elizabeth in running the New York Infirmary and College for Women.

As more women entered medical practice during the 1850s, they often chose to treat women and children. Women differed from male doctors in their emphasis on holistic treatments and their sympathetic responses to women's pleas for information regarding contraception.

Near the end of the decade, in 1859, Blackwell lectured in England on medicine as a profession for women. The British Medical Register placed her name on its rolls and the very hospitals that had earlier refused to admit her now welcomed her. Eventually, Blackwell settled in England, her place of birth. Her sister Emily took over managing the New York Infirmary and College for Women. In 1871, Elizabeth founded the National Health Society and in 1875 began to lecture on gynecology. She introduced many other innovations and wrote a number of books before her death in 1910.

Women and Nature

Not all the issues that women tackled had as clear a connection to the "domestic sphere" as did education, childbearing, and medical care. For instance, women extended their efforts to include the natural environments that surrounded their homes.

From the colonial period on, women had shown an interest in the physical world. Some women became amateur botanists, who collected and classified plant specimens. Others sketched and catalogued different species of plants and animals. These activities were considered respectable because women usually pursued them within their own homes and gardens. During the 1830s and 1840s, for example, Orra White Hitchcock, the wife of the first state geologist of Massachusetts illustrated her husband's numerous publications. She went unacknowledged because she was a woman and an amateur.

During the 1840s and 1850s, women explored nature in other socially acceptable ways, including attending lyceum (public, adult education) lectures on scientific topics. Yet a significant number of Americans continued to believe that women's minds could not comprehend scientific knowledge. Many claimed that women were too weak and vulnerable to hike through the great outdoors. Supposedly, women felt safer and more comfortable within the walls of their homes. Besides, the physical landscape supposedly belong to men, ranging from explorers, soldiers, and farmers to railroad builders and mining magnates.

Women often resented such attitudes. Nor were they afraid of nature or disinterested in learning more about it. In fact, some women accused men of treating Mother Nature in a very unladylike fashion. In a search for wealth, too many men mishandled and even raped the environment. As the moral keepers of society, women railed at men's abusive treatment of nature. And as moral guardians, women felt the need to protect and conserve a far larger sphere than the purely domestic one.

In 1850, Susan Fenimore Cooper's *Rural Hours* not only established its author as the first female nature writer in America but urged women to expand their domestic spheres to include the outdoors. As the daughter of writer James Fenimore Cooper, Susan came from a well-established tradition of nature writing. Four years before the appearance of Henry David Thoreau's *Walden,* Cooper's *Rural Hours* became a widely read nature book.

At the same time that Cooper encouraged women to learn more about the physical world, she did not reject things domestic. Instead, she argued that nature provided a family's larger home. If nature was home, Cooper suggested, then the environment was part of women's domestic sphere. She argued that the preservation of nature was indeed a woman's issue. If women were moral and ethical stewards, then they clearly had the responsibility to exercise stewardship over the land.

Cooper even suggested legal and policy reforms. Here, she trod dangerously close to men's customary preserve, politics. Cooper advocated legislation and programs that would conserve nature's bounty rather than destroying it. "Thinning woods and not blasting them," she wrote, would constitute a positive step toward conserving the world that God had created. Not only did Cooper reproach men, she urged women to take interest in regulating and conserving nature's bounty.

Religious Changes

By initiating changes in their lives and in society, women who had been told to be quiet and passive found their voices. Like Cooper, some women spoke through books and essays. Thousands of others, however, joined organizations that offered women respect, notably Protestant churches and revival meetings.

Evangelical religious sects especially granted women a measure of importance through religious conversion, which established women as church members. Rather than being little more than obedient followers of authoritarian ministers, women had increased influence in church affairs. For instance, women could organize their own auxiliaries of men's missionary, tract, and Bible societies. And male ministers continued to feminize their sermons. In place of an emphasis on women's inherent evil as daughters of Eve, ministers now held out the hope of human perfectibility to women. Ministers assured women that, through religion, they could change themselves and others.

New and nontraditional sects also offered women opportunities. Several of them, notably Shakerism, Spiritualism, Christian Science, and Theosophy, believed in the equality of women and men. The Shakers, founded by "Mother" Ann Lee, even tried to free women from the handicaps of marriage and childcare by practicing celibacy. Moreover, such sects believed that women could fill roles in addition to those of wife and mother. They deemphasized the masculine nature of God and rejected the idea that ministers must be male

Consequently, women began to step *behind* the altar. In 1853, the Congregational Church in South Butler, New York, appointed as its pastor Antoinette Brown Blackwell. She had completed the theology program at Oberlin College in Ohio in 1850. Although her professors had allowed Antoinette Brown to preach, they refused to allow her to graduate or obtain a clerical license. In 1854, Brown resigned her position and became a Unitarian. Two years later, she married Dr. Elizabeth Blackwell's brother, Samuel. She devoted the rest of life to reform causes and to writing books, especially on aspects of science. Blackwell is regarded as the first female American minister.

Utopian Societies

Yet other women who wanted to improve American society, as well as their own roles, participated in Utopian societies. These were nonreligious, communal groups who tried to find a better system of labor and production than existed in the United States at the time. Typically, they supported the equality of women and men, thus attracting the support of women. For example, after Brook Farm was established outside of Boston in 1841, transcendentalist writer and social reformer Margaret Fuller (see below) helped plan the experiment although she did not live there.

Other female participants in the Brook Farm experiment pointed to the commune's many attractions. They claimed that performing domestic labor communally lightened their individual work. And when they performed heavy labor, they were paid at the same rate as were men. Women could vote on community matters and hold influential positions. Finally Brook Farm offered a stimulating intellectual atmosphere, reformism being the favorite topic of discussion. One young woman explained that, "The very air seemed to hold more exhilarating qualities than any I had ever breathed."

Other Utopian groups experimented with unconventional forms of marriage. Notably, Oneida, founded in upstate New York in 1848, practiced a complex form of communal marriage. Under this system, all members cohabited with each other and cared for the children as a group. The idea was to free women from life-long service to men. In addition, members "improved" themselves through "joint" sessions, in which everyone aired their feelings. Oneida lasted for four decades, far longer than other similar ventures. Oneida's most lasting contribution was the attractive and functional silverware its members designed and manufactured—which is still on the market today.

Such reform communities seemed strange and even uncivilized to outsiders. Some people wondered why, for instance, intellectual women and men who had enjoyed the advantages of Boston would go to Brook Farm, where they took part in farm chores and other menial work. After a while, some members of Brook Farm asked themselves the same question. Oneida sparked more emotional responses from outsiders, who opposed the community's "loose" sexual practices. Oneida's critics branded it a "free-love," and thus immoral organization.

Experimental utopian societies did, however, make an attempt to deal with the vexing questions of women's restricted roles and responsibilities. That outsiders reacted with such disdain to them was in some ways an indication that the time had not yet come for Americans to destroy the old model of the American woman.

Benevolent Societies

Meanwhile benevolent societies continued to expand during this era. Not only did the membership of such groups grow, but the organizations dedicated themselves to an unbelievably wide range of social problems. Although most organizations continued to maintain that women had domestic natures, they argued that women's sphere should be enlarged to include neighborhoods and communities. Middle- and upper-class free black women felt an especially strong need to help the poor and otherwise disadvantaged of their race. In New York, the African Dorcas Society provided clothing for poverty-stricken black school children. Among white women in New Jersey, the Newark Female Charitable Society provided assistance to needy whites of the community.

Gradually, white women discovered that their primary technique of "visiting" a needy individual or family and offering occasional help was not enough. Although needy people appreciated the food and clothing that reformers supplied on these visits, most did not seem anxious to read the Bibles that came with the food, or to absorb such middle-class values as cleanliness, hard work, and avoidance of strong drink that female reformers preached. Women soon realized that it was necessary to remove people from bad conditions, ranging from filth to starvation, and to teach them middle-class values, as well as marketable skills, if their "relief" was to prove meaningful. Consequently women turned more and more to establishing "homes" and other institutions in which to board and educate the needy.

The policy of such institutions was to help the "worthy poor," meaning women who went to church, kept their children clean, and had done nothing to invite their wretched conditions. Such homes featured programs that indoctrinated inmates with middle-class values and taught them marketable skills that would keep them from falling back into poverty. Reeducation, then, became central to the policies of charitable associations.

Frequently, such homes and asylums became complex, as well as influential, parts of their communities. These organizations included boards of directors, treasurers and other officers, as well as public relations programs. Generally, they sought incorporation by the state so that female executives could operate free of the restraints of coverture.

Nor could women leaders be criticized for acting in unladylike ways. Sarah Josepha Hale's Boston Seaman's Society was one example. Originally designed to help the bereft widows of seamen support themselves, the Seaman's Aid Society grew into a nonprofit business, vocational training program, school, and home. In nearby Rhode Island, the Providence Employment Society started out during the 1830s by extending help to exploited seamstresses. Because the members of the Providence organization wanted to provide a model, they soon established a small garment business that paid fair wages and provided good working conditions to their charges.

Black women also believed in the advantages of benevolent institutions, but because there were fewer of them, their resources were relatively limited. African American women proved themselves effective fund-raisers, however, especially through holding charity fairs, at which they sold clothing and craft items. From their efforts came such institutions as asylums for black orphans and work-training homes for poor black women. Meanwhile, the Union Anti-Slavery Sewing Society formed in Rochester, New York, to make and sell items at fund-raising fairs. Its proceeds went to the cause that free women of color ranked of utmost importance, the abolition of slavery.

Moral Reform

Moral reform societies attracted thousands of women. They encouraged women not only to attack social ills, but to shape the cultural values of people outside their families. Moral reform groups focused on "fallen women," that is, prostitutes. Unlike an earlier era, however, when prostitutes were condemned as seducers of men, moral reformers portrayed men as the seducers of young women who, once corrupted, remained fallen.

Moral reformers thus launched a two-pronged attack on prostitution. One angle involved trying to convince prostitutes of the "evil" in which they lived and to rescue them from a life of "sin." Most prostitutes, however, remained unmoved by such arguments. Although prostitution may have been a moral issue for female reformers, many prostitutes saw their work in purely economic terms. Many women of the streets realized, some from firsthand experience, that women's factory and domestic jobs simply did not pay a living wage. The second theme of moral reform involved advising women regarding men. Women were cautioned to watch men's behavior at all times. According to a writer in the *Advocate of Moral Reform,* published by the New York Female Moral Society, women must view the "whole tribe of profligate and licentious men with marked contempt" and continuous vigilance. It was men, after all, who supposedly had seduced and abandoned women, thereby forcing them into prostitution.

When some men responded to the charges against them with rude laughter, offensive jokes, and counterattacks on female reformers, they only served to further convince reformers that they were correct in their assessment of male character in the first place. Even the few men who wished to join moral reform societies usually confronted closed doors, for women thought all men untrustworthy allies regarding this issue.

Throughout the 1830s, members of the New York Female Moral Society, as well as similar groups all over the country, employed their own style of "visiting"; they sang hymns and prayed at brothels, almshouses, and jails; talked with prostitutes; and solicited data and case histories relating to sexual abuse and other domestic evils. They also petitioned state legislatures, asking for the passage of legislation that would "suppress crimes against chastity." In 1840, when the New York Female Moral Society reorganized into the nationwide American Female Moral Reform Society, its auxiliaries numbered 555. In 1848, the group gained a corporate charter and renamed itself the American Female Guardian Society.

As in other reform movements, moral reformers came to the realization that homes and other institutions were necessary to bring about meaningful change. As a result, female moral reformers opened refuges for women in need. In New York, this took the form of a House of Reception, a home for prostitutes. In Boston, women reformers founded a not only a Home for Unprotected Girls but a Refuge for Migrant Women and an Asylum for the Repentant. Although these women still preached, they also offered asylum. In fact, by the 1850s, women reformers spent more time on building institutions that they did visiting the objects of their charity.

Prison and Asylum Reform

Women convinced of their moral righteousness and their mission to reform attacked a wide range of social ills. Increasingly, they reached far beyond their own lives for issues to resolve. As fast as a problem came to public attention, female reformers thought of ways to attack it. For example, when it became public knowledge that prisons lumped together women and men, children and adolescents, and the mentally disturbed, female reformers saw a need to separate these inmate populations and institute programs meaningful to each. Women were especially upset that female prisoners of all races had no protection from sexual attacks by male inmates or male guards. Nor were incarcerated women given any care during pregnancy. Because most state and federal authorities considered prisoners beyond hope, especially women who had fallen so low, in any attempt to revise the treatment of prisoners and mental patients, women set out to apply their own moral powers of persuasion.

As a result of women reformer's goading, the first women's prison appeared as early as 1835. Unfortunately, the new Female Prison of Mount Pleasant, New York, was not a widely imitated model. The need for separate women's prisons was still not widely accepted, while other social problems pushed the issue of women's prisons into the background.

During the 1840s, however, prison reform attracted a growing number of concerned women who wanted to help. For instance, female reformers, including Protestant missionaries, "visited" female prisoners in the Tombs, one of New York City's jails. Other women joined the Female Department, an auxiliary of the Prison Association of New York. Out of this and other women's groups came a concerted effort to establish separate women's prisons operated by women and committed to the introduction of inmate education. Like other reformers, these women came to the conclusion that buildings and rehabilitation programs were more effective than just "visiting."

Other women prison reformers worked on behalf of the mentally ill. One such crusader, Dorothea Dix, truly was a reformer at heart. At age fourteen, Dix had taught school in Worcester, Massachusetts. A few years later, she opened a school in Boston. Dix also had an interest in natural science and wrote a number of books on the subject. When she traveled in Europe in an attempt to improve her own health, Dix visited the York Retreat, established by Quakers as an asylum for the "insane." After returning to the United States, Dix discovered she had inherited enough money to support her for life.

Dix, however, could not remain idle, and she began to teach Sunday school to women in the East Cambridge House of Correction. In doing so she discovered that because mentally disturbed persons were considered beyond help, they were left totally unclothed and in darkness. They also lacked basic sanitary facilities and heat. Some were even chained to the walls and beaten. In horror, Dix, with a group of other reformers, toured Massachusetts prisons. Everywhere she visited she saw the mentally ill receiving similar treatment: "confined in cages, closets, cellars, stalls, pens, chained, naked, beaten with rods, and lashed into obedience." In 1843, Dorothea Dix presented her report to the Massachusetts legislature. She asked for the construction of sufficient facilities to house the mentally ill and other disadvantaged people separately from convicted felons and murderers. Dix then went on to Rhode Island and New York to perform the same grisly service. Ultimately all three states responded by funding new mental hospitals.

During the 1840s and 1850s, Dix continued her work on behalf of the poverty-stricken insane in the United States and Great Britain. As a result of her one-woman crusade for prison reform, other women joined her cause. During the 1850s, women's prison reform associations proliferated. Also, individual women accepted appointments to state prison boards, especially in Connecticut, New York, and Massachusetts. Still, the American penal system outside of New England proved detrimental to women, especially those of color. Although Dix had raised people's awareness of the problem, much remained to be done.

Alcohol Abuse

As with penal reform, once women began to consider the extent of drinking in the United States, they learned to identify a host of alcohol-related problems. Female reformers realized that numerous wives and daughters suffered mistreatment at the hands of intoxicated husbands and fathers. They recognized that because most women and children depended on men economically, alcoholic men could financially destroy families. One New England minister explained that as far as female reformers were concerned, alcoholism was the "destruction of all domestic peace, the wreck of all conjugal and maternal hopes."

As a consequence, female reformers defined alcoholism as largely a male problem and the solution as largely a female duty. A widely read temperance novel, *Ten Nights in a Barroom,* agreed. In this allegorical tract, a hapless daughter who has entered a barroom to plead with her unemployed and abusive father to stop drinking and come home is hit by a glass flung in anger. Within a short time, the drunkard's daughter is dead. Although the moral of this story might be that women and children should stay out of taverns, the author argued that drinking destroyed families and hurt innocent children. The novel emphasized the necessity for moral women to guide Americans' behavior.

In response to these appeals, women joined such groups as the Daughters of Temperance in unprecedented numbers. By 1840, the Daughters of Temperance was one of the largest organizations for women, with a membership of thirty thousand. Members of Daughters of Temperance chapters held temperance meetings—or local rallies—and organized such state gatherings as the Women's Temperance Convention, which met in New York in 1852. Women banded together to pray and sing hymns outside, or sometimes inside, saloons. Through the use of such moral suasion, women hoped to convince men to sign pledges of self-control or total abstinence. They felt certain that female morality would triumph over what they called "Demon Rum."

People who made such pledges sometimes honored them. More frequently, however, people forgot promises made in the midst of an emotional demonstration and returned to drinking. In time, reformers realized that more than moral suasion was necessary. A growing number of reformers concluded that it would take legislation to separate confirmed drinkers from their favorite beverages. Therefore, women began to collect signatures on petitions asking state legislatures to adopt prohibition laws.

At this point, however, women temperance reformers found themselves stifled: the temperance movement had turned to legal action but women could not vote! Although female reformers could continue to exercise their moral powers against alcoholism by protesting in front of saloons or circulating petitions, they could not cast ballots for or against prohibition laws, or vote prohibitionist candidates into office. Political action had to come from such men's groups as the American Temperance Society. During the 1840s, women felt left out of the very cause that they increasingly saw as their own. When, in 1846, Maine passed the first state law banning the manufacture and sale of alcoholic beverages, women had no direct hand in the action.

In addition, men's temperance groups seldom let women join their ranks. In 1852, after male members of the Sons of Temperance denied female representatives of the Daughters of Temperance the right to speak in an 1852 men's meeting, women delegates walked out in protest. They then called for and convened a Women's Temperance Convention in New York, where they expressed not only temperance sentiments but early woman's rights attitudes as well.

As the temperance battle heated up, women tried to maintain their influence in the movement by turning moral suasion into physical force. Tired of praying and singing, women resorted to personal confrontation and extralegal force. During the 1850s, groups of women entered saloons and personally destroyed stocks of liquor. In these actions respectable and influential women became vigilantes who literally brandished hatchets to protect their homes and families from the evil of alcohol. Still moral suasion and even violence were not enough; women now realized that they needed the vote if their voices were to be heard along with men's.

A similar pattern occurred among African American women, who also believed in the temperance cause. Some joined black men's temperance organizations, although the largest of these, the New England Colored Temperance Society, refused to accept women as members. During the 1830s, black women initiated temperance programs in churches, clubs, and communities. During the 1840s, some temperance-minded black women joined with white women, especially in Utica, New York. In part because most white women's organizations did not welcome blacks as members, during the 1840s and 1850s black women formed their own temperance societies, particularly in Philadelphia where a substantial number of free middle- and upper-class blacks lived. As in other reforms, many African American women preferred to work in black-only groups. They believed that alcohol, prejudice, and poverty formed a circle of despair in the black community and thus demanded specialized approaches.

The lesson of the temperance movement for African American reform women was more even more distressing than it was for white women. Not only did black men reject reform-minded black women, but so did white women. As a result, women of color realized that the battle for black woman's right would be an especially long and difficult one.

Women in Abolitionism

As important as all the antebellum reform causes were, one issue stood out above all the others: slavery had to be destroyed in a country that thought of itself as democratic and egalitarian. Yet the abolition of slavery was the most difficult reform to achieve. Many white northerners preferred to ignore slavery's presence. Other people clung to racist beliefs and attacked abolitionists personally, stoned or burned the halls in which they spoke, and broke up abolitionist rallies.

Consequently, even women who strongly believed in the cause of abolitionism hesitated to enter such a violent fray that might put them in compromising, unladylike situations. In addition, abolition of slavery would most definitely require political action. Thus, numerous women felt that abolitionism was a cause best pursued by men, who were already publishing antislavery newspapers, holding demonstrations, and forming antislavery organizations. Yet the cause of abolitionism was too important for many other women to ignore. To them, it was the ultimate moral issue that demanded their attention.

The female wing of the abolitionist crusade came largely from free black and upper-class white women in the North. In fact, as early as 1832, free black women in Salem, Massachusetts, had formed the first female abolitionist society. Yet abolitionism brought black and white women together closer than did any other reform issue. As a result, the Salem group became racially integrated in 1834. At the same time, other biracial abolitionist societies appeared in Boston and in Lynn, Massachusetts, Rochester, New York, and Philadelphia, Pennsylvania. Still, some women's groups remained white only. Many white women who had not yet truly confronted the extent of their own bigotry opposed the integration of their groups. Thus, black women's and white women's abolitionism sometimes proceeded on separate tracks. With or without their white sisters' help, for free women of color, abolitionism remained the most pressing cause of all.

Unsurprisingly, the Quaker center of Philadelphia, which counted a high number of free black women among its population, became a hub of abolitionist efforts. There the Forten family was especially active. Sisters Sarah, Harriet, and Margaretta Forten helped found the Philadelphia Female Anti-Slavery Society. After Sarah married Joseph Purvis in 1838, she continued to work on behalf of African Americans. In 1838 and 1839, Harriet Forten served as a delegate to the Anti-Slavery Convention of American Women. Later, both she and Margaretta combined abolitionist writing and speaking with extensive committee work.

Other free black abolitionists included teacher, journalist, and lawyer Mary Ann Shadd Cary, speaker and author Sarah Parker Remond, and lecturer, writer, and poet Frances Ellen Watkins Harper. Of these, Harper gained the most public notice. Her books of poetry, *Forest Leaves* and *Poems on Miscellaneous Subjects,* sold thousands of copies. She also wrote for such antislavery publications as the *Liberator* and the *Christian Standard.* During the 1850s, Harper lectured on her poetry, abolitionism, and woman's rights throughout New Jersey, Pennsylvania, Ohio, and even parts of the South.

One of the best-known black female abolitionists was Harriet Tubman, who became a famous conductor on the Underground Railroad. Born a slave in Maryland, Tubman fled to Philadelphia in 1849. In 1850, she returned to Maryland to guide her sister and her two children north to freedom. The following year, Tubman helped a brother and his family escape slavery. Tubman made at least nineteen trips into slave territory and freed as many as three hundred people. Known as the "Moses of Her People," in 1860 Tubman was a wanted woman in the South; she had a reward of $40,000 on her head.

Of course, these African American abolitionists faced enormous hurdles. Besides racial prejudice that limited their activities, they often found themselves barred as women from speaking, writing, and organizing. Being black and female created problems not faced by white female reformers. The tale of Sojourner Truth is especially instructive. Born a slave in New York and originally named Isabella, she fled from her owner in 1827, just before the passage of the New York Emancipation Act of 1827 was passed. As a free woman, Isabella successfully sued for the freedom of her son, who had been sold illegally into slavery in Alabama. In 1829, she arrived in New York City with two of her children and obtained work as a domestic servant. In time she became a preacher and participated in the effort to turn prostitutes to religion.

In 1843, Isabella took the name Sojourner Truth and set out on foot to preach throughout New England. Three years later, she became an enthusiastic supporter of the abolitionist movement. In spite of threats and physical attacks, she toured the Midwest lecturing against slavery. A large, powerful woman with a deep, resonant voice, Sojourner Truth was one of the abolition movement's most effective speakers. At one speaking engagement in Indiana she literally bared her breast to disprove allegations that she was a man in disguise.

In addition to such female abolitionists of color, white women energetically championed the cause of antislavery. Because these women viewed slavery as a moral wrong, they felt compelled to exercise their moral powers against it. The Boston Female Anti-Slavery Society declared that "as wives and mothers, as daughters and sisters, we are deeply responsible for the influence we have on the human race. . . . We are bound to urge men to cease to do evil and learn how to do good."

White women felt a growing sense of identification with black women. In 1837, abolitionist Angelina Grimké told a white women's antislavery convention that they were "sisters" to slave women. As women, she continued, slaves have a right to look to white women for "sympathy for their sorrows, and effort and prayer for their rescue." Others argued that if one woman suffered sexual degradation, it hurt womankind, and if one mother faced depreciation, then all mothers lost stature. Abolitionist women hoped that if they helped free the slaves, social liberation would be extended to white women as a logical and just outcome of their efforts.

At first, white women's abolitionist societies engaged in fund-raising and exhortation, but they soon adopted more aggressive tactics, including holding national conventions and speaking on the public platform. When the Grimké sisters dared to mount the public platform and speak to "promiscuous" audiences, composed of women and men, people came as much to see the show as to hear the abolitionist message. It has been estimated that in 1837, the sisters spoke in six months time to some 40,000 people.

Women abolitionists also lobbied legislatures to pass desired laws. Female reformers were willing to participate in the political process to this extent, but only a few had come around to wanting the vote and other political privileges for themselves. Yet women increasingly resented the limitations placed on their activities due to their gender. In 1837, one woman's convention proclaimed that "the time has come for woman to move in that sphere which providence has assigned her, and no longer remain satisfied in the circumscribed limits which corrupt custom and a perverted application of Scripture have encircled her."

Because not all Americans believed that women should actively engage in public controversy, women's involvement in abolitionism created controversy of its own. The Grimké sisters' lecturing and political reform activities especially led to a heated discussion of women's roles and responsibilities. In 1837, a group of Congregationalist ministers in Massachusetts issued a "Pastoral Letter" protesting the sisters' "unfeminine" conduct. The letter said in part: "We invite your attention to the dangers which at present seem to threaten the female character with widespread and permanent injury. The appropriate duties and influence of women are clearly stated in the New Testament. The power of woman is her dependence, flowing from the consciousness of that weakness which God has given her for her protection."

Abolitionist leaders feared that such invective and attendant controversy would jeopardize the antislavery crusade, so they begged the Grimké sisters to ignore it. Sarah and Angelina replied that they could "not push abolitionism forward until we take the stumbling block out of the road." In other words, they were determined to exercise their moral powers and, if necessary, to fight for their own rights so that they could attack slavery.

Like Sojourner Truth, the Grimké sisters now espoused woman's rights. In 1838, Sarah stated the sisters' position in her pamphlet, *Letters on the Equality of the Sexes, and the Condition of Woman.* She minced no words in presenting the case: "I ask no favors for my sex. I surrender not our claim to equality. All I ask of our brethren is that they take their feet from off our necks, and permit us to stand upright on the ground which God has designed us to occupy." Shortly thereafter, Angelina married abolitionist reformer Theodore Dwight Weld. The newly wed couple and Sarah settled in New Jersey, where they continued to work for the causes of antislavery and woman's rights.

During the 1840s and 1850s, thousands of women followed the courageous example of Sarah and Angelina Grimké by joining the abolitionist movement. Because they could not vote, they chose instead to petition Congress to pass laws restricting slavery. Although gathering names on petitions entailed hard work, onerous travel, and frequent scorn, these women persevered and collected hundreds of thousands of signatures that Congress could not ignore. In addition to petitioning, abolitionist women lectured, helped slaves escape via a network known as the Underground Railroad, and wrote books and pamphlets.

One of the most eminent of the abolitionist writers was Harriet Beecher Stowe. Coming from a family of reformers and deeply interested in social reform herself, Stowe directed her early writings toward the issues of temperance, higher wages for seamstresses, and improved educational opportunities for women. She later became involved in the abolitionist movement and wrote several antislavery novels. In 1852, she achieved worldwide acclaim with her highly influential *Uncle Tom's Cabin,* and in 1856, she published another "slavery" novel, *Dred: A Tale of the Great Dismal Swamp.*

Women's Frustrations

The woman's reform movement had several important themes. One of these concerned female morality. Not only were women innately moral, they had a divinely inspired mission to instill virtue in others. This "virtue" was based on middle- and upper-class Protestant values seldom meaningful to people of other classes. As women grew frustrated at the widespread resistance to reform they increasingly turned to buildings—homes and other institutions—as the answer. Female reformers hoped that separating people from harsh environments and teaching them marketable skills would bring about the kind of pervasive reform for which they worked. In the process, numerous women became articulate, aggressive, and well trained in business and political procedures.

A second and subtler motif was that "the other sex"—men—were not only less moral than women but were often the root of the nation's social problems. By such lamentable behavior as avoiding church services, drinking to excess, and seducing innocent women, too many men became weak vessels, wanting fulfillment with female piety and piousness. Rather than looking up to men, female reformers looked down on them.

Third, although the work of voluntary associations had drawn women out of comfortable homes to experience firsthand the stench and filth of prisons, taverns, and riotous crowds, few people seemed to appreciate women's efforts. Again, men appeared to be the culprits. Reformer Susan B. Anthony complained that American men left the dirty work of society to women: "Men like to see women pick up the drunk and falling. . . . That patching business is 'woman's proper sphere.'"

Fourth, women felt cheated when they gradually discovered that most reform ideas needed the strong arm of legal provisions to succeed. Although women had been told to use their moral power to clean up American society, it now appeared that such cleaning up demanded political powers, of which women had none. Instead, "the other sex" controlled the vote and office holding. What a dilemma confronted female reformers! They wielded little political influence because they could not own property, vote, or hold office. In addition, they frequently endured criticism for speaking in public and entering the halls of Congress with their petitions. Yet how were they to function as effective reformers without sufficient weapons or power? And how were they to activate their moral force? If they truly were the moral guardians of society, then they required the freedom to exercise their salutary influence on American society.

Unsurprisingly, the woman's rights movement grew out of the frustrations of female reformers, especially those in the temperance and abolition crusades. In the temperance movement, women responded to their lack of power by becoming supporters of woman's rights. A temperance journal, *The Lily,* edited by Amelia Bloomer, began as a newspaper dedicated to "temperance and literature." In 1852, *The Lily*'s new masthead declared the publication "devoted to the interests of women." Thus, women who began their careers as temperance reformers frequently ended them in the woman's rights campaign. Many of these women experienced an increasing enmity toward men, whom they saw as oppressors blocking them from their political rights. At the same time, these women began to define themselves not as submissive domestic beings but as effective shapers of society. In general, then, women's experience with temperance reform caused large numbers of them to question their place and to challenge domestic ideology.

In the abolitionist movement a similar evolution occurred. Women abolitionists especially felt thwarted because they were trying to eradicate what they defined as a huge moral wrong. Their encounters with an economic and political system in which they had little influence led women to believe that they must fight for their own rights. If they were to help free the slaves, women had to free themselves first. As Angelina Grimké put it, "The investigation of the rights of the slave led me to a better understanding of my own." Thus, during the 1840s, numerous abolitionists added the issue of women's rights to their platforms. For some, gaining rights seemed a practical matter; they simply wished to do so in order to proceed with their reforms. For others, achieving their rights constituted an ethical issue that would allow them to carry out their moral responsibilities to the nation.

The limits on women abolitionists became especially obvious in 1840, after the national antislavery organization split into male-only and male-female factions over the so-called woman question. The integrated group sent female delegates to a world antislavery convention in London in 1841, where male delegates seated the women behind a curtain and denied them the right to vote. When the women delegates walked out in indignation, a number of sympathetic black and white men joined them. As a result of this upsetting incident, delegates Lucretia Mott and Elizabeth Cady Stanton agreed that a women's protest meeting was needed in the United States. Mott, Stanton, and others recognized that their reform efforts would continue to confront obstacles until women had such rights as speaking, voting, and holding public office.

Seneca Falls

It was not until 19 July 1848 at Seneca Falls, New York, that the first woman's rights meeting occurred. Although Elizabeth Cady Stanton's husband Henry fled town in embarrassment, Lucretia Mott's husband James agreed to chair the convention. The meeting attracted approximately three hundred people, including about forty men.

After many speeches, including one by black abolitionist Frederick Douglass on behalf of woman suffrage, delegates paraphrased the Declaration of Independence in a plea for equality and expanded rights for women, including the right to vote. It read in part: "We hold these truths to be self-evident: that all men and women are created equal: that they are endowed by their Creator with certain inalienable rights: that among these are life, liberty and the pursuit of happiness." It also condemned unfair practices of men: "The history of mankind is a history of repeated injuries and usurpations on the part of man toward woman, having in direct object the establishment of an absolute tyranny over her." Sixty-eight women and thirty-two men signed this Declaration of Sentiments and Resolutions, the first formal declaration regarding woman's rights in the United States.

The actions taken at Seneca Falls resonated with women, both black and white. In 1850, the black abolitionist Sojourner Truth adopted the cause of woman's rights. Because she had experienced frequent dis-

crimination as a female reformer, Sojourner Truth added woman's issues to her speeches. In 1852, at a woman's rights meeting in Akron,
Ohio, she delivered her famous "Ain't I A Woman" speech in which she
pointed out that chivalry and true womanhood were not very meaningful concepts to most women, especially black, laboring, and poor
women. She argued adamantly for rights for black women because she
believed that "if colored men get their rights and not colored women
theirs . . . the colored men will be masters and it will be just as bad as it
was before."

Also in late 1850, Amelia Bloomer, the temperance reformer, editor,
and suffragist living in Seneca Falls, adopted a reform outfit composed
of a short skirt and Turkish-style pantaloons. Bloomer's intent was to
show that women could be active and able human beings when not
hampered by restrictive fashions of the day such as corsets, petticoats,
and floor-length skirts. Women who followed Bloomer's lead and became "Bloomer girls" by adopting similar dress explained that they
hoped for better health, freedom of movement, and even equality by
freeing themselves from the dictates of fashion. The Bloomer outfit, especially the trousers, created such controversy that most women abandoned it by the end of the decade.

As woman's rights gained supporters, the popular press heaped unsparing ridicule on the Seneca Falls convention and the demands of its
delegates. Also in 1850, James Gordon Bennett of the *New York Herald*
asked, "What do the leaders of the woman's right conventions want?
They want to be members of Congress, and in the heat of debate subject themselves to coarse jests and indecent language."

Not all men, however, were as sharp in their response as was
Bennett. In 1851, a New York minister who had initially opposed
woman's rights came around to supporting it. He observed that both
women and men had devised the traditional division of labor between
the sexes. Rather than subjugating women, he argued, this separation of
tasks had been intended to protect women from danger and performing
heavy labor. He concluded that the time might be right for sweeping
social changes, but that women should not see men as their enemies.
Two years later, however, abolitionist and social reformer William Lloyd
Garrison claimed that men were indeed responsible for women's oppression. Garrison saw women as "the victims in this land," having
been sacrificed to "the tyrannical power and godless ambition of man."

Apparently, the call for woman's rights received many responses. It
was clear that a momentous issue had been raised, and one that would
not be easily settled.

Woman's Rights Demands

Even though woman's rights may have appeared a foolish and trivial issue to some people, for its advocates, both female and male, it held se-

rious and far-reaching implications. For instance, married women's property rights meant a great deal to women who lost control of their property or were left destitute by mismanagement or death of a husband. Thus, legislation protecting married women's property was of prime importance to supporters of woman's rights. Although several states discussed such legislation during the 1830s and New York actually considered such a statute in 1836, the state of Mississippi passed the first Married Women's Property Law in 1839.

Soon, woman's rights advocates argued for modification of women's property laws in all states. Among these was a Jewish woman of Polish birth named Ernestine Rose. First a temperance and abolitionist reformer, Rose had become committed to woman's rights as early as the 1840s. In New York state, Rose circulated petitions and spoke in support of a newly introduced women's property bill. When the legislature finally passed a limited bill in 1848, it marked the beginning of changes in women's ownership of property. Shortly afterward, Pennsylvania passed a similar bill. Other states gradually followed.

Another important issue for champions of woman's rights during the 1840s and 1850s was political privileges for women. Outraged that the brand of "democracy" championed during the Age of Jackson applied only to white males, women came to believe that suffrage entailed more than the right to cast a ballot. Female reformers viewed the right to vote and hold office as the only way to achieve their goals. And numerous suffragists came to believe that women's entry into the political arena was the path to the ultimate goal: equality with men. In 1859, a female physician addressed a special session of the Indiana General Assembly, convened to hear the grievances of Indiana women. She pleaded with her "brothers in the Senate and House of Representatives" to "remove the political disabilities" that retarded women's progress.

On a more abstract level, woman's rights advocates hoped for a thorough rethinking of the doctrine of separate spheres that said wives and mothers should remain within the confines of their homes. Rather, women wanted access to the larger world, including schools and colleges, paid employment, the professions, and the right to divorce abusive or alcoholic husbands. Although the woman's rights movement focused on property and political rights, the agenda encompassed profound social and economic change.

Woman's Rights Ideology

In the process of defending their demands, champions of woman's rights developed an intricate ideology during the 1840s and 1850s. First, doctrines established during the American Revolution contributed ideas regarding equality, human perfectibility, and the right and duty of citizens to participate in their own governance. Woman's rights' theorists argued that if such rights belonged to Americans, then they certainly belonged to women who were Americans.

Second, the philosophies of British reformers fed the American woman's rights crusade by openly discussing women's issues and helping foster a climate that made reform thinkable and even possible. In the 1830s, for example, the Scottish-born Frances Wright broached such topics as equality, improved education, divorce, and birth control in her popular lectures. Also, English author Mary Wollstonecraft's *Vindication of the Rights of Woman* (1792), one of the earliest arguments for the equality of women, was widely read in America during the 1840s.

Third, American writers and speakers offered their own perspectives and philosophies on the subjugation of women. Margaret Fuller, known as the "high priestess" of the transcendentalist movement, addressed the issue of equality. As editor of the transcendentalist journal *The Dial* during the 1840s, Fuller maintained that women should be allowed to expand their strengths and interests, just as men did. Released in 1845, Fuller's *Woman in the Nineteenth Century* was the first American book to examine woman's place in society. It sold out its first printing within a week and created a spirited debate in the *New York Daily Tribune,* with reform editor Horace Greeley supporting Fuller.

Another American writer and speaker, Elizabeth Cady Stanton, concentrated her efforts on gaining the ballot for women. Because Stanton believed that liberation lay in political participation, she especially advocated woman suffrage. In 1850, Stanton met Susan B. Anthony, who soon became Stanton's closest collaborator. Henry Stanton reportedly told Elizabeth, "You stir up Susan and she stirs up the world." During the 1840s and 1850s, Anthony did indeed prove herself an effective orator and an efficient organizer for temperance, abolitionism, and woman's rights. A Quaker schoolteacher and manager of the family farm, Anthony never married and was thus free to travel and speak as she pleased. Like Stanton, Anthony emphasized the right to vote: "Suffrage involves every basic principle of republican government, all our social, civil, religious, educational, and political rights."

Lucy Stone also contributed to the ideology of woman's rights. After attending Oberlin College in the 1840s, Stone became an abolitionist speaker and soon came to deplore the idea of Civil Death and the limitations it placed on women. When she married Henry Blackwell (brother of physicians Elizabeth and Emily) in 1855, Stone kept her family name and entered into a well-publicized marriage contract that read in part: "we deem it a duty to declare that this act [marriage] implies no sanction of, nor promise of voluntary obedience to such of the present laws of marriage, as they refuse to recognize the wife as an independent, rational being, while they confer upon the husband an injurious and unnatural superiority."

Lucretia Mott also came to woman's rights through abolitionism. As an official minister in the Society of Friends (Quakers), Mott had a deep religious belief in justice and equality for all people. During the 1850s, she turned her Philadelphia home into an Underground Railroad station and, in addition to caring for six children, traveled extensively to lecture on abolitionism and woman's rights. She frequently employed Biblical evidence to argue that the inferior status of women was neither natural nor divinely ordained. Rather than promoting woman suffrage, Mott concentrated on a new view of women as responsible, self-sustaining individuals.

African American women contributed to the emerging ideology as well. Although many black women considered antislavery a more pressing cause, some espoused woman's rights as well. For example, abolitionist and journalist Harriet Purvis, her sister Margaretta Forten, and Mary Ann Shadd Cary, Harriet Tubman, and Sojourner Truth all helped lay the groundwork for black feminism. Given their opposition to slavery, it is little wonder that African American feminists envisioned a humanistic community in which every individual would be encouraged to fulfill his or her potential.

During the 1850s, the energy and ideas of these woman's rights leaders helped create a dynamic and visible movement. Hundreds of woman's rights meetings occurred each year, and the "woman question" was widely and hotly debated. Still, woman's rights appealed primarily to white middle- and upper-class women. Thus, issues important to working, immigrant, poor, Native American, African American, and such other women of color as those of Haitian and Jamaican heritage continued to receive little attention. In addition, the existence and repercussions of classism and racism was absent from the rhetoric of most of these reformers. Rather than examining the economic and political structure of the United States, woman's rights' leaders frequently identified men as the enemy. By scapegoating men, they underestimated an economic system that kept people of certain classes and races at the bottom of the economic ladder, and thus poor, uneducated, inarticulate, and seemingly inferior. Woman's rights' theorists typically failed to understand the impact of political power concentrated in the hands of a few. They believed that by gaining the right to vote for themselves, they would be able to equalize the American political system. They limited their view to gender, while they ignored such other factors as race, ethnicity, and social class that also demanded equalizing.

Still, certain issues finally had been pinpointed and openly discussed. The American public had been forced to increase its awareness of the ills afflicting women. In addition, women reformers had learned organizational and speaking skills, attracted a number of male supporters, and forced legislators to accept and at least consider their petitions. As a result, the groundwork of an American feminist movement was in place.

Racism

In campaigning for reform causes, few women had really taken into account the long-ingrained racist attitudes of most white Americans. It was one thing to abolish slavery and quite another to convince white and black peoples to accord each other a measure of respect, much less to live side-by-side as equals. Speeches, tracts, and newspaper articles reveal that although most white Americans might have appreciated the moral point of emancipating the slaves, few intended to become friends and neighbors to African Americans.

In New York City during the 1830s and 1840s, for example, reformers debated everything from radical abolitionism to urban poverty, but they could not agree on the meaning of equality between African Americans and white Americans. Journalists and others wrote about the dangers of "amalgamation," or dating and marriage between black and white people. The gist of their message was that interracial relationships, especially black-white marriages, would destroy New York City's social and racial hierarchy. Nor did most New Yorkers envision an egalitarian system in which African Americans would attend schools with white children or black workers would receive equal pay with white laborers for equal work.

Employed Women

Another neglected area was female wageworkers. Although female reformers had both dedication and energy, they simply could not address every flaw in American life. Moreover, some problems regarding women had not yet come to public attention because they were of relatively recent development.

Despite their intense interest in change, middle- and upper-class women reformers seldom recognized the difficult conditions facing white and black women who worked outside their homes for wages. These employed women labored behind factory walls, did piecework on their kitchen tables, roamed city streets as prostitutes, or toiled in other women's kitchens and sculleries. The situations of these employed women often remained unpublicized, while their predicaments often appeared to be self-inflicted. Even the campaign against prostitution was a moral issue for most reformers, rather than an attempt to help working women.

Consequently, workers themselves had to come to grips with the dilemmas of a recently industrialized society. During the mid-1830s, some women workers unsuccessfully devoted their energies to campaigns for higher wages, shorter hours, and improved working conditions. In spite of these ills, other women continued to flock to factory jobs, hoping for higher wages than they currently earned. Even during the Panic of 1837 and the ensuing economic depression, women left other occupations for factory employment. In 1839, one mill worker lamented that "there are very many young ladies at work in the factories that have given up millinery dressmaking and school-keeping for to work in the mill."

When the depression extended into the late 1830s and early 1840s, wages fell and unemployment spread. In New York and other major cities, bread riots became the order of the day. By 1843, the panic finally eased. Although most women returned to work, they earned less than $2 per week, hardly a living wage, even in the 1840s.

Unemployed and underpaid women workers sought assistance from benevolent women's societies and other charity organizations. One of these was the Mother Society in New York City, devoted to helping poor blacks and unemployed black women. Other employed women argued that they needed some type of labor organization. In 1845, an operative in the Lowell mills, Sarah Bagley, acted on this idea by founding the Lowell Female Labor Reform Association, which advocated the ten-hour workday.

In 1845, Bagley expanded her outreach. She left her job in Lowell to organize branches of the Female Labor Reform Association in Waltham and Fall River, Massachusetts, and Manchester, Nashua, and Dover in New Hampshire. In the labor newspaper, *Voice of Industry,* Bagley complained about an increased work pace and asked Massachusetts legislators to investigate conditions in the mills. The legislators refused to act.

Society in general, and male union members in particular, frowned upon women's participation in unions. Unwilling to accept the reality of women's employment, these people hoped that women workers would soon return to their "proper" places in the home. Working men also feared women because women accepted low wages. These men did not yet realize that organizations of both women and men might establish fair wages for all workers.

Such prejudice did not prevent numerous women workers from joining men's labor unions, participating in strikes, or forming their own organizations. In 1845, the shoe binders at Lynn, Massachusetts, established a Producers Cooperative. During the late 1840s and early 1850s, many of the 181,000 women workers in the clothing, shoe, wool, straw hat, printing, and other industries attempted organization and walkouts.

At the same time, household workers and home pieceworkers had little opportunity to organize, strike, or otherwise protect themselves from exploitation. Some made ends meet by taking aid from charitable societies or by hiring out their children. Others turned to prostitution. In 1858, an estimated six thousand prostitutes existed in New York City, one for every sixty-four adult males. Over half of these women had earned one to two dollars a week as seamstresses, dressmakers, hat trimmers, milliners, tailors, servants, and factory workers before becoming prostitutes, and 63 percent of those who worked as prostitutes had been born in other countries.

This latter statistic indicates the tremendous difficulty immigrant women faced in finding employment. Usually lacking industrial skills and, except for English immigrants, unable to speak the language of their new country, these women fell prey to unscrupulous and mercenary employers who forced them to accept less than subsistence wages and work in dreadful conditions. Others became pieceworkers or domestic servants at unbelievably low wages.

During the 1840s, one quarter of a million women, or one-tenth of the adult female population, worked as domestics. Irish immigrants constituted the majority of domestic workers, while other Irish women worked in the needle trades or as prostitutes. Stranded in urban areas by their lack of funds and kept at the bottom of the economic ladder by anti-Catholic prejudice, Irish and large numbers of other immigrant women were unable to migrate to rural areas where they might put their agricultural skills to use.

Among all these employed women, only factory women had the proximity (to one another), opportunity, and group consciousness to campaign for reform. Although many had come willingly to factories to escape the boredom and drudgery of farm life, they had not intended to exchange one bad situation for another. Female operatives resented exploitation in the form of low wages, high hours, and gender-segregated tasks.

During the late 1850s, more women joined men's strikes or staged their own walkouts. A few even began to recognize that the success of the woman's rights movement might facilitate labor reform. One early labor leader, Harriet Farley, a former mill operative at Lowell, became an avowed woman's rights advocate. In 1850, Farley wrote that "it has been impossible for me to consider so long the 'Rights and Duties of Mill-Girls' without opening my eyes to the vista just beyond the rights and duties of woman." Farley deplored the socialization of "masculine" men and "feminine" women that ignored the common ground between the two genders. In her view, women could support themselves without losing their womanhood: "I have seen that they do not become less worthy and interesting when they become more useful and independent."

Ten years later, in 1860, labor issues came to a head when five hundred men and one thousand women held a huge rally during a strike in Lynn, Massachusetts. In the middle of a terrible blizzard, the women cheered the reading of a special poem, "The Song of the Shoemakers Strike." Some twenty thousand more workers throughout New England joined this labor protest, known as "The Revolution in the North." From this came few actual gains, but it gave workers a new sense of empowerment and confidence to act on their own behalf.

Farm Women

Women who labored on the nation's farms confronted a number of problems that remained largely unpublicized. Farm "wives," for example, frequently found their duties "burdensome" and unhealthy. Some even thought of themselves as beasts of burden, much like a cow or plow horse, but with their own specialized work to perform,

Thousands of other women worked on farms as hired laborers during the late 1830s, 1840s, and 1850s. Often newly arrived immigrant or free black women, these hired hands did not disdain field work. They had performed heavy agricultural tasks in their countries of origin or in the South and were thus willing to join men in the fields.

The numbers of female farm hands increased as agricultural specialization developed. Wheat, corn, chicken, and dairy farms all demanded hired labor, female and male. Immigrant women especially proved themselves invaluable as grain, dairy, and chicken farmers. In 1857, the *Illinois Farmer* pleaded: "We want a supply of young women from the butter regions of Eastern States to come here and also from the Dairy Districts of England, Scotland, Ireland, and Germany."

Still, although farmers usually recruited immigrant, free black, and poor women as field hands, field work was considered appropriate work for all women during periods of labor shortages. Even farm wives and daughters had to work in the rows on occasion. Like their counterparts in domestic labor, these women had little opportunity to organize for their own sake and had to depend on outside forces for any hope of reform.

Women in the West

Native American Women

As traders, missionaries, and settlers continued to cross the California and Oregon trails, they created a state of near chaos among many Native peoples. Indians who crossed the so-called Trail of Tears experienced a destructive transformation. At the same time, other American Indian women saw their influence and customs erode further. Missionary schools especially trained Native women in customary white women's subjects, especially homemaking. Missionary teachers also punished students for speaking their Native dialects or wearing traditional clothing in a concerted effort to make them "white."

Indian women agriculturalists lost their traditional work, farming, and the status and power it brought them. Even as early as the 1840s and 1850s, settlers effectively began to scatter such farming tribes as the Bannocks of Oregon and southern Idaho, as well as the Utes of Utah and Nevada. Beginning in 1841, a wave of white migrants who intended to settle permanently and establish farms in California took to the overland trail. During the late 1840s and 1850s, the discovery of gold and silver in California, Colorado, Nevada, and Idaho dispossessed additional thousands of Native Americans as greedy whites swarmed Indian lands in pursuit of riches.

The U.S. government compensated displaced Native Americans by giving them supplies and summary cash payments known as bounties and annuities. Such goods and monies often found their way into the pockets of corrupt officials and government Indian agents, however. As a result, most Indians continued to live in poverty. A ninety-year-old Chiuructo Indian living in Sonoma, California, lamented that "before the whites arrived here we had much food and a very good life."

Rather than watch their families starve or disperse, Native women often urged their bands and tribes to fight back. One much-publicized confrontation between U.S. soldiers and Native Americans occurred in Minnesota in 1861. The resultant mass hangings of Sioux Indians who resisted U.S. government land policies left many Native women and their children to fend for themselves.

As American settlers flooded into the Pacific Northwest, similar conflicts occurred. Although missionaries had gone to Oregon during the 1840s intending to educate Indians and convert them to Christianity, they had little success deflecting clashes between Natives and settlers. One settler in the Nisqually Valley of present-day Washington State related a common scenario, the deterioration of good relations: "The Indians were very kind to us, protecting us from unfriendly tribes and doctoring us when sick . . . but those times soon passed with the coming of other emigrants, who through mistreatment of the Indians caused hatred between the whites and the Indians."

Hispanas

Spanish-speaking women, who were also native to western areas, similarly faced new dilemmas during the 1840s and 1850s. During the 1840s, for example, conflict escalated between Tejanos (Mexicans in Texas) and the Americans who, since the Battle of San Jacinto, ruled the Republic of Texas. In 1845, the United States annexed Texas as a slave state. The following year the U.S. government entered into war with Mexico, which still claimed ownership of Texas.

Texas and the Southwest (the former El Norte) soon fell into American hands. Colonel Stephen W. Kearney established American rule in Santa Fe in August 1846. A Santa Fe native recalled that the American soldiers' swearing, drinking, and brawling appalled and frightened her family and neighbors. According to her, Hispanics found it hard to believe that Kearney brashly seized the former Mexican governor's office and even sat in his chair. She added that many Mexicans talked heatedly of revolting against the conquering Americans and retrieving their former lands.

On 13 August 1846, Americans similarly seized San Francisco and annexed California to the United States. When the U.S. Congress ratified the Treaty of Guadalupe Hidalgo to end the War with Mexico on 10 March 1848, the United States acquired approximately one-half of Mexico's territory. According to the treaty, Texas now formally belonged to the United States, as did Arizona, California, and New Mexico.

Also in 1848, workers digging a millrace on the American River near Sacramento, California, discovered flecks of gold. Soon, especially during 1849 and 1850, hopeful Americans, Canadians, and Europeans flooded into California's goldfields. Here they appropriated Hispanic lands. Whites warned Hispanic miners, who accounted for 8 to 9 percent of all miners, to leave the mines. Thousands of Hispanas saw their family's lands confiscated, their livelihoods destroyed, their pastoral way of life eroded, and their families scattered.

In Texas, Tejanos also lost their land, both through legal and extralegal means. Meanwhile, in New Mexico, 80 percent of original residents eventually became landless through confiscation or illegal seizure by whites. Despite a provision in the Treaty of Guadalupe Hidalgo guaranteeing New Mexicans all the rights and privileges of U.S. citizens, a number of social, economic, and legal provisions restricted them and their privileges. At least in part, negative beliefs regarding local peoples underlay such actions. To justify their actions, many whites characterized New Mexicans as lazy and immoral: people who could never achieve what white people would if they had the land in question.

In 1851, the U.S. Congress passed the Gwinn Land Act and appointed a land commission to provide a means for Spanish-speaking people to hold on to the land they claimed. Because the commission favored American claimants and the process consumed huge amounts of time and money, most *Californios* (native Californians) eventually lost their land titles. One woman lamented her loss of three ranches to an American settler: "I find myself in the greatest poverty living by the favor of God, and them that give me a morsel to eat."

In addition to legislation, other factors hurt Hispanics. The luxurious living of upper-class Hispanics, years of drought, high taxes, and litigation regarding the division of *ranchos* among numerous heirs had weakened Hispanics' hold on their lands. In addition, the inroads that shrewd American traders made into local commerce undercut the Hispanic economy. By 1860, despite continuing immigration from Mexico, Americans and other newcomers outnumbered Hispanics in the Southwest. Especially in Los Angeles, San Antonio, Santa Fe, and Tucson, previously the most populous Mexican towns in the Southwest, whites now formed the majority of the population.

As a result, Hispanas found their lives drastically changed. They were now subject to American laws, policies, and gender expectations. Although special provisions were adopted to protect Hispanas, such policies were seldom enforced. Now, Hispanas had no more influence than did white women. Also, in Los Angeles, San Antonio, Santa Fe, and Tucson, Hispanas held more paid employment and headed more households than they had before American conquest. Despite the dislocations they suffered, Hispanas clung to patriarchal values. They adhered to the concept of *la familia,* an extended kin network that could include *compadres,* or friends, and demanded loyalty before an individual's own welfare or success. In other words, Hispanas strongly resisted becoming pseudo-white women.

White Women

Across the California and Oregon trails coursed thousands of white women. In 1843, 1,000 migrants assembled in Independence, Missouri. They covered 2,000 miles to reach their final destination, Fort Vancouver on the Columbia River in Oregon country. In 1845, another 3,000 migrants entered Oregon. During the 1850s and early 1860s, settlers began to inhabit the vast and semi-arid Great Plains.

Of these migrants, perhaps as many as one-third to one-half were women, who soon discovered numerous freedoms and opportunities that had not existed in their former homes. For instance, schools throughout the West welcomed female students. When the first tax-supported university in Iowa, now the University of Iowa, opened its doors in 1856, it accepted 124 students—83 males and 41 females.

In addition, western women who chose to marry—and not all did so—could often strike a good bargain. They offered their own experience, skills, and labors and, in turn, looked for good health, perseverance, and practical expertise in potential husbands. Still, couples often courted in haste. In a society where males far outnumbered females, matches frequently occurred without parental guidance or sufficient forethought.

Some women of the Church of Jesus Christ of Latter-day Saints, or Mormons, constituted an exception to this process because they practiced plural marriage. Only a small percentage of Mormons adhered to plural marriage and, among those families that did, the wife, or wives, had to grant a husband permission to marry another wife. Also, many of these Mormon women maintained that they preferred polygamy because it lightened their workloads, provided several "mothers" for their children, and supplied them with additional women in the household to share their emotional and psychological burdens. In 1857, one Mormon woman explained that plural marriage freed her to "work out her individual character as separate from her husband."

Western marriages and families, both monogamous and polygamous, experienced a huge number of stresses. Despite the positive aspects of western settlement, many factors exercised negative pressure: the demanding physical environment, financial worries, lack of support from kin and from religious institutions, and changing expectations of marriage. In addition, alcohol abuse was rife in frontier regions, as was the use of violence to settle disputes.

When their marriages foundered, numerous western men and women deserted their mates or applied for a divorce. Because western divorce laws were generally more liberal than those in the Northeast and the South, the divorce rate in the West far outdistanced the divorce rate in other regions of the country. In fact, during the 1850s the then-western state of Indiana was widely known as a divorce mill—an early forerunner to Reno.

Female divorce petitioners increasingly complained that their husbands physically or verbally abused them. More and more courts accepted this grievance as grounds for divorce. Male divorce petitioners frequently accused their wives of stepping out of bounds and of being strong minded. As these complaints suggest, the customary female ideal—that of an obedient, passive, docile, and quiet woman—began to break down in the West before the Civil War.

If western women asserted themselves it was because most recognized their own worth. Women who worked in their homes and gardens from sunup to sundown recognized that they were crucial contributors to their families' ventures. As one Illinois woman put it, "While the men were learning to farm, the women and children actually supported the families. . . . The women were not unaware of this fact and were quite capable of scoring a point on occasion when masculine attitudes became too bumptious."

Growing numbers of western women worked outside the home. Unlike the East, in the West more women taught school than did men. Many taught in missionary schools established for Native American pupils. Other women worked in an incredible variety of jobs, including boardinghouse keepers, domestics, doctors, editors, entrepreneurs, missionaries, milliners, ministers, nurses, shop clerks, and writers. Although women often met with prejudice and criticism, they continued to work. As a California book sales agent of the 1850s remarked, she had to steel herself daily to enter offices and restaurants to seek out potential customers—mostly men.

Western women increasingly engaged in reform and club activities. They, too, were far from immune to the argument that women must serve as moral guardians of home and family. Thousands of women, including rural women, joined church auxiliaries, book clubs, hospital aid associations, musical groups, and western chapters of the Women's Christian Temperance Union. As they battled to improve their communities and help less fortunate people, these women discovered their own skills and abilities. They soon learned that they could capably run meetings, handle funds, and cast votes.

This expansion of women's roles and contributions encouraged many women to seek additional changes. During the 1840s and 1850s, the discussion of woman's rights, including woman's right to own property and to vote, gained momentum in western states and territories. Jane Grey Swisshelm, editor of the *St. Cloud Visiter* (Minnesota), used the pages of her newspaper to argue for woman's rights, specifically improved education for women and woman suffrage. Her cause was not always popular. On more than one occasion, Swisshelm found her property vandalized or her press thrown in the river. Yet after every such affront she persevered and set up business once again.

Black Women

Not all western women received the right to obtain a better education, hold a well-paid job, seek membership in a club, or exercise the right to vote in local elections. African American women often found themselves excluded from rights and privileges that white women took for granted. Women's clubs accepted only members with the same skin color. Schools often barred nonwhite or non-English-speaking girls from attendance. Employers usually gave preference to white, English-speaking women. As a result, the western experience of a woman of color could differ radically from that of a white woman.

Still, a significant number of black settlers participated in the westward migration. Local manuscript census records indicate that slave women played an important part in settling the West. Even states that proclaimed themselves antislavery in sentiment had slaves in their population. Owners usually described these people as servants rather than slaves, although the terms of servitude were essentially the same as slavery. Frequently newspaper advertisements sought the return of a runaway "servant." One owner claimed that his black, thirteen-year-old servant had been "decoyed" away by a "meddling person." He declared that "it would be an act of charity to her could she be restored to him."

Unlike slaves, free women of color usually went west by choice. They frequently settled in towns rather than rural areas. They often took jobs as unskilled laborers and domestic servants. Typically, free women of color received less pay and worse treatment than did their white counterparts. Many employers refused to hire black women at all. In addition, businesspeople frequently denied them service and landowners refused to rent their property to them.

Despite the difficulties, a sizable number of African Americans and black women of other backgrounds established themselves in the West. During the 1830s, a Mississippi River steamboat cook nicknamed "Black Ann" not only supported herself but bought her children out of slavery. Another named Elizabeth Eakins bought land in Owen County, Indiana, in 1839, paying $1.25 per acre. Another free black family converted their home into a station on the Underground Railroad and helped white abolitionists move fugitive slaves to Canada. Yet other women of color opened boardinghouses, restaurants, laundries, and similar businesses. African American women far outnumbered men in the teaching profession. Clearly, these and other black women maximized their opportunities when they occurred.

Asian Women

Like African Americans, Asian people encountered problems in the American West. Asian women, including Chinese and Japanese, had long lived in Hawaii, but only a few had settled on the mainland. Then war and poverty in China spurred a large number of Chinese, especially men, to migrate to the United States. In 1851 approximately twenty-seven hundred Chinese landed in the United States, many of them Cantonese from Guangdon (Kwangtung) Province on the southeastern coast of China. The following year over twenty thousand others did so. Some 77 percent of Chinese immigrants permanently located in California, while others went to Idaho, Montana, Nevada, Oregon, and Washington.

A few of these immigrants were women. Some helped men colonize the fishing villages of Monterey, California. Several other Chinese women went to rural areas as farm wives. The majority of the early Chinese immigrants were single men, discouraged by low pay from bringing women as wives from China. State antimiscegenation laws barred Chinese men from marrying white American women. Other Chinese were married men who had left their wives and families in China. Employers, who viewed these men as temporary and migratory laborers, had little interest in helping them attract their wives and families to the United States. The low wages they paid encouraged Chinese men to keep their families in China, where the cost of living allowed their American wages to stretch farther.

These and other forces created a demand for Chinese prostitutes. After 1840, employers began to import Chinese women. Poverty-stricken families sold their daughters into indentured servitude, while other families were duped into parting with daughters. By the 1850s, Chinese societies known as *tongs* supplied West Coast brothels with Chinese women. Women who worked as prostitutes demonstrated a variety of responses to their situations. Some died before the end of their four- or five-year term. Others became small entrepreneurs—such as shop or boardinghouse keepers catering primarily to the Chinese community. These women sometimes made a profit and achieved influence in their communities. Yet others fled, especially to Protestant-sponsored mission rescue homes, or married and left the business of prostitution behind them.

In 1860, only 1,784 Chinese women lived in the United States, compared to 33,149 Chinese men. In such cities as San Francisco, approximately 85 percent of Chinese women were indentured servants working as prostitutes. Others were wives and daughters of men of the merchant class. These women usually spent cloistered lives caring for their families in segregated areas known as Chinatowns. Other less-fortunate women worked for low wages sewing, washing clothes, rolling cigars, or making such goods as brooms and slippers. Yet others were farming wives and daughters, who, much like white women, helped with agricultural and related tasks.

Numerous examples demonstrate that such women made the best of their situations. For instance, Polly Bemis, a former prostitute turned homesteader in Idaho, became a legendary figure, known for her compassion and courage. In another case, Mary Bong married an older man and went to Sitka, Alaska, where she established a successful business. Although white people nicknamed such women as "China Polly" or "China Mary," both Polly and Mary, as well as hundreds of other Asian women, were determined to find the "Gold Mountain" they had heard so much about before leaving Asia. If success meant hard work, then they would turn their hands to it. The conditions they faced in the new home might have been especially hard for Asian women, yet the American West offered them more opportunities than had their former homes.

For many Americans, the age of reform meant little more than newspaper headlines or perhaps the occasional annoyance with reformers' rantings. They were busy living their own lives. Or perhaps they preferred to think of the United States in happier terms. During the 1850s, Frances Flora Palmer, a noted and widely popular lithographer at the firm of Currier and Ives, captivated Americans with her cheerful and reassuring farm scenes, winter landscapes, railroad trains hurtling across the terrain, and pioneers trekking westward.

Other Americans, however, had a newly expanded awareness of social problems. They knew with certainty that their great nation had its imperfections. Even though the Panic of 1837 and a plethora of reform movements had stimulated many changes for the better, slavery still blemished American democracy. In addition, women, who contributed heavily to the nation's economic system, had received little in the way of rights or other compensation. Additional problems persisted as well. By 1861 many Americans at least recognized the existence of injustice. What they would do to redress it further was, as of yet, unknown.

One thing was clear. For decades, American reformers had been speaking, writing, and holding public demonstrations at a fevered pace. They had, in the parlance of the day, pulled at the very "woof-and-warp" of American society. Unsurprisingly, those years of intense, often frantic reformism had set the stage for some kind of emotional confrontation.

Study Guide

Checklist of important names, terms, phrases, and dates in Chapter 4. Think about what or who each was and why she, he, or it was significant.

antebellum South
"black codes"
Milla's Midnight School
Harriet Brent Jacobs's *Incidents in the Life of a Slave Girl*
New Orleans
Frances Kemble
Mary Boykin Chestnut
southern women's charitable associations
Women as Moral Guardians
Caroline Lee Hentz
Lydia B. Sigourney
E. D. E. N. Southworth
Elizabeth Fries Lummis Ellet
women's auxiliaries
Catharine Beecher
normal schools
Almira Lincoln Phelps
Lancaster Industrial School
Institute for Colored Youth
Sarah Mapps Douglass
Fanny Jackson Coppin
voluntary motherhood
birth-control methods
Elizabeth Blackwell
Emily Blackwell
Susan Fenimore Cooper's *Rural Hours*
Antionette Brown Blackwell
Oneida Community
"visiting"
"worthy poor"
American Female Moral Reform Society
Female Prison of Mount Pleasant, New York
Dorothea Dix
Daughters of Temperance
moral suasion
Philadelphia Female Anti-Slavery Society

Mary Ann Shadd Cary
Frances Ellen Watkins Harper
Harriet Tubman
Sojourner Truth
exhortation
Massachusetts Pastoral Letter
Letters on the Equality of the Sexes, and the Condition of Women
Underground Railroad
Harriet Beecher Stowe
"the other sex"
The Lily
Amelia Bloomer
1841 World Antislavery Convention in London
Lucretia Mott
Elizabeth Cady Stanton
1848
Seneca Falls, New York
Bloomer outfit
Ernestine Rose
Susan B. Anthony
Lucy Stone
black feminism
Sarah Bagley
Lowell Female Labor Reform Association
Harriet Farley
"The Revolution in the North"
farm "wives"
Trail of Tears
bounties and annuities
Treaty of Guadalupe Hidalgo
Gwinn Land Act
concept of *la familia*
Church of Jesus Christ of Latter-day Saints, or Mormons
missionary schools
Jane Grey Swisshelm
Chinatowns
Polly Bemis
Mary Bong

Chapter 4 issues to think about and discuss:

- In what ways did the Panic of 1837 intensify reformism in the United States?
- In what ways did the slave system become more rigid during the antebellum era? What factors were responsible?
- Divorce is usually seen as a social problem. Why did various groups of women view divorce as a "relief" and a reform?
- For what reasons did men accept, and even support, women's claim to heightened morality?
- In what ways was Susan Cooper's *Rural Hours* a breakthrough for women interested in nature and environmental problems?
- In what ways did "feminized" religious messages underwrite female reformism?
- Why did female moral reformers think they had a right to judge prostitutes and men?
- How did temperance and abolitionist reform not only lead women into woman's rights, but make women's rights seem like a highly just and moral cause?
- What qualities and characteristics did white and black female reformers share? How did their situations differ?
- Why did some Americans oppose the goals of the pre–Civil War woman's rights movement? What did these people have to lose if things changed?
- Women tried to bring about change in many areas at once. Would it have been better for them to concentrate on one or two issues at a time?
- Reform movements seem to go on year after year, decade after decade. Once a social problem is identified, what stands in the way of its quick resolution?
- What does the statement "Hispanas had no more influence than white women" mean?

Suggestions for Further Reading

Women in the South

Bardaglio, Peter W. "Rape and Law in the Old South: 'Calculated to excite indignation in every heart,'" *Journal of Southern History,* 60 (November 1994): 749–772.

Bleser, Carol, ed. *In Joy and in Sorrow: Women, Family, and Marriage in the Victorian South, 1830–1900.* New York: Oxford University Press, 1991.

Burnham, Dorothy. "The Life of the Afro-American Woman in Slavery," *International Journal of Women's Studies* I (July/August 1978): 363–77.

Campbell, John. "Work, Pregnancy, and Infant Mortality Among Southern Slaves," *Journal of Interdisciplinary History* 14 (Spring 1984): 793–812.

Censer, Jane Turner. "'Smiling Through Her Tears': Ante-Bellum Southern Women and Divorce," *American Journal of Legal History* 25 (January 1981): 24–47.

Clinton, Catherine. "Equally Their Due: The Education of the Planter Daughter in the Early Republic," *Journal of the Early Republic* (Spring 1982): 39–60.

—. "Fanny Kemble's Journal: A Woman Confronts Slavery on a Georgia Plantation," *Frontiers* 9 (1987): 74–79.

Coryell, Janet L., Martha H. Swain, Sandra Gioia Treadway, and Elizabeth Hayes Turner, eds. *Beyond Image and Convention: Explorations in Southern Women's History.* Columbia: University of Missouri Press, 1998.

DeCredico, Mary A. *Mary Boykin Chestnut: A Confederate Woman's Life.* Madison, WI: Madison House, 1996.

Farnham, Christie Anne. *The Education of the Southern Belle: Higher Education and Student Socialization in the Antebellum South.* New York: New York University Press, 1994.

—, ed. *Women of the American South: A Multicultural Reader.* New York: New York University Press, 1997.

Faust, Drew Gilpin. *The Ideology of Slavery: Proslavery Thought in the Antebellum South, 1830–1860.* Baton Rouge: Louisiana State University Press, 1981.

Hine, Darlene Clark, Wilma King, and Linda Reed, eds. *"We Specialize in the Wholly Impossible": A Reader in Black Women's History.* Brooklyn, NY: Carlson Publishing, 1995.

Hudson, Larry E., Jr. *To Have and to Hold: Slave Work and Family Life in Antebellum South Carolina.* Athens: University of Georgia Press, 1997.

Jennings, Thelma. "'Us Colored Women Had to Go Through A Plenty': Sexual Exploitation of African-American Slave Women," *Journal of Women's History* 1 (Winter 1990): 45–76.

Johnson, Walter. *Soul by Soul.* Cambridge, MA: Harvard University Press, 1999.

Jones, Jacqueline. "'My Mother Was Much of a Woman': Black Women, Work, and the Family under Slavery," *Feminist Studies* 8 (Summer 1982): 235–69.

—. *Labor of Love, Labor of Sorrow: Black Women, Work and the Family from Slavery to the Present.* New York: Basic Books, 1985.

Lebsock, Suzanne. "Complicity and Contention: Women in the Plantation South," *Georgia Historical Quarterly* 74 (Spring 1990): 59–83.

Leslie, Kent Anderson. "Amanda America Dickson: An Elite Mulatto Lady in Nineteenth-Century Georgia," in *Southern Women: Histories and Identities,* edited by Virginia Bernhard, Betty Brandon, Elizabeth Fox-Genovese, and Theda Perdue. Columbia: University of Missouri Press, 1992.

Malone, Ann Patton. *Sweet Chariot: Slave Family and Household Structure in Nineteenth-Century Louisiana.* Chapel Hill: University of North Carolina Press, 1992.

McLaurin, Melton A. *Celia, A Slave.* Athens: University of Georgia Press, 1991.

McMillen, Sally G. *Motherhood in the Old South: Pregnancy, Childbirth, and Infant Rearing.* Baton Rouge: Louisiana State University Press, 1990.

—. *Southern Women: Black and White in the Old South.* Wheeling, IL: Harlan Davidson, Inc., 1992.

Moss, Elizabeth. *Domestic Novelists in the Old South: Defenders of Southern Culture.* Baton Rouge: Louisiana State University Press, 1992.

Newcomer, Susan. "Out of Wedlock: Childbearing in an Antebellum Southern County," *Journal of Family History* 15 (1990): 357–68.

O'Brien, Michael, ed. *An Evening When Alone: Four Journals of Single Women in the South, 1827–1967.* Charlottesville: University Press of Virginia, 1993.

Pease, Jane H., and William H. Pease. *Ladies, Women, and Wenches: Choice and Constraint in Antebellum Charleston and Boston.* Chapel Hill: University of North Carolina Press, 1990.

Shammas, Carole. "Black Women's Work and the Evolution of Plantation Society in Virginia," *Labor History* 26 (Winter 1985): 5–28.

Sharpless, Rebecca. "Southern Women and the Land," *Agricultural History* 67 (Spring 1993): 30–42.

Sterling, Dorothy, ed. *We Are Your Sisters: Black Women in the Nineteenth Century.* New York: W. W. Norton, 1984.

Tobin, Jacqueline L. and Raymond G. Dobard. *Hidden in Plain View: A Secret Story of Quilts and the Underground Railroad*. New York: Anchor Books, 1999.

Walters, Ronald C. "The Erotic South: Civilization and Sexuality in American Abolitionism," 87–98, in *Procreation or Pleasure? Sexual Attitudes in American History*, edited by Thomas L. Altherr. Malabar, FL: Robert E. Kreiger Publishing Company, 1983.

White, Deborah Gray. *Ar'n't I a Woman? Female Slaves in the Plantation South*. New York: W. W. Norton & Co., Inc., 1984.

Winter, Kari J. *Subjects of Slavery, Agents of Change: Women and Power in Gothic Novels and Slave Narratives, 1790–1865*. Athens: University of Georgia Press, 1994.

Women in the North

Albert, Judith Strong. "Margaret Fuller's Row at the Greene Street School: Early Female Education in Providence, 1837–1839," *Rhode Island History* 42 (May 1983): 43–55.

Aptheker, Herbert. *Abolitionism: A Revolutionary Movement*. Boston: Twayne Publishers, 1989.

Bardes, Barbara, and Suzanne Gossett. *Declarations of Independence: Women and Political Power in Nineteenth-Century American Fiction*. New Brunswick, NJ: Rutgers University Press, 1990.

Bartlett, Elizabeth Ann, ed. *Sarah Grimké: Letters on the Equality of the Sexes and Other Essays*. New Haven, CT: Yale University Press, 1988.

Basch, Norma. "Invisible Women: The Legal Fiction of Marital Unity in Nineteenth-Century America," *Feminist Studies* 5 (Summer 1979): 346–66.

——. *In the Eyes of the Law: Women, Marriage, and Property in Nineteenth-Century New York*. Ithaca, NY: Cornell University Press, 1982.

——. "Equity vs. Equality: Emerging Concepts of Women's Political Status in the Age of Jackson," *Journal of the Early Republic* 3 (Fall 1983): 297–318.

Bednarowski, Mary Farrell. "Outside the Mainstream: Women's Religion and Women Religious Leaders in Nineteenth-Century America," *Journal of the American Academy of Religion* 48 (June 1980): 207–31.

Berg, Barbara J. *The Remembered Gate: Origins of American Feminism*. New York: Oxford University Press, 1978.

Blackett, R. J. M. *Building an Antislavery Wall: Black Americans in the Abolitionist Movement, 1830–1860*. Baton Rouge: Louisiana State University Press, 1983.

Blocker, Jack S., Jr. *American Temperance Movements: Cycles of Reform*. Boston: Twayne Publishers, 1989.

Borish, Linda J. "'Another Domestic Beast of Burden': New England Farm Women's Work and Well-Being in the Nineteenth Century," *Journal of American Culture* 18 (Fall 1995): 83–100.

Boylan, Anne M. "Women and Politics in the Era Before Seneca Falls," *Journal of the Early Republic* 10 (Fall 1990): 363–82.

Brekus, Catherine A. *Strangers and Pilgrims: Female Preaching in America, 1740–1845*. Chapel Hill: University of North Carolina Press, 1999.

Brenzel, Barbara. "Lancaster Industrial School for Girls: A Social Portrait of a Nineteenth-Century Reform School for Girls," *Feminist Studies* 3 (Fall 1975): 40–53.

Bunker, Gary L. "Antebellum Caricature and Woman's Sphere," *Journal of Women's History* 3 (Winter 1992): 6–43.

Capper, Charles. *Margaret Fuller: An American Romantic Life. Vol. I. The Private Years*. New York: Oxford University Press, 1992.

Casper, Scott E. "An Uneasy Marriage of Sentiment and Scholarship: Elizabeth F. Ellet and the Domestic Origins of American Women's History," *Journal of Women's History* 4 (Fall 1992): 10–35.

Cazden, Elizabeth. *Antoinette Brown Blackwell*. Old Westbury, NY: Feminist Press, 1982.

Clinton, Catherine. *The Other Civil War: American Women in the Nineteenth Century*. New York: Hill and Wang, 1984. Chapters 2–4, 6–8.

Cohen, Sherrill. *The Evolution of Women's Asylums Since 1500: From Refuges for Ex-Prostitutes to Shelters for Battered Women*. New York: Oxford University Press, 1992.

Conrad, Susan P. *Perish the Thought: Intellectual Women in Romantic America, 1830–1860*. New York: Oxford University Press, 1976.

Daniels, Christine and Michael Kennedy, eds. *Over the Threshold: Intimate Violence in Early America*. New York: Routledge, 1999.

Douglas, Ann. *The Feminization of American Culture*. New York: Alfred A. Knopf, 1979.

Dublin, Thomas. *Transforming Women's Work: New England Lives in the Industrial Revolution*. Ithaca, NY: Cornell University Press, 1994.

DuBois, Ellen Carol. *Feminism and Suffrage: The Emergence of an Independent Women's Movement in America, 1848–1869*. Ithaca, NY: Cornell University Press, 1978.

Dudden, Faye E. *Women in the American Theatre: Actresses and Audience, 1790–1870*. New Haven, CT: Yale University Press, 1994.

Eckhardt, Celia Morris. *Fanny Wright: Rebel in America*. Cambridge, MA: Harvard University Press, 1984.

Foster, Lawrence. *Women, Family, and Utopia: Communal Experiments of the Shakers, the Oneida Community, and the Mormons*. Syracuse, NY: Syracuse University Press, 1991.

Friedman, Jean E. *The Enclosed Garden: Women and Community in the Evangelical South, 1830–1900*. Chapel Hill: University of North Carolina Press, 1985.

Ginzberg, Lori D. "Moral Suasion Is Moral Balderdash: Women, Politics, and Social Activism in the 1850s," *Journal of American History* 73 (December 1986): 601–22.

——. *Women and the Work of Benevolence: Morality, Politics, and Class in the Nineteenth-Century United States*. New Haven, CT: Yale University Press, 1990.

——. *Women in Antebellum Reform*. Wheeling, IL: Harlan Davidson, Inc., 2000.

Gollaher, David. *Voice for the Mad: The Life of Dorothea Dix*. New York: Free Press, 1995.

Greene, Dana. "'Quaker Feminism': The Case of Lucretia Mott," *Pennsylvania History* 48 (April 1981): 143–54.

Groneman, Carol. "Working-Class Immigrant Women in Mid-Nineteenth Century New York: The Irish Woman's Experience," *Journal of Urban History* (May 1978): 255–73.

Hansen, Debra Gold, *Strained Sisterhood: Gender and Class in the Boston Female Anti-Slavery Society*. Amherst: University of Massachusetts Press, 1993.

Hardesty, Nancy A. *Women Called to Witness: Evangelical Feminism in the 19th Century*. Nashville: Abingdon Press, 1984.

Hersh, Blanche G. *The Slavery of Sex: Feminist-Abolitionists in Nineteenth-Century America*. Urbana: University of Illinois Press, 1978.

Hill, Marilynn Wood. *Their Sisters' Keepers: Prostitution in New York City, 1830–1870*. Berkeley: University of California Press, 1993.

Hoffman, Nancy. *Woman's "True" Profession: Voices from the History of Teaching*. Old Westbury, NY: Feminist Press, 1981.

Isenberg, Nancy. *Sex and Citizenship in Antebellum America*. Chapel Hill: University of North Carolina Press, 1998.

Ireland, Robert M. "Frenzied and Fallen Females: Women and Sexual Dishonor in the Nineteenth-Century United States," *Journal of Women's History* 3 (Winter 1992): 95–117.

Jeffrey, Julie Roy. *The Great Silent Army of Abolitionism,* Chapel Hill: University of North Carolina Press, 1999.

Jensen, Joan M. *Loosening the Bonds, Mid-Atlantic Farm Women, 1750–1850.* New Haven, CT: Yale University Press, 1986.

Kelley, Mary. "The Sentimentalists: Promise and Betrayal in the Home," *Signs* 4 (Spring 1979): 434–46.

——. *Private Woman, Public Stage: Literary Domesticity in Nineteenth-Century America.* New York: Oxford University Press, 1984.

——. "Reading Women/Women Reading: The Making of Learned Women in Antebellum America," *Journal of American History* 83 (September 1996): 401–24.

Kolmerton, Carol A. *Women in Utopia: The Ideology of Gender in the American Owenite Communities.* Bloomington: Indiana University Press, 1990.

Lerner, Gerda. *The Grimké Sisters from South Carolina: Pioneers for Woman's Rights and Abolition.* New York: Schocken Books, 1971.

——. "The Political Activities of Antislavery Women," 112–28, in *The Majority Finds Its Past,* edited by Gerda Lerner, New York: Oxford University Press, 1979.

Mabee, Carleton, with Susan Mabee Newhouse. *Sojourner Truth: Slave, Prophet, Legend.* New York: New York University Press, 1993.

Matthews, Glenna. *The Rise of the Public Woman: Woman's Power and Woman's Place in the United States, 1630–1970.* New York: Oxford University Press, 1992.

Matthews, Jean V. "Consciousness of Self and Consciousness of Sex in Antebellum Feminism," *Journal of Women's History* 5 (Spring 1993): 61–78.

McCall, Laura. "'The Reign of Brute Force is Now Over': A Content Analysis of Godey's Lady's Book, 1830–1860," *Journal of the Early Republic* 9 (Summer 1989): 217–36.

——. "'With All the Wild, Trembling, Rapturous Feelings of a Lover': Men, Women, and Sexuality in American Literature, 1820–1860," *Journal of the Early Republic* 14 (Spring 1994): 71–89.

McDannell, Colleen. *The Christian Home in Victorian America, 1840–1900.* Bloomington: Indiana University Press, 1986.

Morantz, Regina Markell, and Sue Zschoche. "Professionalism, Feminism, and Gender Roles: A Comparative Study of Nineteenth-Century Medical Therapeutics," *Journal of American History* 67 (December 1980): 568–88.

Osterud, Nancy Grey. "Gender and the Transition to Capitalism in Rural America," *Agricultural History* 67 (Spring 1993): 14–29.

Perkins, Linda. *Fanny Jackson Coppin and the Institute for Colored Youth, 1837–1902.* New York: Garland, 1987.

Rosenberg, Rosalind. *Beyond Separate Spheres: Intellectual Roots of Modern Feminism.* New Haven, CT: Yale University Press, 1982.

Ryan, Mary P. "The Power of Women's Networks: A Case Study of Female Moral Reform in Antebellum America," *Feminist Studies* 5 (Spring 1979): 66–85.

Samuels, Shirley. *The Culture of Sentiment: Race, Gender, and Sentimentality in Nineteenth-Century America.* New York: Oxford University Press, 1992.

Scott, Anne Firor. "Almira Lincoln Phelps: The Self-Made Woman in the Nineteenth Century," *Maryland Historical Magazine* 75 (September 1980): 203–16.

Sklar, Kathryn Kish. *Catharine Beecher: A Study in American Domesticity.* New York: W. W. Norton and Company, 1973.

——, and Thomas Dublin. *Women and Power in American History: A Reader.* Vol. I. Englewood Cliffs, NJ: Prentice-Hall, 1991. Parts 16–18.

Sterling, Dorothy. *Ahead of Her Time: Abbey Kelley and the Politics of Antislavery.* Lexington: University Press of Kentucky, 1994.

Terborg-Penn, Rosalyn. "Discrimination Against Afro-American Women in the Women's Movement, 1830–1920," 17–27, in *The Afro-American Woman: Struggles and Images,* edited by Sharon Harley and Rosalyn Terborg-Penn. Port Washington, NY: Kennikat Press, 1978.

Vertinsky, Patricia. "Sexual Equality and the Legacy of Catharine Beecher," *Journal of Sport History* 6 (Spring 1979): 38–49.

Walsh, Mary R. *"Doctor's Wanted: No Women Need Apply": Sexual Barriers in the Medical Profession, 1835–1975*. New Haven, CT: Yale University Press, 1977.

Weiner, Nelia Fermi. "Of Feminism and Birth Control Propaganda, 1790–1840," *International Journal of Women's Studies* 3 (September/October 1980): 411–30.

Wellman, Judith. "The Seneca Falls Women's Rights Convention," *Journal of Women's History* 3 (Spring 1991): 9–37.

Wessinger, Catherine, ed. *Women's Leadership in Marginal Religions: Explorations Outside the Mainstream*. Urbana: University of Illinois Press, 1993.

Yee, Shirley J. *Black Women Abolitionists: A Study in Activism, 1828–1860*. Knoxville: University of Tennessee Press, 1992.

Yellin, Jean F. *Women and Sisters: Antislavery Feminists in American Culture*. New Haven, CT: Yale University Press, 1990.

——. *The Abolitionist Sisterhood: Women's Political Culture in Antebellum America*. Ithaca, NY: Cornell University Press, 1994.

Women in the West

Bean, Lee L., Geraldine P. Mineau, and Douglas L. Anderton. "High-Risk Childbearing: Fertility and Infant Mortality on the American Frontier," *Social Science History* 16 (Fall 1992): 337–63.

Beecher, Maureen Ursenbach. "Women's Work on the Mormon Frontier," *Utah Historical Quarterly* 49 (Summer 1981): 276–90.

Bledsoe, Lucy Jane. "Adventuresome Women on the Oregon Trail, 1840–1867," *Frontiers* 7 (1984): 22–29.

De León, Arnoldo. *The Tejano Community, 1836–1900*. Albuquerque: University of New Mexico Press, 1982.

——. *Mexican Americans in Texas: A Brief History*. Wheeling, IL: Harlan Davidson, Inc., 1993. Chapter 3.

Dysart, Jane. "Mexican Women in San Antonio, 1830–1860: The Assimilation Process," *Western Historical Quarterly* 7 (October 1976): 365–75.

Embry, Jessie L. "Effects of Polygamy on Mormon Women," *Frontiers* 7 (1984): 56–61.

——. "Mothers and Daughters in Polygamy," *Dialogue* 18 (Fall 1985): 99–107.

González, Deena J. "La Tules of Image and Reality: Euro-American Attitudes and Legend Formation on a Spanish-Mexican Frontier," 57–69, in *Unequal Sisters: A Multicultural Reader in U.S. Women's History*, edited by Vicki L. Ruiz and Ellen Carol DuBois. 2d ed. New York: Routledge, Chapman, & Hall, 1994.

Griswold del Castillo, Richard. *The Los Angeles Barrio, 1850–1890: A Social History*. Berkeley: University of California Press, 1979.

——. *La Familia: Chicano Families in the Urban Southwest, 1848 to the Present*. Notre Dame, IN: University of Notre Dame Press, 1984.

Hirata, Lucie Cheng. "Free, Indentured, Enslaved: Chinese Prostitutes in Nineteenth-Century America," *Signs* 5 (Autumn 1979): 3–29.

Jameson, Elizabeth. "Women as Workers, Women as Civilizers: True Womanhood in the American West," *Frontiers* 7 (1984): 1–8.

Kaufman, Polly Welts. "A Wider Field of Usefulness: Pioneer Women Teachers in the West, 1848–1854," *Journal of the West* 22 (April 1982): 16–25.

——. *Women Teachers on the Frontier*. New Haven, CT: Yale University Press, 1984.

Levy, Joann. *They Saw the Elephant: Women in the California Gold Rush*. Hamden, CT: Shoe String Press, 1990.

Mikesuah, Devon A. *Cultivating the Rosebuds: The Education of Women at the Cherokee Female Seminary, 1851–1909.* Urbana: University of Illinois Press, 1993.

Miller, Darlis A. "Cross-Cultural Marriages in the Southwest: The New Mexico Experience, 1846–1900," *New Mexico Historical Review* 57 (October 1981): 335-60.

Myres, Sandra L. "Mexican Americans and Westering Anglos: A Feminine Perspective," *New Mexico Historical Review* 57 (October 1982): 317–33.

Peters, Virginia Bergman. *Women of the Earth Lodges: Tribal Life on the Plains.* North Haven, CT: Archon Books, 1995.

Riley, Glenda. "'Not Gainfully Employed': Women on the Iowa Frontier, 1833–1870," *Pacific Historical Review* 49 (May 1980): 237–64.

Schlissel, Lillian. "Family on the Western Frontier," 81–92, in *Western Women: Their Land, Their Lives,* edited by Lillian Schlissel, Vicki L. Ruiz, and Janice Monk. Albuquerque: University of New Mexico Press, 1988.

Thomas, Sr. M. Evangeline. "The Role of Women Religious in Kansas History, 1841–1981," *Kansas History* 4 (Spring 1981): 53–63.

Tong, Benson. *Unsubmissive Women: Chinese Prostitutes in Nineteenth-Century San Francisco.* Norman: University of Oklahoma Press, 1994.

Yasui, Barbara. "The Nissei in Oregon, 1834–1940," *Oregon Historical Quarterly* 76 (1975): 225–57.

5

"Womanly Strength of the Nation": The Civil War and Reconstruction

1861 to 1877

In April 1861, the American nation split into warring factions, the United States of America and the Confederate States of America. During four years of hostilities lasting until 1865, the North lost some 364,000 lives and the South, 265,000. This was not what American women had wanted or expected. They had asked for reform, especially the abolition of slavery, not a national bloodletting. The war created a number of dilemmas for women, northern and southern, white and of color, but they rose to the challenges.

The Civil War determined that the American states were to remain united and, to use a modern term, multicultural. The war forced the nation to make some hard choices. The postwar period of Reconstruction offered Americans the opportunity to confront other decisions and set a constructive pattern for the decades to come. Because most Americans were unwilling or unable to act in positive ways, the era of Reconstruction shook American society and government to its foundations, as well as caused important changes in the lives and roles of American women. The model of womanhood, already somewhat unstable as a result of reformers' attacks, experienced further blows. Although postwar women took a number of steps forward, they also took a few steps back.

Nor did the American West escape unscathed. Westerners not only participated in the war but faced difficult conditions during Reconstruction. As white settlers became a dominant force in many parts of the West, peoples of color often suffered. Despite its reputation for equality and democracy, the West failed to achieve any more harmony among disparate groups of people than did the rest of the nation. And whether or not conditions were hospitable for women frequently depended on their race, ethnicity, and social class.

Through wartime strife and the subsequent effort to rebuild the nation, the resiliency of gender expectations and social constructs regarding women proved remarkable. Although the invented American woman tottered a bit, the model staunchly resisted collapse.

226

Civil War, 1861–1865

Forsaking Woman's Rights

When the Civil War erupted in 1861, women faced three immediate crises. The earliest of these was the necessity to lay aside all their reform efforts except abolitionism. Although woman's rights' leaders had invested years of hard work and anguish in their cause, they now turned their eyes to the war. As part of their contribution to the war effort, women's rights leaders disbanded their formal, organized campaign.

Virtually all women's rights advocates agreed that abolishing slavery and bringing fighting to an end had to claim the nation's complete attention. Some took a practical approach to the issue. In 1861, one woman wrote that it was "unwise" to argue for women's rights "when the nation's whole heart and soul are engrossed with the momentous crisis and nobody will listen." In addition, even though the Civil War had not started as a war to free slaves, female reformers planned to push it in that direction.

As a result, women's rights' leaders made abolishing slavery the top priority. Their activities were instrumental in defining the war as one waged to end slavery and helped to push President Abraham Lincoln toward declaring emancipation. In 1863, woman's rights leaders Susan B. Anthony, Elizabeth Cady Stanton, Ernestine Rose, and Lucy Stone issued a call for a women's meeting in New York City on 14 May. Literally thousands of women responded. They organized, on the spot, the National Woman's Loyal League. When abolitionist Angelina Grimké Weld took the platform and spoke eloquently for supporting a war for freedom, cheering delegates agreed to collect one million signatures on petitions supporting congressional approval of the Thirteenth Amendment to the U.S. Constitution. The Thirteenth Amendment would constitutionally abolish slavery.

With Elizabeth Cady Stanton as president and Susan B. Anthony as secretary, the Loyal League soon had five thousand members. Of these, two thousand volunteers gathered 400,000 signatures by the time the League dissolved in 1864. In the process, thousands of women learned how to speak in public, organize committees and meetings, and raise petitions. Women may have set aside woman's rights for the moment, but the skills they developed in the interim would prove useful once they redirected their energies toward woman suffrage.

On the Homefront

The second crisis that women encountered was the very preservation of their homes, families, and communities as men left for the front. Women were critically important on the homefront during the war years. In the North, they took jobs in arsenals and munitions factories and were more visible than ever in textile mills (essential for supplying the cloth for uniforms) and other industrial employment. They invaded the offices of the Union government to become clerks known as "Government Girls." In rural areas, women ran farms and other family businesses. Northern women were relatively fortunate that they lived and worked in a prosperous and well-populated area of the country and that most of the war's battles were fought far from their homes.

In the South, harsher conditions faced women, as the war was largely fought on their home turf. Like their northern counterparts, southern women kept farms, plantations, and businesses going. The departure for the front of three out of four white men of military age left many women to perform unfamiliar tasks and heavy labor. Consequently, women went into the fields as workers and overseers of slaves. Although women feared slaves, most learned how to enforce authority, sometimes by brandishing a whip or a revolver. Other women worked for wages, including as clerks in the Confederate Department of the Treasury, as underpaid seamstresses in the Confederate Clothing Bureau in Richmond, and as ordnance workers who prepared cartridges for pittance wages. Still others took jobs with the Confederate Army that ranged from clerk to engineer. And in large numbers, southern women became teachers.

In addition, and perhaps worst of all, because most battles occurred in the South, southern women often had to face the terror of war in their own backyards. The absence of men necessitated women acting as guards and soldiers in defense of their families and farms. From Georgia to Mississippi, women wielded weapons to repel attacks by unprincipled white men and dispossessed Native Americans. The fear of rape and death for them and their daughters turned many a woman's dreams into nightmares.

When the Union's naval blockade of April 1861 cut off the primarily agrarian South from its sources of war supplies, Confederate women turned their homes into crude factories to produce what goods they could with limited materials. Moreover, they frequently pursued a "scorched earth policy," that is, they burned their own crops and killed their own stock to keep them out of Yankee hands.

Southern women also took up arms. They learned how to use rifles so they could resist invasions. In several towns, southern women organized local defense units. In 1865, a group of women under a woman's command lined up for battle as Union troops approached their town of LaGrange, Georgia.

Many of these women were formerly members of a "genteel elite," but war-time conditions and economic need clearly took priority over the standards of womanhood that formerly would have prevented them from pursuing their own means of sustenance and support. It must have seemed to the planter-class women that all other groups of women except them stood to gain from the war. For if the Confederacy won, the ravaged nation would have to go it alone. If the Confederacy lost, the South would be little more than a poor cousin to the flourishing North and West.

As early as 1862 and 1863, southern white women grew disillusioned with the war. Those women living in nonslaveholding areas were especially critical of the conflict. Others complained that the war was not turning out to be the brief and successful rebellion that many southern men had predicted. As women lost fathers, husbands, and sons, or saw them come home without arms or legs, they questioned how such a brutal conflict could be in their interests. Elite white women had already seen the source of their wealth eroded by the war. Others watched as their slaves revolted; inwardly, some women even cheered the slaves on. Regardless of their sentiments, there was nothing women could do except persevere.

In spite of women's heroic actions, however, by 1864 and 1865 incredible want and poverty existed throughout the Confederacy. In 1864, a Virginia woman wrote to her soldier husband: "Chrismus is most here again, and things is worse and worse. . . . Everything me and the children's got is patched. . . . We haven't got nothing in the house to eat but a little bit of meal. I don't want you to stop fighten them Yankees till you kill the last one of them, but try and get off and come home and fix us all up some and then you can go back and fight them a heep harder. . . . We can't none of us hold out much longer down here . . . my dear, if you put off a-comin' 'twon't be no use to come, for we'll all hands of us be out in the garden in the old graveyard with your ma and mine."

Also in 1864 and 1865, an unprecedented number of white women had to support themselves and their children by seeking paid employment in positions ranging from seamstresses to salespeople. Thousands more took teaching jobs in white schools or alongside the "missionary" teachers flocking in from the North to teach in schools established by the Union government for freed blacks after the Emancipation Proclamation of January 1863. Although female teachers had been a rarity in the pre–Civil War South, by the end of the war as many women as men taught in southern schools.

Despite their efforts, women were not always able to stave off the specter of starvation. As early as 1863, women in the Confederate capital of Richmond, Virginia, organized a protest asking for public relief in the form of food and other supplies. The protest soon turned into a riot, during which women looted local merchants for badly needed food supplies.

Soon, "women riots" and "female raids" occurred with regularity in such cities as Savannah, Georgia, and Mobile, Alabama. Women intended their violence as protest against ineffective Confederate food-distribution programs and merchants who took advantage of war-time shortages by charging outrageously high prices for basic items. During these outbursts, angry women seized not only bread, but wheat, corn, and other foodstuffs to feed themselves and their hungry families.

A Savannah woman arrested for participating in a bread riot and brought to trial distributed small cards that said, "Necessity has no law & poverty is the mother of invention." She argued that southern women had tried "fair words" to no avail. Thus, they were driven to using sticks and stones to break shop windows in order that they and their children might survive for one more day. If the Confederate government would not help them, women would help themselves.

During the last years of the war, desperate southern women continued to pillage and riot for bread in such southern cities as New Orleans and Atlanta. Such extreme actions by white women revealed not only the extent of poverty in the Confederate states, but the depths of despair to which its women had sunk.

It is little wonder that in the face of such problems, southern women's efforts in support of the war had died. In mid-1864, a Montgomery, Alabama, woman admitted publicly that "the Aid societies have died away; they are name and nothing more." Instead, women now searched for male relatives on battlefields littered with the wounded and dead. One woman who looked for a wounded cousin said that she came upon men "in every stage of mutilation." She left the battlefield convinced that "nothing is worth a war!"

Undoubtedly, most southern white women were pleased to see the war end in 1865, even though they were on the losing side. At least the killing had stopped. Most had no idea of the further terrors that would confront them during the years of Reconstruction.

Black Women's Efforts to Aid the War

The third crisis women encountered was supplying food, clothing, and medical goods to the troops. Because the war included many factions and was fought on many fronts, it touched the lives of the majority of American women. Women of different races and different regions had to convert their skills as domestic artisans and supervisors to war-time production. They soon recognized that the war had divided American women into different camps than had existed before the war. Black women, North and South, now stood united in their hope of abolishing slavery, while white women, North and South, were estranged by the line between the Union and the Confederacy. Now, it seemed to African Americans, white women were enemies, often working at cross-purposes in their particular war-relief efforts.

Because of the new order of things, black women everywhere proved themselves heroic in furthering the cause of freedom for their people. In the South, numerous black slave women disrupted plantation work and initiated work stoppages in the fields. Others ran away from farms and plantations, especially after the Emancipation Proclamation granted them freedom in 1863. Some joined communities on the Sea Islands of South Carolina and elsewhere that offered farmland, education, and civil rights to former slaves. Moreover, black women, who, at great costs to themselves, urged their men to join the Union troops as soldiers, took over men's jobs, kept families afloat, provided the army with supplies, and nursed the wounded. In the North, free black women joined the war effort by supplying sanitary goods, speaking against slavery, gathering names on antislavery petitions, and volunteering as teachers.

All of these women now faced a way of life they had never before seen, or even thought possible. Those who fled to cities or followed Union troops in hopes of handouts discovered what starvation and disease really was. Those who met with physical abuse and rape at the hands of Union and Confederate soldiers lost their faith in white men as saviors. Others, however, for the first time in their lives, received politeness and respect from white men. Those who saw their sons hung as Confederate spies or marched off to service in Union armies understood the meaning of despair. Those who worked in military hospitals watched powerless to help as surgeons sawed off men's limbs, blood running across the floor. Still, they believed that freedom from slavery was worth such suffering.

A black woman from Georgia, Susie Baker King Taylor, kept a diary of her remarkable service as a Union nurse. After first teaching black children at the request of Union forces, she began to work as a nurse and laundress. For her own protection, Taylor learned how to handle a musket. Taylor served with Clara Barton on South Carolina's Sea Islands, bandaging the wounded and consoling the dying. She feared that by witnessing so much misery she had lost her feelings and sensitivity. "It seems strange," she wrote, "how our aversion to seeing suffering is overcome in war—how we are able to see the most sickening sights, such as men with their limbs blown off and mangled by the deadly shells, without a shudder." Although seriously hurt in a boat accident, Taylor remained with her regiment until the fall of Charleston in 1865.

Names of other black women who participated in the war effort sound familiar, for they were the abolitionist advocates of the pre–Civil War years. For example, Philadelphia abolitionist Charlotte Forten was a volunteer teacher, representing the Pennsylvania Freeman's Relief Associations at Port Royal, South Carolina. She also served as a newspaper correspondent who shared her war-time experiences and observations with thousands of interested readers. In 1864, Forten's essays, "Life in the Sea Islands," appeared in the *Atlantic Monthly*. Forten sketched a powerful portrait of southern black people showing them as ready to learn, work, and become full American citizens.

Meanwhile, another Philadelphia abolitionist, Mary Ann Shadd Cary, served as a Recruiting Army officer who enlisted black volunteers in the Union army. Although other women worked as unofficial recruiters, Cary was the only one who received an official appointment. She even went west and brought back men to Boston. Cary seemed to have a knack for picking good men because her recruits were usually judged the "best lot" brought to headquarters.

Harriet Tubman, the Underground Railroad's most famous "conductor," offered her services to the Union as a scout and spy. Still a woman of great fortitude and cleverness, Tubman conducted secret missions that supplied information vital to Union troops' successful raids of arsenals, warehouses, and forts along the Combahee River in South Carolina. Although she had a bounty on her head placed by the Confederate government, she passed back and forth over enemy lines in great peril, but without injury. Of one battle that resulted in the deaths of nearly 1,500 black troops, Tubman wrote: "Then we saw the lightning, and that was the guns; and then we heard the thunder, and that was the big guns; and then we heard the rain falling, and that was the drops of blood falling; and when we came to get in the crops, it was dead men that we reaped."

In addition to these notable women, thousands of other black women applied their energy and talent when and where they could. One of these was Mary Elizabeth Bowser, a former slave who became a servant in Jefferson Davis's home. There Bowser read military plans and collected useful information for the Union. As she dusted, Bowser simply looked at documents, committing them to memory on the spot. Each evening Bowser would go to Union sympathizer Elizabeth Van Lew's home, where the two women translated the information into code and dispatched it to Union generals.

Throughout the conflict, women also helped "contrabands," as runaway slaves, the property of people in rebellion against the United States, were called during the Civil War. The Contraband Relief Society of Washington, D.C., composed of forty black women, supplied the refugees who streamed north or into Union army camps with sorely needed food and clothing. After the Emancipation Proclamation of 1863, women also helped newly freed women and men. The Colored Ladies' Sanitary Commission of Boston sent $500 to help freed slaves in Savannah, Georgia. Other similar groups helped the former bondspeople by establishing schools, locating housing for widows and orphans, and giving them bandages and medicine.

Black women in both the North and South began to provide education for black children. After the Union declared the education of black Americans a priority, Mary Chase, a free black woman from Alexandria, Virginia, established on 1 September 1861 the first day school for contrabands. Later that month, the American Missionary Association (AMA) engaged a young free black woman to teach classes at Fortress Monroe in Virginia. The African Civilization Society supported yet other black schools and teachers.

The number of black women teachers grew during the war years. In 1864, a free black woman who had studied at Oberlin College asked for the support of the American Missionary Association so that she could teach in the South. "No thought of suffering, and privation, nor even death, should deter me from making every effort possible, for the moral and intellectual elevation of these degraded people," she asserted. She received $10 a month plus board for her efforts. Another free black woman received $15 a month for teaching day, evening, and Sunday schools, visiting black families, assisting the ill, and helping at a nearby hospital.

As the stories of such women demonstrate, black women fully participated in the war.

White Women Helping the Union

White women operated somewhat differently, concentrating their efforts on either the Union or the Confederate cause. During the spring of 1861, northern women congregated in homes, hotels, and churches to preserve fruit, roll bandages, and sew shirts. In April of 1861, three thousand New Yorkers met in Cooper Union to form the New York Women's Central Association for Relief. Such groups held charity fairs and other fund-raising events to collect money with which to buy supplies for ill-equipped troops and military hospitals. In virtually every state, these organizations offered women the opportunity to serve as officers and members of finance committees and sit on boards of directors. Late in 1861, the U.S. Sanitary Commission began to coordinate the efforts of seven thousand Union aid societies.

Such women's groups sent tremendous quantities of supplies to Union troops and military hospitals. Organized in 1862, the Weldon, Pennsylvania, society contributed $17,000 worth of goods in one year. Other local societies began to establish "refreshment saloons" in the North to aid passing military personnel. Two Philadelphia saloons shipped more than $80,000 in supplies and served more than 600,000 meals by 1864.

Yet when representatives from women's groups traveled to the front to assist in distributing supplies they found that havoc prevailed. Some hospitals had received far more goods than they needed. Others had received nothing. And sometimes troop movements had shunted aside supply wagons, which sat in the rain or sun until their cargo had spoiled. Thus, these women acted as forwarding agents, regulating the efforts of women's groups to prevent duplicated deliveries in some cases and shortages in others, and routing supply wagons away from roads used to move troops and munitions.

One of the most active and effective of these women was Annie Turner Wittenmyer of Keokuk, Iowa, who served as forwarding agent for aid societies throughout Iowa. In 1862, Iowa officials recognized Wittenmyer's efforts by appointing her a State Sanitary Agent. When one morning Wittenmyer walked into an overcrowded hospital and discovered her own wounded brother eating hardtack and greasy bacon from a metal tray, she began to campaign for "diet kitchens" that would serve patients healthful fare. In 1864, she established the first diet kitchen, but her cause was far from achieved. Wittenmyer frequently fought with hospital agents, cooks, and doctors who laced coffee grounds with sawdust or sand to make them last longer, and she tried to stop hospital cooks from preparing and serving tainted meat to wounded soldiers.

Even more well known is Clara Barton, who assisted the efforts of the U.S. Sanitary Commission. A former schoolteacher, Barton soon earned the names "Angel of the Battlefield" and "American Nightingale" for her colossal efforts. The Civil War taught her about corruption, lack of supplies, and carnage so great that, in her words, "I wrung the blood from the bottom of my clothing before I could step." Because Barton's war time experiences convinced her of the need for a national, ongoing relief organization capable of offering aid during wars and other national disasters, she later founded the American Red Cross.

Supplying Union Medical Personnel

In the years before the war's beginning, women had begun to gain acceptance as nurses. In 1850, the Massachusetts legislature had established the New England Medical College and urged potential nurses to attend lectures. In addition, Catholic sisters provided nursing care and many hospitals employed charwomen in a quasi-nursing capacity. With the outbreak of war, however, none of these resources could meet the demands of military hospitals. Nurses were quickly trained in short courses or at the front.

Dr. Elizabeth Blackwell, who recognized the need for better instruction for medical personnel, established in 1861 a training program for nurses. Blackwell applied for the position of Superintendent of Women Nurses, but as a "female doctor," she appeared suspect to many people and thus failed to gain appointment. Instead the position was secured by Dorothea Dix. As Superintendent of Women Nurses, Dix recruited only women who were at least thirty years of age and "plain in appearance." Dix feared that young, attractive nurses might arouse their patients' amorous interest and create chaos in the hospitals. This policy caused great bitterness among younger women eager to contribute their services to the war effort.

The diaries of Civil War nurses reveal the horrors they experienced. One Massachusetts woman, who served in 1862 and 1863 in a Washington hospital, wrote in August 1862, "We have just cleaned and dressed over a hundred men from the Harrison's Landing—poor, worn fellows!" A month later, she described a young man who was shot through the lungs yet survived the night: "We considered him the greatest sufferer in the house, as every breath was a pain." As a strong abolitionist, she explained that she could endure the hardships associated with nursing because "this is God's war. . . . The cause is that of the human race, and must prevail."

Another Massachusetts war nurse similarly revealed in letters the terrible conditions she found in military hospitals. After a tour of Union hospitals in 1863, she instituted a letter-writing and canvassing campaign in Illinois to amass needed supplies. Her description of a hospital in which she served graphically reveals the horrible conditions: "It was a miserable place. . . . The cots were placed inside the tents, on unplanked ground. . . . The hospital swarmed with large green flies, and their buzzing was like that of a beehive. . . . Many of the patients did not lift their hands to brush away the flies that swarmed into eyes, ears, noses, and mouths."

Among Union nurses, Mary Ann Bickerdyke was especially well known. Called "Mother" Bickerdyke, this Quaker woman gained a reputation as a tireless worker and a fearless administrator in nineteen battlefield hospitals between 1861 and 1865. A coworker claimed that Bickerdyke was not afraid of anybody, including the high-ranking generals. "But Lord, how she works!" she marveled.

For their Herculean efforts, female nurses received compliments from people ranging from wounded soldiers to President Abraham Lincoln. It was not until 1892 that the U.S. Congress finally granted nurses formal recognition for their invaluable services by giving them a pension of $12 a month.

Female doctors fared even worse. At the outbreak of the Civil War, neither the Confederacy nor the Union commissioned women physicians. Although such women as Elizabeth and Emily Blackwell practiced as physicians in the North, widespread resistance to female doctors continued. During the war, however, people who began to recognize the medical competence of women and the nation's need for more physicians supported the idea that women should have access to formal medical training. Such arguments led to the founding of the Chicago Hospital for Women and Children and the New York Medical College for Women, both in 1863.

The following year, Mary Edwards Walker, M.D., who had graduated from Syracuse Medical College in 1855, received a commission from the Union as assistant surgeon, the first woman to perform such duties in the American armed services. The U.S. Congress awarded Walker the Congressional Medal of Honor, which it later rescinded, probably in light of her strident reform campaigns, especially for woman suffrage and women's health, and her habit of wearing male attire. Well after Walker's death in 1919, Congress restored the medal to her.

Providing Other Services for the Union

Women offered their talents in many other ways as well. The demands of war opened previously banned activities to women. For instance, female authors wrote on politics and war. Julia Ward Howe employed poetry to arouse her readers' love of country. Howe penned her most famous work, the poem "Battle Hymn of the Republic," in 1861 and set it to music in 1862. Other women authors were responsible for an outpouring of books, pamphlets, and tracts designed to raise funds or shape public opinion. Yet other women published personal diaries, reminiscences, and novels written during the war years.

A few women even served as spies, couriers, guides, scouts, smugglers, informers, and saboteurs. In Richmond, Virginia, Elizabeth Van Lew posed as an eccentric known as "Crazy Bet." Under this guise, she rescued Union prisoners from Richmond's war prisons and operated as a spy on behalf of the Union.

Meanwhile, some women went to the front as soldiers. Disguised as men, about four hundred women fought in the Civil War between 1861 and 1865. One Michigan woman served undetected for two years as a male nurse, spy, mail carrier, and soldier.

Assisting the Confederacy

A similar effort took place in the South, where white women had a reputation of being even more combative and angry than southern men. Some passionately supported the slave system, but most simply felt outraged at the way the South had been treated. They believed that the federal government had misused the South, leaving the South no choice but succession from the United States. Yet others thought of the war as romantic or had great loyalties to the culture in which they had been raised.

Consequently, many southern women became compulsive about providing war supplies to Confederate troops. In 1861, a Virginia woman who spent every morning sewing clothes for soldiers proclaimed that, "Our needles are now our weapons." Like Union women, Confederate women organized fairs, raffles, concerts, and plays to raise money to purchase needles, thread, and cloths, as well as to buy the goods they could not, or could no longer, produce themselves.

Women's contributions to poorly supplied Confederate troops were quite remarkable. In one month in 1863, the Center Ridge, Alabama, group sent "422 shirts, 551 pairs of drawers, 80 pairs of socks, 3 pairs of gloves, 6 boxes and a bale of hospital stores, 128 pounds of tapioca and $18 for hospital use." Other local societies established "wayside homes" throughout the South to aid passing military personnel.

Supplying Confederate Medical Personnel

From the war's beginning, southern women visited medical hospitals, offering to read to patients, write letters for them, or pray with them. Late in 1862, the Confederate Congress finally agreed that women could work in official capacities in medical hospitals. Because middle- and upper-class white women felt that the care of men's bodies was "indelicate," they served in supervisory capacities, removed from actual patient care. Yet female administrators saw a great deal. Phoebe Yates Pember, a hospital matron near Richmond, Virginia, indicated that conditions were no better in Confederate hospitals than in Union facilities. Railing especially against drunken surgeons, Pember recorded incompetence, laziness, and discrimination against her as a woman administrator. By 1863, wartime prices were so high in Richmond and her salary so meager that she wrote articles for magazines or did copy work for the War Department at night to supplement her pay.

The daily work of bandaging, feeding, and bathing patients usually fell to slaves or poor white women. In some cases, women who had followed their husbands to the front visited the hospital each day to care for their wounded spouses. A few well-born white women resented this division of labor along racial and social class lines. "Are the women of the South going into the hospitals?" She was saddened that the answer was no. Still, some white women boldly took on the job of nursing mutilated men who often died in their hands.

Providing Other Services for the Confederacy

As in the North, southern women produced patriotic songs and literature. Next to "Dixie," the most popular song was "The Bonnie Blue Flag," which appeared in 1862 with words written by a southern woman.

Female spies also assisted the Confederacy. The Washington society hostess, Rose Greenhow, effectively relayed intelligence to Confederate leaders in code until her house arrest in late 1861 and her subsequent dispatch to Richmond. Greenhow's efforts reportedly helped the South win the First Battle of Bull Run in July 1861. Belle Boyd gained prominence as a Confederate spy and courier in Virginia before she was betrayed and arrested in July 1862.

Women were especially effective as couriers and smugglers because hoopskirts, bustles, and false hairpieces could conceal anything from messages to pistols. Both northern and southern soldiers soon overcame their modesty, however, and by late 1861 thoroughly searched these good Victorian ladies or hired matrons to do so. Louisa Buckner of Virginia was one of the many women arrested after such a search. She carried concealed in her skirt more than one hundred ounces of quinine intended for a Confederate hospital. Still, many ingenious women successfully slipped through enemy lines with goods hidden in crinolines, hoop skirts, parasols, and false-bottom trunks.

In addition, a number of southern women fought for the Confederacy, especially during the first year of the war. One Mississippi woman enlisted with her husband and remained in the military after he was killed at Shiloh. Other women masqueraded as men in order to see combat. Some of these used fictitious names, while others took the names of deceased male relatives. When their secret was discovered, they were sent home without the formality of discharge papers. Nonetheless, a few of them managed to serve for years without blowing their cover. A "Lieutenant Harry T. Buford" was really a Cuban-born black woman who grew up in New Orleans. During her various exploits on behalf of the Confederate cause, her ruse was so successful that some women, thinking her a man, even flirted with her.

Three Steps Forward, Two Steps Back: Reconstruction, 1865–1877

Freedwomen

On 9 April 1865, the Civil War finally came to a halt with Confederate general Robert E. Lee's surrender at Appomattox Courthouse, Virginia. For some women, notably slave women, the war had wrought a revolution in their legal status. When the reunited nation entered Reconstruction, a period in which the federal government intended to put the United States back together and heal its wounds as quickly as possible, women of all backgrounds and races hoped to witness the development of new ways of thinking and acting. Some women's wishes came true: progress indeed characterized their postwar lives. Other women, however, now faced a struggle to survive. For most, some things changed for the better, but a lot remained to be done.

For black women, who had constituted the majority of the African American population on the larger plantations and the minority on the smaller farms in the South, the war radically altered their situations. All black women were finally free of the shackles of slavery. In 1863, the Emancipation Proclamation had freed the slaves living in the Confederate states; then, in 1865, the Thirteenth Amendment to the U.S. Constitution prohibited slavery throughout the nation forever.

Unarguably, freedom offered definite advantages to black women workers. Many could now define their working hours to some extent or change employers. They also had the right to appeal to authority when dissatisfied with their conditions. Formal complaints indicated widespread problems, but they were different from those that arose under slavery. Employers commonly withheld pay to control black women workers and sometimes reacted to them with violence, but women now resisted, filed complaints, moved to other plantations, or took different jobs. Wages remained low and conditions difficult, but black women were no longer chattels.

In addition, marriage was now a legal institution for former slaves. This resulted in a widespread move to formalize individual marriages and establish stable families that included both parents. Massive marriage ceremonies involved as many as sixty or seventy couples, while other former slaves worked diligently to locate spouses or children who had been sold away from them, some traveling from state to state and advertising in newspapers.

African American marriages and families might have gained legal recognition, but the economic insecurity of the black family remained. Consequently, a large number of newly freed black women labored for wages in order to supplement their families' inadequate incomes. Black men who viewed women's labor outside the home as a holdover of slavery nonetheless had to watch their wives seek paid employment.

Sharecropping proved especially hard on freedwomen in the South. The system of sharecropping, in which black workers raised crops on white-owned land and "shared" the crop with the land's owner as payment for its use, was a compromise solution after the war's end. Although sharecropping offered black women more time for domestic labor and protected them to a degree against sexual exploitation by white men, many freedwomen discovered that they still had to work in the fields if their cotton, tobacco, or rice farms were to produce any profits. In addition, white landowners recognized black men as the heads of households, thus undercutting women's power and authority in family decisions.

The lives of black women were hard in numerous other ways. In practice, racial boundaries actually tightened after the war. For instance, black women were denied access to vocational training and the right to hold certain jobs. In addition, black men received privileges that were not extended to black women. While black men received the right to vote and to hold office in the late 1860s, black women acquired no political rights. Black men could own land, but black women seldom had the means to do so.

Also, freedwomen still found themselves vulnerable to sexual aggression by both black and white men. In 1866 in Memphis, Tennessee, for example, a gang of white men anxious to reestablish white power over African Americans broke into the home of two freed women and raped them both. Such outrages occurred frequently in following years. And when the Ku Klux Klan, the Knights of the White Camellia, and other white-supremacy groups formed, their members not only threatened and attacked black women, but sometimes raped them as well.

A large number of rural black women tried to improve their lot by migrating to southern cities. Here they found poor housing, limited job openings, and low wages. In Jackson, Mississippi, and Galveston, Texas, black washwomen went on strike to boost their wages to $1.50 per day. White officials arrested the strike leaders and threatened to require license fees of all washwomen. Domestic servants fared even worse. They worked long hours, seven days a week, for which they received low pay supplemented by castoff clothing and leftover food.

Some urban black women escaped these evils by selling such goods as spruce beer, peanuts, blueberries, strawberries, and vegetables in local markets. Those women who could raise the necessary capital opened restaurants, grocery stores, and boardinghouses. Despite independence, these urban black women found that their lives were still hard.

Nor did black women who migrated to northern cities after the Civil War necessarily find the opportunities for which they had hoped. Like their southern counterparts, they were usually limited to domestic, menial, and service jobs with long hours and poor pay. In 1871, a northern black woman complained in the Philadelphia *Post:* "Why is it that when respectable women answer an advertisement for a dressmaker, they are invariably refused, or offered a place to cook or scrub, or to do housework: and when application is made to manufactories immediately after having seen an advertisement for operators or finishers, meet with the same reply." These women expressed further dismay when they learned that, although they paid taxes, their children were denied admission to tax-supported schools because of their race.

When Reconstruction formally ended in 1877, half of adult black women held jobs, especially as washwomen, domestics, nursemaids, and seamstresses, the same tasks black women had performed as slaves. Such work was time consuming and back breaking, leaving black women little time or energy to work for reform on their own behalf.

Helping Freedwomen

During the Civil War, the United States suffered tremendous property damage, extensive loss of life, and a blow to its national spirit that would take generations even to begin to heal. After the end of the war, black Americans especially needed immediate medical assistance, food, and housing, as well as education, vocational training, and jobs.

Many women participated in the effort to aid newly freed slaves by working for the tax-supported Freedmen's Bureau, established in 1863 as a temporary agency charged with assisting newly freed slaves by supplying them food, medicine, housing, and education. The Freedman's Bureau provided $3 million to help give basic education to between 150,000 and 200,000 freed men and women. By 1869, the year the in which Congress terminated the Freedmen's Bureau, women accounted for half of the agency's nine thousand teachers.

Yet other women, especially educated black women, moved south to work as missionary teachers in black charity schools. Typically, they taught children during the day, adults at night, and held Sabbath schools on Sundays. In New Orleans and Charleston, freedmen's schools employed only black teachers. And in Savannah, Susie King Taylor extended her Civil War service staying on to teach black children. Such black teachers from the North often experienced discrimination in the South. They earned less than did white women teachers, but paid more for their lodgings. They often lived and dined in segregated quarters. In 1868, black teacher Sara Stanley was prohibited from marrying a white teacher.

A huge number of white and black women offered additional assistance through other voluntary organizations. The most notable of these was Josephine Griffing, who between 1863 and 1872 served as the general agent for the Freedman's Relief Association in Washington, D.C. This benevolent association differed from the government-funded Freedmen's Bureau in several ways. With contributed funds, Griffing established sewing and other vocational schools for black women and sought employment and housing for black families. She argued that the Congress should relocate newly freed southern families to northern and western states at government expense. Although Griffing arranged jobs and housing for seven thousand black Americans in and around Washington, D.C., her western relocation plan helped only a few thousand blacks.

Southern White Women

The years of Reconstruction, when Union troops occupied the South and ruled according to martial law, held out far less promise to southern white women. Most of them recognized that the South's social order had to be redefined. Yet it was not a good time for white women to push for autonomy or to challenge long-standing attitudes. Southern men who returned alive were humiliated; they had failed to protect their families and the southern way of life. Rather than shattering men any further, white southern women had to reconstruct men's confidence and assist in the renegotiation of such issues as who had veterans' rights, who could vote, and how much a former slave owner should pay freed slaves.

In addition, formerly elite plantation ladies had to learn a whole range of new tasks, including how to perform domestic chores without the help of servants. Many had to contrive new ways to bring in small amounts of cash, perhaps by selling eggs and butter, writing for local newspapers, or teaching school. Some had to run entire plantations without the aid of husbands, brothers, and sons who had been disabled or killed during the war. As they moved into the fields and various aspects of farm operations, these women proved themselves as worthy workers and managers. For the first time, white southern women gained respect as farmers, for their labor and any cash income they produced were crucial to keeping the southern agricultural economy afloat.

One notable female farmer was Frances Butler, the daughter of British actress Frances Kemble and Georgia planter Pierce Butler. When her father died shortly after the war, Butler took over the management of his rice and cotton fields on the Sea Islands of Georgia. She negotiated labor contracts with black workers, then acted as her own manager. Butler's operation was able to pay out wages without resorting to sharecropping. Nonetheless, it would be quite some time before Frances Butler was able to sleep without the reassuring bulge of a pistol under her pillow.

Because most of the South lay in economic ruin, women of other classes had to seek jobs that paid wages. They worked as clerks, teachers, and industrial laborers to help support their families. The thousands who failed to find employment had to depend on rations from northern-based charity groups. In addition, southern white women lived in fear of the African American soldiers who patrolled neighborhoods, towns, and cities as part of the federal government's occupation of the South. In 1866, when black males obtained the right to vote, many white women, who still could not vote, felt additional resentment and outrage.

In addition, white women soon discovered that white men wanted to continue to "protect" them. The patriarchal ideal of a man caring for and sheltering his wife did not die easily. Nor did some white women wish patriarchy to disappear. The war years had convinced these women that they did not care to shoulder the responsibilities of men. Other white southern women resented what seemed to be a prevalent male attitude. After all, these women asked, had they not proven themselves during the war years? Had they not kept farms and families going? Had they not gone to the edge in their sacrifice and efforts?

The answer to each question had to be yes. White southern men had a deep reason for protecting white women, a reason not easily talked about except in hushed whispers or at all-male gatherings. Many white men increasingly viewed freed black men as sexual threats. They recognized that because the war had depleted the supply of eligible white men in the South, some white women might seek African American mates. If a number of white women had chosen to establish relationships with free and enslaved black men before the war, what would happen now that black men were free agents?

One solution was to pass additional laws preventing black men from even daring to look at white women. In 1863, the same year that the Emancipation Proclamation freed the slaves in the Confederate states, the word "miscegenation" was invented to demean interracial relationships. Although war-time anxieties regarding black men's sexuality certainly had existed, after the war white men's fear of black men reached dangerous levels. Southern states added yet more laws and harsher punishments designed to eliminate black/white relationships. Illegal attacks and hangings (lynchings) of black men further terrorized the black population.

After the war, white southerners were so sensitive to the topic of relationships involving black men and white women that a British visitor to the South reported that, "Americans are not squeamish as to jokes; but you must not jest in their society about the love of black men for white women." Such white supremacist organizations as the Ku Klux Klan were quick to pledge themselves to protect "white womanhood."

In reality, there is no evidence that black men typically lusted after white women. Despite the stereotypes to the contrary, very few black men stalked white women with the idea of rape in their minds. For one thing, African American men recognized that involvement of any kind with a white woman could result in great pain and even death. For another, those who did establish liaisons with white women found that antimiscegenation legislation barred interracial marriage. In addition, threats of tarring-and-feathering, castration, or lynching frequently stood in the way of a racially mixed couple. In 1866, for example, a Virginia black man failed to show up for his wedding to a white woman because a group of white men had prepared for him "a coat of tar and cotton."

In following years, the Klan and other similar groups reserved their worst tortures for black men involved with white women. Another way of discouraging interracial unions was to accuse the black man of rape and lynch, or hang him without a legal trial. To a lesser extent, terrorist groups "warned" white women, either through nighttime visits or severe beatings, that their behavior must stop. Some women who bore mulatto children committed infanticide rather than admitting that a child's father was an African American and having to face the consequences.

Clearly, the degradation and defeat that the war years imposed on white southern men, coupled with the jubilation of African Americans at finally tasting freedom, created a highly volatile situation between white and black men in the South. In a sense, white women became a symbol of everything white men had lost: wealth, land, an enslaved work force, political power, a reassuring racial hierarchy, and, perhaps worst of all, their honor and credibility as men. As a result, white southern women became pawns in a deadly power game.

Revising Domestic Ideals

Because the Civil War years had so dramatically altered the United States, a major revision of the stereotyped American woman seemed to be at hand after the war's end. Some northern white women even hoped that women might be granted the right to vote at the same time that former black male slaves received citizenship and suffrage.

During Reconstruction, ideas about American women would indeed undergo many modifications, but not drastic ones. When Catharine Beecher and Harriet Beecher Stowe collaborated in writing their *Principles of Domestic Science* in 1870, they revealed typical attitudes of the era. They outlined the American woman's "profession" as "the care and nursing of the body in the critical periods of infancy and sickness, the training of the human mind in the most impressible period of childhood, the instruction and control of servants, and most of the government and economies of the family state."

Beecher and Stowe added that, although they sympathized with "every honest effort to relieve the disabilities and sufferings of their sex," they believed that most of women's problems stemmed from the disregard in which most Americans held domestic endeavors. If, they argued, women received training for their prescribed domestic duties just as men did for their trades and professions, family labor would no longer be "poorly done, poorly paid, and regarded as menial and disgraceful." The sisters' rationale for domestic training would soon help underwrite the development of the science of home economics.

Numerous other Americans felt that women should return happily to their homes now that the war had ended and focus their full attention on domestic matters, but many women were uncomfortable with this return to domestic ideals. Because of their work with such groups as women's aid societies, sanitary commissions, and the National Women's Loyal League, women had found that they could effectively speak in public, raise money, handle finances, and serve as executive officers of large organizations, skills hardly useful at home. Those whose husbands died in the war now acted as the arbiters, decision makers, and disciplinarians in their families; circumstances kept these women from staying in the background. And many women had to support, or help, support their families. Thus, although many women physically returned to their homes after the war's end, they found it difficult or impossible to resume prewar behavior.

White Women's Education

As before the war, white female reformers targeted improved education and the right to teach as two of their most important objectives. They were not about to let the gains they had made slip out of their grasp. Nor were they willing to let war-time changes drift away. Rather, they hoped to use the skills they had obtained or honed during war as a stimulus for further breakthroughs.

Certainly, the situation regarding teaching had changed during the war years. In 1860, women teachers had accounted for 25 percent of the nation's teachers. After the war, this figure grew rapidly, for many Americans believed that women's natures were especially suited to teaching impressionable children. For instance, in 1865, the *New York Times* commented that teaching was a work "to which intelligent women are preeminently adapted" and "a duty in which many more ought to be engaged." By the late 1870s, women composed 60 percent of the nation's teaching force. From these women came pressure for better education. Women teachers, with little or no training for their professions, demanded admission to existing colleges. They also asked for the founding of normal (teacher-training) schools and women's colleges.

The response was positive. As early as 1865, Vassar College in Poughkeepsie, New York, opened its doors to a class of thirty-five women. The Vassar curriculum, in an attempt to emulate those offered to male students, included philosophy, Greek, Latin, German, French, English, mathematics, astronomy, physics, chemistry, hygiene, art, and music. At first, the Vassar faculty was composed largely of men. This situation caused Sarah Josepha Hale to write many editorials and letters in protest, and to urge other women to do so as well. Finally, the college hired Maria Mitchell, who in 1850 had been elected to the American Academy of Arts and Sciences for her discovery of the comet that bears her name. As professor of astronomy at Vassar, Mitchell trained the first group of women astronomers in the United States.

Smith College and Wellesley College offered similar programs when they opened in 1875. Unlike Vassar, these colleges had a pool of professionally trained women scholars from which to hire faculty. Wellesley was especially successful in recruiting female faculty members. Wellesley thus provided the opportunity for young women to learn from the first generation of American women who held advanced degrees, especially in botany and psychology.

In the South similar trends developed. Many middle- and upper-class women who had to help support their families entered the teaching profession. This movement of southern women into the classroom soon resulted in a demand for teacher-training schools in this region. In 1875, a normal school opened in Nashville with thirteen women in its student body and two women on its faculty. Several fine southern women's colleges were established during the postwar years, including Agnes Scott, Goucher, Randolph-Macon, and Sophie Newcomb.

In the mid-West, women eagerly enrolled in land-grant colleges. Funded by the Morrill Act in 1862, land-grant colleges were coeducational. Because these schools attempted to give women and men equal education, some odd programs sometimes resulted. At Iowa State College (present-day Iowa State University), the school's "equality" policy resulted in uniformed women toting rifles and drilling in military science programs. In 1869, however, Iowa State replaced military science with domestic science for its female students.

Changes in women's sports accompanied these educational developments. Vassar College furnished facilities for gymnastics, bowling, horseback riding, swimming, skating, and gardening. In 1866, several Vassar women formed a baseball club that played every Saturday afternoon. One young woman commented that "the public so far as it knew of our playing was shocked."

Yet the acceptance of athletics at such schools as Vassar as instrumental in encouraging thousands of women to try their skill at sports. Ice and roller skating were favorites. Bowling became popular, and in 1868, *The New York Clipper* reported that a woman bowled 290- and 300-point games in the same evening. Later, in 1874, Mary E. Outerbridge of New York introduced tennis into the United States. Hampered by long skirts, corsets, and large hats, women played tennis with ladylike grace but little agility. Also in the mid-1870s, archery tournaments provided the first organized sport for women. In an even more progressive vein, croquet allowed women and men to compete in the same game.

Along with education and sports came a self-improvement fad. Hundreds of handbooks on diet, appearance, hygiene, digestion, and female health rolled off the presses in an attempt to convince wan, corseted women to become active, well-rounded American girls and women. One type of guidebook suggested the use of mechanical aids such as nose pinchers, shoulder braces, and massage rollers. Yet others urged women to buy a variety of cosmetics and medicines. Of these, Lydia E. Pinkham's Vegetable Compound, produced by a family business founded in 1875, achieved great renown. Another type of advisor took the natural route, however. These counselors recommended hobbies, reading, and physical activity to women who hoped to better themselves.

Women Writers

After the Civil War, women became authors in growing numbers. They had to challenge a long tradition that said women could only write about such "women's" topics as love, families, and children. During the conflict, women had written about war and politics, describing nauseating scenes of men dying, as well as corpses piled upon corpses. Women had seen, and written about, revolting examples of government corruption, at home and at the front. Why, women authors wondered, should they have to return to prewar limitations?

During the 1860s and 1870s, the period in which she wrote many of the 1,775 poems she produced in her lifetime, Emily Dickinson of Amherst, Massachusetts, assaulted the conventions that hemmed in women writers. She took as her motifs such topics as death, immortality, nature, and passion. Dickinson bowed, however, to social custom that frowned on women publishing such work, releasing only six poems while she lived. Later, Dickinson's works were not only published but received critical acclaim. Today, Dickinson is ranked as the first "serious" American woman poet.

Another well-known woman writer of the era was Louisa May Alcott, who through her work lit here and there small flames of feminism. As a daughter of the transcendentalist Bronson Alcott and the reformer Abigail Alcott, Louisa grew up with a decided mind of her own. She not only wanted to be a writer, but a writer who made a difference. Alcott wrote several novels, dozens of thrillers, short stories, and a diary of the time she spent as a Civil War nurse, but it was her novel *Little Women* that captured public attention.

In 1868 and 1869, Alcott published *Little Women* in two parts. She used this family-oriented, domestic tale to follow the progress of four sisters from girlhood to womanhood. In it, she revealed her interest in alternative roles for women. She created the strong-willed Jo who proclaimed, "Don't shut yourself up in a bandbox because you are a woman, but understand what is going on, and educate yourself to take part in the world's work, for it all affects you and yours." Alcott portrayed the central character of Jo as a restless, searching individual. At the end of the story, however, Jo succumbs to marriage and domesticity.

Both Dickinson and Alcott represent writers fighting to understand women's issues and women's proper role in post–Civil War society. Each, in their own way, gave in to traditional standards of women's behavior. Meanwhile, other women writers took nature as their subject. Although the conservation movement had not yet emerged in America, already women were observing and writing about the physical environment. Women's nature writing typically avoided the two themes of conquest and domination of the land that appeared in many men's books of the era. While male writers tended to argue for "progress" and the use of natural resources, women generally focused on the beauty and spiritual aspects of nature.

Women interpreted the physical environment as female, using female images to describe landscapes. Too, female nature writers viewed the outdoors as welcoming of women, especially those strong and independent enough to meet nature's challenges. Because women had been told that they should fear the wilderness, as they were especially vulnerable to its forces, female writers re-envisioned nature. Rather than rejecting their domestic worlds, however, women writers simply expanded the domestic realm to include the outdoors. If women were to guide family members as they ventured into nature, then nature must fall into women's sphere.

Beginning in the early 1860s, writer Helen Hunt Jackson explored and expanded this subtle argument with great skill. When, in 1867, Jackson moved to Colorado Springs, she delighted in exploring and, despite her long skirts and petticoats, in climbing mountains. In the Colorado landscape, Jackson found both grandeur and the presence of God. She produced a spate of essays, poems, and travel sketches about Colorado, all the time describing nature in terms that would resonate with female readers. Jackson especially employed such women's metaphors as birth, family, and death. In 1876, she wrote an article for the *Atlantic Monthly* about the "silence of the wilderness." Again, she used female images to characterize nature: "This is silence like that in which the world lay pregnant before time began."

Like other early female nature writers, Jackson demonstrated that women could enjoy nature firsthand, describing nature in terms that made particular sense to women. For Jackson, such terms as "Mother" Nature and the "virgin" wilderness had special meaning; they marked and recognized what she believed was the female spirit in all of the natural world.

Art and Music

After the Civil War, Americans held slightly different attitudes toward female artists and musicians, increasingly viewing art and music as "feminine" realms. Some claimed that a woman's inherently delicate and sensitive nature lent itself to artistic and musical production. Others, who thought of art and music as embellishments and refinements in life, identified both endeavors as a traditional part of woman's sphere.

As they always had, American women continued to produce a tremendous amount of folk art in their homes during this era. Through their ingenious designs, quilts especially recalled recent history such as the Underground Railroad, the Slave Chain, and Sherman's March to the Sea. Meanwhile, the new attitude toward art underwrote several important changes for aspiring women artists. Gradually, art schools admitted women to life drawing classes with nude models. Women could also seek training in cities and other countries, well away from the supervision of their families. In 1874, when the Art Students' League organized in New York City, its members included women.

One example of the "new" woman artist was Harriet Hosmer of Watertown, Massachusetts. During the 1850s, Hosmer had studied in Rome with respected sculptor John Gibson. This experience did not make Hosmer into an ardent woman's rights advocate, however. Rather, she believed that "every woman should have the opportunity of cultivating her talents to the fullest extent, for they were not given her for nothing." By the late 1860s and early 1870s, Hosmer's commissions ranged from San Francisco to London.

As a sculptor of international repute, Hosmer enjoyed a rich social life, yet declined to accept any of her suitors. At the age of twenty-four, she wrote to a friend, "an artist has no business to marry." She added that male artists might marry, but not a woman "on whom matrimonial duties and cares weigh more heavily . . . for she must either neglect her profession or her family, becoming neither a good wife and mother nor a good artist." Hosmer's decision was consistent with that of other women in her field; more than half of mid-nineteenth-century women artists chose to remain single rather than attempt to combine their demanding careers with marriage.

Hosmer encouraged the work of Edmonia Lewis, a New Yorker of black and Chippewa Indian parentage. Lewis studied briefly with a Boston sculptor in the early 1860s, then went to study in Rome in 1865. By the 1870s, Lewis had established a solid reputation in both the United States and Europe. Her works enjoyed quite a success at the Centennial Exposition of 1876 in Philadelphia. Because women had been denied exhibit space in the main exhibition hall, they collected money to erect a woman's pavilion. There they displayed women's art, including Lewis's sculptures.

In the field of music, women composers similarly demonstrated that women could produce fine work. During the 1860s, Faustina Hassae Hodges, daughter of organist Edward Hodges and an organist herself, composed ballads and piano pieces. One of her songs, "Rose Bush," reportedly sold 100,000 copies. Frances Raymond Ritter, a composer and music professor at Vassar, included among her work *Some Famous Songs: An Art-Historical Sketch* (1878) and *Ballads* (1887). Few American female composers of symphonies and concertos have been identified, but neither were there many American male composers. Well into the late nineteenth century, classical music in America concentrated on European repertory by male composers.

Science and Technology

During the postwar years, widespread prejudice and discrimination prevented women from entering technological and scientific fields. A well-bred lady did not even admit her interest in such matters. A mid-nineteenth-century editor remarked that "if an unfortunate female should happen to possess a lurking fondness for any special scientific pursuit she is careful (if of any social position) to hide it as she would some deformity."

In spite of this discouraging climate of opinion, some women continued to pursue their scientific interests. During leisure hours, they collected plant specimens, studied them under the microscopes they had set up in their parlors or sitting rooms, and classified them. If anyone questioned a woman's interest, she could simply reply that she was furthering her education, for her own benefit and that of the children she raised. A number of such women discovered plants native to the United States that had never before been catalogued. Women were seldom theorists, but neither were male botanists of that time theoretically oriented.

Kate Furbish of Maine especially built a reputation as an innovative botanist. In 1873, her father died and left her a guaranteed income so that she did not have to marry for financial support. She remained single and spent thirty-five happy years collecting and classifying the flora of Maine. Furbish captured in watercolors the plants she found, especially in swamps, which she described as "a delightful retreat." Without financial compensation, Furbish published articles in the *American Naturalist,* lectured widely, and helped found the Botanical Society of Maine. Although an unpaid amateur, Furbish discovered two new plant varieties, both of which were later named for her. Furbish demonstrated that women could not only think in "scientific" ways, but could make significant contributions to their fields.

Women explored science in other ways as well. During the mid-1860s, a number of women formed scientific study groups. Others supported the introduction of more science courses into women's curricula. During the 1870s, women even approached male scientific societies requesting membership; sometimes women were accepted, but only as "corresponding members" who were neither expected to attend the meetings nor allowed to vote.

Other women took an interest in technology and its applications. One way to measure women's involvement in this field is through applications to the U.S. Patent Bureau. Before the Civil War, only fifty-five women had obtained patents, but between 1860 and 1888 nearly three thousand women applied for patents. The Civil War had acted as a watershed, convincing women to strike out on their own behalf. In addition, the growing ability of women to control their own earnings encouraged them to apply for patents on their inventions. Most female patent applicants lived in New York, Illinois, and Massachusetts. They primarily created items that were domestic in nature. Household and clothing innovations, as well as improvements in bandages and other medical devices, accounted for most of women's inventions in this era.

Many other female inventions were patented under men's names. A case in point was Butterick's clothing patterns. In 1867, Ebenezer Butterick, who borrowed the idea for saleable paper patterns from those his wife made from newspaper on her kitchen table, began his business with 12 workers; three years later he employed 140 people. Using treadle-powered sewing machines and Butterick's mass-produced patterns, women could sew their own stylish clothes at home.

Technology offered women such new contrivances for the home as improved lamps and stoves. At first, domestic ideology impeded the adoption of home technology; it preached that only unfeminine, lazy, or incompetent women would use newfangled, mechanical instruments to care for their families. Catharine Beecher was the first to urge women to embrace technology, especially in the kitchen, where, according to her, women spent over 50 percent of their time. In 1869, Beecher even designed a model kitchen with flour and grain bins, a built-in dish-drainer, a cast-iron stove set in a glass-door alcove to contain the heat, and an indoor sink with two pumps, one for rain water and one for well water.

In spite of what society might have believed, individual women demonstrated great aptitude in science and technology.

Women as Paid Workers

In addition to positive changes for women, postwar society saw many problems. Although slavery had been destroyed, all type of social ills demanded attention. Even in the bustling and prosperous North, all was far from rosy with white female wageworkers. The harmful situation facing these women, already exhausted from decades of reform and four years of war, lay boiling just under the surface.

During the 1860s and the 1870s, large numbers of women entered all types of paid employment. Many women filled new jobs—that is, ones that had not been held by men but were created by the growing economy. As such, women found themselves employed in retail sales, office work, cigar making, typography, commercial laundries, and various types of mills. In addition, they continued to dominate the needle trades, such as sewing and shoe binding.

Whether in new jobs or old, whenever women were hired, wages fell. This occurred because employers still believed that a woman's place was in the home. Thus, employers convinced themselves that women who worked outside the home must be occasional laborers interested in "pin money." Actually, numerous women worked to support their families because their husbands had been disabled or killed during the Civil War. In other cases, male workers did not receive a living wage, their wives and daughters having to pull up the slack. Furthermore, the number of single women who had to support themselves was rising.

White working women labored for inadequate wages and in terrible working conditions. A female worker in an iron mill describes the inferno-like atmosphere in which she toiled: "it [the smoke] rolls sullenly in slow folds from the great chimneys of the iron-foundries, and settles down in black, slimy pools on the muddy streets . . . smoke on the wharves, smoke on the dingy boats, on the yellow river." Even in the more traditional areas of textile mills, working conditions literally threatened women's lives.

The terrible situation was revealed as early as 1860 by a disaster in a textile mill in Lawrence, Massachusetts. The 1860 "Slaughter of the Pemberton" exposed the dangers confronted by the nation's employed women. The Pemberton textile mill had been built in 1852 at great expense. With its wide windows and five floors, Pemberton stood as a model for mills in America and abroad. Yet on 10 January of 1860, the structure gave way. Its cast iron pillars buckled and the flooring caved in. The fifth floor toppled into workers on the lower four floors. When a lantern fell, it set fire to oil and bits of cotton that now littered the collapsing building. Pinned beneath the rubble, the terrified women could do little but wait for the flash fire to reach them. A few tried to slit their own throats or pleaded with onlookers to shoot them. When the fire died out, eighty-eight workers lay dead and many more injured, some beyond recognition.

The Pemberton tragedy grabbed front-page headlines. It appeared, newspaper editors caustically noted, that slavery did not exist only in the South. The North's textile mills, once thought to be an ideal place for women to work, operated on wage-slavery. For months, journalists reported the stories of women who worked at Pemberton to help support their families, and who met their deaths there. "A Curse on ye, ye Millionaires," one poem declared, who "sip your wine." Meanwhile, mothers wailed over dead daughters and sons. Although the outcry against insensitive northern industrialists continued throughout the war years, the war itself dominated the nation's attention.

Despite the press of the war, several reformers attempted to alert the American public to the numerous problems facing paid women workers. For instance, Caroline Wells Dall, an author and lecturer, repeatedly argued that limiting women to only a few kinds of jobs ensured low pay due to high competition among many available female workers for the same jobs. Dall pointed out that thousands of underpaid or unemployed women turned to prostitution, at which they could earn more money than they could in the dreary factories. In her best-known work, *The College, the Market, and the Court: or, Woman's Relation to Education, Politics, and Law* (1867), Dall criticized middle-class women for leading lives of frivolity while their sisters labored in sweatshops and lived in poverty.

Taking matters into their own hands, female workers tried to improve their low pay, long hours, and terrible working conditions by seeking some form of labor organization. At first, women turned to men's labor organizations, only to soon learn that they were not welcomed. In fact, when the National Labor Union (NLU) formed in 1866, no women were present. Two years later, under pressure from such suffragists as Stanton and Anthony, the NLU began to admit women members. In 1870, the NLU elected a member of the Sewing Girls' Union of Chicago as second vice president, but overall, women were barely represented in the nation's thirty-two unions. In 1873, a major economic panic brought hard times to workers and an accompanying decline in union membership, especially among underpaid women workers.

At this point, employed women responded to their exclusion from male unions by creating female unions. Although women cigar makers accounted for close to 10 percent of all cigar makers, they were denied membership in the national union. Thus, the Lady Cigar Makers of Providence, Rhode Island, organized in 1864. Another woman's union, the Collar Laundry Union of Troy, New York, also formed in 1864. This group's efforts proved remarkably successful in raising its women members' wages to a level near that of working men.

Middle- and upper-class women still interested in reform after the war founded other types of groups to help working women. Called working women's protective societies, these associations offered services such as legal aid, medical treatment, and advice to employed women. Nonetheless, the chasm between working women and elite women remained a hard one to bridge. As a result, working women relied largely on themselves. Excluded from male unions, they worked through all-female networks. To further their causes, they exerted collective female action such as neighborhood social pressure or group buying power. When shut out of male organizations, female workers developed their own forms of militancy.

Divorce

Another area that needed women's attention was divorce reform, for it appeared that bad marriages could still perpetuate yet another type of slavery. In 1860, woman's rights reformer Elizabeth Cady Stanton publicly condemned the "slavery" of a bad marriage and argued that women had the right to seek liberty from such a union. Stanton declared that divorce was a boon to women, but after the Civil War started in 1861, she set aside her campaign for divorce legislation favoring women.

The Civil War years placed great stress on American families. Under the tensions of war and with men readying to leave for the front, perhaps to never return, many couples married in haste. One observer explained that the war caused an increase in "ill-assorted" marriages between pretty young women and men clad in romantic military uniforms. In addition, the war splintered families. Both men and women went to the front, leaving mates behind. Others took jobs outside the home, while their spouses did their best to keep farms and families intact.

The war-time divorce rate rose slowly but steadily. In 1860, 1.2 out of every 1,000 marriages ended in divorce. In 1864, the ratio had risen to 1.4, and in 1866 to 1.8. In addition, the figures showed that more divorces went to women than to men, about two-thirds of all cases. Not many African Americans pursued "white," or formal, divorces, but westerners appeared to be flocking into divorce courts. In sum, Americans obtained far more divorces than any other nation in the world.

Even though many Americans were shocked by the increase in the rate of divorce, Elizabeth Cady Stanton continued to call for easier access to divorce. After the war's end, Stanton devoted an increasing number of articles and speeches to condemning patriarchal marriage. Instead of patriarchy, Stanton hoped for marriages between equals. She used the pages of *The Revolution,* a woman's rights journal that she edited, to advance her position regarding divorce, proclaiming that each "slave" who fled a "discordant marriage" gave her joy. She predicted that, "With the education and elevation of women we shall have a might sundering of the unholy ties that hold men and women together who loathe and despise each other."

While not all woman's rights leaders shared Stanton's views, many who did endorsed ease of divorce because it offered escape for the wives of alcoholics. According to common belief, drinking husbands fell into drunken rages and beat their wives and children. "A wife he thrashes, children lashes," was a saying of the era. Gradually, state legislators responded to such pressures. By 1871, thirty-four states, two-thirds of which lay in the South and West, had added drunkenness to their list of grounds for divorce.

Controlling Childbearing

Related to divorce was women's desire to gain control over their bodies, especially in the matter of reproduction. They had no wish to become slaves to husbands or to large numbers of children. During the war years, birth control by abortion increased. This trend alarmed those who still believed that it was a woman's responsibility to bear many children. Others feared that the population of the United States would be seriously depleted if women practiced birth control.

Accordingly, a number of medical practitioners and concerned citizens accelerated their opposition to planned parenthood and birth control. In 1862, an Ohio obstetrician introduced the first statute prohibiting contraception and abortion. By 1865, Americans pointed to the number of lives lost during the Civil War and wondered how long it would take to replenish the population.

Thus, the American Medical Association launched a full-scale campaign against birth control and abortion headed by Anthony Comstock. In 1873, these events culminated in the Congress passing the Comstock Law, which made it a federal crime to send obscene materials, defined to include birth-control information and devices, through the U.S. mail. Because manufacturers of birth-control products could no longer mail their wares to customers, this restriction also ended the widespread publication of birth-control advertisements in newspapers and effectively dampened public discussion of birth control.

Despite the Comstock Law and similar state provisions, thousands of women continued to seek abortions and birth-control information. Elizabeth Cady Stanton encouraged women to use some form of birth control. She argued that women were entitled to choose how many children they would bear. At the same time, an industrial, urban economy made the rearing of large numbers of children more expensive and difficult than it had been on farms. Therefore, while technology had not yet offered dependable birth-control devices, it had helped motivate women to search for them.

At the same time, gynecology became a medical specialty. Although specialties were often looked on as quackery, medical practitioners gradually recognized that grown men's bodies could not be used as a norm for all people. Medical schools now began to offer courses with titles such as "Diseases of Women and Children," which tried to cover female anatomy and illness. With the growth of medical knowledge and technology came the realization that so-called "female complaints" related to women's reproductive systems were not necessarily incurable. During the 1870s, a few courageous surgeons even experimented with the surgical removal of diseased ovaries. Only slowly, however, did gynecology gain favor among physicians and the public, but at least a "science of women," as it was then called, had made an appearance.

Alcohol Abuse and Temperance

Yet another domestic problem that women wanted to resolve was the heavy drinking of alcoholic beverages. Because the relationship between alcohol and family abuse continued to pose a problem for women and children, the postwar temperance movement attracted thousands of female supporters. Out of local bands of women who had once prayed in saloons or destroyed stocks of whiskey came the National Women's Christian Temperance Union (WCTU). Founded in 1874, the WCTU chose Annie Turner Wittenmyer of Iowa as its first president.

To Wittenmyer, the temperance crusade offered women the opportunity to fulfill their moral obligations by liberating humankind from alcohol. In an 1877 address Wittenmyer stated her position: "The drink system is the common enemy of women the world over, and the plans we inaugurate, will be eagerly sought after by the women of all civilized nations, and as the success of all moral reforms depends largely upon women, the world will halt, or move in its onward march toward millennial glory, as we halt or march." The WCTU quickly grew to become the largest woman's organization in the nineteenth century.

Women Prisoners

Other reforms fell farther outside women's supposedly domestic sphere, yet continued to claim women's reform efforts. Although women's attempts at prison reform had started before the Civil War, the situation of female inmates in prisons and reform schools generally remained wretched.

The case of Clara Temple Leonard, a reformer who worked with the Dedham home for Discharged Female Prisoners in Massachusetts, is instructive. During the 1860s, Leonard visited female prisoners and observed the horrible situations in which they lived. In 1869, Leonard called for a separate women's prison under female supervision. To her dismay, Leonard soon discovered that women who lacked the vote had little influence on penal theory and practice.

Not until 1874 did the Massachusetts legislature appropriate $300,000 for a woman's prison at Sherborn. When the prison finally opened in 1877, its male superintendent assured the public that prison officials now taught women inmates "how to work, how to read and write, and how to apply themselves industriously to their given tasks," but it seemed clear to most reformers that far more change was needed.

Law

Another area in which women had little impact was the study and practice of law. During the 1860s, the legal field continued to reject women's participation. State licensing bodies uniformly barred women from taking the required examinations.

One of the few to challenge restrictions on women was Arabella Babb Mansfield. In 1869, she applied for admission to the Iowa bar. An Iowa judge sympathetic to woman's rights ordered the bar to allow Mansfield to take the examinations. One of her examiners noted that Mansfield passed the bar exam with high honors, giving "the very best rebuke possible to the imputation that ladies cannot qualify for the practice of law." Mansfield never practiced law, however. Because of the prejudice against women lawyers, she chose instead to teach at Iowa Wesleyan and later at DePauw University in Indiana.

In the same year that Mansfield became the first licensed woman lawyer in the United States, Myra Bradwell applied to the Illinois Supreme Court for a law license. Bradwell had studied law with her husband while founding and editing the very successful *Chicago Legal News.* An avowed suffragist, Bradwell had drafted several bills to expand women's property rights. In 1869, Bradwell took the licensing examination and passed it with honors, but Illinois denied her a license to practice law because she was a woman. Bradwell appealed her case to the United States Supreme Court, which tossed the matter back to the state of Illinois. Bradwell would not obtain a license until 1890, four years before her death.

During the 1870s, other women fought to become "firsts" in the legal field. In 1871, Phoebe Couzins became the first woman to receive a formal law degree when she graduated from Washington University in St. Louis. The state of Missouri licensed Couzins, but she never practiced law. Instead, she became a leading figure in the national woman suffrage movement.

A year after Couzins's graduation, in 1872, Charlotte E. Ray of New York City graduated from Howard University in law and was admitted to the Washington, D.C., bar. She was the first black woman lawyer in the United States and the first woman admitted to practice in the District of Columbia. The private practice that Ray established failed, however. Too much prejudice existed against women attorneys, much less black women attorneys, to allow Ray to succeed. She moved to New York City, where she taught in a Brooklyn schools for several years.

Apparently, the field of law was so crusty with tradition that women had a difficult time breaking through. Even when they did get the necessary training, discriminatory attitudes prevented them from practicing their chosen profession.

Religion

An unexpected area of resistance to women in the postwar period was in the area of religion. Although most sects had long since feminized their membership and messages, they still barred women from voting and holding congregational offices. As a result, women chose a common alternative: they formed their own groups within churches.

Beginning in 1861, women in thirty-three denominations founded segregated missionary societies. These women-only groups met to pray, study, and raise funds for domestic and foreign mission work. By the 1870s, hundreds of similar missionary societies existed. They not only proved themselves highly effective in fundraising but in training women for leadership positions.

Some women wanted more. They planned to defy the widespread prohibition of women as ministers and religious leaders. In 1863, Olympia Brown graduated from St. Lawrence University's theological school in Canton, New York, as a Universalist minister, the first woman ordained by full ecclesiastical jurisdiction. In 1867, Brown left her pulpit temporarily to campaign unsuccessfully for woman suffrage in Kansas. The following year, 1868, Brown helped found the New England Woman Suffrage Association. When she married in 1873, Brown retained her birth family's name rather than adopting that of her husband. Although she continued parish work for several more years, she resigned her pastorate in Racine, Wisconsin, to become a full-time woman's rights organizer. Brown worked on behalf of woman's rights for almost sixty years.

Other women exerted their leadership rights outside the mainstream, especially by founding their own communities. Probably in 1867, Martha McWhirter helped found the Woman's Commonwealth in Belton, Texas. Under McWhirter's guidance, this Christian, socialist, feminist, and celibate community achieved financial success. Its unorthodox nature drew searing criticism and disdain from clergy, family members, and neighbors. In response, the woman-only community later moved to Washington, D.C., where it remained in force until the 1980s.

Women's Service Organizations

Perhaps the most significant occurrence after the Civil War was the formation of women's service clubs. Literally thousands of women turned to clubs and associations as an outlet for their energies and interests. Many women, such as those on farms and in factories, hoped to solve some of the problems facing them and their families. Other women who had learned organizational skills wanted to utilize them for the good of American society. And almost all of these women planned on furthering some aspect of women's rights.

Often, such women joined men's organizations. In some cases, male leaders now recognized the ideas, energy, and sheer numbers of members that women could supply. In addition, some male leaders supported woman's rights principles as just ones in a democratic society. For instance, when a new farm organization called the Patrons of Husbandry, commonly known as the Grange, organized in 1867, its local units welcomed women members. Women not only seized but broadened this opportunity. As early as the 1870s, women held local leadership positions and began to pressure local Granges to add woman suffrage planks to their platforms. At its first national convention in 1873, the Grange passed a resolution admitting women to the national unit on a limited basis. The following year, the Grange's Declaration of Purposes charged members with developing "proper appreciation of the abilities and sphere of women." Thus, through the Grange, farm women not only attacked farm-related problems but furthered women's agendas.

Similarly, employed women took matters into their own hands. In 1867, young working women in Boston founded the Young Women's Christian Association (YWCA) to assist young, single working women. During its early years, the YWCA focused its efforts on "white, native-born women dispossessed of their status by the need or desire to work." As the YWCA grew, it established boardinghouses with matrons and curfews for "respectable" working women.

At the same time, middle- and upper-class white women started a club movement that had incredible potential for reshaping American society. During the 1860s, the women's club movement erupted in a number of eastern cities. Many of the founders of women's clubs were educated women who before the Civil War had been active in temperance, abolitionism, woman's rights, and other reforms. After war's end, they did not intend to sit at home doing embroidery and overseeing servants. In Boston, for example, in February of 1868 reformer Caroline Severence and poet Julia Ward Howe founded the New England Woman's Club (NEWC). In addition, female professionals were unwilling to remain in the background, letting their male colleagues gain all the privilege. Only a month after Severence and Howe took action in Boston, journalist Jane Cunningham Croly found herself shut out of the New York Press Club's male-only reception for the famed English writer Charles Dickens. Croly responded by founding Sorosis, a female-only group.

Such women's clubs had two dimensions, one of which was educational and cultural. Club members read and discussed books, established libraries, performed plays, and collected and studied plant specimens. The second goal of women's clubs was the performance of public service. For instance, members addressed social problems by raising money for the needy and initiating such community improvement projects as establishing parks.

Women's organizations seemed innocent enough: they simply gave women of leisure something to do and, at the same time, encouraged neighborhood development. Social commentators of the day seldom even remarked on women's clubs. Yet any perceptive person would have realized that a rapidly growing network of assertive women would not long confine their efforts to reading great books. Rather, they would want to expand their rights, especially in the political realm dominated by men. In fact, post–Civil War women's clubs put in place a solid foundation for a full-blown and well-organized women's reform effort that would encompass causes ranging from temperance to woman's suffrage. In a sense, female reform activity of the prewar era had been a dress rehearsal for the women's club movement of the postwar years. During the 1860s and 1870s, women regrouped and reorganized for the arduous campaign that lay ahead of them.

Woman's Rights Renewed

Given the lack of political gains women derived from the Civil War, it is little wonder that the women's rights movement soon resurfaced. As early as 1865, women's rights' leaders who had hoped for great changes as an immediate result of the war met with disappointment. They were stunned to learn that abolitionists were far more concerned about ensuring the freedom of former slaves than with improving the status of women. Abolitionist leaders feared that raising women's rights issues in 1865 would complicate, or even prevent, the passage of legislation to protect blacks. Although the United States ratified the Thirteenth Amendment abolishing slavery in December 1865, additional protective and civil rights legislation for African Americans was under consideration. Its supporters argued that one step should be taken at a time and that women's turn would come eventually. Even the famous black leader Frederick Douglass, who had been sympathetic to women's rights, declared in 1865: "This is the Negro's hour."

In 1866, Congress passed the Fourteenth Amendment, which, when ratified, would extend political privileges to white and black men but not to white or black women. The amendment supported the continued disenfranchisement of women by specifically defining citizenship rights as "male," the first time that this word had appeared in the U.S. Constitution. Women's rights leader Frances Gage scathingly wrote, "can any one tell us why the great advocates of Human Equality . . . forget that when they were a weak party and needed all the womanly strength of the nation to help them on, they always united the words 'without regard to sex, race, or color?' Who ever hears of sex now from any of these champions of freedom!"

Elizabeth Cady Stanton direly predicted, "If that word 'male' be inserted, it will take us a century at least to get it out." Stanton's and other leaders' concern over women's political exclusion erupted at the first major women's rights convention held since the beginning of the war. Meeting in New York City in 1866, delegates listened to a number of speakers, including forty-one-year-old black poet and antislavery lecturer Frances Ellen Watkins Harper. Along with others such as Mary Ann Shadd Cary and Sojourner Truth, Harper saw the need for black and white women to work together. Convention members agreed and unanimously decided to approve the pursuit of suffrage for black American men and for women as their primary goals.

After the convention, leaders duly organized the American Equal Rights Association (AERA) to work toward these objectives. In 1866 and 1867, the new organization lobbied and petitioned to have race and gender restrictions deleted from state constitutions. In 1867, the association supported two suffrage bills in Kansas, one for black men and one for women. When abolitionist leaders failed to support the Kansas woman-suffrage bill, the association decided that it was time to part company with their former allies. The following year, the ratification of the Fourteenth Amendment gave the vote to black men. Suffrage was now solely a woman's issue.

Female suffrage leaders soon discovered that many disagreements regarding how woman suffrage might best be achieved existed in their own ranks. As a consequence, two opposing groups emerged. In 1869, Stanton and Susan B. Anthony formed the National Woman Suffrage Association (NWSA) in Washington. It excluded men from membership and concentrated its efforts on getting the Congress to pass an amendment granting women the right to vote. The NWSA published a newspaper coedited by Stanton and Anthony called *The Revolution*. The newspaper's masthead read: "Men, Their Rights and Nothing More, Women, Their Rights and Nothing Less." In addition to working for the immediate enfranchisement of women, the NWSA supported equal pay for equal work, childcare centers for working mothers, and more equitable divorce laws.

Also in 1869, such woman's rights leaders as Lucy Stone and Julia Ward Howe organized the American Woman Suffrage Association (AWSA) in Boston. Unlike the NWSA, the AWSA encouraged men to join and focused members' efforts on gaining woman suffrage on a state-by-state basis. The AWSA published a newspaper called *The Woman's Journal* designed to counteract what AWSA leaders called the "radicalism" of *The Revolution*.

When these two rival organizations formed in 1869, public opinion on the issue of extended rights for women was mixed. In 1867 and 1868, Kansas woman-suffrage amendments had failed. In 1868, a woman-suffrage amendment introduced in Congress had also floundered. In 1869, Wyoming Territory granted women the right to vote, followed in 1870 by Utah Territory. Although these latter actions were encouraging, they failed to create a landslide toward woman suffrage. Rather, in 1870 the Fifteenth Amendment stipulated that a citizen's right to vote could not be denied on the basis of race or color; the amendment ignored the issue of gender.

Other voices soon supported the call for woman suffrage. Support seemed to come from all sides, some of them totally unexpected. In 1869, two years after he failed to secure woman suffrage in the British Reform Bill of 1867, English philosopher and politician John Stuart Mill published *The Subjection of Women in England*. When Mill's book reached the United States, American readers discovered that Mill believed true social satisfaction depended on the happiness of women, including their equal access to education and legal rights.

The Quaker lecturer and suffragist Anna Dickinson also called for woman's rights. During the Civil War, Dickinson lectured eloquently not only on antislavery but on political and military affairs. She had further shocked people by campaigning on behalf of political candidates in 1863. After the war, dressed in elegant gowns accented by extravagant jewelry, Dickinson lectured on injustices to women. Known as the "Queen of the Rostrum" to some, Dickinson exhibited the "worst possible taste" in the eyes of others.

Also somewhat embarrassing to suffrage leaders were the activities of an articulate and dramatic woman, Victoria Claflin Woodhull, who became the nation's first female stockbroker in 1870. In addition to lecturing frequently on woman's rights, Woodhull ran for president of the United States in 1872. Along with her equally colorful sister, Tennessee Claflin, Woodhull attracted a good deal of attention to the suffrage movement. The sisters' antics convinced a lot of people that woman suffragists were highly eccentric. In spite of the controversy that continually swirled around them, Woodhull and Claflin drew notice to the woman's rights cause and effectively demonstrated that women could enter such male-only areas as finance and politics.

Another determined woman, Virginia Minor, took a different approach. In 1872, Minor sued the state of Missouri for refusing to let her vote. Because married women were unable to bring suit on their own, Minor worked in conjunction with her attorney husband. They carried the case to the Missouri Supreme Court and the U.S. Supreme Court. In the case of *Minor* v. *Happersett* in 1874, Chief Justice Morrison R. Waite ruled that the state had the power to grant or deny suffrage, and that the U.S. Constitution "does not confer the right of suffrage upon any one." Eight other male justices concurred and wrote: "If the courts can consider any question settled, this is one."

In the South, the Rollins sisters of South Carolina's black elite argued for woman's right to vote on several different levels. Charming and well educated, the four Rollins sisters held a political salon, wrote books, and spoke to southern men about woman's rights. In 1869, Louisa Rollin, a dedicated feminist, even spoke to the all-male South Carolina legislature on behalf of woman suffrage. In 1870, her sister, Charlotte (Lottie) Rollin, chaired the organizational meeting of the South Carolina Woman's Rights Association in Columbia. During the early 1870s, Charlotte chaired woman's rights' meetings and served as state delegate to the American Woman Suffrage Association.

White southern women such as Sarah Ida Fowler Morgan of South Carolina publicly declared their advocacy of women's rights. Through editorials in the Charleston *News and Courier* during the 1870s, Morgan examined the "woman question" in great detail. Writing under the pseudonym "Mr. Fowler," Morgan supported employment, singlehood, and equality for women. Instead of focusing on woman suffrage, however, Morgan maintained that the women's movement should pursue economic independence for women. Although such women spoke out all over the postwar South, their voices were often silenced by the numerous other problems of Reconstruction.

Women in the West

Native American Women

At the same time that the eastern portion of the United States attempted to settle issues regarding white and black Americans, the West confronted its own racial and class conflicts. Although western areas had contributed people and supplies to the war effort, they were generally too distant from the fighting front to participate directly. During both the war and Reconstruction, some western states did, however, request the assistance of troops to put down Indian attacks. Although white westerners bemoaned their situations, Indians had even more about which to complain.

By the 1860s and 1870s, white settlement had disrupted Native American communities, wars had torn apart their families, and government imposition of white values further reduced the status of Native women. Along with Native men, women were increasingly confined to reservations where malnutrition, famine, and disease further lessened their numbers. Their children attended reservation schools, which attempted to erase Indian children's culture and their pride in it. Although such schools probably stressed domestic education for its female pupils in order to make them submissive, not just to their future mates but to government authority as well, Native girls found many ways to subvert the system. Female students in early Indian schools resisted regimentation in dress, hair styles, and language. Behind the white matron's back, they whispered in their own languages, "lost" such articles at hair ribbons, and warned each other of a matron's approach after lights out.

Despite the attempt to make Indian women into pseudo-whites, American Indian women of the Plains and in some Far Western tribes continued to exercise a measure of control over their lives. White observers often assumed that Native women were degraded in their traditional cultures because they performed all domestic and most agricultural labor while men engaged in hunting and warfare. Actually, this division of labor extended respect and the right of decision making to both sexes.

In addition, Indian women exercised real choice regarding family issues. For instance, Indian women had power over the frequency of childbearing. They reportedly used herbal birth control. Also, because many Indian women were not required to resume sexual relations until they had finished nursing, they avoided another pregnancy by nursing their most recent child for years. In addition, most Indian cultures stressed the need for both partners to derive satisfaction from marriage. Because divorce was usually simple to obtain, Native women could escape abusive, lazy, or intemperate mates without losing their children and personal property.

Furthermore, some American Indian women continued to wield influence within their tribes. Occasionally, Plains Indian women served as shamans, medicine people, and warriors. Matrilineal tribes such as the Mandans of the Dakotas and Tlingits of the Pacific Northwest vested land in the eldest female of the family. Ownership of land, fields, gardens, houses, and stock passed through female descendants. American Indian women frequently functioned as decision makers and sat on the council of elders, participating in rulings that concerned both wars and hunts. During the 1860s and 1870s, for example, Yakima women played an important role in the reservation economy in what is now Washington State.

A Sioux named Eagle Woman well demonstrated such influence and ability. Uprooted in 1868 from her home near Fort Rice in the Dakota Territory, Eagle Woman decided to help her family and her people adjust to life on a reservation. For the next twenty years, the widowed Eagle Woman (also known as Mrs. Picotte-Galpin) ran a trading post, supported her children, helped others in need, and acted as a liaison between the Sioux people and U.S. government agents.

Another example of a woman who asserted herself was Buffalo Calf Road of the Cheyenne Indians. Although the Cheyenne expected women to act docile and deferential toward men, numerous Cheyenne women broke and rode horses, hunted, and fought in battles. They formed women's associations, including quillers' societies and a secret military society. Buffalo Calf Road distinguished herself by fighting at the Battle on the Rosebud River in June 1876, and by rescuing her brother from enemy fire. Buffalo Calf Road fought a week later against General George Armstrong Custer and his troops at the Little Bighorn River, where she earned the honorary name Brave Woman. Two years later, Buffalo Calf Road led Cheyenne women against the U.S. Army in Nebraska. She died in 1879 of diphtheria.

Still, as lines of forts and increasing numbers of government officials, settlers, and miners arrived in the Great Plains and the Far West, it became clear that Native women of the West would share a fate similar to that of the Algonquian tribes along the East Coast. Moreover, few reformers recognized the plight of Indian women or spoke on their behalf. Even though thousands of white families employed these women as cooks, nursemaids, and washwomen, most seemed oblivious to their problems.

Hispanas

A similar situation existed between Spanish-speaking and white women. Brought together by such situations as employment (white woman hiring Hispanas as domestic help or farm hands) and intermarriage, Hispanas and white women shared recipes, childcare ideas, and fashions, yet in other ways they lived separate lives. Apparently, gender did not provide a strong enough bond to overcome racist sentiments. Thus, Hispanas were left to confront major social changes on their own.

By 1870, people of Spanish heritage lived on ranches, farms, or in segregated urban areas called *barrios*. In Los Angeles, for example, they increasingly lived in a barrio called Sonora Town. Because the birthrate began to stabilize after 1860, the Hispanic population grew primarily from immigration, which remained relatively low during the post–Civil War period. By 1870, Los Angelinos with Spanish backgrounds accounted for only 28.5 percent of the city's total population (down from 30.9 percent in 1860).

In addition, the developing western economy increasingly colonized Hispanics as a manual, low-paid workforce. Numbers of Hispanic property holders decreased, while those working at manual labor increased to 80 percent of the workforce in 1870 (up from 62 percent in 1860). This decline in the Hispanic middle and upper classes, accompanied by a growth in the working classes, created a changed situation for many women. Because male workers often earned inadequate wages, women had to take paid employment as well, usually as domestic servants, nursemaids, laundresses, and prostitutes. Some even broke with tradition by becoming actresses and theater impresarios.

Moreover, a growing number of women headed households: before the War with Mexico, only 13 percent had done so; after the Civil War, approximately 25 percent did so. Because of religious restrictions, divorce was atypical. Rather, the change probably resulted from men seeking jobs away from home and a higher death rate for men than for women. As a result, the female-centered family became an important institution in the Spanish-speaking community in Los Angeles.

The Hispanic family changed in other ways as well. Women escaped arranged marriages by forming more common-law marriages, which California began to recognize in 1862. In 1861 and 1864, other state laws undercut the community property provisions that had passed from Mexican law into California law. As a consequence of the new stipulations, wives' property at their death no longer went to their children but reverted to their husbands. Nor was all of a husband's property subject to inheritance by his survivors.

At the same time, intermarriage with Anglo settlers increased. Before the Civil War, only one Hispanic marriage in ten involved a white mate. After the war, nearly one in three wed a white person. Unlike earlier white settlers, most of these white spouses had little interest in adopting local culture and customs. More frequently, Hispanas, who often hoped to improve their social and economic status through intermarriage, adopted white ways instead. As a result they tended to bear fewer children than they might have in earlier decades and sent their children to English-language public schools.

Clearly, Hispanas, especially those of the working and lower classes, were losing a great deal: the support of extended kinship family systems and a network of godparents and *compadres*. Hispanas also worked in greater numbers outside the home for low wages. Fewer women had time to serve their communities as low-paid or volunteer teachers, *parteras* (midwives), and *curanderas* (healers). Increasingly, they saw their traditional culture attacked by a state "Sunday law" that prohibited bullfights, horse races, cockfights, and other traditional *Californio* pastimes. They also feared for fathers, brothers, husbands, and sons who were now subject to local vagrancy laws that could result in the imprisonment of unemployed men. Moreover, women lived with the threat of whites lynching Hispanic men, a practice deplored in the Spanish-language press as *"los linchamientos."*

Similar changes occurred in other Hispanic centers such as Tucson, Santa Fe, and San Antonio. Especially in San Antonio, the largest Spanish-heritage city in the United States, urban industrialization drew women out of their homes into paid employment and altered the structure of the traditional family. A growing number of Tejanas sought paid employment, working primarily as unskilled laborers or as *vendedoras* in local markets. Others turned their homes into restaurants or boardinghouses.

By the 1860s, women headed over 30 percent of Hispanic families in San Antonio. This usually occurred because men had no choice but to seek employment as migrant field hands or return to Mexico to work, thus leaving family authority in the hands of the women. Tejano families usually lived in *jacales* (timber dwellings), or, in west Texas, in adobes. Women continued to use a *mano* (grinding stone) to grind corn in a *metate* (stone vessel). From this they prepared staples of their diet, *tortillas* and *tamales,* to which they added *frijoles, chiles,* meat, and fish.

From Los Angeles to San Antonio, Hispanas generally proved themselves able to maintain their families in the face of numerous difficulties, to hang on to aspects of traditional culture, and to preserve a semblance of the extended kinship system. They paid the price, however, of working an extended day, often toiling for wages outside the home and performing extensive domestic labor in poor quality housing and communities neglected by municipal officials.

White Women

During the same era, white women in the West grew in number and variety of personalities, philosophies, and occupations. Certainly by the 1860s and 1870s, all types of women lived in the West. Some resided in the raw towns that composed the urban frontier. In town and countryside, single women sought employment, husbands, or both. In cowtowns and gold camps, prostitutes waited for men to complete a trail drive or strike ore. Some women, like the popular trail guide Mountain

Charley, even donned male clothing and assumed male roles. Other women had landed in the West from such places as Canada, Mexico, Germany, Holland, England, Ireland, Sweden, Norway, and Asia. Yet others came as members of such religious groups as the Presentation Sisters in the Dakotas, or the Church of Jesus Christ of Latter-day Saints (or Mormons) in Utah. Others, like Abigail Scott Duniway of Oregon, ardently advocated woman suffrage.

After the Civil War, virtually no western area was without women. Female migrants even entered the mining, lumbering and farming areas of the Far West. Some had traveled across the Isthmus of Panama or "around the horn" of South America, but most had journeyed west across overland trails. In some cases, women became discouraged, frightened, and determined to return to their former homes as soon as possible. In other cases, however, women found the hardships of the overland trip less severe than they had feared. En route female travelers traded with American Indians, who seldom were as fierce as women had been led to believe. As one woman later wrote: "We suffered vastly more from fear of the Indians before starting than we did on the plains." Yet other women raved about the beauty of the prairies, plains, and mountains, and extolled the "wonders of travel."

Women participated in cattle ranching, especially in Texas, and in farming and homesteading throughout the West. On the Great Plains, wives often managed isolated homesteads by themselves while their husbands worked elsewhere to raise the necessary capital for seed, equipment, and building materials. Other women labored alongside their fathers or husbands in "breaking" a claim for cultivation. During the 1870s, one Dakota woman graphically described the demands placed on women settlers: "I had lived on a homestead long enough to learn some fundamental things: that while a woman had more here than in any other part of the world, she was expected to contribute as much as a man—not in the same way, it is true, but to the same degree . . . the person who wasn't willing to try anything once wasn't equipped to be a settler."

Growing numbers of single women took up western land. The Homestead Act, passed by Congress in 1862, offered a settler a free quarter-section of land on the condition that she or he "improve," or cultivate it for a period of five years. A sample of land office data for Colorado and Wyoming indicates that the number of female homestead entrants ranged from 11.9 to 18.2 percent of the total. The data further indicate that 42.4 percent of women succeeded in placing final claims—or "proving up"—on their homestead as opposed to only 37 percent of men. One Dakotan judged these "girl homesteaders" an "interesting segment of the population."

Some Plains and Far Western women had lifestyles similar to those of earlier frontierswomen on agrarian frontiers, but others lived more novel lives. An army wife of the early 1860s enjoyed her rough and erratic life in frontier forts. She traveled around Kansas and Oklahoma in an army ambulance without much discomfort, or any danger from Indians. She basked in the attention paid her as one of the few women in camp and decided that "there is considerable romance in my manner of living."

In 1866, General William T. Sherman urged officers' wives to accompany their husbands to western forts. Sherman promised these women "healthful" conditions and "absolute peace." Although these two conditions seldom existed, officers' wives found that they wielded authority, at least in the social realm. Inside the fort, these women organized dinner parties, card parties, and elegant dances. Outside the fort, they arranged picnics, horseback riding excursions, and trading trips to Native American settlements. In between, they formed reading groups, literary societies, and educational programs for adults and children. Women also promoted such religious activities as Sunday school and prayer service. In other words, officers' wives pursued the same activities as other middle- and upper-class white women, but they did so in the more rudimentary surroundings of western forts and outposts. It was clearly women's task to bring white civilization to the West's military garrisons.

During the 1860s and 1870s, some officers' wives took on official duties during their husbands' absences and kept their husbands' policies in place. One woman who was aware of her husband's sympathy for "buffalo" or black soldiers of his regiment enforced his principles while he was in the field. She even intervened in legal cases regarding African American soldiers, ordering their release from the guardhouse until proper trials could be held. Not all army women were this strong in mind and body, however. In 1874, an Arizona army wife wrote: "I concluded that my New England bringing up had been too serious. . . . Young army wives should stay at home with their mothers and fathers, and not go into such wild and uncouth places."

Other western women with unusual lifestyles included those who took jobs in service industries, including dance halls, saloons, and brothels. Many "soiled doves" who provided companionship and sexual services were hardworking laborers and business entrepreneurs. In 1867 Irish immigrant Mary Josephine Welch, for example, settled in Helena, Montana, where she established the Red Light Saloon. Soon known as "Chicago Joe" after her last hometown, Welch hired women as dollar-a-dance workers in her saloon. These women, known as "hurdy-gurdy girls" after the popular stringed instrument of the day, earned up to $50 an evening. In 1873, however, in an attempt to attract a stable family population, Montana passed legislation against dance halls.

Frontierswomen were not only a diverse group but often a politically active one as well. They hoped to achieve more freedom for women than was accorded them in the North and the South. During the 1860s, for example, Kansas suffragist Clarinda Nichols wrote and spoke in an attempt to whip up support for women's right to vote. In 1861, Nichols played a significant role in the constitutional convention that gave Kansas women the right to vote in school elections.

Later in the decade, in 1869, Wyoming Territory gave women the right to vote. Supposedly, this occurred because of the urging of Esther Morris and others, who argued that woman suffrage would attract more women to Wyoming. These newcomers would balance the current population ratio of six men to one woman and become a "law and order" faction in unbridled Wyoming society.

Utah followed with its own woman suffrage law in 1870. Some believe that leaders of the Church of Latter-day Saints passed such legislation hoping to shore up their political power against the influx of male non-Mormons, or Gentiles, to the area, figuring that Mormon women would vote in favor of polygamy, the extremely controversial institution of plural marriage practiced by some Mormons at the time.

Whatever the motives, woman's suffrage appeared in the West before it did elsewhere in the nation.

African American Women

Black women, disillusioned with southern plantations or urban areas in the South and North, also turned their faces westward during the late 1860s and 1870s. As pioneers and Exodusters (communities of black immigrants, especially in Kansas), they soon discovered that they could not escape racial prejudice. It followed them even into the most progressive of western communities. Once again blacks were relegated to farm labor and domestic service. In one Iowa town, a black woman who worked as a washwoman for many of the community's white women lived by herself in poverty despite continuous labor and was patronizingly called "Nigger Ellen" by townspeople.

Yet it was a hopeful time west of the Mississippi River. In Texas, the first Freedman's Bureau school opened in Galveston. Between 1865 and 1870, the bureau founded approximately one hundred schools in Texas. Other groups who helped black Texans included northern missionaries, the American Bible Society, the African Methodist Church, as well as a number of white Texans. Although the Ku Klux Klan and other groups opposed educating African Americans in the Lone Star State, Texas had one of the most impressive records of all states. As early as 1866, Texas led the rest of the states in numbers of bureau schools established. Two years later, Texas indicated that there were more female black students enrolled than male. The black illiteracy rate dropped, while teacher-training programs supplied growing numbers of black female teachers. By 1877, over three-quarters of school-age African Americans attended school.

In addition, a number of black women achieved economic success in the West. One of the most renowned of these was Mary Ellen Pleasant, who arrived in San Francisco during the Gold Rush, probably in 1849. She claimed to have been born in Philadelphia in 1814, the daughter of a free black woman and a wealthy white planter. She married Alexander Smith, an abolitionist and prosperous Cuban planter, who willed his estate to her. She later married John James Pleasant, worked for abolitionism in Canada during the 1850s, and returned to San Francisco during the 1860s, where she became a restaurateur and investor. In addition to elegant restaurants and boardinghouses, Pleasant ran laundries that employed black women and men. She used her wealth to build a striking mansion, but she also helped other African Americans find jobs and gain civil rights.

Another similar case was "Aunt" Clara Brown, who purchased her freedom during the 1850s. In 1859, Brown convinced a group of gold seekers to hire her as a cook and accompanied them across the Great Plains to Denver. Brown soon moved to Central City, where she established a laundry, worked as a nurse, invested in mining claims, and organized a Sunday school. By 1866, Brown had amassed savings of $10,000, which she used to bring relatives and others to Colorado.

Asians and Asian Americans

After the Civil War, the number of Asian peoples in the American West grew. In 1868, China and the United States signed the Burlingame Treaty, which established reciprocal trade, travel, and immigration but did not provide citizenship for Chinese residing in the United States. Despite this significant omission, between 1870 and 1877, over 100,000 Chinese arrived in the continental United States. More than 90 percent of these immigrants were men who worked as miners, railroad builders, factory workers, entrepreneurs, vendors, fishermen, and agriculturalists. By the late 1870s, California contained more than 70,000 Chinese men and less than 4,000 Chinese women. In other parts of the country, Chinese men totaled approximately 30,000 and women fewer than 1,000.

Chinese women ranged from a growing number of middle- and upper-class wives, usually living in Chinatowns and sometimes assisting in family businesses, to a declining number of prostitutes in such urban areas as San Francisco, farm women in rural areas, and fishing village women along the West Coast. In 1870, a small number of Chinese women worked as unskilled laborers, especially as domestic servants, laundresses, and seamstresses. Ah Yuen of Evanston, Wyoming, for example, hired out as a cook in mining and railroad camps during the 1860s and 1870s. She outlived three husbands and, in later years, made it a point to participate in Evanston's annual Cowboy Days celebration.

Single Chinese men occasionally married Native American, African American, or Spanish-heritage women. Most, however, established split households by marrying Chinese women still residing in China. To ensure their daughters a source of income, families willingly married them off to Chinese men living in the United States. For years afterward, husbands worked in the United States while wives survived, and even raised families, in Chinese villages on the meager financial assistance that their men sent home to them. Consequently, the primary goal of many Chinese couples was to reunite and establish whole families.

During this era, the U.S. Asian population diversified, largely because Japanese immigration to the United States began. In 1868, 148 laborers migrated to Hawaii's sugar cane fields. The following year a Japanese band performed in San Francisco's Woodward Gardens, perhaps as goodwill ambassadors. Those Japanese who followed usually settled in urban areas called Little Tokyos. This early migration included some female *Issei* ("first generation" Japanese in America), who eventually bore *Nisei* ("second generation") offspring. Besides being wives and mothers, Issei women helped establish and run family businesses. Because they lived in segregated areas, however, few learned English or interacted much with Americans. They left it to their Nisei offspring to obtain education and to revise the old cultural patterns that bound their Issei mothers.

By 1877, when President Rutherford B. Hayes ordered the removal of the army of occupation from the South and technically brought Reconstruction to a close, women clamored for all manner of additional changes in American society. The Civil War had made it clear that the country would remain united and that slavery was dead forever. The war years left many concerns unresolved. Among these were civil rights for African Americans, woman's rights, American Indians' place in society, and the intemperate use of alcoholic beverages. For all its high hopes and administration, the Reconstruction era had done little more than complicate these and other issues.

As a result, numerous American women stood poised in 1877 to initiate further, more far-reaching change in the prevailing social system. For one thing, they planned to accelerate their efforts to move into jobs, professions, and others endeavors previously dominated by men. For another, they hoped to remodel permanently the image of American womanhood. Women of all backgrounds not only had a long list of changes they wanted implemented in post-Reconstruction American society, but they were determined to work hard and speak out to get what they wanted.

Study Guide

Checklist of important names, terms, phrases, and dates in Chapter 5. Think about what or who each was and why she, he, or it was significant.

Civil War, 1861–1865
Reconstruction, 1865–1877
National Woman's Loyal League
Thirteenth Amendment
"Government Girls"
"scorched earth policy"
missionary teachers
Emancipation Proclamation of 1863
"women riots" and "female raids"
Susie Baker King Taylor
Mary Ann Shadd Cary
Mary Elizabeth Bowser
"contrabands"
Harriet Tubman
Contraband Relief Society of Washington, D.C.
Annie Turner Wittenmyer
Clara Barton
Mary Ann Bickerdyke
Mary Edwards Walker, M.D.
Phoebe Yates Pember
Rose Greenhow
Belle Boyd
sharecropping
white-supremacy groups
Freedman's Bureau
Josephine Griffing
Freedman's Relief Association
Frances Butler
"miscegenation"
Principles of Domestic Science
Vassar College
Maria Mitchell
Emily Dickinson
Louisa May Alcott
Little Women
Helen Hunt Jackson
Harriet Hosmer
Edmonia Lewis
Kate Furbish
Butterick's dress patterns

"Slaughter of the Pemberton"
Lady Cigar Makers of Providence, Rhode Island
Collar Laundry Union of Troy, New York
working women's protective societies
birth control by abortion
Comstock Law
National Women's Christian Temperance Union (WCTU)
Clara Temple Leonard
Arabella Babb Mansfield
Myra Bradwell
Phoebe Couzins
Charlotte E. Ray
Olympia Brown
Patrons of Husbandry, or the Grange
Young Women's Christian Association (YWCA)
women's club movement
New England Woman's Club (NEWC)
Sorosis
Fourteenth Amendment
American Equal Rights Association
National Woman Suffrage Association (NWSA)
American Woman Suffrage Association (AWSA)
Wyoming Territory, 1869
Anna Dickinson
Victoria Claflin Woodhull and Tennessee Claflin
Rollins sisters of South Carolina
Sarah Ida Fowler Morgan
Eagle Woman
Buffalo Calf Road
"Sunday law"
los linchamientos

Homestead Act of 1862
"girl homesteaders"
"Chicago Joe"
Clarinda Nichols
Esther Morris
Exodusters
Mary Ellen Pleasant

"Aunt" Clara Brown
Burlingame Treaty
Chinese split households
Little Tokyos
Issei
Nisei

Chapter 5 issues to think about and discuss:

- How were women's roles different and similar during the American Revolution and the Civil War?
- How did the lives of black women change as a result of the Civil War? If you were one of these women, would you prefer to have lived before or after the war? Why?
- How did the lives of white women change as a result of the Civil War? If you were one of these women, would you prefer to have lived before or after the war? Why?
- After the Civil War, Africans Americans were free people. Why did the concept of equality of the races fail to grow during the postwar years?
- For what reasons did the Civil War fail to destroy the concept of true womanhood?
- In what ways did women writers and artists expand their horizons after the Civil War?
- What steps *should* an enlightened government have taken after the "Slaughter of the Pemberton"? Why did U.S. leaders fail to enact such programs?
- In what ways were women's reform issues after the Civil War different from, or similar to, today's feminists' demands?
- Such social "evils" as drunkenness, race relations, and limited woman's rights, which female reformers attacked before and after the Civil War, are still problems today. Can any of these problems ever be resolved to the satisfaction of the majority of Americans?
- What factors caused the North, South, and West to differ so greatly from each other?
- How was it possible that post–Civil War white women and those of color worked together yet remained so separated?
- How were army wives in western forts similar to early white women who came to colonial America?
- Even as the number of peoples of color increased dramatically in the West, white people remained dominant there. How were whites able to accomplish this?
- Had women, white and of color, made any substantial progress between the founding of Jamestown in 1607 and the end of Reconstruction in 1877?

Suggestions for Further Reading

Women during the Civil War

Aron, Cindy S. "'To Barter Their Souls for Gold': Female Clerks in Federal Government Offices, 1862–1890," *Journal of American History* 67 (March 1981): 835–53.

Attie, Jeanie. *Patriotic Toil: Northern Women and the American Civil War.* Ithaca, NY: Cornell University Press, 1998.

Bacon, Margaret Hope. "'One Great Bundle of Humanity': Frances Ellen Watkins Harper," *Pennsylvania Magazine of History and Biography* 113 (January 1989): 21–43.

Blanton, DeAnne. "Cathay Williams: Black Woman Soldier, 1866–1868," *Minerva: Quarterly Report on Women and the Military* 10 (Fall/Winter 1992): 1–12.

——. "Women Soldiers of the Civil War," Prologue 25 (Spring 1993): 27–34.

Burton, David H. *Clara Barton: In the Service of Humanity.* Westport, CT: Greenwood Publishing, 1995.

Campbell, D.C., Jr., and Kym S. Rice, eds. *A Woman's War: Southern Women, Civil War, and the Confederate Legacy.* Charlottesville: University Press of Virginia, 1996.

Clinton, Catherine, and Nina Silber, eds. *Divided Houses: Gender and the Civil War.* New York: Oxford University Press, 1992.

Culpepper, Marilyn Mayer. *Trials and Triumphs: Women of the American Civil War.* East Lansing: Michigan State University Press, 1991.

Endres, Kathleen L. "The Women's Press in the Civil War: A Portrait of Patriotism, Propaganda, and Prodding," *Civil War History* 30 (March 1984): 30–53.

Faust, Drew Gilpin. "Altars of Sacrifice: Confederate Women and the Narratives of War," *Journal of American History* 76 (March 1990): 1200–28.

——. *Mothers of Invention: Women of the Slaveholding South.* Chapel Hill: University of North Carolina Press, 1996.

Hall, Richard. *Patriots in Disguise: Women Warriors of the Civil War.* New York: Paragon Books, 1993.

——. "Women in Battle in the Civil War," *Social Education* 58 (February 1994): 80–82. Special edition of Social Education on "Women in Wartime"; includes articles and lesson plans regarding women in this and other wars.

Hamand, Wendy F. "The Woman's National Loyal League: Feminist Abolitionists and the Civil War," *Civil War History* 35 (May 1989): 39–58.

Johnson, Michael P., and James L. Roark. *No Chariot Let Down: Charleston's Free People of Color on the Eve of the Civil War.* Chapel Hill: University of North Carolina Press, 1984.

Kaufman, Janet E. "'Under the Petticoat Flag': Women Soldiers in the Confederate Army," *Southern Studies* 23 (Winter 1984): 363–75.

Kunkle, Camille. "'It is What it Does to the Souls': Women's Views of the Civil War," *Atlanta History* 33 (Summer 1989): 56–70.

Massey, Mary Elizabeth. *Bonnet Brigades: American Women and the Civil War.* New York: Alfred A. Knopf, 1966.

Oates, Stephen B. *A Woman of Valor: Clara Barton and the Civil War.* New York: Free Press, 1994.

Painter, Nell. "Sojourner Truth in Memory and History: Writing the History of an American Exotic," *Gender and History* 2 (Spring 1990): 3–16.

Schultz, Jane E. "Race, Gender, and Bureaucracy: Civil War Army Nurses and the Pension Bureau," *Journal of Women's History* 6 (Summer 1994): 45–69.

Venet, Wendy H. *Neither Ballots nor Bullets: Women Abolitionists and the Civil War.* Charlottesville: University Press of Virginia, 1991.

Whites, Leeann. *The Civil War as a Crisis in Gender.* Athens: University of Georgia Press, 1995.

Women during Reconstruction

Abram, Ruth J. *"Send Us a Lady Doctor": Women Doctors in America, 1835–1920.* New York: W. W. Norton, 1985.

Adreadis, A. Harriette. "The Woman's Commonwealth: A Study in Coalescence of Social Forms," *Frontiers* 7 (1984): 79–86.

Andrews, William D., and Deborah C. Andrews. "Technology and the House-wife in Nineteenth-Century America," *Women's Studies* (1974): 109–28.

Banner, Lois W. *Elizabeth Cady Stanton: A Radical for Women's Rights.* Boston: Little, Brown and Company, 1980.

Barry, Kathleen. *Susan B. Anthony—A Biography: A Singular Feminist.* New York: New York University Press, 1988.

Basch, Norma. "Invisible Women: The Legal Fiction of Marital Unity in Nineteenth-Century America," *Feminist Study* 5 (Summer 1979): 346–66.

——. "'Relief in the Premises': Divorce as a Woman's Remedy in New York and Indiana, 1815–1870," *Law and History Review* (Spring 1990): 1–24.

Beezley, William H., and Joseph P. Hobbs. "'Nice Girls Don't Sweat': Women in American Sport," *Journal of Popular Culture* 16 (Spring 1983): 42–53.

Berch, Bettina. *The Endless Day: The Political Economy of Women and Work.* New York: Harcourt Brace Jovanovich, Inc., 1982.

Berkeley, Kathleen C. "'The Ladies Want to Bring About Reform in the Public Schools': Public Education and Women's Rights in the Post–Civil War South," *History of Education Quarterly* 24 (Spring 1984): 45–58.

Blocker, Jr., Jack S., ed. "Annie Wittenmyer and the Women's Crusade," *Ohio History* 88 (Autumn 1979): 419–22.

Boydston, Jeanne, Mary Kelley, and Anne Margolis. *The Limits of Sisterhood: The Beecher Sisters on Women's Rights and Women's Sphere.* Chapel Hill: University of North Carolina Press, 1988.

Brown, Minnie Miller. "Black Women in American Agriculture," *Agricultural History* 50 (January 1976): 202–12.

Bulger, Margery A. "American Sportswomen in the 19th Century," *Journal of Popular Culture* 16 (Fall 1982): 1–16.

Bynum, Victoria E. *Unruly Women: The Politics of Social and Sexual Control in the Old South.* Chapel Hill: University of North Carolina Press, 1992.

Cameron, Ardis. *Radicals of the Worst Sort: Laboring Women in Lawrence, Massachusetts, 1860–1912.* Urbana: University of Illinois Press, 1993.

Carrell, Kimberley W. "The Industrial Revolution Comes to the Home: Kitchen Design Reform and Middle-Class Women," *Journal of American Culture* 2 (Fall 1979): 488–99.

Cayleff, Susan E. *Wash and Be Healed: The Water-Cure Movement and Women's Health.* Philadelphia: Temple University Press, 1987.

Cogan, Frances B. *All-American Girl: The Ideal of Real Womanhood in Mid-Nineteenth-Century America.* Athens: University of Georgia Press, 1989.

Collier-Thomas, Bettye. "The Impact of Black Women in Education: An Historical Overview," *Journal of Negro Education* 51 (Summer 1982): 173–80.

Cowan, Ruth Schwartz. "From Virginia Dare to Virginia Slims: Women and Technology in American Life," *Technology and Culture* 20 (January 1979): 51–63.

Dill, Bonnie T. "Our Mothers' Grief: Racial Ethnic Women and the Maintenance of Families," *Journal of Family History* 13 (1988): 415–31.

Diner, Hasia R. *Erin's Daughters in America: Irish Immigrant Women in the Nineteenth Century.* Baltimore: Johns Hopkins University Press, 1983.

DuBois, Ellen C. *Feminism and Suffrage: The Emergence of an Independent Women's Movement in America, 1848–1869.* Ithaca, NY: Cornell University Press, 1978. Pages 53–78.

—. "Outgrowing the Compact of the Fathers: Equal Rights, Woman Suffrage, and the United States Constitution, 1826–1878," *Journal of American History* 74 (December 1987): 836–62.

Edwards, Laura F. *Gendered Strife and Confusion: The Political Culture of Reconstruction.* Champaign: University of Illinois Press, 1997.

Elbert, Sarah. *A Hunger for Home: Louisa May Alcott and Little Women.* Philadelphia: Temple University Press, 1984.

Endres, Kathleen L. "'Strictly Confidential': Birth Control Advertising in a 19th-Century City," *Journalism Quarterly* 63 (Winter 1986): 748–51.

Epstein, Barbara Leslie. *The Politics of Domesticity: Women, Evangelism, and Temperance in Nineteenth-Century America.* Middletown, CT: Wesleyan University Press, 1981.

Gollaher, David L. *A Voice for the Mad: The Life of Dorothea Dix.* New York: Free Press, 1994.

Gordon, Jean. "Early American Women Artists and the Social Context in Which They Worked," *American Quarterly* 30 (Spring 1978): 54–69.

Gordon, Linda. "The Long Struggle for Reproductive Rights," *Radical America* 15 (Spring 1981): 74–88.

—. "Voluntary Motherhood: The Beginnings of the Birth-Control Movement," 131–47, in *Family Life in America, 1620–2000,* edited by Mel Albin and Dominick Cavaloo. New York City Revisionary Press, 1981.

Gray, Barbara L. "Organizational Struggles of Working Women in the Nineteenth Century," *Labor Studies Journal* 16 (Summer 1991): 16–34.

Gutman, Herbert G. "Persistent Myths about the Afro-American Family," *Journal of Interdisciplinary History* 6 (Autumn 1975): 181–210.

Harris, Barbara J. *Beyond Her Sphere: Women and the Professions in American History.* Westport, CT: Greenwood Press, 1978.

Hedges, Elaine. "The Nineteenth-Century Diarist and Her Quilts," *Feminist Studies* 8 (Summer 1982): 293–308.

Hewitt, Nancy A., ed. *Women, Families, and Communities: Readings in American History.* Vols. I and II. Glenview, IL: Scott, Foresman, 1990. Part 5 and Part 1.

Hine, Darlene Clark, Wilma King, and Linda Reed, eds. *"We Specialize in the Wholly Impossible": A Reader in Black Women's History.* Brooklyn, NY: Carlson Publishing, 1995.

Hodes, Martha. *White Women, Black Men: Illicit Sex in the Nineteenth-Century South.* New Haven, CT: Yale University Press, 1997.

Horton, James O. "Freedom's Yoke: Gender Conventions among Antebellum Free Blacks," *Feminist Studies* 12 (Spring 1986): 51–76.

Jones, Jacqueline. *Soldiers of Light and Love: Northern Teachers and Georgia Blacks, 1865–1873.* Chapel Hill: University of North Carolina Press, 1980.

Kasson, Joy S. *Marble Queens and Captives: Women in Nineteenth-Century American Sculpture.* New Haven, CT: Yale University Press, 1990.

Kessler-Harris, Alice. *Out to Work: A History of Wage-Earning Women in the United States.* New York: Oxford University Press, 1982.

Kitch, Sally L. *This Strange Society of Women: Reading the Letters and Lives of the Woman's Commonwealth.* Columbus: Ohio State University Press, 1993.

Kohlstedt, Sally Gregory. "In From the Periphery: American Women in Science, 1830–1880," *Signs* 4 (Autumn 1978): 81–96.

Kugler, Israel. *From Ladies to Women: The Organized Struggle for Women's Rights in the Reconstruction Era.* Westport, CT: Greenwood Press, 1987.

Lupton, Mary Jane. "Ladies Entrance: Women and Bars," *Feminist Studies* 5 (Fall 1979): 571–88.

McBridge, Mary G., and Ann M. McLaurin, "Sarah G. Humphreys: Antebellum Belle to Equal Rights Activist, 1830–1907," *Filson Club Historical Quarterly* 65 (April 1991): 231–51.

Morantz, Regina Markell. "Feminism, Professionalism, and Germs: The Thought of Mary Putnam Jacobi and Elizabeth Blackwell," *American Quarterly* 5 (Winter 1982): 459–78.

———. *Sympathy and Science: Women Physicians in American Medicine.* New York: Oxford University Press, 1985.

Morello, Karen Burger. *The Invisible Bar: The Woman Lawyer in America, 1638 to the Present.* New York: Random House, 1986.

Morris, Robert C. "Freedmen's Education," 462–68, in *Black Women in America: An Historical Encyclopedia,* edited by Darlene Clark Hine. Brooklyn, NY: Carlson Publishing Inc., 1993.

Murphy, Lucy Eldersveld. "Business Ladies: Midwestern Women and Enterprise, 1850–1880," *Journal of Women's History* 3 (Spring 1991): 65–89.

Pursell, Carroll. "Women Inventors in America," *Technology and Culture* 22 (July 1981): 545–49.

Reverby, Susan M. *Ordered to Care: The Dilemma of American Nursing, 1850–1945.* Cambridge: Cambridge University Press, 1987.

Rogers, Gayle J. "The Changing Image of the Southern Woman: A Performer on a Pedestal," *Journal of Popular Culture* 16 (Winter 1982): 60–67.

Russett, Cynthia Eagle. *Sexual Science: The Victorian Construction of Womanhood.* Cambridge, MA: Harvard University Press, 1989.

Ryan, Mary P. *Women in Public: Between Banners and Ballots, 1825–1880.* Baltimore: Johns Hopkins University Press, 1990.

Scott, Anne Firor. *The Southern Lady: From Pedestal to Politics, 1830–1930.* Chicago: University of Chicago Press, 1970.

Smith-Rosenberg, Carroll. *Disorderly Conduct: Visions of Gender in Victorian America.* New York: Oxford University Press, 1985.

Stage, Sarah. *Female Complaints: Lydia Pinkham and the Business of Women's Medicine.* New York: W. W. Norton & Company, 1979.

Stanley, Amy Dru. "Conjugal Bonds and Wage Labor: Rights of Contract in the Age of Emancipation," *Journal of American History* 75 (September 1988): 471–500.

Sterling, Dorothy, ed. *We Are Your Sisters: Black Women in the Nineteenth Century.* New York: W. W. Norton & Company, 1984.

Streitmatter, Rodger. *Raising Her Voice: African-American Women Journalists Who Changed History.* Lexington: University Press of Kentucky, 1994.

Turbin, Carole. *Working Women of Collar City: Gender, Class, and Community in Troy, New York, 1864–1886.* Urbana: University of Illinois Press, 1993.

Underhill, Lois Beachy. *The Woman Who Ran for President: The Many Lives of Victoria Woodhull.* Bridgehampton, NY: Bridge Works, 1995.

Walsh, Margaret. "The Democratization of Fashion: The Emergence of the Women's Dress Pattern Industry," *Journal of American History* 66 (September 1979): 299–313.

Wertheimer, Barbara Mayer. *We Were There: The Story of Working Women in America.* New York: Pantheon Books, 1977.

Wertsch, Douglas. "Iowa's Daughters: The First Thirty Years of the Girl's Reform School of Iowa, 1869–1899," *Annals of Iowa* 49 (Summer/Fall 1987): 77–100.

Zorina, Khan B. "Married Women's Property Laws and Female Commercial Activity: Evidence from United States Patent Records, 1790–1895," *Journal of Economic History* 56 (June 1996): 356-88.

Women in the American West

Agonito, Rosemary, and Joseph Agonito. "Resurrecting History's Forgotten Women: A Case Study from the Cheyenne Indians," *Frontiers* 6 (Fall 1981): 8–16.

Albers, Patricia, and Beatrice Medicine. *The Hidden Half: Studies of Plains Indian Women*. Washington, DC: University Press of America, 1983.

Bakken, Gordon Morris. *Rocky Mountain Constitution Making*. Westport, CT: Greenwood Press, 1987. Chapter 8.

Bargo, Michael. "Women's Occupations in the West in 1870," *Journal of the West* 32 (January 1993): 30–45.

Barnhart, Jacqueline Baker. *The Fair but Frail: Prostitution in San Francisco, 1849–1900*. Reno: University of Nevada Press, 1986.

Beesley, David. "From Chinese to Chinese American: Chinese Women and Families in a Sierra Nevada Town," *California History* 67 (September 1988): 168–79.

Beeton, Beverly. *Women Vote in the West: The Woman Suffrage Movement, 1869–1896*. New York: Garland Publishing, Inc., 1986.

Bookspan, Shelley. *A Germ of Goodness: The California State Prison System, 1851–1944*. Lincoln: University of Nebraska Press, 1991.

Butler, Anne M. *Daughters of Joy, Sisters of Misery: Prostitutes in the American West, 1865–1890*. Champaign: University of Illinois Press, 1985.

——. "Still in Chains: Black Women in Western Prisons, 1865–1910," *Western Historical Quarterly* 20 (February 1989): 19–35.

Chan, Sucheng. "Chinese Livelihood in Rural California: The Impact of Economic Change," *Pacific Historical Review* 53 (August 1984): 273–307.

Chaudhuri, Nupur. "'We All Seem Like Brothers and Sisters': The African-American Community in Manhattan, Kansas, 1865–1940," *Kansas History* 14 (Winter 1991–92): 270–88.

de Graaf, Lawrence. "Race, Sex, and Region: Black Women in the American West, 1850–1920," *Pacific Historical Review* 49 (May 1980): 285–314.

Dunfey, Julie. "'Living the Principle' of Plural Marriage: Mormon Women, Utopia, and Female Sexuality in the Nineteenth Century," *Feminist Studies* 10 (Fall 1984): 523–36.

Edwards, G. Thomas. *Sowing Good Seeds: The Northwest Suffrage Campaigns of Susan B. Anthony*. Portland: Oregon Historical Society Press, 1990.

Embry, Jessie L. "Effects of Polygamy on Mormon Women," *Frontiers* 7 (1984): 56–61.

Faragher, John Mack. *Women and Men on the Overland Trail*. New Haven, CT: Yale University Press, 1979.

Foote, Cheryl J. *Women of the New Mexico Frontiers, 1846–1912*. Niwot: University Press of Colorado, 1990.

Foster, Lawrence. "Polygamy and the Frontier: Mormon Women in Early Utah," *Utah Historical Quarterly* 50 (Summer 1982): 268–89.

Freedman, Estelle B. *Their Sister's Keepers: Women's Prison Reform in America, 1830–1930*. Ann Arbor: University of Michigan Press, 1981.

Godfrey, Kenneth W., Audrey M. Godfrey, and Jill Mulvay Derr. *Women's Voices: An Untold History of the Latter-Day Saints, 1830–1900*. Salt Lake City: Deseret Book Company, 1982.

Gray, John S. "The Story of Mrs. Picotte-Galpin, a Sioux Heroine," *Montana, the Magazine of Western History* 36 (Summer 1986): 2–21.

Harris, Katherine. *Long Vistas: Women and Families on Colorado Homesteads*. Niwot: University Press of Colorado, 1993.

Hinckley, Ted C. "Glimpses of Societal Change Among Nineteenth-Century Tlingit Women," *Journal of the West* 32 (July 1993): 12–24.

Hoffert, Sylvia D. "Childbearing on the Trans-Mississippi Frontier, 1830–1900," *Western Historical Quarterly* 22 (August 1991): 273–88.

Hudson, Lynn M. "A New Look, or 'I'm Not Mammy to Everybody in California': Mary Ellen Pleasant, a Black Entrepreneur," *Journal of the West* 32 (July 1993): 35–40.

Jeffrey, Julie Roy. *Frontier Women: The Trans-Mississippi West, 1840–1880*. New York: Hill and Wang, 1979.

Johnson, Susan L. "Sharing Bed and Board: Cohabitation and Cultural Difference in Central Arizona Mining Towns, 1863–1873," *Frontiers* 7 (1984): 36–42.

Lomawaima, K. Tasianina. "Domesticity in the Federal Indian Schools: The Power of Authority over Mind and Body," *American Ethnologist,* 20 (May 1993): 227–40.

Madsen, Carol C. "At Their Peril: Utah Law and the Case of Plural Wives," *Western Historical Quarterly* 21 (November 1990): 425–43.

Maret, Elizabeth. *Women of the Range: Women's Role in the Texas Beef Cattle Industry.* College Station: Texas A & M University Press, 1993.

Marti, Donald B. *Women of the Grange: Mutuality and Sisterhood in Rural America, 1866–1920.* Westport, CT: Greenwood, 1991.

Melville, Margarita B., ed. *Twice a Minority: Mexican-American Women*. St. Louis: C. V. Mosby Co., 1980.

Moynihan, Ruth Barnes. *Rebel for Rights: Abigail Scott Duniway*. New Haven, CT: Yale University Press, 1983.

Myres, Sandra L. *Westering Women and the Frontier Experience, 1800–1915*. Albuquerque: University of New Mexico Press, 1982.

Nomura, Gail M. "Significant Lives: Asians and Asian Americans in the History of the United States West," *Western Historical Quarterly* 25 (Spring 1994): 69–88.

Ong, Paul M. "Chinese Labor in Early San Francisco: Racial Segmentation and Industrial Expansion," *Amerasia* 8 (1981): 69–92.

Painter, Nell. *Black Migration to Kansas After Reconstruction*. New York: Alfred A. Knopf, 1977.

Pickle, Linda Schelbitki. "Rural German-Speaking Women in Early Nebraska and Kansas," *Great Plains Quarterly* 9 (Fall 1989): 239–51.

Riley, Glenda. *Women and Indians on the Frontier, 1825–1915*. Albuquerque: University of New Mexico Press, 1984.

Schlissel, Lillian. *Women's Diaries of the Westward Journey*. 2d ed. New York: Schocken Books, 1993.

Shoemaker, Nancy, ed. *Negotiators of Change: Historical Perspectives on Native American Women*. New York: Routledge, 1995.

——. "The Rise or Fall of Iroquois Women," *Journal of Women's History* 2 (Winter 1991): 39–57.

Shover, Michele. "The Blockhead Factor: Marriage and the Fate of California Daughters," *The Californians* 7 (September/October 1989): 32–39.

Tamura, Eileen H. *Americanization, Acculturation, and Ethnic Identity: The Nisei Generation in Hawaii*. Urbana: University of Illinois Press, 1994.

Williams, Mary L. "Ladies of the Regiment: Their Influence on the Frontier Army," *Nebraska History* 78 (Winter 1997): 158–64.

Index

This is a combined index for Volume 1 and Volume 2.
Volume 2 begins with page 281.

Photograph Credits

Volume 1

Page 155
Top: Pocahontas, after the 1616 engraving of her by Simon van de Passe. National Portrait Gallery, Smithsonian Institution

Bottom: An early Spanish illustration of the "heathens" who came to the Jesuit missions near the modern Arizona-Mexico border in the early eighteenth century. Photo Courtesy of Edward E. Ayer Collection. The Newberry Library, Chicago

Page 156
Top: Mary Gibson Tilghman and sons, 1789. Charles Willson Peale portrait. Maryland Historical Society, Baltimore

Bottom: Batting cotton. Joseph E. Taulman Collection, The Center for American History, The University of Texas at Austin, 3T66, CN 00939

Page 157
Top: Phillis Wheatley (ca. 1753–1784), poet and first African American published author. Library of Congress

Bottom: *The Market Plaza,* by Thomas Allen. Courtesy of The Witte Museum, San Antonio, Texas

Page 158
The Wife, 1831. Illustration from *Godey's Lady Book*

Page 159
The working women of Lynn, Massachusetts protest early 1840s. Walter P. Reuther Library, Wayne State University, the Archives of Labor and Urban Affairs

Page 160
Top left: *Madonna of the Prairie,* painting by W.H.D. Koerner, 1921 Buffalo Bill Historical Center, Cody, Wyoming

Top right: Ma-ke and Kun-zan-ya, St. Louis, 1848. Photo courtesy of Edward E. Ayer Collection. The Newberry Library, Chicago

Bottom: Harriet Tubman. Library of Congress

Page 161
Top: Engraving from *Godey's Lady's Book,* 1845

Bottom: Sarah Josepha Hale, editor of *Godey's Lady's Book.* From *Godey's Lady's Book*

Page 162
Top: A nineteenth-century New England schoolroom, painting by Charles Bosworth, ca 1852. Massachusetts Historical Society, Neg. #666

Bottom: Sojourner Truth (ca. 1797–1883), abolitionist. Library of Congress

Page 163
Top: The water carriers, ca. 1880. Photo by John K. Hillers, Courtesy Museum of New Mexico, Neg. #102081

Bottom: Southern women, photographed around 1860. The Western Reserve Historical Society, Cleveland

Page 164
Top: Indian woman with baby. Photo by Keystone View Co. Courtesy Museum of New Mexico, Neg. #91528

Bottom: Pawnee Indian Wind Lodge, ca. 1868–70. Photo by Wm. H. Jackson, Courtesy Museum of New Mexico, Neg. #58632

Page 165
Top: Apache camp, ca. 1885. Photo by Ben Wittick, Courtesy Museum of New Mexico, Neg.102038
Bottom: "Chicago Joe," Mary Josephine Welch Hensley, who established the Red Light Saloon in Montana before the state outlawed dance halls. Montana Historical Society, Helena, Neg.#944-615
Page 166
Top: Lithograph of a nineteenth-century revival meeting after a painting by A. Rider. Library of Congress
Bottom: Dancing girl, Virginia City, Nevada. Montana Historical Society, Helena. #Pac 74-23
Page 167
Top: Hunting along the Red River, 1870s. State Historical Society of North Dakota, Bismarck, Neg.#A-5089
Bottom: Annie Oakley, early publicity photo, mid-1800s. Annie Oakley Foundation, Greenville, Ohio
Page 168
Top left: Wedding picture, William and Anna Belle Steintemp, 1881. From the Dorothy St. Arnold Papers. Minnesota Historical Society
Top Right: Wedding portrait, Mr. and Mrs. James Sullivan, ca. 1870. Montana Historical Society, Helena, Neg. #952–879
Bottom: Portrait of Old Crow and his wife, 1880. Photo Courtesy of Edward E. Ayer Collection. The Newberry Library, Chicago
Page 169
Former slave, Tillie Brackenridge, in San Antonio, ca. 1900. Mrs. Charles Bush III, copy from the Institute of Texan Cultures, San Antonio, Neg. #85-76
Page 170
Top: Na-tu-ende , Apache, ca. 1883. Photo by Ben Wittick. Courtesy Museum of New Mexico, Neg. #15910
Bottom: Mormon settlers, Arizona, ca. 1885. Photo by Ben Wittick. Courtesy Museum of New Mexico, Neg. #15615
Page 171
Top: Dr. Mary Walker, c. 1865. #fTR 655.11 P743. Gernsheim Collection, Harry Ransom Humanities Research Center, The University of Texas at Austin.
Bottom: American Tennis Club, c. 1887. Gernsheim Collection, Harry Ransom Humanities Research Center, The University of Texas at Austin.

Inventing the American Woman: An Inclusive History, Third Edition
Developmental editor and copy editor: Andrew J. Davidson
Production Editor: Lucy Herz
Proofreader: Claudia Siler
Indexer: Margie Towery
Cover Designer: DePinto Graphic Design
Printer: Versa Press, Inc.